BLOOD AND

VENGEANCE

BLOOD AND

ONE FAMILY'S STORY
OF THE
WAR IN BOSNIA

CHUCK SUDETIC

VENGEANCE

W · W · NORTON & COMPANY

NEW YORK   LONDON

For information about permission to reproduce selections from this book,
write to Permissions, W. W. Norton & Company, Inc.,
500 Fifth Avenue, New York, NY 10110.

The text of this book is composed in 10.5/13 Electra LH
with the display set in Munich Bold
Composition and manufacturing by the Haddon Craftsmen, Inc.
Book design by Margaret M. Wagner
Cartography by Jacques Chazaud

LIBRARY OF CONGRESS CATALOGING-IN-PUBLICATION DATA
Sudetic, Chuck.
Blood and vengeance : one family's story of the war in Bosnia /
by Chuck Sudetic.
p. cm.
Includes bibliographical references and index.
ISBN 0-393-04651-6
1. Yugoslav War, 1991– —Atrocities. 2. Yugoslav War, 1991– —Bosnia and
Hercegovina—Srebrenica. 3. Yugoslav War, 1991– —Personal narratives,
American. 4. Genocide—Bosnia and Hercegovina. 5. Sudetic, Chuck.
6. Srebrenica (Bosnia and Hercegovina)—History.
I. Title.
DR1313.7.A85S83 1998
949.703—dc21 97-46476
CIP

W. W. Norton & Company, Inc., 500 Fifth Avenue, New York, N.Y. 10110
http://www.wwnorton.com

W. W. Norton & Company Ltd.,10 Coptic Street, London WC1A 1PU

1 2 3 4 5 6 7 8 9 0

To my father and mother

i Ljilji, i Sari, i Azri
    od Glogonjskoga rita do Parme
    do Brajton Biča i Senjaka,
    pa i skroz nazad

CONTENTS

Photographs appear following page 190.
Maps appear on pages x-xi, 2, 3, 136, 166, 252.

When I'm asleep, dreaming and lulled and warm,—
They come, the homeless ones, the noiseless dead.
While the dim charging breakers of the storm
Bellow and drone and rumble overhead,
Out of the gloom they gather about my bed.
    They whisper to my heart; their thoughts are mine.

—Siegfried Sassoon *"Sick Leave,"* 1918

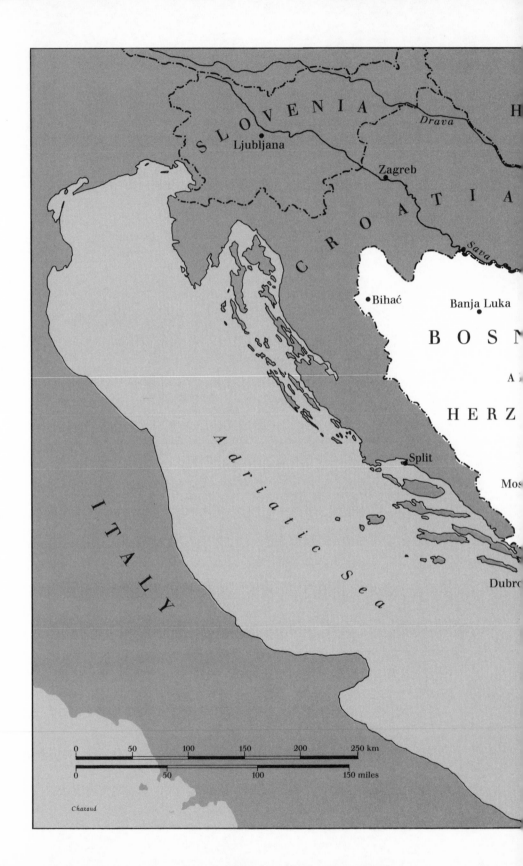

Chazaud

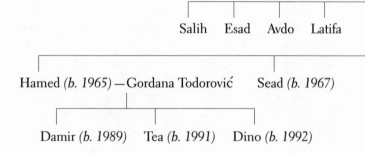

Salih   Esad   Avdo   Latifa

Hamed *(b. 1965)* — Gordana Todorović   Sead *(b. 1967)*

Damir *(b. 1989)*   Tea *(b. 1991)*   Dino *(b. 1992)*

ČELIK FAMILY TREE

☾   ☾   ☾

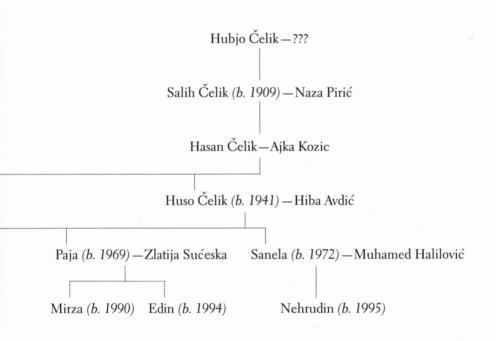

Hubjo Čelik — ???

Salih Čelik *(b. 1909)* — Naza Pirić

Hasan Čelik — Ajka Kozic

Huso Čelik *(b. 1941)* — Hiba Avdić

Paja *(b. 1969)* — Zlatija Sućeska   Sanela *(b. 1972)* — Muhamed Halilović

Mirza *(b. 1990)*   Edin *(b. 1994)*   Nehrudin *(b. 1995)*

MAIN CHARACTERS

Abdić, Fikret (AB-deetch, FEE-kret)—A Communist-era director of an agricultural enterprise who was responsible for a $500-million financial scandal. Leader of a Muslim faction in northwestern Bosnia. Muslim member of the Bosnian presidency after 1990 elections. Carried on trade with the Serbs and Croats before forming a private army and rising against the mostly Muslim army of Bosnia and Herzegovina.

Ahmetagić, Fehim (AH-met-ag-eetch, FAY-heem)—Grandson of Mullah Medo Ahmetagić. Survivor of Zvekara killings in 1941.

Ahmetagić, Hussein—Great-grandson of Mullah Medo Ahmetagić. *Hodža* at Kupusovići mosque until the late 1980s. Left after dispute over water with Branko Mitrašinović.

Ahmetagić, Ibro (EE-bro)—Son of Mullah Medo Ahmetagić and father of Fehim Ahmetagić. Survivor of Zvekara killings in 1941.

Ahmetagić, Meho (MAY-ho)—Grandson of Mullah Medo Ahmetagić, survivor of Zvekara killings in 1941.

Ahmetagić, Mullah Medo (MED-o)—Self-taught Muslim holy man from Vlahovići, a hamlet just down Mount Zvijezda from Kupusovići. Staunch supporter of the Serbian monarchy after World War I. District president during the period between the two world wars. Said to have received the Star of Karadjordje, the highest medal awarded by the Serbian king. Burned alive by Serbian Chetniks during World War II with his wife and other family members.

Akashi, Yasushi—Special Representative of Secretary-General Boutros-Ghali to the UN military force in the former Yugoslavia from December 1993 to October 1995. A staunch opponent of air strikes.

Almir, Hodža (AL-meer)—A Muslim faith healer from a village near Tuzla.

Andrić, Ivo (ANN-dreetch, EE-vo)—Nobel Prize–winning novelist who wrote about Bosnia. Born in the town of Travnik to Catholic parents, and lived in Višegrad under the care of a Muslim woman. Wrote the novel *Bridge on the Drina* about life in Višegrad from the building of the famous stone bridge to the beginning of World War I.

Annan, Kofi—Head of peacekeeping operations for the UN during most of the Bosnian war. Later elected secretary-general of the UN.

Avdić, Avdija (AHV-deetch, AHV-dee-ya)—Father of Hiba Čelik, the wife of Huso Čelik. Former member of the SS's Handžar Division, a quasi-military unit used as a special police in Yugoslavia from 1943 to the end of the war.

Avdić, Husnija (HOOS-nee-ya)—The mother of Hiba Čelik.

Bayezid, Sultan—The son of Sultan Murat. Fought at the Battle of Kosovo, where his father was killed.

Bećirović, Ramiz (beh-CHEER-o-veetch, ROM-eez)—Acting commander of the Muslim military forces in Srebrenica after Naser Orić's departure from the safe area in the spring of 1995. Former head of the Communist national guard in Srebrenica.

Bildt, Carl—Former prime minister of Sweden. Co-chairman of the International Peace Conference for the former Yugoslavia after the departure of David Owen in 1995.

Boutros-Ghali, Boutros—Secretary-general of the UN during the Bosnian war.

Branković, Djurdje (BRAHN-ko-veetch, JOOR-jay)—A Serbian despot who ruled over Srebrenica twice in the fifteenth century. Married to a Greek woman named Jerina, often referred to as Jerina the Damned.

Briquemont, Francis—The Belgian general who commanded the UN military force in Bosnia from General Morillon's departure in July 1993 to early 1994.

Broz, Josip—See Tito.

Čavkušić, Hadžira (CHAHV-koo-sheetch, ha-JEE-rah)—Daughter of Hasib Čavkušić. Friend of Sead Čelik and boyhood love of Milan Lukić. From the village of Kapetanovići, just below Kupusovići.

Čavkušić, Hasib (HAH-seeb)—Father of Hadžira Čavkušić and friend of Huso Čelik. Lived in Steyr, Austria. Friend of the Lukić family.

Čavkušić, Ismet (EES-met)—Husband of Latifa Čelik. Lived in Kamenica, a hamlet about an hour's walk from Kupusovići toward the northwest on Mount Zvijezda.

Čelik, Ajka (Kozić) (CHEL-eek, AYE-ka)—Wife of Hasan Čelik. Mother of Huso Čelik.

Čelik, Avdo (AHV-doe)—An older brother of Huso Čelik. Born in 1937. Lives in Mölln, Austria.

Čelik, Edin (ED-een)—Son of Paja and Zlatija Čelik. Born in 1994 in Srebrenica.

Čelik, Esad (ESS-ahd)—An older brother of Huso Čelik.

Čelik, Gordana (GORE-dahn-ah)—Formerly Gordana Todorović. The author's sister-in-law. Married Hamed Čelik in 1989.

Čelik, Hamed (HOMM-ed)—Husband of Gordana Todorović, son of Huso Čelik.

Left Kupusovići to work as a fruitpicker near Belgrade in 1987. Left Yugoslavia in 1992. Lived in Austria for a year before rejoining his wife and children and moving to Canada in 1993.

Čelik, Hiba (Avdić) (HEE-bah)—Wife of Huso Čelik. Mother of Hamed, Sead, Paja, and Sanela.

Čelik, Hujbo (HOOY-boh)—A contemporary of Mullah Šaban Čelik. The father of Salih Čelik and great-grandfather of Huso Čelik.

Čelik, Huso (HOO-so)—Son of Hasan and Ajka Čelik. Husband of Hiba Čelik. Father of Hamed, Sead, Paja, and Sanela Čelik.

Čelik, Jusuf (YOO-soof)—The first cousin of Huso Čelik's children. Found Chetnik knife inside a cave beside the Čelik house.

Čelik, Latifa (lah-TEA-fah)—Sister of Huso Čelik. Married name is Latifa Čavkušić.

Čelik, Mirza (MEER-za)—Son of Paja and Zlatija Čelik. Born in Višegrad in 1990.

Čelik, Mullah Šaban (MOOL-ah SHAH-bahn)—A stranger who bought Kupusovići with bags of gold ducats after the occupation of Bosnia by Austria in 1878. Built a house next to Juz-bin's mosque.

Čelik, Naza (NAH-zah)—Third wife of Mullah Šaban Čelik and grandmother of Huso Čelik. Left Šaban to marry Salih Čelik. Remarried into the Kupus family after her husband's death during World War I. Died near Srebrenica during World War II.

Čelik, Paja (PIE-ah)—The youngest son of Huso and Hiba Čelik. Husband of Zlatija Čelik and father of Edin and Mirza.

Čelik, Salih (SAH-leekh)—The grandfather of Huso Čelik. Married Mullah Šaban's third wife, Naza. Killed during World War I near Srebrenica.

Čelik, Salih (SAH-leekh)—A brother of Huso Čelik. Named after his grandfather killed during World War I. Left the family after World War II and moved to Croatia.

Čelik, Saliha (sa-LEE-ha)—*See* Muratagić, Saliha.

Čelik Sanela (sah-NELL-ah)—Married name Sanela Halilović. Youngest child and only daughter of Huso and Hiba Čelik. Wife of Muhamed Halilović.

Čelik, Sead (SAY-ahd)—Son of Huso and Hiba Čelik. Left Kupusovići after returning from the army. Worked on the Adriatic coast of Croatia in a shipyard as a laborer until taking a position as a laborer on a merchant ship. Now living in Canada.

Čelik, Zlatija (ZLAT-ee-yah)—Wife of Paja Čelik. Mother of Mirza and Edin. From Odžak.

Chirac, Jacques—President of France. Shifted French policy toward Bosnia in 1995.

Churkin, Vitaly—Russia's special envoy to the former Yugoslavia in 1993 and 1994.

Cot, Jean—A French general who replaced General Wahlgren as commander of the UN military forces in the former Yugoslavia in July 1993.

de Lapresle, Bertrand—A French general who took over the UN military forces after General Cot's departure in 1994. Lieutenant General Rose's superior in the UN military chain of command.

de Vere Hayes, Guy—British deputy to Lieutenant General Briquemont of Belgium in 1993. Offered to remove Naser Orić from Srebrenica.

Delić, Rasim (DELL-eetch, RAS-eem)—Commander of the mostly Muslim army of Bosnia and Herzegovina.

Delić, Sead (DELL-eetch, SAY-ahd)—Commander of the Bosnian army's Tuzla Corps.

Deronjić, Miroslav (DARE-ohn-eetch, MEER-oh-slav)—The head of the Serbian Democratic Party in Bratunac. Participant in the roundup of Muslim men in Bratunac in 1992. Head of the Civilian Affairs Committee of Srebrenica after the town's fall in 1995.

Dudić, Ibro (DUDE-eetch, EE-broh)—The commander of the 282nd Brigade in Srebrenica. Respected by Muslim men as a fighter and as an officer who would not take unnecessary risks.

Dukić, Rajko (DUKE-eetch, RAI-koh)—Head of a mining company in the village of Milići. Financed the Serbian Democratic Party. Friend of Radovan Karadžić.

Eagleburger, Lawrence—The U.S. deputy secretary of state under the Bush administration. Reputed to be Washington's most knowledgeable person on Yugoslavia.

Erić, Andjelija (AIR-eetch, ann-JELL-ee-yah)—The mother of Nego and Golub Erić. Went to Belgrade and obtained an audience with Tito to beg him to commute her sons' sentence of death.

Erić, Golub (GO-loob)—Grandson of Vaso Erić, son of Mikailo Erić, brother of Nego Erić. Fought in World War II as a Chetnik and a Partisan and participated in the massacre of Muslims in the village of Sopotnik in December 1941. Tried and sentenced to death before Tito commuted his sentence to imprisonment. Honorary commander of the Serbian fighters in Kravica at the beginning of the Bosnian war. Killed in action in May 1992.

Erić, Jakov (YAHK-ov)—The son of Vaso Erić. Chief agent for Narodna Odbrana in Kravica. Died in an Austrian prison during World War I.

Erić, Jovan (YOE-von)—The son of Vaso Erić. Member of Narodna Odbrana in Kravica. Died in an Austrian prison during World War I.

Erić, Krstina (KERST-een-a)—Wife of Nego Erić. Killed by her husband during the Muslim's Orthodox Christmas attack on Kravica in January 1993.

Erić, Mihailo (me-HIGH-lo)—Son of Zoran Erić, grandson of Golub Erić. Wounded in May 1992. Farmworker who lives in Kravica.

Erić, Mikailo (me-KAHY-lo)—Father of Golub and Nego Erić. Died in an Austrian prison during World War I. Participated in the Narodna Odbrana organization before the assassination of Archduke Franz Ferdinand.

Erić, Nego (NEH-go) — Grandson of Vaso Erić, son of Mikailo Erić, brother of Golub Erić. Fought in World War II as a Chetnik and a Partisan. Participated in the massacre of Muslims in the village of Sopotnik in December 1941. Tried and sentenced to death before Tito commuted his sentence to imprisonment. Died by suicide during the Orthodox Christmas attack on Kravica by the Muslims in 1993.

Erić, Vaso (VOSS-so) — Father of Jakov, Jovan, and Mikailo Erić. Born into a family of sharecroppers in 1844. Became a leader of the Serbs in the village of Kravica after he taught himself to read and write the Cyrillic alphabet. Joined the uprising against Bosnia's feudal landlords in 1875 and fought in the international war that broke out in 1876. Fought against Austria's occupation of Bosnia. Fled Bosnia to Serbia after seditious comments uttered in opposition to Austria's annexation of Bosnia in 1908. Member of Narodna Odbrana and confidant of Major Kosta Todorović.

Erić, Zoran (ZOE-ron) — Father of Mihailo Erić and son of Golub Erić. A peasant and a construction worker. Lives in Kravica.

Franken, Rob — A major in the Dutch army. Deputy to Lieutenant Colonel Karremans at the time of Srebrenica's fall.

Geburt, Thomas — A lieutenant colonel in the Canadian army. The commander of the contingent of Canadian soldiers sent into Srebrenica after it was declared a safe area in 1993.

Golić, Ejub (GOAL-eetch, Ay-yub) — A Muslim military officer in Srebrenica. Killed at Baljkovica during the march out of Srebrenica toward Muslim territory. Considered a hero by the men who made that march.

Halilović, Hajrudin (hah-LEEL-ov-eetch, HIGH-roo-deen) — The brother of Muhamed Halilović, son of Smail Halilović.

Halilović, Muhamed — The husband of Sanela (Čelik) Halilović. Native of Srebrenica.

Halilović, Naza (NAH-zah) — Mother of Muhamed Halilović and mother-in-law of Sanela (Čelik) Halilović.

Halilović, Nehrudin (neh-ROO-deen) — The son of Muhamed Halilović and Sanela (Čelik) Halilović.

Halilović, Sefer (SEF-er) — Commander of the army of Bosnia and Herzegovina in 1993.

Halilović, Smail (SMAH-eel) — The father of Muhamed Halilović and father-in-law of Sanela (Čelik) Halilović. Built hydroelectric dams in Srebrenica.

Hasanović, Avdo (hah-SAHN-oh-veetch, AHV-doe) — Head of Srebrenica's hospital during the Bosnian war.

Hebib, Avdo (HEB-eeb, AHV-doe) — Bosnian police official.

Hochschield, Fabrizio — Head of the Sarajevo office of the UNHCR at the beginning of the Bosnian war.

Hollingworth, Larry—A field officer for the UNHCR. Former British military officer.

Hrebreljanović, Lazar (hreh-brel-YAN-o-veetch, LAH-zahr)—Serbia's most powerful prince at the time of the Battle of Kosovo. Mustered a multinational force to engage the Ottoman army on the feast day of Saint Vitus (Vidovdan), 1389. Legend says he was executed in revenge for the killing of Sultan Murat. Bones said to belong to Prince Lazar were carried around Serbia in 1989 in commemoration of the 600th anniversary of the battle.

Hunt, Swanee—U.S. ambassador to Austria. Member of the Hunt family of Dallas, Texas.

Izetbegović, Alija (eez-zet-BEG-o-veetch, AHL-ee-ya)—Leader of the Muslim Party for Democratic Action. President of the collective presidency of Bosnia and Herzegovina from first free elections in 1990 to the present.

Janković, Mile (YONK-oh-veetch, MEE-lay)—A friend of Paja Čelik from Odžak. Participated in the expulsions of Muslims from Kupusovići and other villages in 1992. Died of cirrhosis in December 1996.

Janković, Stamena (STOM-en-ah)—The wife of Vitomir Janković and mother of Mile Janković.

Janković, Vitomir (VEET-oh-meer)—A Serb from Odžak. Fought as a Chetnik at beginning of World War II and participated in the Zvekara killings before going over to the Partisans. Despised by Serbs on Mount Zvijezda for allegedly informing on Chetniks. Head of the farmers' co-op in the Kupusovići area and janitor of the primary school in Odžak. Died in the early 1980s and buried in Odžak.

Janvier, Bernard—Lieutenant general in the French army. Commander of the UN military force in the former Yugoslavia in 1995. Staunch opponent of air strikes. Proposed the withdrawal of UN troops from the safe areas in Bosnia.

Jerina the Damned (YER-een-a)—A figure in the folklore of eastern Bosnia. Said to have created Mount Zvijezda and drawn the Roman Signs. In all likelihood, the name Jerina is drawn from the name of the Greek wife of a medieval Serbian despot, Djurdje Branković.

Juz-bin-Kulaga (YOOZ-bean-COOL-ah-gah)—Said to have been an Ottoman military commander who received land on Mount Zvijezda and built the mosque in Kupusovići. Said to be buried in the graveyard beside the mosque.

Kapetanović, Jusuf (cop-pay-TAHN-oh-veetch, YOU-suf)—A friend of Huso Čelik who lived in the hamlet of Kapetanovići. Taken away by Milan Lukić's men in Potočari after the fall of Srebrenica.

Kapetanović, Meho (MAY-hoo)—A grandson of Jusuf Kapetanović. Taken away by Milan Lukić's men at Potočari.

Kapetanović, Mujo (MOO yoe)—Postmaster at Prelovo. Brother of Jusuf. Disappeared after fall of Srebrenica.

Kara Marko—The local leader of Serbian uprising in Srebrenica area in 1804–13. Fled to Serbia after the uprising's collapse.

Karadjordje, or *Black George* (KAH-rah-george)—The leader of the first Serbian uprising against the Ottoman Empire from 1804 to 1813. Beheaded by the leader of the second Serbian uprising, Miloš Obrenović.

Karadjordjević, Aleksandar (kah-rah-GEORGE-e-veetch)—The Serbian king who ruled over Yugoslavia after World War I and declared a dictatorship in 1928. Assassinated in Marsailles in 1934.

Karadjordjević, Petar II—King of Yugoslavia. Son of Aleksandar. Went into exile after Nazi invasion of Yugoslavia in 1941.

Karadžić, Radovan (KAH-rah-jeetch, ROD-o-von)—The president of the Serbian Democratic Party in Bosnia from 1990 to 1996. The predominant Serbian political leader in Bosnia before and during the Bosnian war. Indicted for genocide and crimes against humanity by the International War Crimes Tribunal in The Hague.

Karremans, Ton—Lieutenant colonel in the Dutch army. The commander of the Dutch army contingent in Srebrenica at the time of its fall in 1995.

Kemura, Hadži Sulejman Efendi (KEM-oor-ah)—The leader of Yugoslavia's entire Muslim religious community. Opened Juz-bin's mosque in Kupusovići after its restoration in the 1950s.

Kešmer, Behadil (KESH-mer, bay-HAHD-eel)—A Muslim peasant who lived in Žlijeb, a few hundred yards from the Čelik house.

Koljević Nikola (COLE-ye-veetch, NEE-cole-ah)—A Shakespeare professor who bailed Radovan Karadžić and Momčilo Krajišnik out of jail in the early 1980s and went on to become one of the leaders of the Serbian Democratic Party after 1990. Committed suicide the autumn of 1996.

Kozić, Adem (KOH-zeetch, AH-dem)—A cousin of Huso Čelik. Killed by Milan Lukić's gang in 1992.

Kozić, Ajka—See Čelik, Ajka.

Kozić, Amir (AH-meer)—A cousin of Huso Čelik. Father of Bedži, Deba, and Džemal Kozić. Went to work in Austria during the 1970s.

Kozić, Bedži (BEH-jee)—A friend of Paja Čelik.

Kozić, Deba (DEB-ah)—A friend of Paja Čelik.

Kozić, Džemal (JEM-ahl)—A friend of Paja Čelik.

Kozić, Hanifa (HAH-nee-fa)—The wife of Adem Kozić and mother of Munevera and Hasan. Expelled from Kupusovići by Lukić's gang. Lived out the war in a camp in Turkey.

Kozić, Šemsa (SHEM-sah)—A woman who lived in Kupusovići and cast out the spell on Saliha Muratagić's cow in the mid-1980s.

Krajišnik, Momčilo (CRY-eesh-neek, MOME-chee-low)—The second-most-powerful Serb leader in Bosnia and Herzegovina during the war.

Krstić, Radislav (KERST-eetch, ROD-dee-slav)—A Serb commander whose men executed Muslim prisoners captured after the fall of Srebrenica. Now commander of the Bosnian Serb army's Drina Corps in the town of Vlasenica. Wounded in the leg early in the Bosnian war.

Kupus, Hasib (COO-poos, HAH-seeb)—A cousin of Huso Čelik. The retired police chief in Bijeljina at the time the town was attacked in 1992. Murdered, presumably by Ražnatović's men, in April 1992.

Kupus, Mujo (MOO-yo)—Kupusovići's wealthiest peasant and the Muslim who contributed the most to the restoration of Juz-bin's mosque.

Lazar—*See* Hrebreljanović, Lazar.

Levinsen, Anders—The field officer of the UNHCR in Tuzla at the time Srebrenica was under attack in early 1993.

Lukić, Mikailo (LUKE-eetch, mick-AYE-low)—A cousin of Milan Lukić. The head of Serbia's secret police in the town of Bajina Bašta.

Lukić, Milan (MEE-lahn)—A school friend of Huso Čelik's son Sead. Commanded the militia unit that expelled and murdered thousands of Muslims from the Višegrad district. Participated in the killing of Muslims at Srebrenica.

Lukić, Rale (RAH-lay)—An uncle of Milan Lukić. Lost his father to Muslim members of the Ustaše in August 1941. Lives in Steyr, Austria.

Lukić, Sredoje (SRED-oh-yeh)—A cousin of Milan Lukić. Held by the Šabanović brothers in the Višegrad dam in April 1992. A participant in the expulsions and murders of Muslims in Višegrad in 1992.

Mardel, Simon—A physician for the World Health Organization who hiked over a mountain to get into Srebrenica in the late winter of 1993.

Markov, Miloš (MARK-ov, MEE-losh)—A medieval fighter of Turks. The namesake for the Milošević clan of Montenegro.

Marković, Mirjana (MARK-ov-eetch, MEER-ya-na)—The wife of Slobodan Milošević. Daughter of Moma Marković, who was named a national hero after the victory in World War II by the Communist Partisans. A professor of Marxism-Leninism.

Marković, Moma (MO-ma)—National hero of World War II. Father of Mira Marković, the wife of Slobodan Milošević.

Mehmed Pasha Sokolović—*See* Sokolović, Mehmed Pasha.

Meholjić, Hakija (MEH-hole-eetch, HOCK-ee-ya)—The police chief in Srebrenica during the Bosnian war.

Mendiluce, José Maria—The Spanish head of the UNHCR in Yugoslavia. Witnessed Serb gunmen in Zvornik putting children under the treads of tanks and running them over.

Mihailović, Draža (mee-HIGH-low-veetch, DRA-zha)—The royalist commander of the Chetnik forces during World War II. Executed by Tito's government in 1946.

Miletić, Vera (MEE-let-eetch, VAY-ra)—The mother of Mirjana Marković, the wife of Slobodan Milosević. Executed by pro-Nazi Serb police while being held in custody in 1944.

Miličević family (mee-LEE-chev-eetch)—A Serb family from a village above Odžak. Some men of the family became members of Milan Lukić's gang during the Bosnian war.

Milošević, Slobodan (mee-LOSH-ev-eetch, SLOW-bow-dahn)—The president of Serbia before and during the Bosnian war. Later president of Yugoslavia.

Milovanović, Milan (mee-low-VON-o-veetch, MEE-lahn)—The second-in-command of the Bosnian Serb army after General Ratko Mladić.

Mitrašinović, Branko (meet-rah-SHEEN-o-veetch, BRON-ko)—A Serbian friend of the Čelik family who lived above Kupusovići in the hamlet of Odžak.

Mitrašinović, Pantelija (pon-TELL-ee-ya)—A Serb who lived in a village above Odžak and carried lumber and contributed money for the building of Saliha's house. Sons killed in the Bosnian war.

Mitrašinović, Petra (PET-ra)—The wife of Branko Mitrašinović. Hiba Čelik's best friend.

Mitrašinović, Radislava (ROD-ees-slav-a)—The daughter of Vladimir Mitrašinović. The woman who was living in the Čelik house while the Čeliks were in flight during World War II.

Mitrašinović, Vladimir (VLAH-dee-meer)—The father of Branko Mitrašinović. Took part in the killings at Zvekara cave in 1941. Tried to apologize at the reopening of the Kupusovići mosque after World War II.

Mladić, Ratko (MLODD-eetch, ROT-ko)—General in the Bosnian Serb army. Commander of the Bosnian Serb forces from May 1992 to mid-1996. Indicted for genocide and crimes against humanity by the International War Crimes Tribunal in The Hague.

Morillon, Philippe—The French army general who commanded the UN military force in Bosnia and Herzegovina from fall 1992 to summer 1993.

Mujkanović, Mustafa (mooy-KAHN-o-veetch, MOOS-ta-fa)—A Muslim *hodža* tortured and executed in the school gymnasium in Bratunac in May 1992.

Murat, Sultan—The Ottoman sultan whose forces defeated the Serbs at the Battle of Kosovo on June 28, 1389. Killed by a Serb assassin during the battle.

Muratagić, Avdo (MOOR-ot-og-eetch, AHV-doe)—Saliha Muratagić's son. Cousin of Huso Čelik's children.

Muratagić, Saliha (sah-LEE-hah)—The cousin of Huso Čelik whose parents and siblings were killed in Chetnik massacres in 1941 and 1943. The mother of six children.

Abandoned by her husband. She lived in the Čelik house until the early 1980s, when Huso and the neighbors built her a house of her own.

Nicolai, Cees—A Dutch army general who was a deputy to General Rupert Smith, commander of the UN military force in Bosnia and Herzegovina in 1995.

Nikolić, Jovan (NEEK-oh-leetch, YO-von)—The Serb military commander at Kravica. Wounded in a Muslim attack on Glogova in December 1992. A nephew of Nego Erić.

Njegoš (Petar II Petrović-Njegoš) (NYEH-gosh)—A Montenegrin prince and Orthodox bishop who wrote poetry advocating the extermination of Muslims from Serb lands.

Novaković family (no-VOCK-o-veetch)—A Serb family from Pozdrčići, a hamlet just west of Kupusovići. Male members of the Novaković family were Chetniks during World War II and members of Milan Lukić's gang during the Bosnian war.

Obrenović, Miloš (oh-BREN-o-veetch, MEE-losh)—The leader of the second Serbian uprising in 1815. Beheaded Karadjordje. Arranged for the expulsion of Muslims from Serbian territory in the 1830s.

Ogata, Sadako—The UN High Commissioner for Refugees.

Omerović, Fadila (OH-mare-oh-veetch, fa-DEAL-ah)—A Muslim woman in Srebrenica. The best friend of Dragica Vasić.

Orić, Mevludin (OAR-eetch, mev-LOO-deen)—A Muslim man who survived the execution field at Križevačke Njive.

Orić, Naser (OAR-eetch, NASS-air)—The commander of the Muslim military forces in Srebrenica. Removed from Srebrenica by helicopter in spring 1995.

Owen, David—The co-chairman of the UN peace conference on the former Yugoslavia. Appointed at the London conference in August 1992. Resigned in May 1995.

Palić, Avdo (POLL-eetch, AHV-doe)—The commander of the Muslim military forces in Žepa.

Panić, Milan (PONN-eetch, MEE-lahn)—The Serbian-American prime minister of Yugoslavia in 1992.

Pavelić, Ante (PAH-vell-eetch, ON-tay)—Croatia's Fascist dictator during World War II. The leader of the Ustaše who carried out genocidal killings of Serbs during the war.

Pecikoza, Stanko (PET-si-koz-a, STAHN-ko)—The head of the Serbian Democratic Party in Višegrad before the Bosnian war. Murdered by Serbs.

Pepić, Milojica (PEP-eetch, meel-OY-eet-sa)—A Serb from the village of Pozdrčići who tried to direct the Čeliks into a trap.

Pepić, Petar (PEP-eetch, PEH-tar)—The father of Milojica Pepić. Saved Paja and the other Čeliks as they were fleeing Kupusovići.

Pirić, Fehrat (PEER-eetch, FAIR-hot)—The first Muslim reported killed in the Višegrad district during the Bosnian war. Executed by a Yugoslav army soldier.

Plavšić, Biljana (PLAHV-sheetch, BEEL-ya-na)—A member of the ruling presidency of the self-declared Bosnian Serb republic in Bosnia. An ardent Serb nationalist.

Princip, Gavrilo (PREEN-tseep, GAV-ree-low)—A Serbian terrorist. Assassin of Archduke Franz Ferdinand in Sarajevo on June 28, 1914.

Putnik, Vojvoda Radomir (POOT-neek, VOY-voe-dah ROD-o-meer)—A Serbian army general. Serbian army commander during World War I.

Radovanović, Arsen (rod-oh-VAHN-oh-veetch, ARE-sen)—The son of Dragojle and brother of Dragoljub Radovanović of Odžak. A Serb friend of Huso Čelik. Participant in the fight in the Odžak schoolhouse in the mid-1950s. Offered to help get Huso Čelik out of Bosnia at the beginning of the Bosnian war.

Radovanović, Borislav (BORE-ee-slav)—The brother of Arsen and Dragoljub Radovanović and a neighbor of the Čeliks.

Radovanović, Dragoljub (DRAH-go-loob)—One of the Čelik's neighbors and a close friend of Huso and Hiba Čelik. Participated in the schoolyard fight in Odžak in the mid-1950s. Son of Dragojle Radovanović, who participated in the Zvekara killings in 1941 and became good friends with the Čeliks after World War II.

Ražnatović, Željko (razh-NOT-o-veetch, ZHEL-ko)—Also known as Arkan. The commander of a unit of Serb irregulars who carried out brutal attacks on civilians in Croatia in 1991 and Bosnia in 1992–95. A former contract killer for Communist Yugoslavia's secret police. Suspected of having committed war crimes.

Rizvanović, Nurif (reez-VON-ov-eetch, NOOR-eef)—A Muslim who was reportedly arrested and killed by other Muslims after he infiltrated into Srebrenica from Tuzla with several hundred fighters.

Rose, Sir Michael—The commander of the UN military force in Bosnia in 1994. Former British army lieutenant general. Former commander of the SAS.

Šabanović, Avdija (shah-BAHN-oh-veetch, AHV-dee-ya)—A militia leader in the Muslim Party for Democratic Action in Višegrad at the beginning of the war. Led the takeover of the Višegrad dam in April 1992. Now living in Goražde.

Šabanović, Murat (MOOR-aht)—A leader of the Muslim militia in Višegrad before the beginning of the war. Participated in the takeover of the Višegrad dam in April 1992. Now living in Chicago.

Sadić, Hasim (SAH-deetch, HAH-seem)—Bosnian army commander in Tuzla area. Condemned evacuation of Muslims from Srebrenica in 1993.

Savović, Branimir (SAH-voh-veetch, BRON-ee-meer)—A leader of the Serbian Democratic Party in Višegrad.

Silajdžić, Haris (SILL-aye-jeetch, HARR-ees)—Foreign minister of Bosnia, and later prime minister of Bosnia and Herzegovina.

Simatović, Franko (stah-MOT-o-veetch, FRONK-o)—The commander of Slobodan Milošević's police militia unit. Worked closely with Željko Ražnatović during the 1991 war in Croatia and the Serb attacks on Muslims in the Drina River valley that began the Bosnian war in March and April 1992.

Smith, Leighton—American admiral, commander of NATO's forces in southern Europe.

Smith, Rupert—The British army lieutenant general, commander of the UN military force in Bosnia and Herzegovina during 1995. His superior was Lieutenant General Janvier.

Sokolović, Mehmed Pasha (so-COAL-o-veetch, MEH-med POSH-a)—The grand vezier of Suleiman the Magnificent and other Ottoman sultans in the sixteenth century. Born in Sokolovići, a village up the Drina from Višegrad and near the town of Rudo. Taken away by the Ottoman authorities in payment of the "blood tax" and converted to Islam. Ordered the stone bridge over the Drina to be built at Višegrad. Restored the independence of the Serbian Orthodox Church, which later bequeathed a Serbian national identity to many Orthodox Slavs in Bosnia and other areas of the Balkans. Considered a hero by the Serbs even though he was a Muslim. Appointed his brother patriarch of the restored Serbian Orthodox Church. Assassinated by another convert to Islam from eastern Bosnia.

Stambolić, Ivan (STOM-bow-leetch, EE-van)—A law school friend of Slobodan Milošević and nephew of Serbia's Communist strongman in the 1970s. Paved the way for Milošević's rise into positions of responsibility in Serbia. Ousted by Milošević in 1987.

Štitkovac, Enver (SHTEET-ko-vots, EN-ver)—The commander of the local military police in Žepa. Ran the black market and trade connections with the Serbs. Reportedly drove to Sarajevo in a Volkswagen after Žepa fell to the Serbs.

Stoltenberg, Thorvald—A Norwegian politician and the co-chairman of the UN peace conference on the former Yugoslavia from 1993 to 1995. Replaced Cyrus Vance.

Sućeska family (SOO-chess-kah)—A family from the hamlet of Odžak. Formerly a bey family.

Sućeska, Dževahira (jev-ah-HEAR-ah)—The mother of Zlatija Čelik, Paja Čelik's wife, and Senad Sućeska, Paja's best friend.

Sućeska, Hakija (HOCK-ee-ya)—The uncle of Senad Sućeska. The first Muslim killed in Odžak and Kupusovići during the Bosnian war.

Sućeska, Rasim (RASS-eem)—A native of the village of Žlijeb who worked as a conductor on the Ćiro and perpetrated the brawl at the Odžak schoolyard in the mid-1950s.

Sućeska, Salko (SOL-ko)—The son of Hakija Sućeska. Killed by Lukić's men in Višegrad in June 1992.

Sućeska, Senad—Paja Čelik's best friend.

Sućeska, Zuhdija (ZOOKH-dee-ya)—Huso Čelik's best friend. Father of Paja Čelik's wife, Zlatija, and his best friend, Senad. Died of cirrhosis of the liver before the Bosnian war.

Suleiman the Magnificent—Arguably the greatest of all Ottoman sultans. Died in Hungary in 1566.

Suljić, Osman (SOOL-eetch, OOS-mahn)—Srebrenica's district president during the Bosnian war.

Tirić, Hase (TEAR-eetch, HA-say)—Commander of Muslim militia in Bijeljina. Later commander of the Black Swans.

Tito, Josip Broz—The leader of the Communist Party in Yugoslavia from the 1930s until his death in 1980. The commander of the Communist Partisans during World War II. Yugoslavia's supreme leader after World War II.

Todorović, Kosta (tow-DOOR-o-veetch, COAST-a)—A Serbian army officer responsible for running networks of secret agents across the border in Austrian-controlled Bosnia in the years preceding World War I. Awarded the Star of Karadjordje posthumously.

Todorović, Mara (MAH-rah)—The author's mother-in-law. Born in a village near the town of Bosanska Dubica. Survived an Ustaše attack that virtually wiped out her entire family. Saved from an Ustaše concentration camp by an Italian family that needed a housemaid and moved to Belgrade after World War II.

Todorović-Sudetic, Ljiljana (LYEE-lya-na)—The author's wife.

Tolimir, Zdravko (TOLL-ee-meer, ZDROV-ko)—General in the Bosnian Serb army. A deputy to the Bosnian Serb commander, Ratko Mladić.

Topalović, Brane (tow-POLL-o-veetch, BRON-ey)—The name of a Serb who, according to eyewitnesses, killed Muslim prisoners in the gymnasium of a Bratunac school in April and May 1992. Still lives in a town in Serbia just west of Belgrade.

Tursunović, Zulfo (TOOR-soon-o-veetch, ZOOL-fo)—The Muslim military commander in the southwestern corner of the Srebrenica enclave near the village of Sućeska.

Ustić, Akif (OOS-teech, AH-keef)—Naser Orić's right-hand man in Srebrenica until fall 1992. Killed in an ambush with about twenty of his men.

Vance, Cyrus—The U.S. secretary of state in the Carter administration. The co-chairman, with David Owen, of the UN peace conference for the former Yugoslavia. Resigned in May 1993.

Vasić, Dragica (VAS-eetch, DRAHG-eet-sa)—The Čeliks' Serb neighbor in Srebrenica.

Vasić, Veljko (VEIL-ko)—The Serb husband of Dragica Vasić. A secret operative for Marshal Tito's Partisans during World War II. Head of Srebrenica district after the war. His mother and sister and five nieces and nephews were killed by the Ustaše during World War II.

Vasiljević, Mitar (vas-EEL-yev-eetch, MEE-tar)—A Serb waiter at the hotel beside Mehmed Pasha's bridge in Višegrad. A member of Milan Lukić's gang.

Voorhoeve, Joris—Defense minister of the Netherlands. Called off the NATO air strikes against the Serbs after the fall of Srebrenica.

Wahlgren, Lars Eric—A Swedish army general who commanded the UN military force in the former Yugoslavia. Fired without notice for opposing the UN resolution declaring Srebrenica and other regions in Bosnia to be safe areas.

Wörner, Manfred—Secretary-general of NATO.

Zekić, Goran (ZECK-eetch, GORE-on)—The leader of the Serbian Democratic Party in Srebrenica. Killed by Naser Orić's men in a roadside ambush above Srebrenica in 1992.

Zekić, Zagorka and *Slobodan* (ZECK-eetch, ZAH-gore-ka and SLOW-bow-dahn)— Serb neighbors of the Čeliks who were murdered by Muslims in Srebrenica in January 1993.

Zelen, Ljilja (ZELL-en, LYEE-lyah)—The wife of Radovan Karadžić, the leader of the Serbian Democratic Party in Bosnia. The daughter of a Serb whose family was decimated by the Croatian Fascist Ustaše during World War II.

PROLOGUE

The opening months of the second year of the war in Bosnia, May and June of 1993, seemed to be a season for promises, big and small. I was in Sarajevo one evening late in that season when I remembered I had an appointment at a government building in the city's center and had to get there to keep a promise I had given my wife weeks earlier. The appointment had nearly slipped my mind, and I was irritated that it hadn't. I was tired. A drizzle hung in the air. And now I had to drag myself out of my room and try to make contact by ham radio with someone I knew but felt little connection with. The radio operators had postponed the appointment twice already. Drumming up some excuse to postpone it again would have been easy, and I've forgotten why I didn't.

I was making, and keeping, few personal promises back then. From a Cleveland suburb bursting with kids and housewives and working fathers, I had found my way into a mercenary, monomaniacal existence and had shoved family obligations to the bottom of my list of priorities. It was my fifth year in Yugoslavia, and I was making my living by reporting about the war for the *New York Times*. There were many incentives for staying on the road, for staying in Bosnia to work. I earned real money only if I found stories that got into print, and in all the world Bosnia was the place to find compelling stories. But it was not only the money that kept me going back. Even in peacetime, back before the war when I was a student in Yugoslavia, traveling through Bosnia's mountains had been an adventure for me, a journey back in time through the legacies of three extinct empires, one Islamic, one Eastern Orthodox, one Roman Catholic; a journey into a world run by a bankrupt Communist mafia and its secret police; a journey through wild natural beauty into a moribund world of semiliterate, hard-drinking peasant men, a world of superstitions, tattooed women, and a cult of the dead, a world where living memories and bedtime stories merged history into the landscape itself. Once the war began, there was an addictive, groin-tingling excitement to working in Bosnia. I relished the hunt for stories and words that would show the horror and the scandalous injustice of the destruction of Bosnia and the war's primary victims, the Muslims. This was easy enough. But I always felt that my stories and words failed to plumb the deep structure of Bosnia itself, especially peasant Bosnia, lumpen Bosnia, the Bosnia the war had ravaged most.

There is a method to presenting the reality of war in *Times* style, a restrictive method but a perfectly valid one just the same. It focuses mainly on institutions and political leaders and their duties and decisions, while leaving the common folk to exemplify trends, to serve as types: a fallen soldier, a screaming mother, a dead baby—literal symbols, the kind Pablo Picasso used to render the Fascist bombing of Guernica during the Spanish civil war. This method is described by various terms: detachment, disinterestedness, dispassion, distancing, and others with negative prefixes engineered to obliterate any relationship between observer and observed. When I went to Bosnia to work, I used to imagine I had entered a great grassland teeming with life. "I build a tower hundreds of feet high," I told one of my friends. "I climb it every morning and observe the wildlife devouring one another and struggling to survive down below. And from that distance, I write about what I see, send my story, have something to eat, and go to sleep." I once walked through a town littered with the purple-and-yellow bodies of men and women and a few children, some shot to death, some with their heads torn off, and I felt nothing; I strolled around with a photographer, scratched notes, and lifted sheets covering the bodies of dead men to see if they had been castrated; I picked up a white flag from the ground near the twisted bodies of half a dozen men in civilian clothes who had been shot next to a wall, and then I carried the flag home and hung it above my desk. I once saw soldiers unload babies crushed to death in the back of a truck and immediately ran off to interview their mothers. I accidentally killed an eighteen-year-old man who raced in front of my car on a bike; his head was smashed; I held the door when they loaded him into the backseat of the automobile that carried him to the emergency room of Sarajevo's main hospital; I expressed my condolences to his father; then I got a tow back to my hotel, went to my room, and sent that day's story to New York.

My observation tower had begun to wobble by then, but I managed to maintain a distance for another eighteen months, and no one could have kept me from going back to the war. It was exhilarating. It was my addiction, my mania. It even simplified life and gave it meaning. Only when I traveled home to my wife and daughters in Belgrade did the pent-up stress and anger and guilt erupt. I would slam doors, smash dishes, and swear for a few days, lobotomize myself with rented videos for a week or so, and head back to

Bosnia to detach myself from my family and emotions and take up the hunt for stories and words for another month or two.

I HAD already filed my story on that drizzly Sarajevo evening in June 1993 when I remembered my appointment and my promise to my wife, Ljiljana. I had told her before I left Belgrade that I would do my best during that trip to Bosnia to track down a man named Huso Čelik, a Muslim man with crossed eyes, a laborer in the brickyard of a construction company whom I had met twice in Sarajevo before the war. There was a family connection. Ljiljana is a native Yugoslav, a Serb born and raised in Belgrade; her only sister, Gordana, had married Huso Čelik's eldest son, Hamed. No one had heard from Huso or the rest of his family since they disappeared in the Bosnian mountains during the opening months of the war. Anger, uncertainty, and a thirst for vengeance were poisoning Hamed's mind. A few months after the war began, he was fired from his job in Belgrade; a couple of days later, one of his Serb neighbors threatened to shoot him because he was a Muslim; then he left Gordana and their children and went to Austria to live with his uncle and await an immigration visa to Canada. Muslim refugees passing through Austria brought Hamed tales of the war and rumors about his family. They said a Serb gang led by a man named Milan Lukić, a school chum of Hamed's younger brother, had driven out all the Muslims from his family's hamlet. They said Hamed's father had died of a heart attack, his youngest brother had been killed, and his sister wounded. Soon Hamed's relatives and their Muslim neighbors in Austria were cackling about Hamed's Serb wife. In Belgrade, the Serbs started asking why Hamed had left his wife alone to wrestle with three kids in one room of her mother's two-room apartment.

I knew hundreds of similar stories, and after the first dozen or so they were hardly news. In that first year of the war, nationalist Serb gunmen bent on dismembering Bosnia had uprooted hundreds of thousands of Muslims and killed tens of thousands more, the vast majority of them civilians and prisoners. The survivors were scattered all over Yugoslavia and the rest of Europe. I had made an effort to ask around for Huso in refugee shelters. I inquired with government officials and occasionally scanned lists of the displaced and the dead. Some nights, I tuned in to local radio talk shows dedicated solely to greetings and messages from callers searching for their lost relatives; but this was like listening to someone read a telephone book. Finally, a friend in the government set up a time slot for me to speak by ham radio with a man named Huso Čelik who had turned up in a place called Srebrenica, a town just inside Bosnia's border with Serbia.

When I walked out of the drizzle and into the government building, a security guard pointed me toward the radio room. I figured the radio operators were not going to give me much time, so I rehearsed my questions as I climbed a staircase and set off down an empty corridor. The Serb army besieging Sarajevo had cut off the city's running water, and the air in the corridor was sticky with the odor of the shit that had piled up in the toilets all day. I found my way through the stench to an alcove where an antenna cable emerged from under a closed door, ran across the corridor, and climbed out through an open window. The radio operators asked me to wait outside for a few minutes, and I leaned out the window to breathe. "First," I thought, "I have to make sure it's the right Huso Čelik."

The operators already had Srebrenica on the air when they called me into the room. The tuner had a piece of paper covering it to hide the frequency. A garbled voice I would never have recognized emerged from the ether.

"Hallo," I said. ". . . over."

More garble I could not understand came through the crackling speaker.

"Hallo. Hallo. Where are you from? Over."

". . . up . . . sovići."

It sounded right.

"Where do you work? Over."

"Vr . . . nica. Vra . . . ca."

It was Hamed's father, all right. Vranica was the name of the construction company where Hamed had taken me to meet his father a few weeks before the war. When the signal cleared up, Huso wasted no time rattling off each family member's name. Hamed's mother, Hiba, was well. His sister had never been wounded. His brother was alive. I passed along regards from everyone in the outside world.

"Tell them we're alive and well," Huso said. "If you can, come and see us."

"I'll try," I answered, though I knew even then I would never make it.

"And bring cigarettes," Huso said, "only cigarettes."

"I understand."

"And please, try and get us out of here."

The radio operators motioned that my time was up, and we signed off. Sarajevo had no telephone links with the outside world then, so I sent a sparse message over a satellite to the *Times*'s foreign desk in New York before getting something to eat and going to sleep. My friends in New York forwarded it to Ljiljana in Belgrade so that she could call Hamed with the good news that the Čeliks were alive and the bad news that they were trapped in a town that had become something worse than a concentration camp.

I had spent much of that spring writing about how the army of the Bosnian Serbs had goaded tens of thousands of displaced Muslims into Srebrenica, battered them with artillery, demanded their surrender, and threatened to massacre the town's menfolk once the place fell. The ambassadors of the countries sitting on the United Nations Security Council had saved Srebrenica from a bloodbath by hastily declaring it to be a "safe area" and by pledging to protect it with NATO jets if the Serbs attacked again. This was the biggest promise of that season.

❨   ❨   ❨

TWO years later, in June of 1995, one of many seasons for broken promises arrived in Bosnia. Huso and the other Čeliks were still trapped in Srebrenica, living off humanitarian aid, smoking homegrown tobacco and pumpkin leaves, waiting out the war. Hamed had made it to Canada with Gordana and their three children; he had tried to slip cash inside Polaroid snapshots enclosed in Red Cross letters he sent to Huso from Toronto, but all of the money was stolen. Ljiljana and I had been back in New York with our two daughters for five months by then; I had exhausted myself in Bosnia, took a staff job with the *Times* that promised a secure future, and made the mistake of assuring my wife I could set the unresolved question of the war on a shelf beside my white flag and live happily in an ocean-front apartment, with weekends free for romping on the beach and trying to catch the Browns and the Indians on television.

Word of the Serb army's attack on Srebrenica came to us on the television news. Hamed glued himself to CNN around the clock and called me a few times during the five days of the offensive to see if I knew anything more than the television was reporting. The UN was releasing precious little of what it knew about the attack. I remember hearing and reading speculation by UN officials that the Serb army was only trying "to squeeze" the Srebrenica "safe area." I recognized the scent of the cheap red herring that had been dragged around Bosnia for years already by UN diplomats and military officers to cover up the sticky odor of the powerful nations of the Security Council breaking their word. Hamed and I swore together in rage. We predicted what would happen; anyone who knew page one about Bosnia could have predicted what would happen. We waited to see who would make it out alive.

A few hours after Srebrenica's fall, Serb soldiers had thousands of the town's Muslim women, children, and old people surrounded on the grounds of a decrepit battery factory next to a UN military base. The soldiers had arrived at the factory amiably enough. They gave Muslim children cookies, pieces of candy, and chunks of bread. One Serb even kissed his former neighbor on the cheeks before he escorted him away. Gunshots rang out. Women wailed. Soon the place was reeking of shit and urine. Soldiers on horseback began herding the crowd into a tighter circle. Women who went to fetch water spotted the bodies of dead boys in a creek. German shepherd dogs chased down men who had bolted into the nearby woods. One woman hung herself inside a factory building.

Huso and Hiba knew the Serb gunmen who led away a dozen of their neighbors from back home. Two of the Serbs had grown up in villages just down a dirt road from the Čelik place. Their leader, a lean, good-looking young man who was wearing a tight black shirt and baggy fatigues with a long knife in a scabbard hanging from his belt, had been the schoolmate of Hamed's younger brother. It was Milan Lukić. He assured Huso and the other Muslim men that everything would be fine. He said he had chartered a special bus for the Muslims from his district and picked out a dozen of them to come and get the tickets for everyone else. Huso believed Lukić. Huso even volunteered to go along with the rest of the Muslim men when Lukić and the other Serbs led them away. "I'm ready to go right now," Huso said. But the Serbs told Huso to sit down.

He shuffled back into the crowd and bundled himself up inside a worn-out army jacket as if he were freezing in the summer heat. He lit a cigarette, then griped about pains in his chest and swelling in his legs. Hiba was irritated with him. She was afraid the women nearby in the crowd would see him paralyzed with fear and hear him whining like a child. She assured him that everything would be fine. She told him they were not alone.

❴   ❴   ❴

IN September of 1995, at the beginning of a new season for promises in Bosnia, I took a month's leave from my job in New York and traveled back to Bosnia to meet the Čeliks who survived the slaughter at Srebrenica, the largest mass killing in Europe since the Communists took over Yugoslavia after World War II. I brought them a wad of cash, cartons of Marlboro, a stack of Canadian immigration forms, and suitcases stuffed with clothes, shoes, and toys. I also came to collect the Čeliks' memories for a story for *Rolling Stone* magazine about how the UN and the powerful countries of the world had ignored their promises and abandoned the Muslims of Srebrenica to the Serbs' tender mercies.

We talked for days in the kitchen of a gritty farmhouse, swatting mosquitoes and sipping coffees and colas and an occasional plum brandy. The Čeliks spoke with hardly a pause, and I found it strange that it was taking so long to tell the stories. Slowly I realized this was because their stories carried me far beyond a chronology of a massacre and an international scandal. The stories flashed me back to a time before the Čeliks groped their way through the mountains to Srebrenica. The stories told of life along a troubled border long before the Bosnian war. They described a hamlet with a funny name and wives with no husbands and sons with no fathers. They spoke of a weather-beaten schoolhouse, a man with a hidden cannon, beehives that flew through kitchen windows, and a woman who galloped around on a tree branch to remove a hex from a mad cow. They turned back time to another war, and another; to invasions and rebellions; to heretics, dervishes, pashas, and sultans; to slaves and sharecroppers and a swindler with three wives. When I started talking with Serbs from around Srebrenica and the villages near the Čeliks' old home, I realized their stories dovetailed with the Muslims' and also began with memories of a time long before the war, memories of fistfights, funerals, and feasts, of great-great-grandfathers who struggled to be free of feudalism, of great-grandfathers who helped ignite a world war, and of grandfathers who fought to survive Fascist butchery, who exacted blood vengeance to appease their dead, and who suffered defeat and buried their guns for another day.

Here was the deep structure. Here, with a myriad of characters and contradictions, were images of the peasant Bosnia destroyed by the war; images that were not symbols, not the fallen soldier, the crying mother, the dead baby of *Guernica*, but portraits of people, of individuals, going about their lives in quiet desperation like the roly-poly women, the grizzle-bearded, drunken men, and the prankster children of Brueghel; images that gave a glimpse of how peasant Bosnia had come to be, how it survived the seasons and the centuries and the wars, how it struggled to lift itself from poverty and ignorance, how its bitter, living memories were stirred as the Communist world collapsed, and how a small group of men bent on taking and keeping personal power ignited its passions and blew a country apart.

The old addiction, my mania, seized me once again, and I broke the promise I had made my wife. Within a few months I had quit my job and we had packed our apartment into a storage warehouse in Cleveland and moved back to our old neighborhood in Belgrade. I took off alone for one last stint in Bosnia for the sake of a few stories and words that might lay some living memories of the dead and of a dying world silently to rest.

CHUCK SUDETIC
Senjak
July 15, 1997

PART ONE

DYING EMPIRES, DEADLY MYTHS

BOSNIA

Srebrenica

Podravanje

Zlovrh

Žepa
Slap
Ferry

Kamenica
(Hiba's)
Rujišta

Odžak
Kupusovići
Žlijeb

Prelovo

to
Sarajevo

Skelani

Bajina
Bašta

Dam
Drina

Steel
bridge

Tara Mt.

Zvijezda Mt.

SERBIA

to Užice

Višegrad

Dam
Mehmed
Pasha's
Bridge

Dobrun

Drina

0   10 km

0   5 miles

Chazaud

1

Huso Čelik entered the world, grew to manhood, and raised his family in eastern Bosnia, on the upper reaches of Mount Zvijezda, or Star Mountain. This mountain is a bulwark of earth and limestone, and its crest has marked out one stretch of Bosnia's border with Serbia for much of the last six hundred years.*

Signs of this border's troubled past abound on Mount Zvijezda. Amid its meadows are the stone ruins of an army barracks and the crumbling trenches where border guards once fought and died. There is a vacant, weather-beaten building that was once a customhouse, and far below it lies an empty meadow known by all the locals as the Customs Area. There are ancient gravestones decorated with daggers and swords and inscribed in languages no longer spoken on the mountain. Etched into its living rock are crude stick-figure eagles with proud, outstretched wings; mystical swastikas; and horse soldiers with helmets and drawn swords. The peasants call these pictographs "the Roman Signs" and believe they are almost as old as the mountain itself. Someday, the peasants say, someone will come and decipher the secret meaning of the Roman Signs. Then a massive river will gush forth from the rock and devastate the land for miles around.

Parents and grandparents have prepared generations of Mount Zvijezda's children for the uncertainty of life on the border by telling them stories of the soldiers and the bandits and the greedy landlords who have ravaged the place over the years. They have told and retold their memories of fathers and mothers, uncles and aunts, and grandfathers and grandmothers who died by violence and whose deaths were never avenged. They have discreetly pointed out killers still living within shouting distance, still working their fields and tending their flocks, still smiling as they stroll by the house on their way home. These tales have taught generations of the border's children that a smile may always be something other than a smile. They have ingrained in them the assumption that Mount Zvijezda might well have never seen a generation come and go in peace since its creation.

---

*The side of the Mount Zvijezda described corresponds to the area known locally as Višegradska Župa.

EVEN the children on Mount Zvijezda can tell snippets of the story of Jerina the Damned, the legendary villainess who created the mountain. Jerina was foreign born, the wife of a hated despot who once ruled the countryside for miles around. She henpecked her husband and built the mountain as part of a fortress to defend her husband's territory against invaders and brigands. Jerina, the legend goes, used black magic to fashion from water alone an entire legion of giant soldier-slaves. Each morning, rain or shine, she ordered these slaves to line up in long human chains and pass boulders from one to the next. Month after month, Jerina's slaves toiled. Year after year, they piled up the boulders and secured them with stones and dirt until they had formed a wall rising some three thousand feet above the valley floor and extending for twelve miles more or less from south to north. Every few miles along the top of the wall, Jerina's slaves built up rounded peaks that jut skyward like watchtowers. Between these towers, the slaves left passes accessible only by steep footpaths that rise like stone stairways. On the sides of the mountain, the slaves also cut fissures and tight passages into the white rock. These open into an underworld of caves and grottoes, ice-cold subterranean rivers, and vertical shafts that plunge into pitch-black pits that seem to have no bottom.

Jerina had the western wall of Mount Zvijezda buttressed with terraces of earth anchored by outcroppings of rock. These terraces are cut by creeks that turn into angry torrents after each snow melt and rainstorm. Covering the terraces are forests of beech, oak, and pine as well as rolling pasturelands, meadows, and rows of pear, apple, and plum trees that mark off vegetable patches and small fields of potatoes, wheat, and spindly corn. Unpredictable gusts of wind blow down from the top of the mountain wall and up from the valley floor. The air carries the aroma of manure, pine resin, and wood fires along with the gurgle of falling water, the screech of birds of prey, the tinkle of cowbells, and the "Yeoooo! Yeoooo" of peasant men and women summoning one another as they tend their flocks or work their fields.

Life on Jerina the Damned's mountain has made these peasants cautious even in their singsong calls to one another. I once heard Huso Čelik's lifelong friend, a Serb named Dragoljub Radovanović, yodel to his wife, Zora, one spring afternoon. The Bosnian war had ended by then, or seemed to have ended. Zora and her sister were down in a meadow below their cinderblock house. They were using a pair of paper scissors to shear their sheep and were stuffing the fleece into plastic bags. "Yeoooo! Yeoooo!" Dragoljub called down to them. "Come on hoommme! Someone's commme to visit. Commme seeee! Someone's commme to visit."

I had brought someone with me—Hamed's mother, Hiba. The glaucoma had fogged up Dragoljub's eyesight so badly by then that he had had to put on his glasses even to try make out who it was climbing the path toward his house.

It took him a few seconds more to recognize Hiba. He had known her for years, but she had disguised herself. She had not covered her squirrel-colored hair with a kerchief, and she was wearing a skirt instead of *dimije*, the billowy bloomers tied at the ankle that Muslim women on the mountain had always worn. Dragoljub was discreet. He did not shout out the visitor's name when he called to Zora. The other Serbs in the village would have heard him. No good would have come of it. "We'rrre commmmmin'," I heard Zora yodel from the meadow below. "We'rrre almmmmmoooossst dooonnne." She never yelled up to ask who had come to visit.

AT the foot of Mount Zvijezda's western slopes, far beyond yodeling range from Dragoljub's house, the turquoise waters of the Drina River flow northward, parallel to the mountain for its entire length. Jerina the Damned had to keep the river from flooding her land. So she channeled the Drina out through the walls of her fortress by cutting a forbidding gorge that separates Mount Zvijezda from Zlovrh, or Evil Mountain, its twin to the north. The gorge begins at a riverside village known as Slap, right where the Drina makes an unnaturally sharp eastward turn. A few miles farther downstream, Mount Zvijezda drops the burden of the Bosnian-Serbian border onto the Drina's back, and the current carries the border for the rest of the river's journey northward.

At about the time of the birth of Christ, legions of foreign soldiers conquered Bosnia and merged it into the vast blend of tribes, peoples, city-states, and colonies called the Roman Empire. The Romans built villas and roads in the Drina valley over the next four hundred years. Latin became the language of the land. Caravans traveling northward from the Adriatic seacoast loaded their cargo onto rafts and steered them downstream or followed a minor trade route beneath Mount Zvijezda and along the Drina's right bank. Ferrymen transported some of these ancient travelers and their pack animals across the river near Slap. After reaching the left bank, the caravans entered a narrow valley now known as Žepa. Then they zigzagged their way up the side of Zlovrh before descending through a forest into a mining town that had grown up around rich silver and lead deposits. The Romans called this mining town Domavium. Their slaves, mostly prisoners of war and their offspring, dug the silver, smelted it, transported it down the Drina on barges, and minted coins from it.

The Drina's long experience as a border began during Roman times, in A.D. 395, when the sons of Emperor Theodosius split the empire and used the river to mark the frontier between its Latin-dominated western half and its Greek-dominated eastern half. Within a few centuries, the Western Roman Empire collapsed into the chaos of the Dark Ages. Barbarian invaders from the

East, including Croats, Serbs, and other Slavic tribesmen, wiped out Bosnia's Latin-speaking Christians and plundered their towns, churches, and villas in the Drina valley. Bandits halted the caravan traffic. The Roman roads fell into disrepair. Domavium's mines closed. And the Slavic tongue replaced Latin as the language of the land. Domavium's name was recast using the word *srebren*, the Slavic adjective for silver, and the town came to be called Srebrenica.

No single empire held sway over southeastern Europe during the centuries after the conversion of the barbarian Slavs to Christianity and the Great Schism of A.D. 1054, when the Roman Catholic pope and the patriarch of the Eastern Orthodox Church tore the main body of Christianity in half and left Bosnia dangling in the middle. The Slavic princes and feudal landholders who ruled Bosnia in the Middle Ages prospered for a time by reopening Srebrenica's silver mines. But they soon found themselves under pressure from the east by the Orthodox princes and despots of medieval Serbia and from the north and west by the Roman Catholic kings of Hungary and the feudal leaders of Hungary's vassal state, Croatia. The names of many of these rulers — King Sigismund, Djurdje Branković, Despot Stefan, and many others — have long since faded from the memory of most of the peasants on Mount Zvijezda. But the mountain folk perk up and smile when they hear the familiar name of Jerina the Damned, as if this foreign-born villainess who conjured up an army of giants from water to build Mount Zvijezda embodied all of the evil incarnate in all of the men who ever ruled over it, as if Jerina had come to represent the danger that would make an old Serb with glaucoma afraid to shout to his wife that a Muslim woman had come back to the village for a visit.

"Oh, that Jerina the Damned, that Jerina the Damned," the toothless mouth of one of the Čeliks' great-uncles once sighed when I asked him about her. His nickname was Penzija, "The Pension," and he was about ninety years old and almost cut off from the world by deafness. "She is damned, that Jerina," he repeated.

"Why? Why is she damned?" I asked.

"Huh?"

"Why?" I shouted. "Why is she damned?"

"She is damned and has always been damned. The people damned her. And that's all I can say about it."

❨   ❨   ❨

JERINA'S bulwarks failed to protect Bosnia from the last great incursion against Europe from the East, the invasions of Ottoman Turk armies into the southeastern corner of the continent beginning in the fourteenth century.

The Ottoman Turks evolved from an obscure band of nomads who fled the Mongol invasion of the Central Asian steppes in the early thirteenth century. They took refuge on a rocky plateau in central Anatolia and began, under a sultan named Osman, to expand their territory westward at the expense of their new Orthodox Christian neighbors. Within a few decades, the descendants of Osman had assembled a military juggernaut that fed itself on conquest, plunder, and tribute, and they laid the foundation for the second lasting empire, after Rome, to master the Balkan peninsula. The Ottoman Turks tore apart Orthodox Byzantium, the remnant of the Eastern Roman Empire that had been worn threadbare by centuries of internal strife and an invasion by Roman Catholic crusaders. On Vidovdan, the feast day of Saint Vitus, June 28, 1389, the Turks barely defeated a Serbian-led Christian army in a battle at Kosovo that would become the grist of the Serbian nation's founding myth centuries later. After a setback at Belgrade in 1456, which has been marked throughout Christendom ever since by the tolling of church bells at noontime, the Ottoman armies overran the rest of Orthodox Serbia. Sultan Mehmed marched his armies across the Drina into Bosnia in 1463 and put its princes and feudal landholders to the sword. Ottoman seamen seized one seaport after another, harassed shipping on the Mediterranean Sea, and took control of the overland trade routes to China and India. This prompted the Catholic king and queen of Spain, the same Ferdinand and Isabella who had expelled the Muslim Moors from their last handhold in western Europe, to take a gamble on Christopher Columbus to find them a new trade route to the Far East. Three decades after the discovery of America, the Ottoman armies conquered Hungary and threatened to lift the star and crescent of Islam over even more of European Christendom. Only then, only when minarets were casting their shadows on the rolling plains before Vienna—and just a few hundred miles from Renaissance Venice and Florence—did Austria's ruling family, the Habsburgs, summon the will to mold from a rabble of jealous princes and petty despots a Roman Catholic empire capable of warding off the prospect of imminent destruction.

Bosnia's medieval princes had received scant support from the Roman Catholic world in defending their lands from the Ottoman forces. Most Bosnians were crude shepherds and peasants, tenant sharecroppers who had no idea of nationhood. They had never shown much obeisance unto the established Christian churches and paid even less heed to the Catholic and Orthodox warriors and merchants who invaded their land and sometimes sold their kinfolk into slavery. Many of eastern Bosnia's landholders and peasants were members of a home-grown Bosnian Christian Church, a sect persecuted by the popes of Rome *and* the Serbian Orthodox bishops as heretical.

After the Ottoman invasion, Bosnia's peasants became the sharecroppers of

Muslim landlords, soldiers rewarded by the sultan with temporary custody of estates seized from Bosnia's ousted feudal families. The dues the Christian sharecroppers owed their new masters actually decreased from what they had been paying before the conquest, and peace returned to the land for the first time after decades of turmoil. Over the centuries, many Bosnian Slavs accepted the religion of their foreign conquerors. The song of the muezzins called the new faithful to prayer each day from minarets. The young boys were circumcised each spring by traveling barbers. Consumption of pork was forbidden. And every woman covered her face with a veil from her sixteenth birthday to the end of her life. Conversion to Islam brought reduced taxes and the full benefits of citizenship in a vigorous, overarching power that seemed predestined to conquer the continent. Muslims willing to fight found opportunities to rise to positions of authority in the military and acquire wealth by pillage and plunder. But the vast majority of the converts were, and would continue to be, peasants and herdsmen who were as dirt poor, illiterate, and ignorant as their neighbors who chose to remain Roman Catholics or Orthodox Christians.

Although Islam was the official religion of the Ottoman state, the sultan exercised religious tolerance. He resettled in Bosnia's towns many of the Jews expelled by Ferdinand and Isabella from Spain in 1492. The Greek patriarchs of the Eastern Orthodox Church found a new patron in the sultan, who gave them political and judicial jurisdiction over most of the Christians within the realm, an authority they had never enjoyed under the Christian emperors of Byzantium. The sultan exempted his Christian subjects from serving in his military but required them to pay higher taxes than the Muslims. For several centuries, the sultan periodically ordered Christian families to surrender to him male children, who were forced to accept Islam and remain imperial slaves for life. These boys were schooled in Turkish, Arabic, and other languages and given elaborate training in the military arts and statecraft. Some were inducted into the most elite unit of the imperial army, the Janissaries, while others were assigned to administer the sultan's government. These slaves enjoyed privileges and so much potential for upward mobility that some Christian families volunteered their sons for the sultan's "blood tax." Since freeborn Muslims were barred from the government and the Janissaries, Muslim parents sometimes bribed the sultan's tax collectors to take their boys or secretly left their sons uncircumcised and gave them to their Christian neighbors so that they could, in turn, hand the boys over in payment of the tax.

❛ ❛ ❛

THE limestone mosque a minute's walk away from the Čelik family's homestead on Mount Zvijezda is the largest mosque in the entire district. It stands at the intersection of two rocky trails, and all of the peasants living nearby call this place "the Cross." The Serbs say the mosque was built atop the ruins of an Eastern Orthodox chapel, and they argue that the Cross would never have gotten its name if it had not been for the crucifix that once stood atop the chapel. The Muslims, however, insist that the mosque was built from the ground up by a certain Juz-bin-Kulaga, the commander of thousands of Ottoman soldiers, who was granted land on Mount Zvijezda by the sultan. Juz-bin, they say, was laid to rest next to the mosque under a gravestone whose top had been chiseled into the shape of a turban. No one remembers when or how Juz-bin died. No one even remembers whether he was still alive on a fateful summer day when the local *hodža*, the Muslim clergyman assigned to the mosque, climbed the spiral stairway inside the minaret, peered out over the fields and meadows from its circular porch, and called the faithful to the afternoon prayer.

"*Allahu ekber!* God is great!" the *hodža* sang. Then he noticed something unusual down below and paused for an instant. "*Allahu ekbe* . . . Yeoooo! Yeoooo! Therrre's a cooow in the caaabbage paaatch! Yeoooo! Yeoooo! Get the cooow! Get the cooow!"

Elsewhere in the realm of the sublime sultan, perhaps, such sacrilege would have caused a scandal and a swift meting out of punishment. But the sides of Mount Zvijezda rumbled with laughter, and the Muslim and Orthodox peasants bestowed upon the hamlet next to Juz-bin's mosque a new name that has made people cluck about that cow in the cabbage patch ever since. Kupusovići, they called the place. KOO-poos-oh-vee-chee, Hamlet of the Cabbage People.

ITINERANT dervish mystics and the *hodžas* who served at Juz-bin's and other nearby mosques provided the only education on Mount Zvijezda, and its Orthodox Christians went without schooling entirely. A handful of the Muslim men learned to read the Arabic of Islam's sacred book, the Koran, and to write their Slavic language in the Arabic script; a rare one among them would master the Persian of the Sufi mystics and poets. The *hodžas* and other self-taught Muslim holy men known popularly as mullahs prayed over the sick and worked cures by feeding them pieces of paper on which they had scrawled out passages from the Koran in Arabic letters with goose quills dipped into ink made from grass. Both the Muslims and the Orthodox Christians had women and men who conjured up potions and charms from leaves, rags, fingernails, and ashes and promised that these would ward off disease, break up a marriage, stop a kid from wetting the bed, or dry up the udders on the neighbor's best cow. Old women and men would melt lead and drop it into pails of water, and from the shapes taken by the globs of cooled metal they would tell someone's fortune, exorcise demons, and assuage fears. If a mullah or a *hodža* or a faith healer proved particularly adept, the sick, the barren, the jealous, and the vengeful would ignore their religious differences and seek their help.

The age-old agricultural cycle on Mount Zvijezda turned without interruption. The peasants raised and harvested their crops by means of wooden plows and other primitive implements. The women sheared their sheep, spun and dyed the wool, and wove it into cloth. The proper time for plowing, planting, and harvesting was set according to the saints' days on the Orthodox calendar and, since no one really remembered anyone's birthday, children were told that they came into this world "during the plowing," "with the beans," "with the plums," or, for an unfortunate few, "with the manure." Bosnia's feudal landholders, who were known as beys, *kapetani*, and agas, recruited thousands of Eastern Orthodox peasants from Montenegro and other regions beyond Bosnia's borders to work their fields as tenant sharecroppers. The land-rich and money-poor Muslim landlords on Mount Zvijezda, including the Sućeska beys of Odžak, the hamlet a few hundred yards west of Kupusovići, brought in whole families of Montenegrin tribesmen, a rough-and-tumble highland people who were so poor that they distilled their brandy from grass. They also practiced the most ancient of all methods of maintaining social order: blood vengeance, a custom that requires the men of one family to kill any male member of a second family if someone from the second family has caused the death, even by accident, of someone from the first. It was literally a head for a head, and the retaliation could be carried out at any time and by any means, including a knife to the back. Blood vengeance was a matter of customary law when there was no other law. It was a matter of family honor from which only women and pre-teenage boys were exempted.

The ancestors of today's Radovanović family came to Mount Zvijezda with these Montenegrins. The Lukić family came to Rujišta from a Montenegrin village called Lipovac, and its members worked as sharecroppers for an aga named Zahić. The Čeliks themselves might have come from Montenegro during the same period. After the Orthodox Montenegrins' arrival, Muslims continued to make up the majority population on Mount Zvijezda; but in Bosnia as a whole, the Orthodox soon outnumbered the Muslims and Catholics.

VIŠEGRAD, the town nearest to Mount Zvijezda, grew up on the right bank of the Drina at the site of a medieval ferry landing about ten miles south of Kupusovići. In the sixteenth century, Mehmed Pasha Sokolović, the most illustrious son of the Drina valley, transformed Višegrad into a bustling caravan stopover by spanning the river with a bridge. It is a miraculous bridge, with eleven white stone arches and a marble tablet calling upon Allah to bless it. At its center is a square balcony known as the *sofa*, and there, on the sofa's stone benches, the townsmen of Višegrad gathered in the evenings to discuss the issues of the day. They gazed down into the swirling current of the river as they sipped frothy coffees said to be as sweet as sin, as hot as hell, and as black as a woman's heart.

Mehmed Pasha was born to a prominent Orthodox family from a village up-river from Višegrad. He was handed over to the sultan in payment of the blood tax and rose by his wits, ambition, and luck to become the most powerful minister to perhaps the greatest of all Ottoman sultans, Suleiman the Magnificent. Mehmed Pasha never forgot his home or his Orthodox roots. He used his power to free the Serbian Orthodox Church from Greek domination in 1557. He had his brother appointed patriarch of the restored Serbian Church, allowed it to establish a new patriarchate in Kosovo, and gave it jurisdiction over all Orthodox Christians in Serbia, Bosnia, and other regions of the Balkans. As a result, many Eastern Orthodox peasants and herdsmen in Bosnia came to identify themselves in later centuries as Serbs; and Mehmed Pasha, a convert to Islam who commanded the sultan's army against Christendom, is today regarded by the Serbs as a national hero. Ironically, Mehmed Pasha died from a knife thrust into his heart by another Orthodox convert to Islam, a dervish from eastern Bosnia seeking vengeance for the death of his spiritual master, who had been executed by the Ottoman authorities as a heretic.

Mehmed Pasha's assassination left the Ottoman Empire in the hands of weak-willed rulers and marked the beginning of centuries of decline. Freeborn Muslims, who were less obedient to the sultan than his Christian-born slaves, gradually found their way into the Janissaries and the government administration. The estates granted temporarily to Ottoman soldiers were gradually transformed into hereditary feudal lands, and the landowners now had less reason to fear the whims of the sultan in far-off Istanbul. The Christian tenant sharecroppers who worked these feudal lands were now effectively stripped of the protection the sultan's absolute authority had once provided. And it would not be long before the landowners began demanding that the sharecroppers pay extortionate dues.

❈   ❈   ❈

THE last, desperate lunge by the Ottoman Empire against Christian Europe failed in 1683. Austrian, German, and Polish knights routed a huge Ottoman army besieging Vienna and sent the sultan's forces retreating like a fugitive rabble eastward through Hungary. In 1686, the Austrians and their Catholic allies pried the Ottomans from Hungary's capital, Budapest, and commenced, to Europe's delight, the destruction of the Ottoman legacy on European soil. Budapest's mosques and bathhouses were burned and razed. Muslim families, including the families of army officers who had once been the Ottoman feudal elite in Hungary, retreated into eastern Bosnia and other Ottoman territories and were desperate to reestablish themselves on new land. The Austrians had practically reached the gates of Belgrade by the end of the century, when they paused to conclude a peace treaty. It was then that Russia, the Eastern Orthodox realm of czars who claimed the inheritance of the defunct Eastern Roman Empire, took up its sword and set about carving away new chunks of Ottoman territory. Soon the czar was demanding that the sultan grant Russia a protectorate over the Serbs and the other Orthodox Christians within the Ottoman Empire. Within a few decades, Catholic Austria and Orthodox Russia had begun competing to acquire Ottoman territories in the Balkans.

As the years passed, the sultan lost internal control of his empire. Rampant bribery and other forms of corruption sucked away his state's vitality. Without the incentive of new conquests and plunder, the Ottoman military machine broke down. Local warlords became the de facto sovereigns of huge tracts of imperial territory. Lawlessness consumed the land as these warlords fought among themselves and against troops sent in by the sultan to restore imperial control. Common men resorted to blood vengeance to settle their scores. The conservative Muslim Slav beys, *kapetani*, and agas in Bosnia were desperate to cling to their land and privileges. They stymied attempts by the sultan to reform his government and armed forces, just as the European powers had been modernizing their governments and armies in the wake of scientific advances brought on by the Enlightenment. This eighteenth-century movement in Western Europe stressed individual liberty, secularism, reason, and a spirit of skepticism. It gave birth to the ideals incorporated into the American Constitution and the Bill of Rights.

The Enlightenment also spawned a new state of mind that swept over all of Europe and later became the world's dominant political attitude. This was nationalism. Under its spell individual Frenchmen, Germans, Hungarians, Italians, Serbs, and, somewhat later, Croats, began to sense that they owed their primary loyalty not to emperors, kings, or popes but to their respective *nations*. Soon this new sense of national loyalty developed into a hunger for the formation of "nation-states" independent of Europe's overarching empires. In time, the idea of national unity overwhelmed the Enlightenment ideal of individual liberty, and from there it was a short step to the barbarism of modern warfare, to war waged not by a small class of feudal warriors or mercenaries but by an entire nation. During the French Revolution and the

Napoleonic Wars, for the first time, men were mobilized en masse, willingly or unwillingly, to fight for the glory of France. In time, the other European nations mobilized national armies, and their aim became the creation of nation-states and, too often, the subjugation or extirpation of entire foreign or minority populations within them. Men who refused to participate were castigated as traitors.

With support from Orthodox Russia, the Serbian Orthodox Church had become by the late 1700s the backbone of the emerging Serb nation. The Church had also become more of a nationalist than a religious organization. Serb priests mythologized the defeat at the Battle of Kosovo and demanded that it be avenged. They lauded the centuries-long resistance to the Turks mounted by the Orthodox clansmen in Montenegro and brigands in Serbia, who fought the authorities one day and collaborated with them the next. Priests in Montenegro began preaching a crusade not only to rid Serbia of the Ottoman Turks but to destroy the entire legacy of the Ottoman Empire, just as the Catholic Europeans had done, and to expel or exterminate the Slavs who had converted to Islam.

The Serbs first threw off Ottoman domination in 1804. Russian-backed insurgents led by Karadjordje, or Black George, a prosperous pig farmer with Montenegrin roots, took control of a swath of land in central Serbia that reached to the passes atop Mount Zvijezda. The uprising held out for nine years before the Turks sent Karadjordje fleeing. Ottoman troops, with Muslim Slavs among them, retaliated against the Serb rebels by plundering their villages, enslaving Serb women and children, torturing and executing captured Serb leaders, and, in some places, murdering all males older than fourteen. These atrocities provoked a second Serb uprising, in 1815, which was led by an illiterate peasant named Miloš Obrenović. Obrenović struck a deal with the sultan. The Serb delivered the Ottoman leader the severed head of Karadjordje and vowed to pay the sultan tribute if he would grant the Serbs autonomy in a patch of territory south of Belgrade. The deal held.

After Russia handed the Ottoman army another defeat in 1829, Obrenović, with diplomatic support from Saint Petersburg, arranged for the expulsion of Muslim landowners and peasants from the region where the Serbs had won their autonomy. The Turks, however, were allowed to maintain garrisons in Belgrade and other Serbian towns. And Ottoman border guards now took up positions along the highest reaches of Mount Zvijezda to protect Višegrad and Mehmed Pasha's bridge from Serb militias and prevent them from driving out the Čeliks, the Sućeskas, and the other Muslim families from Kupusovići, Odžak, and the other villages on the mountain's western slopes.

Thirty years later, at about the same time that the U.S. cavalry was herding the native tribes of the American West onto reservations, Serbia's ruling prince,

Miloš Obrenović's son, Mihailo, prepared a general Balkan uprising against the sultan. Under intense diplomatic pressure aimed at averting a regional conflagration, Turkey agreed to withdraw its military garrisons from Serbia's towns. The Muslim townspeople were now expelled from Serbia, and their mosques were razed. These bitter Muslim Slav outcasts left Serbia for Turkey or found refuge on Mount Zvijezda and other areas of eastern Bosnia. By then, Serb nationalist leaders were laying claim to Bosnia and justifying their claim by arguing that medieval Serbia's princes had controlled vast tracts of Bosnian land and that the Orthodox Christians, the largest segment of Bosnia's population, were in fact Serbs. Soon nationalist Croat leaders staked their claim to Bosnia as well, arguing that the whole region had once been Roman Catholic, and therefore Croat. Both the Serbs and the Croats dismissed Bosnia's Muslims as "ethnic Serbs" or "ethnic Croats" whose ancestors happened to have converted to the Muslim faith. The attitudes of the Muslim Slavs themselves were divided. Some Muslims considered themselves to be Serbs, others Bosnians, others Croats, and others "Turks" or simply loyal subjects of the sultan.

By the late nineteenth century, the force that had once unified the Austrian Empire's disparate peoples, the danger of Ottoman expansion, had ceased to exist even as an illusion. The Hungarians, Czechs, Croats, Italians, Slovaks, Romanians, and other nations submerged within the Austrian Empire were clamoring for the creation of their own nation-states. Hungary's status was elevated, and the Austrian Empire became Austria-Hungary. As Russia continued to expand its borders and influence at the expense of the Ottoman Empire, pressure mounted on Austria to do the same. Government officials in Vienna and officers in Austria's army coveted Bosnia and other Ottoman lands. Their ambition to seize these lands put Austria on a collision course with the Serbs and their backers in Russia.

By 1875, the Ottoman Empire had gone bankrupt. Tax collectors in Bosnia resorted to violence in an attempt to seize grain from hungry sharecroppers after a crop failure. An armed uprising began with the tolling of church bells. Relations between the Serb and Muslim peasants ruptured in many areas, and the bloodshed dragged Bosnia onto the agenda of the international community for the first time. Serb peasants attacked feudal landowners all over Bosnia, and the landowners struck back by sending out Muslim irregulars who burned hundreds of Serb villages and killed several thousand peasants. Bosnian Serb nationalists proclaimed their loyalty to Serbia. They demanded an end to feudalism. They demanded ownership of the farmland they were working and sought Bosnia's merger into Serbia. After a year of peasant bloodshed, Serbia and Montenegro went to war against the Ottoman Empire in a bid to seize its territory in Bosnia. Russian volunteers rushed to join the fight as if it were an Orthodox crusade, and the Russian government saved Serbia from defeat by intervening militarily and driving back the sultan's troops to the very gates of Istanbul. Half a million Muslim Slavs, about a third of Bosnia's population, now found themselves cut off from the receding borders of the Ottoman Empire; about six thousand of these Muslims were beys, *kapetani*, and agas who owned land tilled by about eighty-five thousand sharecroppers and their families, almost all of them Christian.

Europe's ruling monarchies sought to prevent an explosion of sectarian violence in Bosnia and to maintain a balance of power between Orthodox Russia and Catholic Austria. At a peace conference in 1878, the European powers dashed Serbia's ambition to inherit Bosnia and gave Austria the right to occupy the region for an undetermined period. It took Austria's army only a few weeks to secure Bosnia's borders and crush internal resistance to the occupation, which all but a few Muslims eventually came to accept as the will of Allah. The region's Serbs initially reconciled themselves to Austrian rule but assumed that Austria's Habsburg emperor, Franz Josef I, would abolish Bosnia's Muslim-dominated feudal order and distribute the Muslim estates to the sharecroppers. The Serbs grew bitter, however, when no land reform was forthcoming. Their ambition to link Bosnia with Serbia had dismayed the Austrian emperor. He turned to Bosnia's Muslim elite to garner support for the occupation and allowed them to maintain control of their feudal lands. Thus, Catholic Austria preserved the Ottoman Empire's Islamic legacy in Bosnia instead of destroying it, as its Catholic armies had done in Hungary and as the Serbs had done in Serbia.

❮   ❮   ❮

THE Austrian army stationed guards to keep watch over the border along the top of Mount Zvijezda. In Odžak, the guards built a stone customhouse next to the Radovanović family's homestead and took up residence in an old Ottoman barracks just below the house of a Serb family named Mitrašinović. Each day the guards would climb the steep footpaths to the crest of the mountain wall and check travelers coming across from Serbia. They kept watch for horse and cattle smugglers and searched for men who were dodging the unpopular Austrian military draft. The border guards also registered all the stills on the mountain, and enforced limits on the amount of brandy the peasants were allowed to make.

It was probably sometime in the late 1880s when a lone Muslim who called himself Mullah Saban, and nothing more, crossed the border from Serbia into Bosnia. He soon made his way to Kupusovići and announced that he had bought the place along with most of Žlijeb, a village just within shouting distance to the east. The Čeliks and other sharecroppers in Kupusovići now became Mullah Šaban's tenants. They watched in wonder as he constructed himself a fine house so close to Juz-bin's mosque that the shadow of the minaret fell on it on sunny mornings. He opened a store in a room on the ground floor of the house and sold coffee, sugar, and other staples to his sharecroppers.

Mullah Šaban seemed never to have had a family of his own. But he got along well with the Čelik menfolk and soon adopted their surname despite the fact that they were his tenants. Mullah Šaban Čelik, he now called himself, Mullah Šaban "Steel." He trusted the Čelik men enough to give them a peek at some gold ducats he kept hidden away. They assumed Šaban had stolen the gold. They figured he had kept his real surname a secret because he was on the run from some blood-vengeance vendetta across the border and did not want word of his whereabouts to get back to wherever it was he had come from.

Mullah Šaban wanted desperately to have a son. Every Bosnian man in those days wanted to have a son. Sons were the only fitting heirs for a man's material riches. Sooner or later a man's daughters would run off and marry out of the family. Without a son, everything Mullah Šaban had acquired would be cast to the capricious winds that blew down the mountain. He soon took a wife, a girl named Pemba, and brought her to his house next to the mosque. A year or so went by, but Pemba bore him no children. So Mullah Šaban took a second wife, named Čima, but she too seemed to be barren. The third wife's name was Naza. When she failed to conceive a child, Mullah Šaban bought himself a baby boy from someone on the mountain. Šaban was happy, and all three of Šaban's wives fussed over the baby, but the infant died within a few months.

At that time, and for years afterward, it was the duty of Kupusovići's women to fetch water for their families at a spring next to Juz-bin's mosque. The women would gossip and gabble as they waited to fill their water jugs. They would complain about their aches and pains. They would talk of how they had planted entire fields with seeds that did or did not sprout. They would commiserate with one another on how their drunken husbands beat them and kept them up all night. And they also cackled about Mullah Šaban. They were sure he had been cursed with impotence because he had swindled somebody out of the gold ducats he had stashed in his house. It did not take long for the women to begin jabbering about Šaban's third wife, Naza, and how she had taken a shine to one of Mullah Šaban's sharecroppers, a son of Hujbo Čelik named Salih. And it was not long thereafter that Mullah Šaban caught Naza and Salih together.

"You will go with him," Šaban told Naza.

"No, I will not."

"Bring me branches from an oak tree."

Naza obeyed. It was the duty of a Muslim wife to obey. Always.

Mullah Šaban put the oak branches into the fire in his hearth and blew on the flames. He watched the fire consume the branches and turn them into glowing orange coals. Naza waited. Šaban took his walking stick. He pointed it at his wife as if he were going to beat her.

"You are going with him," Mullah Šaban said. "Dance on the coals and tell me you are going with him."

The woman pressed her bare foot onto the coals before she agreed to leave.

"Go," he said. "Now."

Naza left the house next to Juz-bin's mosque and married Salih Čelik. By him, she gave birth to a son named Hasan and at least five daughters, one of whom died in childhood of a snakebite. Mullah Šaban lived for years in his house with the store on the ground floor, but he passed away without having fathered an heir. As he lay dying, he summoned to his bedside all of his wives, including Naza. He gave each one a third of his property. Salih and Naza Čelik received a plot of land near the Cross. They were tenant sharecroppers no longer.

HASAN ČELIK was born in 1909, according to the birth records anyway. He was a quiet child with olive skin, dark hair, and chestnut eyes. By the time he was born, the Austrians had already introduced some of the miracles of the Industrial Revolution to Višegrad and begun wrenching the people of Mount Zvijezda out of the Dark Ages. After July 4, 1906, the unpredictable gusts of wind blowing up the mountainside began to carry with them the faint whistle of a distant steam locomotive. The tiny train, called by the diminutive "Ćiro," or "Choo-Choo," by everyone who spoke the Serbo-Croatian language, chugged its way from Sarajevo along a band of narrow-gauge tracks that ran through tight tunnels and along the sides of deep river gorges before rattling over the Drina on a new steel bridge and hissing and wheezing its way into Višegrad station. Passengers could now travel between Višegrad and Sarajevo in four hours instead of the two days it had required to make the journey on foot since Mehmed Pasha had built his bridge. The Austrians paid local men money to build the steep stone embankments, blast open the tunnels, and lay the tracks. A few of the Čelik men went to work on the railroad after the line was completed, and other peasants found jobs as lumberjacks or woodcutters in local sawmills that could now ship the area's abundant hardwood to distant markets.

Most families on Mount Zvijezda, however, remained on the periphery of the money-earning world and beyond the domain of steam power, watches, and books. They continued to till their fields with wooden plows drawn by oxen or horses. The Muslim landholders continued to collect their dues, though by now most of them had sunk into a poverty almost as miserable as that of the sharecroppers around them. Many men on the mountain lived for their addiction to their plum brandy. They awoke to it each morning and downed it before going to bed at night. Muslim men reveled in the brandy despite the prohibition on alcohol handed down by the Prophet Muhammad in the Koran, and the Serbs had no such religious prohibition. The peasants had found communion in the brandy for as long as anyone could remember, and this communion, for the time being at least, seemed rooted more deeply than a sense of nation or religion. Rare among them was the man who did not take God's name in vain more often than he prayed to Allah or the Christ Jesus.

The mental calendar of the mountain might just as well have been anchored to the plum harvest and the brandy making in late fall and early spring. Not every one had a still, and, if later custom is any indication, the Čelik menfolk in their baggy trousers, black wool cummerbunds, and maroon fezzes would distill the brandy at the Radovanović place or with the Mitrašinović men. There was nothing much else to be done at brandy-making time, nothing that could not be done drunk anyway, so the men would take turns for days on end feeding branches to the fire, tasting each new batch of brandy, and scooping out the bubbling mash with long-handled ladles when it was done. Sometimes they would sit up all night arguing and swearing on the pussies of each other's mothers. They would roast potatoes on the fire, trade lies, tell tales, and play practical jokes. One of them might pull out a wooden flute and play a tune that began the *kolo*, the dance they all seemed to know without ever having learned it. The Muslim women in their billowy *dimije* and drooping veils would take the arms of their Serb sisters and dance about the yard, two steps forward, left foot behind right, right behind left, one step back, jump, and two steps forward.

❮ ❮ ❮

THE men on Mount Zvijezda were preparing for the fall brandy making in 1908, when Austria touched off an international crisis by announcing that it had unilaterally annexed Bosnia. Serbia girded itself for war before Russia stepped in and calmed the situation by means of diplomacy because St. Petersburg was not prepared to go to war over Bosnia. Within a few months, however, Serbia's army had begun creating networks of secret agents in Bosnia whose goal was to wrest the region from Austria's control. Serbia grew even more bold after popular wars in 1912 and 1913, when the tiny country doubled its size by recapturing Kosovo and other territory from the Ottoman Empire. In May 1914, one of the Serbian army's spy networks smuggled into Bosnia a pistol and a young Bosnian Serb student who could recite by heart epic poems about the medieval battle at Kosovo. On Vidovdan, June 28, this student, Gavrilo Princip, stood on a Sarajevo sidewalk and shot to death the heir apparent to Austria's imperial throne, Archduke Franz Ferdinand, and his wife, Countess Sophie Chotek. Animosities toward Bosnia's Serbs erupted into violence immediately after word spread that the Habsburg archduke and his wife had died. For days, Muslims and Croats looted Serbian Orthodox churches and Serb-owned shops, houses, and apartments in Sarajevo, Višegrad, and other towns.

Under pressure from Germany, Austria declared war on Serbia a month after the assassination. The rival alliances that had pitted Europe's great powers against one another clicked into force, and World War I began. Germany, Austria-Hungary, and Turkey faced off in total war against France, Great Britain, and Serbia's main backer, Russia. Salih Čelik was drafted into the Austrian army and sent from Kupusovići to fight Bosnian Serb insurgents in the mountains just west of the Drina. The bulk of the Austrian forces crossed the river into Serbia, intending to punish it quickly and once and for all. Against all odds, however, the Serbs kicked the Austrians back across the river and overran the western slopes of Mount Zvijezda. All of Višegrad was evacuated across Mehmed Pasha's bridge before the Austrian army pulled out and blew up the stone bridge's seventh arch. Naza packed up Hasan and the rest of her children and fled westward with several thousand other Muslims. The refugees traveled on foot and in oxcarts for days before reaching Bosnia's western edge. When they arrived, Naza got word that Salih had been killed in a clash with a band of Serb guerrillas in the mountains above Srebrenica.

Bitter after its initial defeats, the Austrian army treated Bosnia's Serb population as a fifth column. Vigilante gangs of Muslims and Croats carried out gruesome attacks on Bosnian Serb villages. Austrian police rounded up Serbian Orthodox priests, teachers, merchants, community leaders, and anyone else suspected of belonging to Serb nationalist organizations. Thousands of Serbs were driven into Serbia. Others were pitched into concentration camps or executed by hanging and firing squad. In the end, however, after battling heroically against invasions by Austria and Germany and after losing about a quarter of its population to fighting and disease, Serbia emerged on the victorious side.

The war destroyed or fatally wounded all of the old European empires. It also marked the emergence of a new world power, the United States of America, and the ascendancy of the idea of "self-determination of nations," the right of the nations submerged within the old empires to form independent nation-states. The Austrian Empire was broken up into a patchwork of nation-states, including rump Austria, the country that became the heartland of Nazism. Orthodox Russia fell to the atheist Bolsheviks, and parts of the old Russian empire broke away. The Ottoman Empire shrank into the modern secular state of Turkey. Germany, the nation held to be most responsible for the war, was humbled and required to pay war reparations that created the economic chaos and bitterness that would eventually fuel the rise of Adolf Hitler, the unification of Austria and Germany, and the Germans' second march against the Slavs of eastern Europe and Russia.

Bosnia descended into anarchy after the Austrian authorities withdrew. Serb sharecroppers rebelled against their Muslim landlords, and vigilantes indiscriminately killed Muslim peasants, often in retaliation for the killings of Serb civilians by Muslims and Croats in the service of Austria during the war. Serbs demanded Bosnia's immediate unification with Serbia. Instead, however, a new state was forged from the lands inhabited by southeastern Europe's Serbs, Croats, Muslims, and other Slavs. This new country was supposed to become the nation-state of the "South Slavs," or "Yugoslavs," and was initially called the Kingdom of the Serbs, Croats, and Slovenes. It became the Kingdom of Yugoslavia in 1929, after years of political instability provoked its Serbian king, Aleksandar I Karadjordjević, a direct descendant of Karadjordje, to declare a dictatorship and create a police state.

Most Serb leaders assumed Yugoslavia to be an extension of the old Serbia's territory and a fitting reward for victory in a war that had cost the Serb nation dearly. Serbs took over the new country's administration and bragged that they had "liberated" the Croats, Slovenes, and other Yugoslavs during the World War. Farmlands that had belonged to Bosnia's Muslim beys, *kapetani*, and agas were expropriated without compensation and handed over to their former tenant sharecroppers. Police thugs and the army, whose generals were almost all Serbs, cracked down on nationalist organizations, and especially on Croats who wanted little to do with the new state. Bosnia's mainstream Muslim Slav leaders opted to support the Serb king for fear that Bosnia would be swallowed up by Serbia and Croatia if Yugoslavia disintegrated. Despite this support, Serb extremists showed alarm at the large number of Muslims living within the new state's borders and called for intermarriage to dilute the Muslim population and, if that failed, expulsion of the Muslims or their forcible conversion to Christianity.

No international border ran along the crest of Mount Zvijezda after World War I. The Austrian customhouse and barracks in Odžak stood empty, and "the Customs Area" became an empty meadow. Naza Čelik and the other Muslim refugees had returned to Višegrad to find that three of the arches of Mehmed Pasha's bridge had been blown away. Their homes were still intact, but a cannon shell had carved a chunk of stone from the minaret beside Juzbin's mosque. The traditional agricultural cycle on the mountain began to turn as it always had before the war. The plows were still fashioned from wood. Grain was still harvested with hand scythes and milled at water wheels driven by the mountain streams. Muslim women still covered their faces in public. Herbal treatments, folk remedies, and citations from the Koran scribbled on paper and swallowed were still the only hope for people stricken with tuberculosis, typhus, syphilis, diphtheria, and other diseases.

Few peasants from Mount Zvijezda found jobs even after the government began investing capital in the Višegrad area. A couple of new sawmills opened. A new bomb factory and a chemical plant brought work to several thousand people. The old Austrian customhouse in Odžak became the headquarters for the local precinct, and in 1924 an elementary school opened in the building that had been the Austrian barracks below the Mitrašinović family's house. For the first time, teachers arrived to give reading lessons to the peasant children. Muslim parents refused to send their daughters to school, and many of their sons gave up reading altogether once they finished the fourth grade. The teachers also taught basic arithmetic and Serbian history. They led their pupils on nature excursions through the nearby forests and marched them up onto the crest of Mount Zvijezda. On the sides of Stolac, Zvijezda's highest peak, the pupils sipped water from a spring reputed to be the coldest in all of Bosnia. Nearby, they dropped pebbles into the blackness of a vertical cave. They listened as the stones clicked against the rough sides of the shaft and echoed and echoed and echoed for as long as it took the class to sing a song. They called the cave Zvekara, "the Clicker."

Hasan Čelik was already too old for school by the time the first teachers arrived in Odžak, and he never learned to read. His widowed mother, Naza, remarried after the war and moved into a house a few yards away from the place she had shared with Salih on the Cross. Sometime during the late 1920s, Hasan married Ajka Kozić, a Muslim girl with green eyes and sunken cheeks who came to Kupusovići from a village a mile or so across the mountain. Hasan and Ajka's family grew quickly. Their first child was a son, and, since Muslims are forbidden to name sons after their fathers, they called the boy Salih in memory of his grandfather. A daughter, Latifa, soon followed; then two more sons, Avdo and Esad. Hasan built his family a new house with a stone foundation, whitewashed wooden walls, and a pine-shingle roof. Through the windows, Ajka could gaze out over the Drina valley and hold up her children and show them Zvijezda's stone walls and towers, its rolling terraces, and its patchwork of fields, pastures, and forests. She could show them the handiwork of Jerina the Damned and her legion of soldier-slaves, and the children could feel the unpredictable gusts of wind, smell the aroma of the pine resin and the burning wood, and hear the rustling leaves, the tinkle of cowbells, and the singsong voices yodeling, "Yeoooo! Yeoooo! Coming hooome! Coming hooome!"

By mid-January 1941, Ajka was pregnant again. The baby was expected to arrive with the plums.

2

AJKA gave birth to Huso Čelik on September 11, 1941. When I asked Huso's older brother Avdo to talk about the blessed event half a century later, all he could do was smile and say Huso's eyes became crossed in the earliest days of his life because whenever Ajka nursed him he was always keeping one eye out for her other nipple.

The late summer of 1941 had been unusually hot. The terraces high on Mount Zvijezda had yielded a bumper corn harvest, and the plum branches were heavy with fruit. World War II had come to Yugoslavia five months earlier, and the villages on the mountain had been tense. On a sunny afternoon a few days after Huso was born, gunfire erupted in the forests above Kupusovići. Hasan and Ajka looked up and saw smoke rising above Muslim homes burning in Odžak. They called the children. Ajka packed some food and clothing and wrapped Huso in a blanket. The family fled southward down the mountain until they reached a village close to Višegrad. The shooting lasted until after midnight.

Hasan and the other Muslim men discussed among themselves what to do. They had no weapons to fight back. Their only leader was an aged, self-taught Muslim holy man named Mullah Medo Ahmetagić, who quickly advised everyone not to panic. Mullah Medo enjoyed the respect of everyone on the mountain. He had presided over the local district for years, and in his spare time he had taught many of the Muslim boys to read the Koran. Mullah Medo was also a staunch supporter of Yugoslavia and its Serb king. He had received an award from the king, and it is written in books that the award was the Star of Karadjordje itself, one of the highest honors the king bestowed. Some Muslims from Mount Zvijezda still whisper that Mullah Medo got the award because he had once led nationalist Serb conspirators across the border from Serbia past the Austrian guards and that his home was a safe house at the very time the Habsburg archduke was assassinated. When the shooting erupted on Mount Zvijezda in September 1941, the Muslim men followed his advice. There was no panic. But Hasan and Ajka and many other Muslims did not risk returning to their homes.

HASAN ČELIK would never have begun building a new house in 1940 if he had imagined that World War II would reach his front door. Half of Europe had already fallen to the Nazis when Hasan set to work, but the invasion of Yugoslavia on Palm Sunday, April 6, 1941, was not a foregone conclusion. On the morning of the attack, herdsmen grazing their goats and sheep on the mountain wall above Kupusovići listened for the thuds of aerial firebombs exploding on Belgrade. At night, they climbed the peaks to scan the blackness for the orange glow of fires burning beyond the horizon. Yugoslavia's army disintegrated within days of the attack. Whole brigades surrendered or deserted. Hordes of peasants picked abandoned army horse carts and vehicles clean. The country's sixteen-year-old king, Petar Karadjordjević, fled.

Hitler had little use for Yugoslavia except to neutralize it in order to guarantee the security of the supply lines for the armies he would soon send to invade Communist Russia. He thought he had solved his problem when the Yugoslav government agreed to a limited military pact with Germany in March 1941. But a group of Serbian air force officers, who were encouraged, and perhaps covertly backed, by Great Britain, overthrew the Yugoslav government. Anti-Nazi demonstrators took to the streets of Belgrade waving British and French flags. "Better war than the pact," they chanted. "Better the grave than a slave."

In radio broadcasts from London, Prime Minister Winston Churchill praised the demonstrators as heroes. But their open support for Britain and France infuriated Hitler. Once his army had overrun Yugoslavia, the German dictator decided it would be simple and easy to dismember the country and share its territory with Italy, Hungary, and other neighboring countries. The Germans occupied the larger towns in a shrunken Serbia and installed a puppet government in Belgrade to keep order and round up some 90 percent of Serbia's 15,000 Jews for extermination. Hitler also created the puppet "Independent State of Croatia" and endowed it with all of Bosnia. Respectable Croat leaders declined Hitler's offers to rule the new state, and he settled for Ante Pavelić, a Serb-hating Croat with heavy eyebrows and frowning cheeks who had for years commanded a gang of terrorists known as the Ustaše. He helped plot the assassination in 1934 of King Aleksander I, the same Serb king who had presented Mullah Medo with his award. Most Croats and many Bosnian Muslims were happy to be rid of Serb domination after the Nazi invasion. Their enthusiasm would be short-lived.

After riding into Croatia's capital, Zagreb, on a white horse before ranks of goose-stepping Ustaše, Pavelić set about to create an ethnically pure Croat country across a territory where Croats constituted barely half the population. He dealt with Bosnia's Muslims by declaring them to be "Croats of the Islamic faith" and hailed them as the "flower of the Croat nation" because they had not sullied their bloodline over the centuries by intermarrying. Croatia's Serbs, Jews, and Gypsies were targeted for liquidation and expulsion. A campaign of bestial violence against them began in May 1941. About 80 percent of the 40,000 Jews in the Croatian state were eventually killed. Ustaše death squads, whose members were boiling over with racial hatred for the Orthodox Serbs and often out to settle personal scores or retaliate for the brutality of the Serbian police in the interwar period, raided Serb villages all over Croatia and Bosnia and killed their inhabitants, often by locking the peasants inside their homes or churches and setting them afire. Entire families were herded into concentration camps, where they were massacred with clubs or knives because the Ustaše did not want to waste bullets. The brutality of the Ustaše toward the Serbs shocked even the Germans, and it aggravated German commanders because it drove the Serbs to mount armed resistance.

Dispersed soldiers of the Yugoslav army and Serb civilians desperate to fight for their own survival organized resistance to the Ustaše and the occupying armies over the summer of 1941. Two main resistance movements developed. The first was the nationalist Serb "Chetnik" movement of Draža Mihailović, a Yugoslav army colonel and a former classmate of Charles de Gaulle at Saint-Cyr, the French military academy. The second resistance force was the Partisans of Josip Broz Tito, the man Communist Russia's dictator, Josef Stalin, had picked to the lead Yugoslavia's minuscule Communist Party. Mihailović's Chetniks, who operated from a high plateau just across the Serbian border from Višegrad, were poorly organized and had rare contact with many local Serb resistance groups in far-flung corners of the country. Chetnik commanders loyal to Mihailović often ignored his orders and attacked defenseless villages without his knowledge in response to local demands for blood vengeance and the need to plunder food supplies. Tito's Partisans came on the scene only after June 21, 1941, when Hitler's forces finally marched into Communist Russia. Yugoslavia's Communists had tried to assassinate King Aleksandar in the early 1920s and were banned thereafter. Tito, the son of a Croat peasant and his Slovene wife, was a soldier in the army of Austria-Hungary during World

War I and was taken prisoner on the Russian front. He learned about communism in Russia and enlisted in the Red Guards during the Russian revolution before returning to Yugoslavia.

Mihailović and Tito were natural enemies, but they temporarily found common cause. A sworn anti-Communist, Mihailović enjoyed the backing of Great Britain and the other Allies. He was bent on restoring Yugoslavia's king and the Serb-dominated government's authority, if not throughout the entire country, then at least across territories where Serbs made up the majority of the population. This goal appealed to most Serbs but repulsed most of the old Yugoslavia's other peoples. As the dimensions of the Ustaše terror against Serb civilians became clear, extremist Serb nationalists pressed Chetnik commanders to make their ultimate war aim the creation of a Serb nation-state, a Greater Serbia, and the elimination of the Muslim, Albanian, and Croat minorities within the territory it would encompass. Tito's ambition was to seize power throughout all of Yugoslavia and introduce a Communist regime. The Partisans' war cry, "Death to Fascism, Freedom to the People," attracted recruits from among all of Yugoslavia's peoples. During the first months of the war, the Chetniks and Partisans buried their differences. Their forces mounted armed attacks on the Germans and Italians and won control of much of eastern Bosnia and western Serbia.

Hasan Čelik and his neighbors went about their seasonal routine after the Nazi invasion, planting their vegetable patches and cornfields, tending their flocks and distilling their brandy, as if the war would never find its way onto the slopes of Mount Zvijezda. A small contingent of Ustaše showed up in Višegrad a few weeks after Pavelić took power, and they recruited a handful of local Muslims. Ustaše patrols sometimes used the stone schoolhouse just below Vladimir Mitrašinović's place. They soon began confiscating hunting weapons and pistols and, in the process, beat up and murdered some Serb peasants. Novica Lukić from down in Rujišta was tortured and killed by some Muslims in an Ustaše outpost who wanted to requisition some of his grain; a local Muslim in the Ustaše killed one of the Mitrašinović men from Odžak, and another member of the Mitrašinović family was taken off to Višegrad's bakery and burned alive in its oven. After skirmishes with Serb resistance fighters on the rail line, Ustaše militiamen began attacking Serb hamlets, killing more Serb peasants, and shipping others off to concentration camps. It was then that Chetniks from Serbia struck the Bosnian side of Mount Zvijezda and sent Hasan and his family fleeing with Mullah Medo and the other Muslims.

The Ustaše in Višegrad offered little response to the Chetnik attack. Within a few weeks, the Chetniks had driven all of the Ustaše from Mount Zvijezda and torn up sections of the rail line through the village of Dobrun, which lies at the southern end of the mountain and just inside Bosnia's border with Serbia. The Ustaše commander in Višegrad ordered his men to bolster the town's defenses and effectively ceded Mount Zvijezda to the Chetniks, but he turned their attention to the Serbs west of Višegrad, burning Serb villages and butchering innocent women and children in reprisal for Chetnik ambushes. By mid-October, Chetnik officers loyal to Draža Mihailović had crossed over the mountain from Serbia, recruited and dragooned local Serb peasants into their ranks, and set up a command post in the old customhouse in Odžak.

The Germans responded to the uprisings in Serbia and Bosnia by issuing a warning that they would execute one hundred Serb civilians for every German soldier the resistance killed. Thousands of Serb civilians were shot in reprisal executions, including a group of school pupils and their teachers in the Serbian town of Kragujevac. These killings brought to a head the differences between Tito and Mihailović. Tito fought on, calculating that German retaliation against civilians would alienate the population and win the Partisans fresh recruits; Mihailović, whose people were already facing genocide at the hands of the Ustaše, feared a holocaust and ordered his Chetniks to stop attacking the Germans. From now on, Mihailović's long-term strategy would be to lie low and prepare to seize the country when the Allies either invaded Europe through the Balkans or defeated Germany elsewhere. In the short term, Mihailović collaborated with the Germans and, especially, the Italians. The Chetniks' main enemies became the Partisans, the Ustaše, and Croat and Muslim civilians. Mihailović's men attacked the Partisans on November 1, 1941, at Užice, a Serbian town just over the border from Višegrad. Yugoslavia's civil war had begun.

Italian troops entered Višegrad on November 8 in an effort to bring order to the town and relieve the Ustaše hemmed in there by the Chetniks. The Italians had not come to fight. They protected themselves by digging deep trench works in the hills around Višegrad, then strung in front of them mazes of barbed wire hung with tin cans that would clatter if anyone tried to sneak through. The Italian commanders agreed to let Mihailović's Chetniks run the countryside around Višegrad if they refrained from attacking the town. The Chetniks soon allowed the Italians to evacuate the Ustaše from Višegrad. Once they were gone, Serb men from the outlying hamlets felt comfortable enough to leave their guns at home and carry food to their Serb relatives living in the town.

Within a few weeks, the Chetniks agreed to allow refugee Muslim peasants to return to their hamlets on Mount Zvijezda. Hunger and hygiene were already becoming serious worries in besieged Višegrad. Winter was coming on. The Italians printed up permission slips and handed them out to any Muslims who wished to go home. Miserable refugee families streamed out of town and climbed along the mountain tracks leading toward their houses and fields. Among them were Hasan and Ajka Čelik and their children. The return went without a hitch. After ten days, all but a handful of Muslim refugees had left the town and gone home.

Hasan was kneeling and reciting the Muslims' midday prayer one afternoon later that November when his fourteen-year-old half brother, Ibrišim, came to the door.

"We've got to get out of here," the boy said.

The Chetniks had sent around word that all Muslim men fifteen years of age or older had to register at the old customhouse in Odžak. The men would be sent home once they registered. The house of any Muslim man who did not show up would be burned and the rest of the family held to account.

Naza was at the Čelik house. She ordered her sons to flee through the woods back to Višegrad.

"I will not run from my home any more," Hasan told them. "I cannot run from my home any more. I see that I cannot run from death any more."

There was an argument. The women cried, and Ibrišim ran off. But Hasan refused to budge. In those days, many Bosnian *hodžas* were preaching that the war was simply God's will and that death at the hand of an enemy was God's wrath upon Muslims who had not shown respect for the laws and the holy word of Allah. No one could run from the will of Allah.

Hasan turned to Ajka: "Mother, it's over for me. It is up to you to take care of these children." Hasan then got down on his knees to pray.

A Serb patrol came to the door later in the day. Hasan was still kneeling.

"Enjoy your prayer now because it's your last," a Serb told him. "You must come with us."

Hasan stood up. "Mother, these children . . . don't give them up to live under a strange roof."

Latifa watched and said nothing. Hasan took off his maroon fez and set it on Esad's head.

"Take care of this for me."

The Serbs led Hasan out. "Bring up some food tonight," one of them ordered the women.

The men disappeared up the rocky path toward Odžak and the Chetnik command post in the customhouse. A few dozen Serbs were outside the building. There were some Chetniks from Serbia, and Serb refugees driven by the Ustaše from towns and hamlets across the Drina; but most of the men hanging around were locals from Odžak and nearby Serb villages. At the door to the customhouse stood Dragojle Radovanović, a small, wiry man with a Charlie Chaplin mustache. He jotted down in a notebook the name of every Muslim who went inside. Fehim Ahmetagić, Mullah Medo's grandson, became no. 77. He walked through the doorway and turned to the left into a room. It was already crowded with Muslim men. Here were the Kešmers from Žlijeb, the Kozić and Čelik men from Kupusovići, the Sućeskas from Odžak. The young men from Mullah Medo's hamlet had waited patiently in a line outside the door of the barber's house and had their hair cut before coming. Their mothers had told them to bathe and dress in their best clothes. Their fathers feared that the Serbs would mistreat the womenfolk if the young men ran off, so they led them to Odžak themselves and took their places beside them in the first room to the left of the front door of the customhouse. It had a floor of bare wooden planks. There were glass windows guarded on the outside by Serbs with shotguns. Through the windows the men could see stretches of the Drina valley below.

Before nightfall, Ajka returned home from Odžak crying.

"They've got them locked in there like cattle," she told Naza. Latifa listened. "He wouldn't eat."

Two of the Serbs from Odžak, Vitomir Janković and Vladimir Mitrašinović, took the Muslims in small groups from the customs station after darkness fell. They were led about fifty paces down the path toward the mosque and crowded into a stall where the Austrian border guards had once kept their horses and a cellar below a house belonging to Dragojle Radovanović. The men waited there that night. No one slept.

In the morning, the Serbs brought the Muslims out into the light, one at a time as their names were called from Dragojle's list. Younger Serbs ordered the men to empty their pockets and put their hands behind their backs. Dragojle took a pair of pliers and bound their wrists with wire stripped from a fence. Younger Serbs then tied the prisoners to one another using the black home-spun from the Muslims' cummerbunds. The prisoners were silent and compliant. Anyone who seemed ready to resist was punched or clouted with a rifle butt.

Fehim Ahmetagić heard a deep voice suddenly shout.

"*Pička ti materina*," the voice said, swearing on the pussy of someone's mother. "Who the fuck has this man tied up? . . . Ibro, *pička ti materina*, what are you doing here? You don't belong here."

The voice belonged to a Serb peasant named Milorad, who was well liked on the mountain. He was speaking to Fehim's father, Ibro.

"Get them to let at least one of my sons go," Ibro begged him. Ibro nodded his head toward Fehim and his brother, Meho.

Milorad waved his hunting rifle and told the other Serbs to free Ibro and his sons.

"Who are you to be defending these Ustaše?" one of the Serbs snapped.

"These guys aren't Ustaše," Milorad said. "You might as well let them go and tie me up with the rest of them."

Milorad snipped the wire binding the wrists of Ibro and his sons, then untied the cloth that bound them to the other Muslims. A thousand needles pricked Fehim's chilled hands. He stepped off to the side and waited there as the Serbs brought more prisoners out of the cellar.

"I have done nothing," Fehim said to two Serb friends who dared speak to him.

"It's an order," one of the Serbs answered. "An order from the army."

Milorad led Ibro and his sons into the customhouse and along a short hallway to a room at the back of the building.

"Sir," Milorad said to the commander. "We have taken Mullah Medo's sons and grandsons, sir. Do you know Mullah Medo? Do you know who he is? Do you know the king himself gave Mullah Medo the Star of Karadjordje?"

"We know what kind of man Mullah Medo is," barked another Serb in the room. "But we don't know about his sons. What kind of men are his sons?"

The commander stared at them all.

"Let them go," he said. "Let them go on their way."

"We cannot just let them go on their own," Milorad said. "If they leave here on their own, they'll be dead before they make it past the mosque."

"Take some men. Lead them home. Guard them there."

The Chetniks led Fehim and his father and brother to their house. They tacked a paper notice with an Eastern Orthodox cross above Mullah Medo's door. It said he was not to be touched.

Ajka brought Hasan food that afternoon and told Naza and the children that it was Dragojle who had tied their father's hands with wire.

Later that night some of the Chetniks gathered a few hundred yards above the customhouse. They sat beside Vladimir Mitrašinović's still. Vladimir had a fire going. The brandy was dripping out just fine, and the men got drunk. They laughed. They bellowed out songs about Serb heroes of old, songs about revenge for Kosovo, songs about the reviled Turks and their Christian brothers who had betrayed the Orthodoxy by converting to Islam in centuries past. When the Serbs returned to the customhouse, the Muslim prisoners were sitting and lying on the ground. Their hands were still bound with wire and their arms were still tied together by their cummerbunds. Vladimir had brought the last bucket of plum mash, bubbling hot from the still. He scooped it out with a ladle and poured it down the prisoners' backs.

"Get up! *Pička ti materina!* Get up!"

The prisoners rose slowly to their feet, and the Chetniks ordered them to march. They climbed the rocky trail toward Stolac, the highest of Mount Zvijezda's rounded peaks. Muslim men hiding in the forests heard the Serbs singing and firing their guns at the sky. The prisoners hiked for two hours before they arrived at the mouth of Zvekara, the deep vertical cave where the boys used to throw pebbles and listen to the clicks as they fell. The Chetniks shot some of the Muslims and slit the throats of others. Their bodies were dropped down the shaft. Hasan Čelik had been killed on the march. The Serbs ordered a few Muslims to carry his body, and they dumped it into the cave atop the others. No one escaped.

Muslims hiding in forests and caves listened to Serb voices belch out songs with crude lyrics all over the slopes of Mount Zvijezda for days and nights as the killing continued. Muslims from one village, Prelovo, were driven into a streambed and shot. The Serbs of Rujišta led a group of their neighbors down to the Drina, ordered them to wade into the river, then opened fire. Roving bands of Chetniks threatened to kill any Serbs who protected Muslims. But some Serbs did not let their fear overcome them. A Serb from Žlijeb saved his Muslim neighbors by telling them to flee to Višegrad. Serb women, some of them refugees only recently driven from their homes by the Ustaše, hid their new Muslim neighbors.

The morning after Hasan was taken away, a young man was caught hiding in a stall just below the Čelik house. There was a shout. Ajka, Naza, Latifa, and Salih rushed to the window to watch what was going on outside. In a meadow below the house, a Serb with a gun lunged toward the young man. He fought back. He rushed the gunman. He tackled him to the ground and punched his face. Then he stood up to run. The Serb grabbed his gun again, staggered to his feet, and shot the fleeing man in the back. The Čelik women watched as he approached the wounded man cautiously, shot him in the head, and walked away. The body lay still on the ground. From the window the women could not recognize who it was. Hours passed before one of their friends, a Serb woman, happened by. It was safe for her to go down and take a look. She came back and said there was no more danger. Salih walked down and dug a grave in the meadow where the body was lying. It was for his uncle, fourteen-year-old Ibrišim.

Ajka and Naza had no menfolk left in their families now. They gathered up the children and set out on a trail that runs parallel to a creek flowing down to the Drina. Ajka was hysterical when they came to a footbridge over the stream. She lifted Huso in order to throw him into the water, but the other women grabbed her arms.

"I can't carry this one any more," she pleaded. "I have no milk. I have no food. I have no man."

Naza took the child and calmed her down. They walked on, and hours later they entered the ring of Italian barbed wire around Višegrad and found a place to sleep. Within a few days, Ajka had turned Avdo and Esad over to an orphanage.

HEAVY snows fell on Višegrad that December. Refugees jammed into cellars, shacks, and cattle stalls. Typhus swept through the town and up onto the mountain in January and February 1942. Wooded hillsides within the ring of barbed wire were cut clean by men chopping firewood. When food supplies ran low, Muslim men disguised themselves as women and slipped through the siege line to fetch potatoes and unmilled corn from surrounding villages. They would be hidden for days at a time by Muslim women and girls who had decided that it was better to stay in their villages than face the hardship of the town. Bands of desperate and hungry Serb fighters prowled the mountainside, squeezing the Muslim women and the local Serbs for food. Chetnik commanders ordered the Muslim women not to stray far from their homes and banned the wearing of veils. In mid-March, the Chetniks began killing Muslim women and children on Mount Zvijezda. Some of the victims were forced into the Drina and shot; others were shut up inside houses and burned alive.

In April 1942, the Germans and Ustaše launched an offensive against the Partisans and Chetniks in central and eastern Bosnia that sent thousands of Serb civilians fleeing eastward across the Drina and into empty Muslim houses on Mount Zvijezda. The Ustaše slaughtered many of them on the left bank of the Drina, others panicked and drowned trying to swim the river, and still others were saved by the Germans and penned up in a camp. The offensive reopened the roads from Višegrad to Sarajevo, and Ajka and Naza took Salih, Latifa, and Huso across the Drina and into a house in a village that had been abandoned by Serbs who were among those the Ustaše massacred on the riverbank. The women had to forage for food. Almost every morning, groups of Muslims accompanied by armed escorts set out on a three-day hike northward over Zlovrh to Srebrenica. There they bought, scavenged, or stole food and lugged it back to their families. On her way back from a trip to Srebrenica, Naza's group fell into an ambush near a Serb village called Podravanje. She was shot and left behind.

Now Ajka was alone with her three children. She joined an evacuation to northern Bosnia that the Croatian authorities had organized. She packed up Huso and with Salih and Latifa climbed aboard the Ćiro and traveled to Sarajevo before turning northward. They spent the winter in a Croat house in the town of Bijeljina and in the spring of 1943 moved northward again, to a village in Croatia where Ajka found work as a farm laborer. By then, there were no more Muslims left on the slopes of Mount Zvijezda. A group of Serb men bolted a chain to the circular porch atop the minaret beside Juz-bin's mosque and tried to pull it over as if they were in a kind of tug-of-war. When that failed, one of them took a sledgehammer and knocked away its stones, one at a time from the top down. The mosque's rafters, beams, and roof shingles were stolen, and cattle rustled from the departed Muslim families were corralled inside.

The Chetniks had rounded up the last Muslim women, children, and old people left on Mount Zvijezda in November 1942. They told the Muslims they were going to be taken across the Drina and exchanged for Serb civilians. By then, whole Muslim families had taken shelter near the house of Mullah Medo Ahmetagić, seeking to benefit from the protection he was supposed to have enjoyed. But Mullah Medo, his wife, two of their grandsons, and other members of their family were among the people the Serbs led down to the riverbank and across the Drina. Mullah Medo died with the last of them, burned up in a house doused with gasoline. No one survived.

❮ ❮ ❮

ON September 9, 1943, Italy surrendered to the Allies. The Italian troops in Višegrad had already bought their way out of Bosnia and into Serbia by trading some of their weapons to the Chetniks in exchange for safe passage through a railroad tunnel above Dobrun. Draža Mihailović's collaboration tactics had not gone unnoticed by the Allies, and Winston Churchill was angry. It was becoming evident that Germany would eventually lose the war. Hitler's army in Russia was retreating. The Allied invasion of Europe long awaited by the Chetniks was expected the next spring. Mihailović was anxious to take control of as much territory as possible before the Partisans could grab it. He was also desperate to prove to Churchill that his Chetniks could kill Germans in meaningful numbers and deserved to keep receiving Allied support. Mihailović decided to mount an attack on Bosnia from Serbia. The Allies sent fresh observers to Mihailović's headquarters, and Churchill dispatched one of his old friends, Brigadier Fitzroy Maclean, as the British liaison to the Partisans. Maclean's orders from the British prime minister were to "find out who is killing most Germans, and suggest means by which we could help them kill more."

The Chetnik assaults commenced with the demolition of bridges along the narrow-gauge rail line and culminated with a major attack on Višegrad that began at dawn on October 5. The Ustaše and German forces in the town fled across the Drina within a few hours. Exploding shells and sniper bullets cut to pieces panicked civilians who tried to flee across Mehmed Pasha's bridge after them. Višegrad fell by the afternoon. The Chetnik offensive petered out a few miles to the west, where there was a rout of the retreating German and Ustaše forces and a heavy loss of life among the Muslim civilians who fled with them. Chetnik fighters looted whatever they could from the homes in Višegrad and abandoned their units to carry their booty home. The wanton slaughter of Muslim civilians trapped in the town went on for the next two weeks. Each day, Chetniks dragged Muslims alone or in groups to the *sofa* at the center of Mehmed Pasha's bridge and shot them or slashed their throats and pushed them into the Drina. The killing went on before the eyes of Allied liaison officers who tried in vain to stop the slaughter. One American liaison officer happened by as a Chetnik sergeant was throwing an aged Muslim woman from the bridge, and the officer's Chetnik handler had the sergeant immediately executed before the American's eyes. Within hours of the Višegrad massacre, however, the Allied governments were informed of the killings and advised that the Chetniks were waging an ethnic war, a war to drive an entire ethnic group from recaptured territory. Mihailović tried to tidy up the Chetniks' image. Within a few days, he ordered that all looting be stopped and that relations with the Muslims be "maintained on a high level."

It was too late. Though historians have found no evidence directly linking the Chetnik massacres of Muslim civilians with subsequent Allied decision making, Brigadier Maclean's reports back to Churchill were so devastating that within a few months of the Višegrad killings the Allies had drastically cut military supplies to the Chetnik forces. In November 1943, Tito was named by a Communist-dominated council of anti-Fascist organizations to lead a temporary Yugoslav government and the exiled King Petar was forbidden to return to Yugoslavia. Soon thousands of Chetnik fighters were going over to the Partisan side, and the Allies announced that the Partisans had become the recognized Allied liberation force in Yugoslavia. Mihailović and King Petar persevered for another two years, but they were effectively finished. It was the Partisans who drove the occupying forces from the country. And after the war, Tito thanked Brigadier Maclean for his contribution to the Partisan cause by presenting him with a villa on the Adriatic island of Korčula.

When victorious Partisan troops fought their way into Višegrad on February 15, 1945, they found a few shell-shocked civilians living on the edge of existence. The shelling and fires had left a maze of roofless buildings. Debris littered the stone streets. About half of the people who inhabited the little town and the surrounding district before the war had either perished or disappeared. And five arches of Mehmed Pasha's bridge had been blown into the Drina.

3

AFTER the war, radios and loudspeakers set up in town squares and outside village meeting halls broadcast Tito's will throughout the land. They proclaimed the birth of a new Yugoslavia, a Communist Yugoslavia, and the dawning of the age of "Brotherhood and Unity." The country was subdivided into six republics in an attempt to prevent a return of the kind of Serbian hegemony that had ruined the Kingdom of Yugoslavia. The border between the Socialist Republic of Serbia and the Socialist Republic of Bosnia and Herzegovina ran along the crest of Mount Zvijezda where the old border had run for centuries.*

Displaced persons were told to return to their villages and towns. Everyone was to go home. Everyone was to face his or her neighbors. Tito's police would deal with the incorrigible and the fugitive Chetniks and Ustaše. Anyone who dared utter an unkind word to someone of another nationality would sit for ten days in jail; if the unkind word was about someone's mother, the sentence would be three months.

Word of mouth carried the news of the refugee return out onto the rich plains of Croatia and the farm where Ajka Čelik was living with the remaining members of her family. She traveled to Višegrad after harvest time in 1945 to find out what, if anything, was left of the house Hasan had built them just before the war. On her way to the town, she traveled along a road strewn with the skeletons of dead horses and the rusting hulks of burned-out tanks and trucks. Women and children collected fuel for their wood stoves along the edges of the forests. She walked through the ruins of Višegrad and made her way along the rutted dirt road that led northward along the Drina. She passed houses whose roofs and interiors had been gutted and whose stone foundations had become overgrown with weeds. She ascended the trail that crossed a wooden bridge over a rushing stream. The water gurgled over rocks worn smooth like pillows, and unpredictable winds rustled through the trees. But there was a silence over the land. The tinkle of the cowbells was gone. The singsong calls of the peasants were gone.

As Ajka approached Kupusovići, she saw there was no minaret standing next to Juz-bin's mosque, and she spotted a gaping hole in its roof. Just up the

---

*Herzegovina is a mountainous region wedged between Bosnia, Montenegro, and Croatia's stretch of the southern Adriatic coast. It was named for a Slavic prince, or "herzog," before the Ottoman invasion.

mountain, in Odžak, were the ruins of the customhouse and the school just below the house of Vladimir Mitrašinović, the Serb who had poured the plum mash down the necks of the Muslim men taken away with Hasan. The charred shell of a Muslim home stood on the bluff just above the Čelik place. Then Ajka spotted her own house on the Cross. The pine shingles of the roof were still in place. The whitewashed walls were still standing. Not a windowpane had been shattered.

Ajka approached the house. A woman emerged from inside. They knew and greeted each other. She was a Serb. Her name was Radislava Mitrašinović. She was Vladimir's daughter, and she had kept watch over the Čelik house since Ajka and the children had left. Radislava welcomed Ajka home, and Ajka found that the Radovanović family had safeguarded all of her bedding, her furniture, her farm implements. Not a spoon was missing. Ajka stayed a day or so before returning to the farm in Croatia. She packed up Latifa, Salih, and Huso and made the long journey back to their home and their land and the cycle of peasant life on Mount Zvijezda.

Salih was in his late teens by now, and he wanted no part of his old home. He had seen the world beyond the mountain, the cities and roads, the money-paying jobs, the fertile plains, the places where making a life would be much easier than making ends meet on Jerina the Damned's mountain. Salih feared the mountain. The first autumn of the war still lived for him. His father was dead; the Serb neighbors had taken him away. His uncle was dead; a Serb had shot him down, and it was Salih who had dug his grave in fear and haste and laid him to rest in it. Salih would have nothing more to do with Serbs. He ran away from Ajka on the trip back to Višegrad, but she caught up with him and forced him to continue the journey. He stayed in Kupusovići for a month before he ran off again. Ajka got a letter from him a few years later. He was living in Croatia, in Zagreb. He had found a job and a Croat wife and now had a pair of daughters. He came home once to sign away his right to inherit a share of the land that had belonged to his father so that he could collect some government benefits. He never returned again.

Ajka fed the family on a widow's pension and what food she could scratch from the soil. There was a community of sorts taking shape again in Kupusovići, Odžak, and Žlijeb. Other Muslim widows and their children had moved back into their homes. Some Muslim families shared their houses with displaced Serbs and their children. A few Muslim women were raising Serb orphans, and some Serb women were raising Muslim children whose parents had disappeared. But among the surviving men a silence prevailed about the war and the old customhouse in Odžak and the vertical cave called the Clicker.

Ajka came down with an ulcer the summer after the war and spent a few months in a hospital in Sarajevo. Latifa, now fifteen years old, took over the family. She worked the fields, did the cooking, and looked on as Huso jumped around the yard like a goat. When Ajka returned from the hospital, she brought help. Her name was Saliha Čelik, and she was the fifteen-year-old daughter of one of Hasan's distant cousins. Saliha's father had ended up in the Zvekara cave; her mother, two brothers, and a seven-year-old sister had been burned alive beside the Drina with Mullah Medo; and Saliha herself had lived out the war in an orphanage and worked for a while as a housemaid. She moved into her father's house just below Ajka's, but the women worked the fields and kept house together. They were cut off from the world except for the news they picked up while filling their water jugs at the spring beside Juz-bin's mosque. The village women still chattered on about chores and children. They spoke about what they had seen of the wide world during the war. They talked of their menfolk and what had become of them. They told their children about the Serbs from Odžak and the other nearby villages who had participated in the killings just as every Serb mother told her children about the Muslims who had been Ustaše. And the Serb and Muslim children played together almost every day.

Tito named Boro Princip, a relative of Gavrilo, the archduke's assassin, to run Višegrad immediately after the war. And the Communists warned everyone to be on guard against lurking "enemies of the people." Tales of fugitive Chetniks and Ustaše never stopped circulating on the mountain. People said the Ustaše were regrouping abroad, in Canada, the United States, Western Europe, Australia, and South America. There were Chetniks hiding in the woods and in the caves and grottoes along the mountainsides. They had buried their guns and were surviving with the help of Serb peasants who brought them food at night. People said the Chetniks were biding their time, waiting for a massive invasion to liberate Serbia once Britain and the United States had finished driving the Communists from Greece. One Muslim woman came upon a rifle stashed in the forest and used its barrel to fasten together a yoke for her oxen. Tito's soldiers combed Mount Zvijezda and discovered some of the buried guns. The secret police apprehended Draža Mihailović in the mountains about twelve miles southeast of Višegrad, and he was quickly tried and executed. A few Muslims and Serbs stood up to denounce their Serb neighbors for killing civilians during the war; but only a handful of the men were ever tried and convicted.

Many Chetniks and Ustaše had defected to the Partisans toward the end of the war. Some of these defectors found their way into the Communist administration and police when peace returned, and they helped ferret out Chetnik and Ustaše fugitives. One of the Chetniks who had gone over to the Partisans was Vitomir Janković from Odžak. Vitomir was a husky bear of a man. He wore a thick mustache with turned-up ends and a Serb peasant's cap with a creased brow. After the war, the Communists named Vitomir head of the local farmers' co-op. It was an important job because it gave him some say in the distribution of food and other humanitarian assistance. Vitomir also oversaw the dismantling of the only Orthodox church for miles around, a chapel that had been built during the war by a Chetnik commander with stones from Muslim houses. Vitomir had the stones from the chapel hauled up to a village just below Odžak and used them to construct a building for the the farmers' co-op. Many Serbs silently detested Vitomir. The men of one Serb family particularly hated him because they held him responsible for betraying two of their brothers executed by the Partisans.

❝   ❝   ❝

THE RED CROSS located Esad Čelik a few months after Ajka had returned the family to Kupusovići. Esad was in an orphanage in the far-off town of Travnik and was sent back to Kupusovići immediately. Another few months passed before a woman from a village near Kupusovići recognized Avdo Čelik walking along a street in Sarajevo. She followed the boy as he climbed a steep alley onto a high hill overlooking the city and entered the house of a mullah. Avdo listened as the peasant woman greeted him.

"Good day, *efendi*."

"Good day," the mullah answered.

"I believe this boy is the child of my neighbor."

"Are you certain?"

The peasant woman nodded. Mullah Hafiz Bahrija Avdić studied her face. The mullah was a respected man in Sarajevo, and learned, strict, and decent.

"Come into the house."

His wife served the peasant woman something to drink.

"Please spend the night here," he said. Then he turned to his wife. "Please fix her a bath."

The mullah's wife brought the peasant woman clean towels and fresh *dimije* to wear. The next day the mullah sent the woman on her way, and he gave her a photograph of Avdo and a slip of paper.

"Take this picture and our address," he said. "If the boy's mother is still alive and if you find her, instruct her to come here to me."

"Thank you, Hafiz Bahrija," the woman said. And she left.

It was Avdo's job each morning to pick up bread from the baker's for the mullah's wife. Upon returning home from the bakery one morning a few weeks later, he found the house empty.

"Avdo," he heard someone yell. "Over here."

The mullah and his wife were inside the neighbor's house. Another peasant woman had called. She was standing next to the mullah when Avdo walked into the room. Avdo walked up to the mullah's wife and handed her the bread.

"Don't come to me. This is your mother."

The mullah turned to Ajka. "Do you recognize your child?"

Ajka stared at the boy. He was nine now. She had not seen him for five years.

"I know that one or the other of his eyebrows is bent," Ajka said. "Does he have a scar? My boy cut himself when he was a baby. He fell onto a kerosene lamp, and he has a scar."

Ajka pulled Avdo toward her. She lifted his shirt. There was the scar.

"We brought him from an orphanage near the train station at the beginning of the war," the mullah said. "The orphanage in Višegrad had sent him to Sarajevo with some other children. He had a hernia then. We almost sent him back. But he seemed a good-natured boy. We had a friend who was a doctor at the hospital, and he told us the hernia could be treated easily. So we took him there."

The mullah had taught Avdo to read the Koran and write the Arabic script in the traditional way. If he did not finish his lessons, he would be beaten with a stick or, if it was winter, sent out into the yard to turn blue in the cold.

The mullah addressed Ajka: "You may leave the child with us if you wish. We have taken good care of him, and we can continue to do so. We will raise him well. And I will continue to teach him the word of God."

Ajka agreed to leave her son with Hafiz Bahrija and his wife. She visited Avdo twice during the next two years. When the mullah's wife became pregnant, she wrote to Ajka and told her to come for her son. He was eleven when he returned to Mount Zvijezda.

Avdo had forgotten Kupusovići. He did not know his brothers Huso and Esad or his sister, Latifa. Nor did he know village life or village poverty.

"What is this?" he asked, gazing at his first meager meal of greens and a few onions with corn bread. "Your god is wretched, indeed." He went out to the garden, pulled up some more onions, and started munching on them.

Esad followed him. "What do you think you're doing?" he shouted at Avdo. He started to beat him. "You little fuck." Huso joined in, and Avdo punched them right back. The fights never stopped.

❮ ❮ ❮

IN the fall of 1947, a few Serb teachers from Montenegro arrived on Mount Zvijezda and began holding reading and arithmetic classes in peasant houses. The radios and the loudspeakers had announced that Yugoslavia's vast illiterate masses had to be taught to read if the wisdom of Marxism-Leninism was to reach them. Huso, Esad, and Avdo attended the classes in a house for a few years, and the older men would attend reading lessons at night. Then the local authorities sent orders for the old Austrian customhouse in Odžak to be turned into a primary school. Men from Kupusovići, Odžak, Žlijeb, and the other nearby villages were drafted into a work brigade. They set to work repairing the building. They built classrooms on the ground floor and, on the upper floor, an apartment for a schoolteacher and his wife. The biggest classroom was to the left of the main entrance and enclosed by the same stone walls that had held Hasan and the other Muslims before the Chetniks led them to their deaths. The work brigade put down a new floor of freshly hewn wooden planks. They hammered together wooden benches and installed a chalkboard. On the wall they hung a portrait of a stern-faced Tito wearing a smart uniform. There was no electricity, so the only light came from the three windows that opened onto the grassy yard in front of the school and the expanse of the Drina valley to the south. Against the inner wall was a wood-burning stove that warmed the room during the winter. The stove was tended by the man hired to be the school janitor, Vitomir Janković.

Huso was there for the first day of classes. He wore moccasins like all the other children and carried a chunk of cornbread to eat. A few Muslim parents sat in jail for a spell because they refused to send their daughters to school, but for the most part people now saw the benefit to having all their children learn to read and write, especially because the education was free. The sons and daughters of the Serbs who had fought with the Chetniks now shared the same small wooden school benches with the sons and daughters of Muslim men who had been killed or who had run off to join the Croatian army or the Ustaše. And at their benches, the children learned the melodies of the victors' songs and to sing lyrics like these:

> Oh, that little Partizanka,
> Oh, how she could fight.
> Hey, everyone must hear,
> Hey, everyone must know,
> How that little Partizanka marched,
> How that little Partizanka handled a grenade.
> Oh, that little Partizanka,
> Oh, how she could fight.

The Communists wrote the history of the war, and it was a simple history. The Germans and Italians and their collaborators were to blame for all the fighting in Yugoslavia. Monuments were built for Partisan dead and a few of the Serbs massacred by the Ustaše. But no memorial would ever be built for the thousands of Muslims killed by the Chetniks. No history, no novel, no newspaper article ever mentioned the hundreds of men tossed into the Zvekara cave. The war in which half of Yugoslavia's dead were killed by other Yugoslavs was simply passed off as a war of "national liberation."

In 1948, however, Yugoslavia found itself under an external threat that unified its quarrelsome peoples as never before. A simmering dispute between Tito and Stalin broke into the open after the Soviet dictator tried to quash the political and economic independence that the Yugoslav Communists, and Tito, had enjoyed since the end of the war. On June 28, Vidovdan, Stalin had Yugoslavia expelled from the Cominform, a Soviet-dominated bloc of Communist nations. The Cominform called upon Yugoslavia's Communists to overthrow Tito, and Moscow threatened an invasion to bring Yugoslavia back into the fold. Huso and many Muslims came to adore the defiant Tito as a savior and protector against the foreign threat. The vast majority of Serbs, children and adults, did too. Tito's portrait found a place of honor in the Čeliks' kitchen, as it did in kitchens all over the country, and the portraits stayed there even as Tito tried to ease himself back into Stalin's good graces by applying the strict tenets of Stalin's brand of communism.

Religion was practically banned. Schoolteachers beat Muslim pupils caught attending religion classes or Friday prayers. In 1950, the government banned Koran classes and the printing of Islamic textbooks. Young Muslim women welcomed a ban on wearing veils, and more girls began going to school. But some older Muslim women considered it immodest to show their faces to the world and were arrested and fined or held for a time in jail. The government also tried to clamp down on faith healers. Bosnia still had very few doctors, and if herbal teas and folk medicines failed to cure an ailment, Muslims continued to swallow verses from the Koran written on bits of paper. Muslim men continued to teach their sons the Koran in secret and met openly for Friday prayers despite the hole in the roof of Juz-bin's mosque and the missing minaret. But Huso and the other Čeliks were not among them.

The government was about to collectivize the farmland when economic stagnation, and the danger of popular unrest, forced Tito to abandon further implementation of a centrally planned economy. Tito was desperate for something new to shore up his hold on power, and he embarked upon an economic and social reform program that eventually gave the country's economic enterprises and local governments real control over much of their own affairs. No longer would the state own and operate the industrial enterprises. Now the factories and mines, the buses, the Višegrad steam train, the library books, and the schools became "social property," the property of society as a whole. They belonged to everyone, but their management was entrusted to groups of workers headed by loyal Communists. It was 1954. A recruiter from a mine came onto Mount Zvijezda, searching for strong arms and firm backs. Avdo was seventeen, and underage. So Ajka went to Višegrad's town hall and had Avdo's birth records altered to make it appear that he was twenty. The work was backbreaking, but it was a job and Avdo was away from the mountain. The foreman apologized when he fired Avdo after finding out his real age. By the time he got home, Huso had taught himself to play a simple wooden flute and to carve wooden cigarette holders like Tito's. From maple wood, a wolverine hide, and horsehair, he fashioned himself a *gusle*, a single-stringed musical instrument used to accompany the singing of epic folk poems. Avdo took up the drums, and he and Huso would play when the villagers got together to drink and dance. They earned pocket money and learned to drink.

Brotherhood and Unity broke down in Kupusovići at dusk one dry spring evening in the mid-1950s. Dragojle Radovanović and his sons Dragoljub and Arsen invited their Serb friends to a party at the new schoolhouse in Odžak. All of the village Serbs, young and old, showed up. There were bottles of brandy. Food was laid out on the pupils' benches in the main classroom. Huso was the only Muslim there. He played the flute better than anybody around, and the Radovanović brothers paid him to play for the party. Ajka had ordered Huso to stay away, but he ignored her. There would be brandy and girls, and the money was good. Huso sat down near the front of the room and soon filled the classroom with a repeating melody in ear-piercing tones. A chain of dancing people spiraled around the floor as he played. They stepped in time. Two steps forward. Left foot behind the right. Right behind the left. One step back. Jump. And two steps forward. And on and on and on, circling the room with a person waving a kerchief at the front, the person honored to guide the dance.

The fact that the Serbs had picked the schoolroom in Odžak as the venue for their party and did not invite any Muslims had irritated some of the Muslim young men. Probably nothing would have come of it had a Muslim named Rasim Sućeska not been getting drunk with some friends at a Serb house down in Žlijeb that night. Rasim's father had been killed by the Chetniks, and he grew up to become one of the toughest, hardest-drinking Muslim boys in the village before taking a job as conductor on the Ćiro. He was once called to account for throwing a passenger through the window of the train when he found him without a ticket. Now Rasim and his friends decided to crash the affair at the school.

At one point in the dance, Rasim burst into the classroom. "Hop, hop, mani mani, let the dance be led by the Muslimani!" he shouted as he lunged toward the dancers.

Dragoljub shouted back something insulting about a fez, and one of the

Muslims overturned a bench on which an old Serb woman had been sitting. "Fuck your *alem*," the woman blurted out, cursing the crescent moon ornament that had just been mounted on the tip of the new minaret next to Juzbin's mosque.

"And fuck your altar," a Muslim fired back.

The brawl was on.

Bottles flew through the cigarette smoke and smashed against the walls and through the windowpanes. Serb women climbed out through the windows. Rasim and his friends punched and kicked their way from the door to the closed end of the room. Then they turned and rustled all of the Serb partygoers out the door and into the cool night air. Once outside, the Serbs tore pickets from Dragojle Radovanović's wooden fence and brandished them at Rasim and his gang. Huso was already long gone. He had crawled along the floor to the door of the schoolroom, run down the hill from Odžak, and walked into his house as if nothing had happened.

"Where have you been?" Ajka demanded. "What's going on up there?" Huso slid into a corner of the house and refused to speak.

Rasim and the other Muslims strode proudly into Kupusovići a few minutes later. Behind them trailed one of their comrades who had gotten beaten up after the Serbs caught him tangled up in the wire of a fence.

"Why did you leave me behind, *u pičku materinu?*" the man said after he got himself untangled and ran down to rejoin his friends. "Let's go back up there and kick some ass," Rasim said.

"Leave them alone, Rasim," Ajka implored.

The Radovanović brothers and the other Serbs had by then regrouped and begun taunting the Muslims and flinging stones down toward Kupusovići.

When Rasim and his gang ran up to get them, the Serbs were ready. Rasim was clobbered either by a rock or with a wooden picket. A gash opened in the side of his head. The Serbs pelted the Muslims with stones as they grabbed the dazed Rasim and carried him back down the hill. He ended up with a brain injury that impaired his memory from the moment he was struck until the day he died.

The Muslims marched into the Višegrad police station the next morning and pressed charges against the Serbs for having incited an ethnic riot. Dragoljub and Arsen Radovanović were hauled in for questioning. The Serbs were adamant that it was the Muslims who were at fault.

"We want Huso as a witness," Dragoljub's mother told Ajka.

Ajka refused.

"There is no reason to be afraid. We'll bring him back tonight," the Serb woman promised.

By the time Ajka finally agreed, the Muslims who had started the fight had already gotten to Huso and threatened to kill him if he said anything.

Huso was quiet when he took the stand. "A fight started," Huso said. "I crawled out of the room."

"Did you see anything else?"

"No."

"Anything?"

"No."

Huso stepped down. Everyone knew he had lied. The judge held the Serbs responsible for the brawl, and later Dragoljub's mother came by the Čelik house.

"Oh, Ajka," she said, "memories live for a long time. *Kad tad*, Ajka, sooner or later."

It took only a few weeks, however, for Dragoljub and Arsen to become Huso's friends again.

(((

THE great brawl had come at a time when the Yugoslav government's repression of Islam was easing. By now, the postwar world was divided between the capitalist nations of the West, led by the United States, and the Communist Eastern bloc, headed by the Soviet Union. Tito had dangled Yugoslavia between the West and the Soviet bloc and was playing one side off against the other to his political and economic advantage. He denounced the division of the world into the capitalist and Communist blocs at the same time that he was taking military and economic aid from the West and, in the wake of Stalin's death, patching up ties with the Soviet Union. Simultaneously, he worked to ease Yugoslavia's isolation by helping to create a third bloc, an organization of countries that chose not to be allied with either the West or the Soviet Union. This organization was called the Movement of Non-Aligned Nations, and Tito used Bosnia's Muslims to win the good will of the Islamic countries that joined. When the Muslim leaders of Egypt and Indonesia visited Belgrade, Tito dragged out the leader of Yugoslavia's Islamic community, the *reis ul-ulema*, to meet them. Muslims from Bosnia started showing up on the staffs of Yugoslavia's embassies in Islamic countries.

The time was ripe for repairing Juz-bin's mosque, and when the Muslims began working on it, the local Serbs turned out to help. It was a Serb who donated the lumber to repair the mosque's roof beams and some of the stone for rebuilding the minaret. Serbs passing by the Cross walked over to the mosque, left money donations for its repair, then walked away. One of the Serb peasants who did work on the mosque still carried inside him shrapnel from a war wound, and two of his brothers were Orthodox priests.

The work began and progressed without government permission. The Višegrad police tried halfheartedly to shoo away the Muslim stonemason who had come from across the Drina to lay the stonework for the new minaret. But he kept coming back.

"What are you throwing him out for? If you don't let them fix that roof, I'll take the roof from my own house and put it up there," one of the Muslim peasants shouted at the police.

There was no retaliation against either of them.

The grand opening of the restored mosque came on Friday, October 16, 1959. The sky was as turquoise as the Drina, and the first frost had already come and gone, but the air was warm and fragrant with the smells of Indian summer. The women in Kupusovići began the final preparations early in the morning. There were walnuts to crack and grate, and pastries to bake. The boys and men slaughtered sheep and set them on spits for roasting. Muslim men and women from Žepa took the ferry across the river at Slap and arrived in Kupusovići in a caravan of horses with bridles decorated with tassels and flowers. A crowd, including an Orthodox priest, gathered to greet the *reis ul-ulema* himself, Hadži Sulejman Efendi Kemura, and his retinue of Muslim clergymen when their motorcade from Sarajevo crossed Mehmed Pasha's bridge in Višegrad. Little girls presented the clergymen with bouquets of flowers. The town's Communist boss welcomed the visitors with a reception in his office before the motorcade set off. Miles below Kupusovići, the road gave out and the cars could proceed no farther. So the clergymen mounted horses and were led on the rocky path through Odžak, past the Čelik house and on toward Juz-bin's mosque.

"*Allahu ekber! Allahu ekber!* God is great!" a muezzin cried from the minaret as the caravan drew within sight. A green-and-white flag with the half moon and star of Islam decorated the minaret beside the red-starred flags of Yugoslavia and Bosnia. The *reis ul-ulema* and his party made their way through a crowd of applauding people to the home of Mujo Kupus, the village's wealthiest peasant and the Muslim who had contributed the most to the mosque's repair. There the clergymen rested, drank coffee, and ate pastries.

The ceremonial opening of the mosque followed the rest break. Never had anyone on the mountain seen such a gathering. The crowd stretched up the hillside, far beyond the overgrown stone walls that had been the foundation of Mullah Šaban's house. Vladimir Mitrašinović and other Serbs from Odžak looked down on the crowd from outcroppings of rock.

When the *reis ul-ulema* appeared at the front of the mosque, the Muslims presented him the key, and he held it in his hand while he addressed the crowd.

"I appeal to all of you present here today," he said, "to continue your efforts to strengthen the brotherhood and unity between you and your neighbors. . . . I call on you to keep up the struggle for building an even more radiant future."

The *reis ul-ulema* kneeled and prayed; then he rose and snipped a ribbon stretched across the front door. Once inside, he led the Friday prayers. All the men outside kneeled toward Mecca, the Muslim holy city, and bowed time and again as one, touching their heads to the ground, holding them there, and lifting them in unison as the *reis ul-ulema* completed the prayers.

The crowd applauded as the clerics emerged from the mosque. The clergymen ate lunch and meandered through the crowd, talking with villagers, before they mounted the horses and began the journey down the mountain for the drive back to Sarajevo. The festival around Juz-bin's mosque dragged on even after the send-off. To the music of flutes and drums, girls and boys dressed in folk costumes danced the *kolo*. Women in *dimije* carried around trays of food and drink. Children with bare feet and grass-stained knees gamboled about the meadows. Older boys showed off for the girls. They ran races and competed in stone-throwing contests for towels, shirts, and other prizes. Horses galloped free around the throng of Muslims as the Serbs watched from the hillsides above. The Muslim men were not supposed to be drinking on such a sacred occasion, but some of them slipped away to sneak shots of brandy, and Avdo and other young men were appointed to see to it that no one got into fights or drank too much and caused a scandal.

The party was still in full swing when Avdo and the other security guards spotted Vladimir Mitrašinović walking into the crowd carrying a pair of wool socks as a gift. Vladimir began to speak.

"Good people! Good people!" he said. "Let me through. Please. Please. Let me speak. I must say something to you."

Avdo and the other men gathered around him.

"My neighbors, my neighbors, I have come here to say to you that I ask your forgiveness. I have come to ask that you pardon me for what I did in 1941."

Vladimir looked frightened, desperate. And the Muslims gazed at each other. They grumbled that some priest had probably refused Vladimir absolution until he apologized to the Muslims.

"Vladimir," said one of the Muslims, "it would be best if you got out of here."

"But my soul cannot rest. The memory . . ."

"The guys over there are from Žepa, Vladimir. If they hear you talking any more like this, it will be all the worse for you."

"But . . ."

"Get the fuck out of here, Vladimir."

The frustrated Serb headed out of the crowd carrying the pair of socks. One of the Muslims kicked him as he passed by, and he hustled away and hurried up the hill to his house.

4

THE annual tattooing came to be a ritual across Yugoslavia. It was not the traditional Bosnian-style tattooing performed each year for centuries on the eve of the vernal equinox by Catholic women who scraped lampblack with chicken feathers from the bottoms of iron pans, mixed it with saliva or mother's milk, and fashioned sunbursts and sheaves of wheat on their arms and chests. I have spoken with old peasant women whose hands and arms were covered with these tattoos; they belonged to the last generation to tattoo themselves in the traditional way and said their mothers had instructed them to mark themselves so that Muslim beys would not steal them and keep them as concubines. This new tattooing ritual, by contrast, involved young men, soldiers, who, during fits of boredom, took thick sewing needles and pricked blotches of black writing ink into their forearms. Their design was simpler than the sunbursts and shafts of wheat, and it presupposed an ability to read letters and numbers. First came the year the men had been drafted into the army and had taken their oaths to defend Yugoslavia. Then came letters. "JNA" for the men who preferred the Latin alphabet; "JHA" for those who preferred the Cyrillic. But the initials were always the same: "Jugoslovenska Narodna Armija," "The Yugoslav Peoples' Army." Some true-believer Communists topped the design with a red star. One sorry zealot once even inscribed across his brow "Slava KPJ sa Drugom Titom na Čelu," or "Glory to the Communist Party of Yugoslavia with Comrade Tito at Its Head"; a lawyer friend of mine spotted him in one of Tito's camps for political prisoners.

Tito had personally engineered the army of Yugoslavia, the army of all of Yugoslavia's peoples, to be the engine of Brotherhood and Unity. The radios and loudspeakers proclaimed that all young men would serve. The army would defend Yugoslavia's nations and its socialist order. It would nurture the legacy of the glorious Partisan victory over fascism in World War II. It would bequeath that legacy to the young Serbs, Croats, Muslims, and Slovenes in its

ranks. Allegiance to Yugoslavia and the socialist order would overarch the loyalty of its soldiers to the Serb, Croat, Slovene, and Macedonian nations.

For years it seemed to be so. Each of Ajka Čelik's boys went to the army, and
since they were Bosnians they all had to serve their stints outside of Bosnia. In
1962, Huso was assigned to a barracks in central Serbia, in a leafy little town
called Kruševac. There he learned to shoot. He learned to march and to
salute. He washed dishes and slopped latrines. He drank brandy with his comrades, and he taught himself to play the clarinet. The Croats, Muslims,
Slovenes, and ethnic Albanians in his outfit gave him money to play folk
melodies that reminded them of their mothers, their girls, and their homes on
mountains far from central Serbia.

Huso was away in Kruševac on the autumn afternoon when Ajka complained of pains in her stomach. She crawled into her bed, covered herself
with a quilt, and did not speak a word to anyone for days. No one thought to
go for a doctor. On the last day, Esad and Avdo looked in on their mother. Her
eyes gazed up at them from the bed. "God willing," she muttered. "God willing. . . . Forgive me. I forgive you." She slipped into unconsciousness, and in
a little while she stopped breathing. The women cleansed Ajka's body. They
laid her in a wooden coffin with no lid and covered her with a white sheet.
Avdo and Esad dug her a grave on the hillside beside Juz-bin's mosque, just
above the spring where the women of Kupusovići gathered each day to draw
water. The *hodža* read the prayers. The men lowered Ajka into the earth and
covered her over. They did not mark her grave.

HUSO returned from the army a few months later. His brothers had already
married by then. His sister, Latifa, had found a husband, Ismet Čavkušić, and
had gone to live with him at the northern tip of Mount Zvijezda in a village
called Kamenica. Huso, now twenty-two years old, had grown into a thin
young man who wore a mustache, smoked the harsh local tobacco, and enjoyed drinking bouts with his friends. He had had women to cook for him, to
clean for him, and to wash his laundry every day of his life until the day he left
for the army. Now he was free of the military and without a mother or a sister.
Now he had to find a wife.

Late July was harvest time for the winter wheat in Kamenica. The young
women worked their way through the grain fields in rows, slashing the stalks
with scythes and leaving them on the ground to be tied into bundles and carried off for threshing. The women sang as they toiled. Each night, after the
day's work was done, the women got together in the village. Huso and some
other young men showed up. Huso had come to visit Latifa and Ismet. He

knew there would be young women around, and he brought along his clarinet. He played as the young women locked arms and danced the *kolo*. After the dance, the women sang in harmony for hours. At one point in the evening, Latifa approached sixteen-year-old Hiba Avdić, one of the unmarried young women from Kamenica, and sang to her and the other young girls: "Play, play, my partygoers, I'll leave you the yard, and the window where the young men come calling."

Latifa took Huso aside and pointed out Hiba to him. She had dark brown hair, a beaming smile, and hands already calloused from farm work. "If you want a fine wife, this one is the right one for you," Latifa told Huso. "She's a real *radinkinja*, a real worker."

Latifa had already spoken with Hiba about Huso, and Hiba sang to him while he played.

> Every girl gets the man she picks.
> And I pick the one leading the dance.
> From the time we stop singing to God,
> Our voices lose their harmony.
> But God can make all well again.

Huso and Hiba saw each other five or six times during a courtship that lasted a few weeks. Hiba would give her parents some excuse to drop over to see Latifa. Huso would be there waiting, and they would share a few sentences and maybe a laugh. The young men and women did not shake hands during courtship in those days, and they did not sit closer than a few yards from each other. If they danced the *kolo* with a group of young men and women, they had to hold a kerchief between them so their hands would not touch.

In the late fall, Huso came to Kamenica with half a dozen friends from Kupusovići. It was a gray evening, chilly and damp. Hiba's father, Avdija Avdić, had gone to a nearby village for a reading lesson and was due home at any time. Huso's plan was for Hiba to steal away before Avdija returned. But Avdija spotted the young men as he was walking home. He greeted them as they tried to sidle behind a neighbor's haystack. Avdija did not recognize any of them. He figured they had come to take away a young woman as a bride. But he did not suspect it was his Hiba.

"There are some guys out back behind the haystack," Avdija told Hiba and his wife, Husnija, when he came into the house.

Hiba went about her chores. She gathered her things together without anyone's noticing. A few pairs of *dimije*. Some blouses. Her shoes. Then she slipped out the door, joined Huso behind the haystack, and set off with him across the mountain for Kupusovići. Only a few minutes passed before Avdija and Husnija noticed that Hiba was missing. They thought she had eloped in the opposite direction, down the mountain to Slap, and across the river to Žepa.

"God help her if she went across the Drina," Husnija cried. The people on Mount Zvijezda were dirt poor and ignorant, and they knew they were poor and ignorant. The weight of this knowledge was eased in their minds only by their generally held assumption that the Muslims who lived in isolated Žepa were worse than poor and ignorant—that they were primitives. Over in Žepa, mothers-in-law worked young brides to a pulp. Over in Žepa, the husbands drank themselves to death even faster than the men on the mountain, and they beat their wives until they dropped dead. Over in Žepa, God knows what might happen to a sixteen-year-old girl. Husnija knew that a Muslim man from Žepa had come courting Hiba that summer. He was a big drinker, and his first wife had run off. "God help her if she went over there," Husnija told her husband.

The wedding feast in Kupusovići consisted of a spread of bread, vegetables, meat, pastries, and bottles of plum brandy and cups of frothy coffee. The young men and women of the village danced the *kolo* around Huso's kitchen until midnight and then left the young couple alone to begin married life. About two weeks later, Huso and Hiba made the customary reconciliation with her parents. Hiba saw a friend from Kamenica and told her to tell Avdija and Husnija that she was now living in Kupusovići. Avdija sent back his regards, and Huso, through intermediaries, sent Avdija a couple of button-down shirts as a gift. Hiba visited her parents' home a few days later and gave Husnija bags of sugar and coffee and some fabric to make *dimije*.

"You were too young," Husnija scolded her. "There was no need for you to do this while you were so young."

"He was all by himself. It's a good situation."

"You are only sixteen."

"His mother is dead. There is no mother-in-law, and there is a house."

Hiba brought to Huso the reading skills of a second-grader, a sense of humor, and the equivalent of about ninety dollars in cash. She knew how to knit, how to cook, and how to work the fields. Huso kicked in another fifty bucks, and the household was started.

€   €   €

THE next spring, after the heavy planting was done, Huso left Hiba with Saliha and with Esad's wife, Ajkuna, and joined the great migration of village people to the city that had begun a century earlier in western Europe with the dawn of the industrial age. The subsistence farmers of Mount Zvijezda were becoming wage earners: truck drivers, porters, security guards, factory workers, and miners. The Serb men mainly migrated to Belgrade and other towns in Serbia, and most of the Muslims went to Sarajevo. They left the villages to the old men and the old women, to mothers tied down with small children, to the retarded and the infirm, the drunk and the shiftless. The country's gritty towns grew into gritty cities. Avdo had already gone to Sarajevo with his wife. Esad had found a job setting explosives at a mine in Serbia and walked back and forth over the mountain to get to work. Huso set off down the mountain with a change of clothes, caught a bus to Višegrad, and took the Ćiro to Sarajevo. He worked odd jobs at first, and found steady employment after he got hold of a forged certificate saying he was a qualified bricklayer. He worked for a construction company called Vranica and lived with hundreds of other workers from eastern Bosnia in a company barracks above the old Muslim heart of the city. Huso filled up whatever free time he had with his clarinet, his friends, and bottles of brandy brought from home.

In Sarajevo, the fathers and sons of the city's old families, for some reason, branded the newcomers "Swedes" and despised them for their rudeness, their crass tongues, their naive ambition, and their lack of common sense. "Fuck you, Swedes," the townspeople cursed the arriving peasants, "and fuck that Ćiro that brought you and doesn't take you away forever."

Under the direction of Communist Party bosses, who were mostly citified peasant men like themselves, this lumpen Bosnia built the new neighborhoods of postwar Sarajevo. They added the drab apartment blocks of Grbavica and later the drab high-rises of the city's far-western suburbs. Every Friday night, lumpen Bosnia would head for the gingerbread stationhouse built by the Austrians high above Sarajevo's old Catholic quarter. They would cram aboard the eastbound Ćiro and fight for a space on the wooden benches. The engine whistled and coughed up sulfurous smoke and ash that coated the faces of everybody inside rickety passenger cars. The workmen on board drank and gambled and pissed and cussed, and woe to any well-dressed single women who happened by. Fistfights broke out over a wrong word, a card dealt from the bottom of the deck, unpaid loans, debts left over from the war, and sometimes nothing at all. If one of the Swedes lost his wallet, the first Gypsy to wander within arm's reach might find himself rolling down a weedy embankment. But the Ćiro chugged along so slowly on some stretches of the rail line that anyone thrown off stood a good chance of running back to the train and, if he dared, climbing aboard again.

This was Yugoslavia's gilded age. Tito's hybrid socialist system, which allowed a larger degree of local decision making than any other Communist system, had produced one of the world's fastest-growing economies. New factories and roads had opened. Electrical lines began reaching into the villages. Tito fostered a personality cult for himself, constructed personal villas in each of the country's six republics, and dabbled in foreign affairs, fine wine, and ballerinas. Some Yugoslavs worked very hard, but few worked very efficiently. Communist bosses took control of the decision making for the factories, mines, and local government, and they developed networks of family members and supporters who were given jobs in exchange for their allegiance. These bosses and their networks soon matured into local mafias that controlled the police and the strings of informants recruited in every government department and business enterprise. Malcontents were either bought off with jobs, apartments, and trips abroad or handed over to the criminal courts and prisons. Serbs held the important senior government, police, and enterprise-management positions in Bosnia, and the policies of Bosnia's government were tapered to dovetail with those of Serbia. The old part of Višegrad was ground under, and new buildings were built. A hotel next to the Mehmed Pasha's bridge. A performing-arts center. A sports hall on the riverbank. Very little of the new wealth, however, made its way onto Mount Zvijezda. The mountain had not produced many Partisans like Vitomir Janković, and to the victors and their families had gone the spoils of war.

The socialist economy sputtered in the mid-1960s. Now desperate to get their hands on foreign currency they were unable to earn, the Communists lifted restrictions on foreign travel, allowing Yugoslav men to take jobs abroad and propping up the flagging economy with the money these workers sent from outside the country. Moreover, the local Communist mafias began borrowing funds from foreign banks and funneled much of the money into their own pockets. Calls for reform and free elections were smothered by the police. Tito shunted aside reformist party members and replaced them with second-rate party hacks whose main talents were sycophancy and greed. Serb leaders lost their dominance of much of Bosnia's political and economic life, and Serbs no longer made up the republic's largest ethnic group. The Muslims had a significantly higher birth rate than the Serbs, and immigration by Muslims into Bosnia from other parts of Yugoslavia, and an outflow of Serbs seeking economic opportunities in Serbia and abroad, had made the Muslims more numerous than the Serbs. By 1968, the central committee of Bosnia's Communist Party had declared Bosnia's Muslims to be a distinct nation, an equal partner with the republic's Serbs and Croats. This rankled Serb intellectuals, who began grumbling in private that Tito was anti-Serb.

(((

HIBA Čelik registered her marriage to Huso with the district authorities in Višegrad only when she became pregnant the first time. She gave birth to all of her children at home. Hamed, born in 1965, was the oldest child. Two more sons, Sead and Paja, followed in the next four years. All the boys were circumcised by traveling barbers who toured the mountain each spring when the fruit trees were in blossom.

Huso was drinking heavily by then. In fact, all of the men in the family were drinking heavily, and there were plenty of family arguments. Huso and Avdo would go for spells without speaking. Huso came home only on weekends, and his sons effectively became the third generation of the family to grow up without a father around the house. One weekend afternoon, Huso was sitting at home drinking. He started giving Paja sips of brandy. The little boy got drunk quickly and stumbled around. While Huso was snickering, one of the Radovanović men, a relative of Dragoljub and Arsen, burst into the house. "Fuck your Turk mother," he shouted at Huso. The Serb was drunk too. He ground his teeth as if he were deranged. He felt inside his pocket as if he wanted to pull out a knife. Huso pounced on him. He shoved the Serb outside the door, dumped him head first into a water trough, and went back inside the house swearing.

Huso eventually bought himself a pistol, a Serbian-made revolver that he registered with the police and kept at home. A lot of the peasant men on the mountain had guns. Some of the men were hunters. Others enjoyed shooting bullets into the air at weddings. Stories still circulated all around the mountain that former Chetniks and Ustaše had kept their guns stashed since World War II, and some of the stories were true. One summer, one of Huso's nephews, Jusuf Čelik, crawled down into a cave a few yards from the house and reemerged showing off a long, rusty bayonet. A cannon supposedly hidden by Behadil Kešmer had already become a legend by then. Behadil was a Muslim from Žlijeb, and all the villagers joked about him because he had always been a little slow.

"We know you Muslims are hiding weapons," a Serb would joke to one of his Muslim neighbors.

"Yes, of course we're hiding weapons," the Muslim would answer. "Thousands of weapons. And you all know that Behadil has his cannon stashed away somewhere. He's had it there since the war, and he keeps it cleaned and oiled." No one thought to ask what Behadil might be doing with a hidden cannon or where he planned to get the shells to fire with it. The conversations never got that far before everyone, including Behadil, started laughing. One of the Čeliks' neighbors once leaned out a window when Behadil was strolling by the house.

"Behadil!"

"Yeoooo."

"Where've ya got that cannon?"
"Between my legs!"

HIBA'S last baby, her only daughter, arrived one evening in 1972. The curious boys tried to peek inside the bedroom all afternoon to watch the birth, but Saliha shooed them away and herded them down to her rickety old place below Huso's house and kept them there until it was all over. Huso and Hiba named the baby Sanela, and from the day of her arrival Huso cut down on his drinking. His flute disappeared. He sold his clarinet and his *gusle*. And he started to fix up the house. He took down the pine shingles from the roof and replaced them with terra-cotta tiles. He patched the walls and painted each facing a different color—maroon, white, red, and emerald green.

The first of the twentieth century's technological miracles had reached Kupusovići in 1971 with the electrical line. But the closest gravel road was still an hour's walk away, and no phone line stretched that far up Mount Zvijezda. In 1973, a bulldozer bigger and louder than any machine the children on the mountain had ever seen cut a rocky, single-lane road up to Kupusovići, Odžak, and Žlijeb. The road took the place of the trail running parallel to the stream leading down the mountain. Not since the days of Jerina the Damned's soldier-slaves had so much stone and dirt been moved on Mount Zvijezda. The children jumped from their beds early in the morning and ran off to make sure they did not miss a minute of the excitement. Hamed and Paja took empty sardine cans, tied them together with twine and pretended to build a road of their own out behind the house. When the bulldozer reached Kupusovići, the peasants greeted the operator with cheers and kisses. "*Živeo bulldozer!* Long live the bulldozer!" they cried. Women tossed flowers onto the metal hood covering the rumbling diesel engine. They gave the operator towels and button-down shirts and other gifts suitable for a wedding. The men drank plum brandy toasts, and Paja got to ride up on the seat of the bulldozer next to the operator himself.

IN 1974, Yugoslavia's constitution officially recognized the country's Slavic Muslims as a separate constituent nation. Huso was so impressed that he went to Austria to find work. His brother Avdo had been living in Austria for five years already, in Mölln, a tiny hamlet perched in the Alps. There were construction and assembly line jobs for unskilled laborers in Austria then, and the Bosnians who went north found work through their relatives and friends who had gone before them. Muslims and Serbs from Mount Zvijezda practically colonized the Austrian town of Steyr and nearby villages like Mölln. Avdo found work sewing ski boots together in a factory. Huso's friend Hasib Čavkušic´ got a job in a sawmill. Behadil Kešmer was there with at least one cannon. Hiba's brothers from Kamenica were nearby, along with Huso's best friend, Zuhdija Sućeska, from Odžak, a couple of the Lukić boys from Rujišta, and other Serbs from hamlets down near the Drina. Huso, like a lot of the Bosnian men, did not take to life in Austria. Time was consumed with work and drinking and gambling. Many families broke up.

Saliha had gotten married by then. Her husband had moved into her house below Huso's. This was an unusual arrangement, for it was always the Muslim women who gave up their families and went to live with their new husbands. But Saliha had inherited a house and land that had belonged to her father. Her husband was so poor that he was still practically a serf, a tenant share-cropper who owed his existence to a local farmer. Saliha and her husband had six children before he left for Austria. On one occasion, he sent home Austrian shillings worth the equivalent of a couple of hundred dollars. He visited Saliha and their children two years later and brought along money for the children's schoolbooks and showed off an eight-track tape player. He never told Saliha where he lived or what he did. He never contacted her again.

Down at the spring beside Juz-bin's mosque, the women fetching water and washing their dresses gossiped about Saliha's husband. Everyone said he had found a new wife somewhere in Austria. The women still complained to one another about their husbands' drinking and vomiting all night. They gossiped about how the young women talked only of getting away from the village, of going to Belgrade or Sarajevo, of finding a man who would take them away from the mountain and perhaps even out of the country. They cackled about young women who were having relations with men without getting married to them, and about how that might be better than getting married to a man without ever having touched his hand. They griped about the jealousy of their husbands and about neighbors who had cheated on their husbands in Austria, about husbands who had cheated on their wives, about a Muslim child in the village who was the spitting image of the Serb living just across the road, or about how a child born to a Serb woman looked just like the husband of one of the Muslim women.

HUSO returned to the Sarajevo construction company after a few months in Austria and picked up the old routine. On one winter day, when snow had closed the roads on the mountain, he rode up to the house atop a sledge drawn by oxen. He brought with him a large cardboard carton covered with a blanket. The boys unloaded the box and carefully carried it up a snowy path past the water trough and into the house. Huso cut the box open and un-packed a mammoth black-and-white television set. It was called "The Am-bassador." They set it up in a place of prominence in the kitchen, on the drainboard next to the sink. Huso attached the antenna and plugged it in. At seven-thirty that night, they watched for the first time the program that cast a stronger spell over the Yugoslavs than any faith healer or mystic could ever match: the evening news. Here was Tito meeting foreign dignitaries right in the Čeliks' kitchen. Here was Tito meeting the workers at a factory or a farm complex. Here he was watching folk dancers performing an elaborate *kolo* and talking of Brotherhood and Unity.

Until that first news broadcast, every Čelik who had ever lived had gotten the news almost exclusively by word of mouth; now the television news be-came for them, as for almost all Yugoslavs, word of mouth with pictures. It was not taken without a grain of salt, but it was a tiny grain. The Muslims and Serbs of Mount Zvijezda had learned enough stories from their older relatives to know that the history that came through the television was a lie. The fail-ure of the government to come clean about what had really happened during World War II was eroding its legitimacy in the eyes of the younger generation. The war had not just been a liberation struggle against invaders and their quislings. It had been something far more sinister. It had forced people to take sides. It had brought on circumstances that drove them to commit hor-rible acts and affiliate themselves with men and organizations committed to genocide. It had wounded the Yugoslavs in a thousand different ways, and though the wounds had healed over on Mount Zvijezda and in many other areas of Bosnia, the scar tissue was thin.

Hamed, more than the other Čelik kids, listened to the war stories. Huso knew only what his mother and brothers and sister had told him about the war. But Grandpa Avdija, Hiba's father, had seen it with his own eyes. And he told Hamed tales in such detail that he knew they were true. Grandpa Avdija had escaped being killed by Chetniks twice before fleeing with his wife and mother from Kamenica to Srebrenica in 1942, at about the same time that Hasan Čelik's mother, Naza, was shot and left to die while scavenging for food. Sre-brenica was under Ustaše control, but there were Serbs living and suffering all over the area. In 1943, the Partisans drove the Ustaše from Srebrenica, and Avdija joined a German unit that counterattacked a few days later and drove the Partisans out.

"I said, 'Fuck it, I haven't got anything to eat, and I'm getting pushed all over the place,'" Avdija said. He decided to join a special Muslim military unit the Germans were organizing. It was called the Handžar Division, a division of the SS, the military wing of the Nazi Party that was used as a police-terror squad. The Germans sent the Muslims for four months of training in France in mid-1943. "Then came the uprising," Avdija said. "It was over the summer sometime. Some of our guys killed three or four German officers. The story went around that the French resistance had paid them to kill Germans, but how those French found some of ours who would do it for money I don't know. An order came down that every tenth one of us was to be executed. But it was all smoothed over."

After training, the Handžar Division was sent back to the Balkans to wreak havoc upon the enemies of the Third Reich. Grandpa Avdija went to Bosnia before being transferred into Hungary to fight the advancing Russians. "At the end of the war we ran toward Austria," he said. "We took off our SS uniforms before we got out of Hungary and put on regular German army uniforms. They gave us different military ID cards, and we surrendered to the English at Klagenfurt. We knew we had to surrender to the English. They were better. They didn't ask who you were and what you were, and we were lucky because we had German uniforms. We gave up our weapons there. The English put us into trucks and took us to Italy, to Rimini. Right on the sea."

Having a German army uniform was a stroke of luck at the end of the war because the British army in Klagenfurt handed back to Tito's Partisans thousands of the Chetniks, Ustaše, and other Yugoslavs who had fled across the border from Slovenia. In the last big massacre in wartime Europe, Partisan death squads executed thousands of the prisoners, including wounded men dragged from hospitals and dumped into caves.

"Then Tito announced that all could return to their land, that the people could decide who was guilty and who was not," Avdija said. "I hadn't harmed anyone or killed anyone. I never committed any crime. So I came back. The English escorted us to the border. I came into Yugoslavia on a train still in my uniform. I didn't have anything else. It was 1945, the autumn. Partisan officers were on the station platforms when my train pulled into Ljubljana. They looked over our papers, and I was arrested. I was in a camp in Croatia for a month. Then we loaded ourselves into a train that was so crowded you couldn't scratch yourself or sit down. They gave us something to eat. Then for four days we stayed there, moving for an hour, stopping for an hour. Nothing to eat or drink. When we got to Belgrade, they took us out of the train. The civilians beat us. They threw wooden beer crates at us. Someone would shout, 'These are Pavelić's men.' And they would draw their fingers across their throats."

The Yugoslav police put the prisoners in a camp, and Avdija carried water and wood. "We didn't wash for six months except in the woods, in the streams," he said. "In one month, thirty-six of the men died. There were a lot of Germans among us, just Bosnian Muslims and Germans, and the guards forced us to beat up the Germans. Then one day they came and told us to go home.

Just like that. No notice. Nothing. 'Go home'. It was March 12. I took the Ćiro back to Višegrad." This was clearly not the righteous partisan war of liberation that Hamed had heard about in school.

❦ ❦ ❦

BY 1980 Huso had had enough. Saliha had been living in the basement of his house for two years already. She was down there with her six kids while her tumbledown house rotted away. The rain leaked through the wood shingles on the roof. The walls swayed and squeaked when the winds blew unexpectedly from the valley floor. It was too dangerous to live in. Any storm might blow it over.

Huso went down to a meeting of the precinct council. He needed its approval to make a collection for a new house. The council gave him a receipt book. On the weekends, Huso and Hamed walked up and down the mountain, banging on doors and asking for money: "We're taking contributions. Saliha needs a new house. Anything will do."

Everyone knew Saliha. Everyone knew how she had been orphaned during the war. Everyone knew that her husband had abandoned her with six kids, and they knew she had kept right on going without whining and moaning about it, as if it were the will of Allah and nothing more. All of the neighbors gave money, even some people farther down the mountain. Others promised to come up with building materials. The cement blocks and bags of concrete arrived in two small trucks, and Hamed and the boys unloaded them and stacked them up. The old place came down easily. A good tug on a rope and the walls fell over. The boys set to work with hammers and axes and chopped the wood into kindling.

A few weeks later, a slab of cement had been laid. Stonemasons began building the foundation. Paja and his brother Sead lugged bricks and pans of mortar. Men coming to Friday prayers would stroll over from Juz-bin's mosque, observe the work in progress, make comments, and set coins and cash down on the wall as a contribution. Slowly the stone walls rose, and atop them came rows of cement blocks. Sanela and the other kids played hide-and-seek around the unfinished house. The workmen brought their wives, and drank and sang together. When the men grew bored with the work, they went off to a flat meadow above Branko Mitrašinović's house and kicked a soccer ball around. And Branko, a heavyset man who wore a hat with a visor like a baseball cap, came down with food and tools.

The foundation was settling on Sunday, May 4, 1980. It was a sunny day. Hamed was supposed to go outside to graze the cow, but he wanted to watch a soccer game on television and tricked Paja into tending the cow for him. It was a big game. All of Yugoslavia seems to have been watching it. Hajduk, the team from Split, a city on Croatia's Adriatic coast, was playing at home against Partizan of Belgrade. The television screen went blank during the match. Solemn music started coming through the speaker. About thirty seconds later, an announcement was read by a man with a shaky voice.

"Comrade Tito has died," he said.

The strongman who had ruled Yugoslavia for thirty-five of his eighty-eight years, the man who was the ultimate arbiter of the quarrels between the men governing the country's different republics, was gone. Tito had not groomed a successor. He could never have found one. People all over the country wept. The football players wept. Policemen wept. And the air blowing up onto Mount Zvijezda carried the sound of factory whistles and sirens sounding below in Višegrad.

Huso looked up from the television screen.

"Tito dies," he said, "everything dies." The old man's portrait was still hanging on the kitchen wall.

A FEW weeks after Tito's state funeral, work began on the walls and roof of Saliha's new house. Woodsmen marked out trees in the forest just below Mount Zvijezda's crest and the men hiked up there and cut them down. Pantelija Mitrašinović, one of Branko's relatives, went up with his oxcart and brought the wood down the mountain. When he arrived at the Čelik place, he took a wad of cash out of his pocket and plopped it down on the foundation of the new house. "This is so you will have good fortune," Pantelija said. "So everyone will live in health and happiness."

Grandpa Avdija came and went to work beside Dragojle Radovanović. The two old men drank together and told tales about the work camps after the war.

"I worked in the Barbara mine, near Zenica," Avdija told Dragojle. "It was 1949. An order came. If I hadn't gone, the police would have found a reason to come and take me away. So I went without any complaint."

Dragojle told Avdija that he, too, had gone without complaint and ended up chopping wood for months.

The two men climbed up onto the new ceiling joists to put the roof on the house. They kept drinking and kept jabbering. It must have been the heat, but it was certainly helped by the brandy: Saliha looked over and saw Grandpa Avdija lose his balance and slip over the side of the house. Dragojle grabbed Avdija's legs before he tumbled to the ground, and the Serb held him there, upside down, until Avdija recovered his wits and hauled himself up. They laughed and resumed hammering and sawing, and when the work was done they drank some more and ate the food the women kept bringing out. They took lead pencils, and on the joists supporting Saliha's kitchen floor they wrote their names: Avdija Avdić, the former storm trooper; Dragojle Radovanović, the former Chetnik; Paja and Sead and Hamed Čelik, the sons of Huso Čelik, the man whose mother nearly threw him into the creek the day after Dragojle wrote his father's name in a notebook and helped lead him off to the Zvekara cave.

5

SALIHA'S new house had been standing for a year or so before Vitomir Janković, the school janitor, died of natural causes. Ironically, it was Vitomir, probably the most despised Serb in Odžak, who had the biggest funeral anyone in the nearby hamlets could remember. He had forged a lot of connections in Višegrad after the war, enough at least to get himself a Partisan pension even though half the mountain knew he had been among the Chetniks who killed Hasan Čelik and the other Muslim men dumped into the Zvekara cave. The mourners' parked cars lined the narrow road up the mountain, and every family that drove from down below seemed to have brought a wreath.

The Serb graveyard in Odžak was a shout away from the Čelik place. Paja and other young Muslim boys used to sneak into it at night and tip over gravestones just to cause mischief. This offended the Serbs, and the boys should have known it. The Serbs went to great pains to tend their graveyard, unlike the Muslims, who left most of the graves next to Juz-bin's mosque unmarked and untended because the souls of the Muslim faithful are supposed to go straight on to their heavenly reward without so much as glancing back. Serbs believe in the living dead. They believe that the spirits of their departed linger near the place where they died in body for forty days before moving on to heaven or the netherworld. And they believe that if these spirits are not appeased or avenged during these forty days, they might become vampires and never move on. (The word "vampire" is the only Serbo-Croatian cognate in the English language, not counting *šljivovica*, or plum brandy.) The living placate the souls of their dead relatives and friends by pouring them brandy libations, by leaving them plates of food on their graves, or by lighting them cigarettes and twisting them filter downward into the dirt of their graves so that they can enjoy the smoke just as they enjoyed it while they were still alive.

By the time Vitomir passed on, the generation old enough to have survived World War II was well on its way to dying off. Vladimir Mitrašinović was gone, and nobody remembered his ever having tried to apologize again. Paja would soon carry the wreath at the head of the procession that bore Dragojle Radovanović to his grave. Huso came home from Sarajevo for the funeral of his best friend, Zuhdija Sućeska, who had returned from Austria just in time to die, like so many of his neighbors, of cirrhosis. A few years later, Huso's brother Esad was walking to work alone on the trail over Mount Zvijezda into Serbia when he died, apparently of a heart attack. Some passerby found his body. It was bruised. It looked as if he had struggled against somebody or something and had fallen two or three times onto the rocks, and the women passed around a rumor that he had been killed.

Huso and Hiba went by Vitomir's house to pay their respects to his family before they buried him. A priest showed up and sang prayers as if Vitomir had not been the one who had overseen the dismantling of the Orthodox chapel after the war. Family members passed out chunks of bread and spoonfuls of *žito*, a paste made from unmilled wheat and served at funerals and holidays. The men downed shots of brandy in Vitomir's memory. His wife, Stamena, wept. She cried that Vitomir had died only because some Muslim in the Partisans had beaten him up during World War II. They dug his grave in a family plot next to the road below the house. Serb women wailed in lament as the men lowered Vitomir's coffin into the ground with ropes. When everyone had taken a piece of dirt and dropped it in, men with shovels filled the grave. Vitomir's friends poured shots of brandy onto the mound of fresh dirt. They hammered a cross into the ground at the head of the grave and draped the cross with towels.

Soon after the funeral, word spread that Vitomir had left behind eight hundred liters of brandy in his cellar. His son, Mile, and his friends drank all of it; in fact, they finished it off within a year. They were well on their way when Uncle Avdo, Huso's brother, came from Austria with his wife for a vacation in Kupusovići. A lot had changed on the mountain since Avdo had last visited. Electrical lines were running into all the villages by now. Hydroelectric dams had tamed the Drina downstream from Mount Zvijezda, and a new dam would soon be constructed just above Mehmed Pasha's bridge in Višegrad. The nearest post office, down the mountain in Prelovo, had a telephone, and wishful thinking metamorphosed into a rumor that the government would soon run phone lines up into Kupusovići and the other outlying hamlets. The Ćiro had given way to an asphalt road and a new steel-and-concrete bridge over the Drina. Buses now ran every hour or so from Višegrad to Sarajevo and cut the travel time by an hour. One family in Kupusovići had even bought a compact car, and the snarl of chain saws in the forests and the rumble of a dairy truck coming to collect milk from each village on the mountain now mingled with the sound of the gurgling streams, the tinkling of cowbells, and the singsong calls of the peasants toiling in the fields.

Uncle Avdo and his wife were bouncing along in the beat-up local bus to Višegrad one afternoon during their vacation when the driver recognized him and struck up a conversation: "Avdo, did you hear that Vitomir Janković passed away?"

Avdo looked the driver coldly in the face.

"Vitomir Janković could not have passed away," Avdo answered. "It would be impossible for him to pass away. Vitomir Janković could only have died like a dog."

Avdo had heard of Vitomir's passing when he arrived in Sarajevo from Mölln. He immediately walked up to a newspaper kiosk and bought a greeting card and an envelope. On the card he wrote, "My congratulations on Vitomir Janković's death like a dog." He signed the card, sealed it in the envelope, and addressed it: "Mile Janković, Odžak." Then he walked it over to a post office, dropped it into the mail slot, and made the rounds telling his old pals about what he had done.

Word that Avdo was going around telling his friends about the greeting card reached Huso within a day or so. When he came home that Friday from work, he dropped by the Prelovo post office and pleaded with the postmaster, Mujo Kapetanović, to search the sacks of incoming mail. He begged the postmaster to give the card to him instead of delivering it to Mile. "That card will bring nothing but trouble," Huso explained. "And I've got to live in this place."

Postmaster Mujo failed to find the card. Apparently, it had already been delivered. A few days later, Avdo went back, unrepentant, to his village in Austria. Mile never mentioned the card to Huso. But Huso heaped the greeting-card incident atop everything else he worried about. He could only trust that Mile would know he had nothing to do with it.

HUSO suffered his first heart attack while at work on a construction site in Iraq in 1983. He had been in the Iraqi desert for nine months, working as a surveyor's assistant. The Vranica construction company was profiting from the good relations Tito had fostered with the Islamic oil states in the Non-Aligned Movement. Vranica was building Saddam Hussein some of the underground military bunkers that NATO's air forces would blast to pieces in the Persian Gulf War eight years later.

Huso traveled home to Kupusovići to recuperate from his heart attack for a few weeks before he returned to Sarajevo and a position in the company's brickyard. While he was at home, he described Iraq for Hiba and the kids.

"There's no grass in the desert, just scrub and rock," he said. "The sheep are bigger than any I've ever seen, but there's not a blade of grass." He told them about how Iraqi women married their cousins to keep their families' wealth from being diluted and about how his Iraqi friends paid him a pile of cash for ten liters of his brandy because alcohol is officially banned. Huso said he got to know an Iraqi with seven wives who wore gold rings through their noses. He told everyone that Vranica had arranged an excursion to Baghdad and a visit to a glittering mosque with a gold-plated dome and icicles of gold hanging from its sides. Before they got off their tour bus, the workmen were warned about a Muslim from Bosnia who had been on an earlier tour and had tried to snap off one of the golden icicles; the poor guy got caught, Huso said, and his hand was chopped off right then and there. Huso lifted up his hand and showed off a watch he had purchased in Baghdad for about eighty dollars. It was an "Orient." A "Double X," with a flexible metal band and a stainless steel back. Water resistant. Quartz. Made in Japan. It ran by battery and had plating that made it sparkle like gold. He never went anywhere without the watch and would not let any of the boys touch it.

He may have come back from Iraq with an ailing heart, but he also returned home with a lot more money than he would have been able to earn in Sarajevo. He had enough to lend Branko Mitrašinović's son money for a house and to repay Dragoljub Radovanović some money he had lent Hiba. Huso had enough left over to run a water line from a spring above the Cross into his house and connected the line to a sink and bathtub and a new electric water heater. A lot of the men were installing water lines to their houses then. It made life easier for the women, though Hiba and Sanela still did the family laundry by hand. The running water, however, all but ended the women's daily gatherings at the spring beside Juz-bin's mosque.

Huso had a regular work schedule after his heart attack. Hiba would visit him a few times each year but never for longer than a few days. Her friends were back in Kupusovići, and she refused to leave the kids, not to mention the cows and chickens, with Saliha for too long. Huso tried to persuade Hiba to move the family into an apartment in Sarajevo, but she refused to come down from the mountain. Hiba had known nothing but village life and hated the noise and bustle of Sarajevo. When they argued about it, Huso would throw up his hands and shout and tell her she could move in with Behadil.

Huso kept dividing his time between Sarajevo and Kupusovići. He rented a single room in the barracks and planted himself a vegetable and flower garden outside. Eight hours a day, five days a week, he would check the comings and goings of trucks laden with bricks, sand, concrete, and other building materials. He got off work every Friday at about noon and headed to the bus station for the trip to Višegrad. Sometimes a Serb taxi driver named Drago would give Huso a lift from the Višegrad bus station to Kupusovići. When he did, he often found Hamed, Sead, and Paja playing soccer with the Kozić boys in the field above Branko Mitrašinović's house. Huso would beat his sons for it. He had forbidden them to play soccer because he had to earn the money to pay for the shoes they tore up on the rocky ground above Branko's place. Huso kept a pen knife in his pocket. He used it for whittling. But if he found a soccer ball around the house, he would take the knife and stab holes through the ball and slice it down the side so it could not be patched.

On Saturday mornings, it was Huso's routine to eat fresh wheat bread for breakfast. The angry knocks at the door would usually begin before the bread came out of the oven: "Huso. Come out here and just see what your Hamed has done, *pička mu materina*. Look at this boy!" A mother would show Huso her son's fat lip or black eye. Huso would disappear back inside the house and give Hamed a whipping. From the time Hamed had reached junior high, he was raising hell up and down the mountain. Hay bales and outhouses mysteriously burst into flames on winter nights. Beehives flung themselves through open kitchen windows. Cows wandered into cabbage patches and munched away until their stomachs were ready to explode and someone shouted from up above, "Yeoooo! Yeoooo! Therrre's a cooow in the caaabbage paaatch! Yeoooo! Yeoooo! Get the cooow! Get the cooow!" Hamed once took a long scythe and cut a swath of destruction through Hakija Sućeska's cornfield because he wanted a ready-made shortcut to somewhere through Odžak.

When it came to fist fights, it was everyone for himself and Hamed generally in the middle. He grew burly and started training in karate. When he grew too big for Hiba to handle, she began pitching rolling pins and pieces of firewood at him. The police, most of them Muslims, would sometimes wander up to investigate the juvenile vandalism in the villages on the mountain, and occasionally they would hustle two or three suspects into the woods, rough them up, and leave it at that. Brotherhood and Unity was still the law of the land, but its enforcement had been relaxed. The Muslim kids on Mount Zvijezda now called their Serb schoolmates "Vlahs," a pejorative word meaning "outsiders," and the Serbs called the Muslims "Turks."

Not all memories rest silently, and Hamed never forgot the stories Grandpa Avdija and Uncle Avdo had told him about what Vitomir, Dragojle, and the other Serbs had done to the Muslims during the war. Once, in the woods high up on the mountain, he spotted Dragojle walking home. He followed the old Serb quietly and noticed he had been drinking. "If I push him over a cliff," Hamed thought, "it will look like an accident. They'll think he was drunk . . ." It remained just a thought.

Unlike Hamed, Sead Čelik grew up to be tall and thin like his father, but less burdened by the past. Sead was quiet, and he spent a lot of time after school with a Serb classmate, one of the Lukić boys from Rujišta, Milan Lukić. Milan's father, Mile, was born just before World War II; and his grandfather, Novica, had been tortured and killed in the late summer of 1941 by Muslim members of the Ustaše who had summoned him to their outpost in a lumber camp in Rujišta and ordered him to hand over some food. The Lukićs' Muslim neighbors fed the family for a few weeks before the Chetniks, including some of the Lukić men and Milan's maternal grandfather, took part in the killings of the Muslims on the mountain. Sead and Milan seemed to care nothing for stories of the war. They shared cheese pies at school. They hung out after classes to play soccer and basketball. They rode together most of the way home on the local bus.

Milan was boisterous. He enjoyed the limelight and told lots of jokes to keep himself under it. All the girls at school loved him. And for a while in junior high, Milan loved Hadžira Čavkušić, the pretty black-haired, ebony-eyed daughter of Hasib Čavkušić, a Muslim who had gone to work at the sawmill in Austria and who was friends with one of Milan's uncles in Steyr. It was a Lukić who had warned Hasib's father, Nurko, to flee Rujišta for Žepa just before the Chetniks started killing the Muslims on Mount Zvijezda in 1941; but some of the Lukić men of Rujišta participated in a Chetnik massacre that claimed the lives of Nurko's first wife and all of his children. Milan and Hadžira saw each other a thousand times in the village. But it was puppy love. Milan left home without finishing high school. Sead and Hadžira got word through some friends that he had gone to Serbia for police training arranged by some distant cousins in the police over there; other neighbors, however, heard he was in Belgrade selling soda pop and beer from a cart at the bus station. Milan came back to the mountain from time to time after his high school class had graduated. His neighbors say he returned once from Switzerland showing off gold chains and rings he had stolen from a jewelry store. And at a dance one night at Prelovo, he saved one of his Muslim friends from a knife attack by another Serb who nicked Milan in the back with the blade.

BY now practically all of the young men left the mountain when they finished school. Yugoslavia had defaulted on its loans, the economy was in a free fall, and people were desperate for money-paying jobs. By the late 1980s, there was no chance of landing a job in Višegrad. The local factories were swamped with workers who were doing nothing. The local vocational school kept turning out cooks and waiters, but the nearest restaurant openings were for seasonal jobs serving the mostly German and Italian tourists frolicking on the beaches around Dubrovnik and other vacation towns along the Adriatic coast. Enlisting in the police or the army was as good a way as any to escape the peasant life on Mount Zvijezda.

SANELA habitually switched on the television after school and watched the afternoon shows as she did her chores. Paja would head for the stalls to look in on the oxen and cows. Paja hated school from the first day and never did well. Huso tried to help him by tacking a piece of paper with the multiplication tables on the wall in the kitchen and for a while made Paja stand by the stove until he learned them by heart. It did little good. Paja and his best friend, Zuhdija Sućeska's son Senad, went to school together and caused trouble together. They would sneak into Juz-bin's mosque, climb up the spiral staircase inside the minaret, and shake back and forth until it started swaying like a playground amusement. They snatched eggs from the pigeon nests on the minaret's circular porch and tossed them down onto the heads of men coming out of Friday prayers. One day they set dried chili peppers on fire during class and drove everyone outside with the fumes. On another day, they strolled past the Janković house and serenaded Vitomir's wife, Stamena, as she puttered in the yard:

> Stamena, oh, Stamena
> She leapt into the sky.
> And she singed her pussy
> On a blazing pine.

The next day, the teacher told them to go outside and break off fresh branches from a nearby bush, and they were beaten red.

The boys did odd jobs for the teachers to secure themselves passing grades. When Paja finished the eighth grade, Huso tried to push him to enroll in vocational classes. Something. Anything. But Paja was too far gone. He seemed to want nothing more than to work the family land. Buying a pair of oxen was his idea. They were both piebald, and he named them Šaronja and Balja. Paja fed them, grazed them, cleaned out their stalls, and brushed them down. He would earn money or return favors by using the oxen to plow fields and cart loads of firewood or hay up and down the mountain. One summer, Paja took one of the oxen up onto Stolac and cut and trimmed a pine tree for a new center pole for his hay bale. He had heard stories about Stolac and could see the peak from the house, but he had never been up there before. He slurped water from the spring reputed to be the coldest in all of Bosnia. And he dropped pebbles into Zvekara and listened as they clicked down and down along the sides of the vertical shaft before their echo died out in the blackness.

EVEN in her new house, Saliha never outgrew her old habits. She wore a floral head scarf that almost covered her face like a veil, and she was so superstitious that she would go for days without letting her cow, Milava, out of its stall for fear that someone might put a hex on it. One summer day, Paja went around telling everyone that Milava had gone crazy with cabin fever and that he had heard the cow moan like a bull twelve times without breathing in: "She's inside with her front legs on the wall trying to climb out."

Hiba and Saliha's daughter got an old rag, folded inside it strands of hair, fingernails, garlic, and ashes, and tied it all together with twenty knots. That night they set it on a stone wall next to the door of the deranged cow's stall. Saliha waddled down the next morning and started calling for help: "A hex! A hex!"

Sanela was still a little girl, but she knew that one of the Kozić women, a sturdy, gourd-shaped woman named Šemsa, would know what to do about a hex. Šemsa came running as soon as Sanela told her what had happened. When she arrived at the stall, Šemsa took one glance at the rag and its twenty knots and began searching around the yard. She picked up a long, straight tree branch. Then she slipped it under her billowy *dimije*, lifted it between her legs and started galloping around the yard in front of the stall like a witch straddling a hobbyhorse.

"Šemsa, where are you riding?" Hiba and the other women screeched.

"I'm sweeping away the spider webs."

"Where are you sending them?"

"Down the mountain! Sweep! Sweep! Sweep!"

The gourd-shaped woman's *dimije* and blouse flopped up and down as she galloped around the yard. It took an hour of hard riding before Šemsa and Saliha thought the area had been swept clean enough of spider webs to let the nervous cow out of the stall. The animal calmed down as soon as it got outside. Saliha went back into her house certain Šemsa had worked a miracle.

HAMED left Kupusovići to do his stint in the Yugoslav army in 1985. He was assigned to a commando unit in Kosovo and returned a year later with "JNA" tattooed on his forearm. He soon understood that he would have to leave the mountain again to find a job. Sead had come home from the army as well, and stayed around just long enough to give his army jacket to Huso before leaving to work as a laborer in a shipyard on the Adriatic coast; when that gave out, he went to sea as a hand on a cargo ship. Hamed went off to Dubrovnik that same summer. He had no luck landing a job in the restaurants or hotels there. After a week, he heard that a juice company just outside of Belgrade was looking for fruit pickers. He took a bus to Serbia and signed on. Gordana Todorović, my sister-in-law, was tallying up the bushels of plums picked by the workers that fall when she fell in love with Hamed. Gordana had a degree in agriculture. After the harvest season, she did quality control, and Hamed somehow got himself assigned to the juice cooler where the quality control was going on.

Gordana took a leave from her job to come to America and work as a live-in nanny so that she could save up some money and get married. She earned two hundred dollars a week in cash and had free room and board in a house with a swimming pool right up the road from Richard Nixon's home in Saddle River, New Jersey; that was certainly better than I was doing with my degree in journalism and a couple of foreign languages. I thought Gordana was wacky to trade away her job for a few dollars a month and an uncertain future on the dingy outskirts of Belgrade, but she did it for love, and she did it without looking back.

Romeo and Juliet–style marriages between Serbs, Muslims, Croats, and members of Yugoslavia's other quarrelsome ethnic groups may have become commonplace in the country's urban areas by the mid-1980s, but they rarely came off without commentary from the neighbors. Just before Gordana and Hamed got married, one of the Serb women from the neighborhood tried to convince my mother-in-law, Mara, that Muslim men possess a powerful black magic and that she had better engage a mystic to make sure the spell on Gordana was nothing more than love. Hamed's magic must have been exceptionally potent because it went undetected, and he and Gordana would go on to have two sons and a daughter.

Huso was proud that his son had married a city girl, and a Serb with a college education at that. On Mount Zvijezda, Muslim girls assumed they would marry Muslims, and Serb girls knew they would marry Serbs. Everyone had talked when a Muslim girl from one of the nearby hamlets ran off with her Serb schoolteacher and moved into his apartment down in town. Now Huso went around talking her up with his Muslim and Serb neighbors, and the Serbs all asked when they were going to have a peek at his Vlah daughter-in-law.

PAJA never bothered to get a high school diploma. He grew into a sinewy, reticent man and stayed at home until he was drafted into the army and assigned to patrol Yugoslavia's border with Hungary. He spent a few weeks in the barracks stockade after shooting a guy who had been making out in the dark with his girlfriend near the border, but a military court ruled that Paja's action was justifiable. When Paja got out of the army, he married a village girl, Zlatija Sućeska, the sister of his best friend, Senad. They moved into the three upper rooms of Huso's house, Hiba and Sanela moved into the ground floor, and in 1990 Zlatija gave birth to a boy named Mirza.

Zlatija was a husky girl who got along well with Hiba and Sanela even though they came from three different generations of Muslim women. Zlatija, like Hiba, wore the billowy *dimije* but did not cover her head with a kerchief. Sanela was petite, and she dressed in tight jeans and T-shirts. She liked tying a kerchief around her neck and would not think of wearing one over her head.

"Wear the *dimije,* just once a month," Hiba would yell at her.

"I can't stand those things," Sanela would snarl back. "I can't walk in them. I can't even go to the bathroom comfortably in them."

"Shut up!" Huso would interrupt from somewhere in the house. "Can you see anything beneath what she's wearing?" he said, turning to Hiba.

"I can't," she answered.

"Then let her go ahead and wear the jeans," he said. Then he turned to Sanela. "You can wear those pants. I don't care. But I never want you wearing them in front of me, and I never want to hear that you are wearing jeans that are all torn up. And I never want to see you in tight jeans when your shirt isn't tucked in."

Sanela never went for makeup, but she grew her nails long and kept them painted. This, too, got on Hiba's nerves, but Sanela knew she could get away with it, because Huso was gone most of the time and because she earned good grades in school. She enjoyed reading, performed well in math, and was one of the fastest sprinters on the mountain. Huso could never decide whether he was in favor of the running or not. He hesitated to let Sanela go off with the junior high team to run in other towns. She asked Huso once if she could run with the team at a competition in a town just across the Drina. He agreed, but changed his mind at the last minute, as if he had to exert his authority to prove something. Sanela snuck out of the house and ran in the track meet anyway. When she got home, Huso apologized for not having given her permission to go.

Huso and Hiba decided it would be best if Sanela did not attend high school. Many Muslim girls on Mount Zvijezda did not go to high school. Zlatija had not gone. The high school in Višegrad was a lot farther from home than the junior high in Prelovo. Huso did not like the idea of Sanela's going to school with young men, and he was not ready to spend money on the bus fare to and from Višegrad. Educating girls was still not considered a prudent investment. Sooner or later, an evening would come when even the best-educated daughter would disappear from the house; in a few weeks, a message would arrive that she had married a young man from one village or another, and that would be the end of her.

After her schooling had ended, Sanela spent her days working around the house, hanging out at Saliha's to smoke cigarettes, and spending time with her boyfriend, Samir. Sanela was crazy about Samir. She had started seeing him, and smoking, when she was in the sixth grade. She was thirteen then; and Samir was twenty, and drove a taxi. Their age difference drove Huso mad. Sanela would spend time together with Samir at Saliha's. They would sit up late at night watching television in Saliha's kitchen and put a blanket over the window so it would look as if the place was dark and everyone was sleeping.

Sanela read whatever she could get her hands on, pulp romances and magazines mostly. She nagged Huso until he let her take the yearly high school equivalency exam. She passed, then set her sights on hairdressing lessons.

Sanela also started visiting the mosque. The village got a new *hodža* in the late eighties, Hussein Ahmetagić, the great-grandson of Mullah Medo. The Muslims built Hodža Hussein a new house on the very spot where the minaret had once cast its shadow on Mullah Šaban's place. Hussein and his wife began inviting Sanela over to visit, and Sanela felt uncomfortable when they dropped what they were doing and began to pray. Sanela decided to learn to pray, and Hussein taught her the prayers in Arabic. At first the words were exotic, but meaningless. She had never seen or heard Huso, Hiba, Sead, or Hamed say any prayers; Paja had tried it once, but soon gave it up. Sanela kept at it. The strange-sounding words became etched in her memory. She pushed herself to learn as much as she could and once tried to fast each day from dawn until dusk during the Muslims' holy month, Ramadan. Her stomach throbbed, and her head got light. At the end of the fasting period came the three days of Bairam, the Muslims' biggest feast. Strings of lights would shine from the minaret of Juz-bin's mosque at night. After morning prayers, the women would bring out casseroles and trays with food. The adults would go house to house to visit their friends and eat, and when the adults came home the younger people would make the rounds.

NOT long after the Muslims finished building his house, Hodža Hussein began quarreling with his neighbor Branko Mitrašinović. The water pipe into the *hodža*'s house ran from a well the Austrians had built next to their barracks just below the Mitrašinović place. The local school had used the water after World War I, and Branko took over the well after World War II. Now he objected to Hussein's using the water for his house and garden. "It isn't your water, Branko," the *hodža* told him. "This isn't Kosovo, Branko. You can't keep me from using a well that was never yours." The quarrel spooked Hussein. It was 1989. Something unseen in forty-four years was reemerging in Yugoslavia then: nationalism, Serb nationalism. "Branko will poison the water and my kids will die," Hussein told his father. Soon Hussein left Kupusovići, and Juz-bin's mosque was without a *hodža* for the first time since its reopening.

Huso bought Hiba and Sanela a washing machine that summer. The next spring, Gordana and Hamed came down from Belgrade to show off their first baby, a boy named Damir. Huso was home for a week, and Sead came back from the sea. Paja bought a lamb from Branko Mitrašinović and roasted it on a spit. Branko dropped in to visit, and his wife, Petra, brought along a roll of yarn she had spun herself. Dragoljub and Zora came by. And Gordana was dumbstruck to see the Serbs in the Čelik home, drinking brandy, chatting, giving gifts. Hamed had told her the stories of the war and left matters at that. "How can you even talk to Branko?" she asked after the Serbs had gone home. The other Čeliks shrugged their shoulders. Dragoljub and Branko were the neighbors, like any of the Muslim and Serb neighbors. Dragoljub had lent Hiba money while Huso was in Iraq, and Paja had carried Dragojle's funeral wreath. Branko could get under anyone's skin, that was certain. But Huso had laid the tiles in Branko's bathroom and lent Branko's son money to build a house. And like Huso and Hasan, and Salih and Hujbo, and Čelik men of generations long forgotten, Paja made his plum brandy in a Mitrašinović still every autumn and spring.

PART TWO

FROM THE BONES OF PRINCE LAZAR TO THE WELL-FED DEAD

6

THE KITCHEN window of Huso Čelik's home and windows on many of the other houses on Mount Zvijezda glowed through the darkness with the blue-gray light radiating from the television screens inside. Night upon night, before and after the subtitled episodes of *Dynasty* or broadcasts of soccer and basketball games, the mountain folk sat watching in fascination as the Cold War came to an end and Communist Eastern Europe and Russia launched into transitions as radical as the changes that had swept over the continent after 1878, 1918, and 1945. Huso, Paja, Dragoljub, and the other men sipped their coffees and brandies and smoked their cigarettes. The women washed their dishes and clothes, spun their wool, and fed logs to the fires in their stoves. And together they gasped and cussed in shock, delight, and anxiety. East Germans began pouring over the border from Hungary into Austria, and the Hungarian border guards did not shoot at them. Poland and Hungary escaped the Soviet orbit. Czechs took to the streets of Prague in the "Velvet Revolution," the Berlin wall was battered to bits with sledgehammers, and Germany's reunification seemed a foregone conclusion. In terms the peasant folk could barely grasp came word that Westerners—economists and politicians and diplomats—were pressing the leaders of these Communist countries to introduce free-market capitalism immediately and with little regard for the political and social consequences.

Signs that Yugoslavia was coming apart at the seams had been appearing for years, and at first the show was entertaining. Official taboos were violated left and right, and sacred cows led to public slaughter. A $500-million financial scandal was uncovered at a Bosnian agricultural enterprise, and the republic's Communist godfather was sacked. Dissidents in Slovenia, Yugoslavia's richest and most advanced republic, began demanding free elections and an end to the Communist Party's monopoly on political power. Hot-tempered Serbs from Kosovo, an autonomous province of Serbia whose population is 90 percent ethnic Albanian, griped about discrimination and harassment by the province's ethnic Albanian authorities.

For fleeting moments, despite the anxious voices of the television news reporters, it seemed the coming changes might be beneficial. Yugoslavia could no longer muddle through as it had, and everyone knew that. Inflation had grown so steep that store clerks had to write up new price tags for their merchandise every afternoon. Savings were wiped out. Wages plummeted. Workers pretended to work and pilfered whatever they could grab. The government pretended to govern. Managers of giant public enterprises and generals in the army embezzled as much as their Swiss and Austrian and Cypriot bank accounts could hold.

The personal and social consequences of the economic breakdown soon became clear even to the common folk on Mount Zvijezda. The factories, farm complexes, and mines could no longer pile up losses and count on the government to bail them out by taking foreign loans or by printing currency with nothing backing it. Young professional people could not find work and leapt at any chance to flee abroad. High school graduates who had managed to acquire occupational training were now almost unemployable except as physical laborers toiling for slave wages. Workers who once assumed they enjoyed employment for life were now terrified of losing their jobs; and workers living in small, one-factory towns knew that layoffs would require them to pack up and abandon the houses they or their parents had spent decades building. Everyone grew anxious to see who would decide which workers would be laid off; who would decide the size of the paychecks, the pensions, and the unemployment benefits; who would inherit the assets of bankrupt factories that belonged to everyone and to no one; who would be the winners; who would be the losers; who would be the scapegoats; who would be the new masters.

The Communist bosses running Yugoslavia's republics had clawed at each other's throats along national lines for decades behind closed doors. Serbia's leaders had fought with Croatia and Slovenia to get their hands on investment money for local boondoggle projects, including the construction of a hugely expensive railroad line between Belgrade and the Adriatic through the highlands of Montenegro, some of Europe's roughest terrain. Croatian and Slovenian leaders had haggled over the prices of Serbian raw materials. Practically every republic had wanted to have its own automobile assembly line. Practically every two-horse town miles from the nearest highway could not live without having its own ten-story hotel.

For all that, the Communists carefully nurtured a public image of harmony at the top. For years after Tito's death, the party leadership stage-managed massive stadium rallies to celebrate the great dictator's birthday. They presented one another with war medals to keep the myth of the Partisans alive. They warned of the ever-present danger of nationalism and swore to defend Brotherhood and Unity and the socialist order to the end. When making public calls for urgent economic reforms, they reverted to a wooden language understood by no one, and they blocked promising reform initiatives because applying them would have required loosening the Communist Party elite's monopoly control of the government and the country's industries.

SLOBODAN MILOŠEVIĆ, the prime mover in Yugoslavia's slide into nationalist turmoil, mastered the art of political intrigue in the miasma of deceit that was suffocating the country's Communist establishment. Milošević was born in Požarevac, a small town in Serbia, in August 1941, about three weeks before Huso Čelik came into the world. He married his boyhood sweetheart, Mirjana Marković, the daughter of Moma Marković, one of Tito's political commissars. Her mother, Vera Miletić, was a Communist Party secretary who was arrested and executed during World War II by pro-Nazi Serbian police and posthumously ostracized by the party after the war for having reportedly revealed the identities of members of Belgrade's Communist underground. It remains a mystery to what extent Milošević's ambition was driven by the aspirations of his wife, who has been nicknamed Jerina the Damned, or by the fact that his father abandoned his mother before the two of them committed suicide in separate incidents a decade apart. Milošević's parents were born in Montenegro, and some of his clansmen trace their roots back for generations, to a fighter of Turks named Miloš Markov in the eighteenth century and, beyond that, to Orthodox vassals who took the losing side in the Battle of Kosovo in 1389.

Milošević rose through the bureaucracy of Serbia's Communist Party by riding on the coattails of a law school friend, Ivan Stambolić, the nephew of Serbia's Communist godfather. After putting a political knife into Stambolić's back in 1987, Milošević became Serbia's paramount leader. He quickly dragged all of the Communist Party's national rivalries out from behind closed doors in order to curry favor with the Serb people and use his popularity to augment his power. Within a few months, Milošević had seized political control of Montenegro and Serbia's richest region, the autonomous province of Vojvodina, by mobilizing public opinion against their feckless, faceless, and much hated Communist bureaucracies. He accused the ethnic-Albanian Communist leaders in Kosovo of plotting to cut the province away from Yugoslavia and merge it with neighboring Albania; and in March 1989, he ignored Yugoslavia's constitution and squeezed the last life out of Kosovo's political autonomy. He spat all over the Slovenes and their demands for democratic reform. And while insisting that Yugoslavia could be ruled only by a one-party system, Milošević demanded that the country's deadlocked government of six republics be replaced by a strong, "American-style" federal government based in Belgrade.

Milošević's internal-security ministry recruited unemployed young men into a special police military unit, which was armed and supported by Serb nationalists in the Yugoslav army's officers corps. He used these police units to crush street protests by ethnic Albanians in Kosovo's towns and to spread terror into the province's villages. Scores of Albanians were killed. Tens of thousands of Albanian workers were thrown out of work. The television screens on Mount Zvijezda and all over Yugoslavia showed the pictures of Milošević's troops beating Albanian demonstrators. Before their eyes, Slovenes, Croats, Muslims, and other Yugoslavs saw the reincarnation of the Serb hegemony and police thuggery that had radicalized Yugoslavia in the 1930s and presaged the bloodbath of World War II. Up on Mount Zvijezda, it was clear even to Branko Mitrašinović that he no longer had any reason to let Hodža Hussein draw water from the old Austrian well, and it was clear to Huso Čelik that no good would come from any of it.

Vidovdan, June 28, 1989, was the day Slobodan Milošević chose to drive a ceremonial stake into the heart of Brotherhood and Unity. On that morning, hundreds of thousands of Serbs thronged to the site of the Battle of Kosovo to celebrate its six hundredth anniversary. Beady-eyed Serbian Orthodox metropolitans hovered over Prince Lazar's bones, the remains of the man who had led the Christian armies onto the Kosovo battlefield and had perished there, the remains that the Serbian Orthodox Church had just taken on a pilgrimage around Serbia as if now, in 1989, after six centuries, his death would finally be avenged and he would be able to rest in peace. The royalist iconography of the Chetniks reappeared for the first time since the butchery of World War II. Milošević, Serbia's new warrior prince, descended from the sky aboard a helicopter at exactly high noon. He saluted the crowd as he climbed onto the dais and joined a group of stiff-faced politicians, some security police in dark suits and tinted sunglasses, and a troupe of folk dancers decked out in embroidered costumes. The throng chanted Milošević's nickname: "Slo-bo! Slo-bo! Slo-bo! Slo-bo!" And the nation's leader, jowly and supercilious, stood before them and spoke.

Serbia, Milošević proclaimed, had been reborn. The Serbs, he said, would no longer tolerate having their national muscle restrained. They had to unite as never before: "If our people lost the Battle of Kosovo, it was due not only to the military supremacy of the Turks but to the tragic discord among the leadership of the Serbs. This discord has dogged the Serb people throughout their history, through both world wars and, later, when the Serbian leadership in socialist Yugoslavia remained divided and prone to make compromises at the people's expense. . . .

"The heroism demonstrated here at Kosovo cannot allow us to forget that at one time our people were brave, and dignified, and stood among the few who went into battle undefeated. . . . Now, six centuries later, we are again engaged in conflicts and disputes. These aren't yet armed battles, but such things can't be ruled out."

The people in the throng lavished applause upon their hero. "Slo-bo! Slo-bo! Slo-bo!" they chanted. And over and over they sang a rhyme: "Oh, Prince Lazar, how ill-starred, not to have a Slo-bo marching at your side."

❦ ❦ ❦

EACH day, through the scratchy speaker of a shortwave radio, the BBC brought to my desk the news of the nationalist euphoria sweeping over Serbia. My wife Ljiljana and I were living in Brooklyn then, in a one-room basement apartment on Pembroke Street, just down the beach from Coney Island. I was immersed in books about Yugoslavia and was writing a short history of the country for the Library of Congress in between afternoon runs to the amusement park and back. I had met Ljiljana, learned Serbo-Croatian, and studied some journalism in Belgrade in the mid-1980s thanks to a Fulbright scholarship, and had been trying for three years to find a reporting job that would lead me back to Eastern Europe and eventually to Moscow. The BBC's reports, coupled with the rejection letters, were driving me mad with frustration and jealousy. In Belgrade, the Communists were staging massive nationalist demonstrations; in Kosovo, striking Albanian miners were holed up thousands of feet underground in a protest against the Serbian takeover of their province; the Serbian police were indiscriminately firing heavy machine guns into private homes, and Slobodan Milošević was laying down his marker.

One afternoon, after noticing that the *New York Times* had brushed over some particularly compelling story from Kosovo with a few paragraphs of copy from a wire service, I sent a letter and a résumé over the transom to Joe Lelyveld, who was then the paper's foreign editor; I professed to know something about Yugoslavia and offered to move back to Belgrade and write stories about what was going on. A reply from the *Times* landed in my mailbox a few days later. I assumed it was just another rejection and nearly pitched it into the wastebasket unopened; but the speedy reply and the size and the shape of the envelope — it was small and almost square — were unlike the form-letter rejections I had gotten from the *Times* before, and I opened the envelope out of curiosity. The letter had come from Lelyveld himself; he said what I had offered to do would get me nowhere, but if I wanted to move to Yugoslavia anyway, I should come by for a chat. I had three meetings with members of the foreign staff on West Forty-third Street over the next few months. On my last visit, one of the editors, Tom Feyer, gave me a few tips about how to construct a newspaper story; then he let me read five or six pieces of unedited copy; I left the office confident I could find stories and words that would be decent enough to be edited into shape. I had never worked for a newspaper and knew no one at the *Times* before I sent my letter. No one there had asked me to fill out an application. No one had asked to see a writing sample or a list of references.

Ljiljana and I moved to Yugoslavia from New York in January 1990, a few days after Slovenia's Communists refused to take any more of Milošević's browbeating and walked out of the last congress ever held by Yugoslavia's Communist Party. Belgrade looked the same as ever: dusty, crumbling, shrouded in black and white and gray. The cafés were still jammed. The air was still choked with the smoke of trash smoldering in the street dumpsters and the exhaust blasting from the worn-out diesel engines in the city's buses. The amiable, unpretentious place I had known as a student, however, had been obscured behind a cloud of hysteria kicked up by the propaganda spewing from Milošević's state television network. The "news" broadcasts and evening talk shows had convinced even well-educated Serbs that they were a "chosen people," a "celestial people," and that Tito had actually been an impostor, a Russian Communist agent infiltrated into Yugoslavia by Stalin just to subdue the Serbs and break up the country. People believed that the Serbs had been victims, and only victims, throughout their entire history; they believed they were now being victimized again by a decades-old conspiracy of Stalinists, Masons, Albanian mafiosi, Ustaše émigrés, the pope of Rome, the CIA, the KGB, and neofascists in Germany and Austria who were bent on breaking up Yugoslavia; they believed that Slobodan Milošević, the Serbian Communist Party, and the Yugoslav army were the only forces standing in the conspiracy's way, saving them from rack and ruin. Even casual conversations slid into a harangue against Albanians, Slovenes, Croats, and Germans. Drunks on the street blabbered about a Greater Serbia stretching all the way from Kosovo to Pittsburgh. One pleasant and otherwise reasonable Serb woman broke down in tears when I had the audacity to tell her this conspiracy talk was a lot of hogwash. "You'll see," she sobbed. "The Germans, the Croats, the Albanians, they're going to kill us all. They're going to kill us all! You'll see."

This pathetic lunacy entertained me for a few months before it began grating on my nerves. I fell into the habit of telling taxi drivers to shut up and drive, and I avoided places like the Writers' Club, the traditional night spot for Belgrade's "intelligentsia," because I knew I would not keep my mouth shut. At the same time, however, I was thankful for the hysteria, and had to be. In March 1990, it gave me my first story: a few hundred words about some castle-in-the-sky scheme by Milošević's government to dilute the ethnic-Albanian majority in Kosovo by recolonizing the province with hundreds of thousands of Serbs. A few weeks later, Feyer told me over the phone that I had gotten my first byline with a tale about an Albanian in Kosovo who was traveling from hamlet to hamlet and reconciling blood-vengeance vendettas between rival Albanian families in order to strengthen the opposition to the Serbian government's repression. The hunt for new stories, new ways of showing the realities of Yugoslavia in transition, quickly became an addiction.

When Ljiljana and I moved to Yugoslavia, her sister Gordana and Hamed were living with their son, Damir, in a matchbox apartment a few minutes' walk from my mother-in-law's place in a dusty suburb across the Danube from Belgrade. Gordana was on maternity leave from the juice factory, and Hamed had found a better-paying job welding metal frames for ironing boards. He usually left for work before dawn, and, on the night we met, he came home after dark, took a quick shower, grabbed a beer, and lounged around in a T-shirt and tennis shoes. He didn't talk much, and I wasn't saying much of anything either, probably because I wanted to get home to do some work. If we spoke at all about the political situation, it was to crack jokes or swear at someone. Hamed invited Ljiljana and me to Kupusovići for a visit, but there was never any time and, in those days, not much money. By the springtime, Ljiljana had gotten a job with a Slovenian travel agency leading foreigners on tours around Yugoslavia, and I was on the road all the time as well.

That April was a month of elections. Voters in Slovenia and Croatia brought to power non-Communist governments whose leaders demanded broader autonomy from Belgrade and threatened to secede from Yugoslavia if they did not get it. Milošević had given up on preserving the old Yugoslavia months earlier and had begun working to spread his power base by extending Serbia's borders. He clearly knew there were plenty of Serbs in Croatia and Bosnia who would be willing to kill and die before they would ever accept minority status in independent Croatian or Bosnian states. He knew he could find even more Serbs desperate enough to fight to take over control of the factories, mines, hotels, and stores where they worked.

Milošević found a willing accomplice for his carve-up of Yugoslavia in the person of Croatia's new president, Franjo Tudjman, who had been a political commissar for Tito's Partisans during the war and rose through the ranks of the Yugoslav army to become a general. It remains a mystery to what extent Tudjman's political ambitions were driven by the fact that his parents were found dead in their home soon after the war in an incident that the police officially found to be a murder-suicide (though Tudjman has maintained for years that they were murdered by vengeance-driven Serb Communists). After retiring from the army in the 1960s, he emerged as a Croat nationalist, and his ambition became the creation of an independent Croatian state that would encompass huge tracts of Bosnia, if not all of it. Tito had twice jailed Tudjman for preaching Croat nationalism, and he cut a pathetic image after his release from prison. Nationalist passions in Croatia lay dormant until Milošević's rise, and Tudjman used to hang around in the American library beneath the U.S. consulate in Zagreb, attempting to buttonhole diplomats who were trying their best to avoid him.

From the moment they took power, Tudjman and his nationalist party set about antagonizing the Serb minority in Croatia and effectively driving them into Milošević's hands. In his inaugural address, Tudjman snubbed the republic's Serbs by referring only to Croats. Croatia's internal-affairs ministry announced that it would require all police officers to wear a badge emblazoned with a Croatian coat of arms that was clearly designed to resemble the symbol the Ustaše death squads had worn during their persecution of the Serbs in World War II. Serb-owned beach houses were ransacked and torched, and the police turned up no suspects. The press in Serbia seized upon each of these issues. It warned that another bout of genocide was just around the corner, that the Croatian government was preparing gas chambers and had secretly buried nuclear waste in predominantly Serb-populated areas of Croatia in order to poison the population. By August, Milošević's police ministry and nationalist Serbs in the midlevels of the Yugoslav army's officer corps had instigated an armed uprising against Tudjman's government by local Serbs in the mountain town of Knin, a former Chetnik stronghold that straddles a railroad line and highway linking central Croatia with the Adriatic. Milošević's bid to dismember Croatia and create his own Greater Serbia had begun.

The virus of nationalism spread gradually through the Serb and Croat populations in Bosnia. The Muslims, who now made up over 40 percent of the republic's population, reacted to it by forming a nationalist party of their own: the Party for Democratic Action. Its leader was Alija Izetbegović, a lawyer, and a pious Muslim whose ancestors had been merchants in Belgrade before being driven from their home during the expulsions of Muslims from Serbia in the 1860s. Izetbegović had been an activist in an illegal Muslim student organization that resisted Tito's clampdown on the Islamic faith in the late 1940s. He spent five years in jail after a show trial in 1983 in which he was convicted of "anti-state activity" and "counterrevolution." At issue was an essay, written a decade earlier, in which he advocated democracy and economic reforms and, for Muslims, a moral revival based on Islamic principles. During a republicwide election campaign in the fall of 1990, Izetbegović campaigned for the preservation of Bosnia as a multiethnic, multireligious republic. He wanted Bosnia to remain within a broader Yugoslavia in order to head off the looming threat that the Muslims would be caught in the crossfire of a war between nationalist Serbs and Croats bent on dividing Bosnia's territory. But he warned that if Yugoslavia broke apart, the Muslims would strive to make Bosnia an independent country before they would settle for becoming second-class citizens in a Milošević dictatorship.

Radovan Karadžić, the man picked in Belgrade to lead the nationalist Serb party in Bosnia, the Serbian Democratic Party, was born on June 19, 1945, in Petnjica, a primitive village high on Mount Durmitor in Montenegro. Like the Milošević family, the Karadžić clan of Petnjica boasts a family tree rooted in the heroic past of the Serbian nation. Family members say Ottoman incursions drove their ancestors from a mountain near Kosovo a decade or so before the great battle in the fourteenth century. They also claim that their clan included Vuk Karadžić, a nineteenth-century linguist who transcribed thousands of Balkan legends and heroic epics, reformed the Serbo-Croatian language, translated the Bible, and developed the Serbian variant of the Cyrillic alphabet. Radovan Karadžić aspired to follow in Vuk's literary footsteps and become a poet, but he was looked upon as a bumpkin, a "Swede" like Huso Čelik, when he moved to Sarajevo as a teenager to attend school. He married a medical student named Ljilja Zelen, one of three daughters of a Serb who had established himself well in the Bosnian capital after the Ustaše wiped out his family during World War II. Karadžić went on to study psychiatry and dabbled in poetry. During the student unrest of the late 1960s, he was shunned by his friends for being a secret-police informer. And like the assassin Gavrilo Princip, he memorized the verses of Petar II Petrović-Njegoš, a nineteenth-century bishop-prince of Montenegro, who is hailed as Serbian literature's greatest poet and whose most famous epic lauds the extermination of Muslim Slavs. But Karadžić was not a vulgar anti-Muslim racist. He founded the outpatient treatment center at the psychiatric clinic of Kosevo Hospital, Sarajevo's main hospital. He gave free medical treatment to his neighbors—Muslim, Serb, and Croat—and was not averse to padding his income by peddling bogus medical and psychological evaluations that qualified healthy workers for early retirement and enabled criminals to cop insanity pleas. At about the time of the 1984 Winter Olympic Games in Sarajevo, Karadžić and a partner, Momčilo Krajišnik, a manager at a mining enterprise named Energoinvest, took out a loan from an agricultural-development fund and used the money to build themselves houses in Pale, a Serb village in the mountains above Sarajevo that had been transformed into a ski resort by the Communists. The two men were arrested for fraud and sat in jail for eleven months before another Serb, a Shakespeare professor named Nikola Koljević, bailed them out.

These three men later became key figures in the Serbian Democratic Party, and the party presidency lifted Karadžić out of the penury he was suffering after his jail term. His apartment was a cluttered mess when I visited him and Ljilja for an interview in September 1990. Karadžić was a gracious host. He wasted no time in hauling out a decanter of plum brandy and immediately waved off any possibility that Bosnia could ever become an Islamic state: "Most Muslims here are not fundamentalists. . . . These Muslims are used to the European way of life, an emancipated way of life. These Muslims oppose the fundamentalists."

It was the Croats, the Ustaše, whom Karadžić saw as his enemy. As he was talking, Ljilja chimed in like a taxi driver: "Tell him about the genocide against the Serbs." I held up my left hand, took a sip of brandy and stopped him before he got started. I told him that my mother-in-law, Mara, was born in a Bosnian village that was burned in 1941 by an Ustaše death squad. I told him that her entire family had been killed, that she had been pitched into an Ustaše concentration camp, that her grandmother had been burned up in her house.

"So you're a Serb," said Karadžić, smiling and leaning forward and figuring he had an answer to the most crucial question in this part of the world. "You know, of course, that if your wife is a Serb, then you're a Serb. That's our custom."

"No. I'm a Croat, and Irish, and American," I replied, also smiling.

"But you understand," he said.

I understood what he meant. In Karadžić's mind, the need to avenge the Serb deaths during World War II would justify anything his people might do. In his mind, the blood on the Serbs' hands during the war had been justified by the Ustaše genocide. "The Serbs are endangered again," Karadžić warned. "The most direct danger to the Serb people is that there will be a breakup of Yugoslavia and that part of the Serb nation will become a minority in a new foreign country. This would mean their destruction, culturally, nationally, and spiritually and perhaps even economically and physically.

"Serbs here are ready for war. If someone forces them to live as a national minority, they are ready for war. This nation remembers well the genocide. The memory of those events is still a living memory, a terrible living memory. The terror has survived fifty years. The feeling is present still because they won't allow us to bury the dead."

ON November 9, 1990, after three years of watching the chaos unfold on television each night, the people of Kupusovići and the nearby hamlets strolled over to the main classroom in the whitewashed schoolhouse across from the Radovanović place in Odžak and cast their ballots in the first free, multiparty elections ever held in Bosnia. The election became a demonstration of ethnic loyalty; and when the votes were tallied, Bosnia's nationalist Muslim, Serb, and Croat parties had toppled the republic's Communists. Alija Izetbegović became Bosnia's president, and he formed a government that included members of all three nationalist parties. Izetbegović and Kiro Gligorov, the president of Yugoslavia's poorest republic, Macedonia, worked desperately to keep Yugoslavia from breaking up. They proposed various schemes to save the country: a loose federation of republics, a Canadian-style confederation, and an "asymmetrical" confederation that would have allowed Croatia and Slovenia to become virtually independent but maintain a special relationship with the other republics. It was Milošević, Tudjman, and the Slovenes who rejected each of their proposals. Milošević insisted that Yugoslavia could be a federation under Belgrade's control, a federation under his rule, or nothing at all.

Milošević might never have precipitated a war to seize the territory he coveted in Croatia and Bosnia had anti-Communist Serb nationalists not taken to Belgrade's streets on March 9, 1991, and threatened his hold on political and economic power in Serbia. Belgrade had seen nothing like it since the anti-Nazi demonstrations of March 1941, when the government was overthrown and crowds toting French and British flags marched through the streets shouting, "Better the grave than a slave." Milošević panicked. His riot police attacked the protesters, and the demonstrators countered by rushing police cordons. Milošević first quelled the unrest with a combination of police power and empty promises. Then he deflected the Serbs' dissatisfaction with the Communists and the economic mess at home onto the traditional enemy, the Croats. His television commentators now began warning that the Yugoslav army would go to war to preserve "Yugoslavia's unity" and "defend" Serbs threatened by resurgent fascism in Croatia. Milošević told a meeting of local Serbian political bosses that he would not dispute Croatia's right to secede from Yugoslavia but would not sit back and let Tudjman make off with districts in Croatia that had Serb majorities.

"As you all know, only the strong, and never the weak, can dictate where borders will be drawn. Therefore, we must be strong," Milošević told the local Serbian leaders. "We consider it the legitimate right and interest of the Serb people to live in one state. This is where the matter begins and ends. This legitimate interest of the Serb nation does not endanger any other people. . . . But if we must fight, then by God we will fight. I hope they won't be crazy enough to fight us. Because we may not know how to work well or to do business well, but we certainly know very well how to fight."

A few days later, on March 25, Milošević met President Tudjman secretly at a sprawling horse ranch on the open plains of Vojvodina. There, in one of Marshal Tito's grand old villas, the two leaders conspired to carve up Bosnia and create from its carcass a Greater Serbia and a Greater Croatia. They appointed a secret commission to draw new borders before departing to prepare to do battle over lands they could not agree upon. Slovenia and Croatia declared independence from Yugoslavia in late June 1991. Local clashes, almost invariably sparked by agents from Belgrade and Zagreb, gradually escalated across Croatia. By the autumn the war had begun. And within a month, the UN Security Council had imposed an arms embargo on all the republics of the former Yugoslavia, a decision that gave the Serbs an overwhelming advantage in weaponry and equipment because they controlled the Yugoslav army.

DURING the fighting in Croatia, President Milošević brought stiff pressure to bear on Bosnia's Muslim leaders in an attempt to force them to join his Greater Serbia. President Izetbegović time and again rejected having anything to do with Milošević's plans to include Bosnia in a diminished Yugoslavia. Izetbegović declared Bosnia to be neutral in the Croatian conflict and refused to allow the Yugoslav army to draft Muslim men to fight in Croatia. Milošević responded by imposing economic sanctions on Bosnia. "Islamic fundamentalists" were added to the list of conspirators against Serbia and the Serbs. The Serbian police ministry and the army began delivering guns to Karadžić's Serbian Democratic Party, and his party leaders sold and distributed them to Serb men. Izetbegović's party, too, began haphazardly to prepare the Muslims for war.

On October 14, 1991, the Muslim and Croat parties brought before the Bosnian parliament a proposal to declare Bosnia a "sovereign republic," still formally within Yugoslavia, but competent to take decisions without referring to the federal government in Belgrade, which had become an empty shell with the secessions of Croatia and Slovenia. Radovan Karadžić went to the podium and threatened the Muslims with destruction if they adopted the proposal.

"You want to take Bosnia and Herzegovina down the same road to hell and suffering that Slovenia and Croatia are traveling," Karadžić railed. "Do not think that you will not be leading Bosnia and Herzegovina into hell. And do not think that you will not perhaps make the Muslim people disappear. Because the Muslims cannot defend themselves if there is a war."

Izetbegović followed Karadžić to the rostrum: "His words and his manners show why others refuse to remain in this Yugoslavia. The kind of Yugoslavia that Mr. Karadžić wants, nobody else wants any more, nobody, except perhaps the Serbs. This Yugoslavia and the manners of Karadžić are simply hated by the peoples of Yugoslavia, by Slovenes, Croats, Macedonians, Albanians, Hungarians, Muslims. By Europe and the world. . . . I solemnly state that the Muslims will not attack anyone. However, I state just as solemnly that the Muslims will defend themselves with great determination and that they will survive."

The Serbian Democratic Party's deputies responded by walking out of the parliamentary session. The Muslims and Croats adopted the sovereignty declaration in their absence. About ten days later, the Serb deputies created their own national assembly and passed a resolution underscoring their desire to remain within Milošević's diminished Yugoslavia. The schoolhouse in Odžak was open for voting again on November 9, 1991. This time the nationalist Serbs held a referendum and arranged for more than 100 percent of Bosnia's Serbs to cast ballots saying they would never accept an international border separating them from Serbia.

Izetbegović was now desperate to save Bosnia from dismemberment. He secretly organized a Muslim militia but knew he could not assemble an army or police force strong enough to thwart the Bosnian Serbs and their backers in the Yugoslav army and Serbia's police ministry. The Muslim leader thought he might be able to save Bosnia and its Muslims by appealing for the international community to recognize Bosnia as an independent state and begging for the United Nations to deploy a peacekeeping force to prevent war from breaking out.

International recognition of an independent Bosnia was a perilous issue, an issue world leaders had long sought to avoid addressing. If Bosnia were recognized as an independent country along with Croatia, Slovenia, and Macedonia, it might incite Milošević and Karadžić to begin gobbling up Bosnia's territory; if Bosnia were not recognized with the other republics, it would effectively be handed over to Milošević by default. Izetbegović tried to dodge the question for months by pleading with world leaders not to recognize Croatia or Slovenia until an overall settlement of the Yugoslav conflict could be negotiated.

In November 1991, however, the Yugoslav army and Milošević's special police brought the recognition issue to a head. They overran the ethnically mixed Croatian town of Vukovar after pounding it with howitzers, mortars, and aerial bombs for three months and sacrificing a never publicized number of men in scores of half-baked attempts to storm the place. More than two thousand civilians—Croats, Serbs, Hungarians—were blown to bits in the indiscriminate shelling, and the world did nothing to stop it. Men and officers of the Yugoslav army dragged hundreds of unarmed, draft-age prisoners, including some wounded, from Vukovar's hospital, trucked them into a cornfield, and executed them. Serb irregulars pulled men in civilian clothes out of groups of shell-shocked refugees and shot them dead on the spot.

Though it would be another two years before I would articulate it in this way, it was in Vukovar that I consciously climbed onto an observation tower for the first time to look down on the doings of man in his world as if his race were nothing but the wildlife on a great plain. Vukovar demanded it. The charred, denuded trees; the buildings that seemed to have melted into the streets; the stacks of the dead; a detached leg in a pile of rubble and plaster dust, bloated, and covered by leathery skin as gray as an elephant's; the frozen, yellow-gray grimaces; the purple lips of dead children drawn back over tiny teeth: all of it was abhorrent and all of it was alluring, and it had to be kept away, kept at a distance. I scratched some notes into a steno pad, few adjectives, no reaction, nothing charged.

In the wake of the Yugoslav army's war crimes at Vukovar and the clear evidence that the army's primary objective was to expel forcibly the non-Serb population from the Vukovar area, Croatia's main ally, Germany, redoubled its already stiff pressure on the European Community countries to recognize Croatia as an independent state. The German foreign minister, Hans Dietrich Genscher, soon met with President Izetbegović of Bosnia to discuss his opposition to Croatia's recognition, and this time the Bosnian leader did not raise any objections to it. By mid-December, Germany had bullied the other European nations into accepting a scheme for the recognition of Croatia, Slovenia, and any of the other Yugoslav republics wishing to apply for it. On December 20, Bosnia's presidency voted to apply.

Milošević and Karadžić did not hesitate to go forward with their preparations for war in Bosnia. The Yugoslav army began setting up artillery positions around Sarajevo and other Bosnian towns. Milošević soon had his minions issue a secret order for the transfer into Bosnia of all Serb officers in the Yugoslav army who had been born there. The Bosnian Serbs' renegade national assembly proclaimed the creation of the Serb Republic of Bosnia and Herzegovina, later known as Republika Srpska. And Croat and Serb leaders held meetings in Austria to outline plans for population transfers that would create ethnically pure Croat and Serb territory in Bosnia. All that was left for them to do now was to deal with the Muslims.

THAT winter—I don't remember the month—Ljiljana and I went to a dinner at the home of an American diplomat in Belgrade. The main guest was a State Department official who had just been appointed to supervise the Balkan region. He was making a tour of the area. During the salad and main courses, he went on and on explaining how the United States should not, and would not, get mixed up in "small ethnic wars," "local wars," and that the proper policy toward these conflicts was to contain them and keep arms from flowing into the areas they devoured. I had, and still have, no trouble with the policy of keeping American troops out of the Balkans; but after Vukovar, it became difficult to stomach members of polite society from Washington talking about Yugoslavia and yapping on and on about keeping arms away from people trying to defend themselves when they knew full well that this meant that Milošević and his ilk could have their way with any unarmed homeowner who got in their way. Over dessert, this American official conjured up one rhetorical contortion after another to try and distinguish these "small ethnic conflicts" from the Iraqi invasion of Kuwait without having to admit that the massive, overwhelmingly American military intervention to drive the Iraqis out of Kuwait was about oil and nothing else.

"No," he said, "we should not become involved in these conflicts."

"And what if one side has all the guns and does whatever it pleases with people who have none? And what if we maintain an arms embargo against them, what then?" I asked him.

"Then one side wins," he answered with no hesitation. "One side wins."

7

GUNS. An obsession with guns infected Bosnia's mountain men. They boasted about their guns the way Behadil crowed about the cannon between his legs. They debated the qualities of the different kinds of guns: the reliability of the Nazi-era German pistols and machine guns that many of them had oiled and buried forty-six years earlier; the virtues of a Serbian-made AK-47 assault rifle; the vices of the cheap Romanian AK, whose nickel-plated barrel would overheat and shoot every which way but straight after firing two dozen rounds. The peasant men mulled over how to scrape together the cash to buy guns. The Serbian AK sold for about a thousand dollars, the profit from a few slaughtered cows. A machine gun cost half as much more. Hand grenades went for about twelve dollars apiece.

By the late fall of 1991, Muslims from Žlijeb were no longer sending their children to the primary school over in Odžak. Down in Višegrad, Muslim and Serb men were no longer sitting together in any café except for the bar of the hotel beside Mehmed Pasha's bridge. This café was Višegrad's illegal gun bazaar. You could walk through the metal-and-glass doors any night that winter, cross the dark lobby on a floor slippery with gray slush, turn to the right, descend a few steps, slide open a glass door, and enter a brightly lit room choked with cigarette smoke. The men there would sit at card tables and talk in low voices. One of the waiters, a dark-skinned man whose name was Mitar Vasiljević, would make discreet inquiries. He hardly bothered to strip the coffee-stained tablecloths or empty the aluminum ashtrays.

Serb gun sellers from Karadžić's party say they knew the Šabanović brothers of Višegrad, Avdija and Murat. The Muslim brothers ran a couple of one-room grocery stores in Višegrad, which made them respected "businessmen" in town. They were born near Višegrad right after World War II, but their family was new to the area. Their father had been driven out of Serbia in the 1930s and had joined a Muslim militia attached to the Ustaše during the war. Avdija and Murat grew into barrel-chested men who did not mince their words and were quicker to take action than to think about its consequences. Avdija spent time in jail for getting drunk and killing a friend at a wedding in the 1970s. Murat was even more boisterous. He proudly wore the name of the sultan who led the Ottoman army against the Serbs in the medieval battle at Kosovo, and he proudly named his own son Bayezid after the son of Sultan Murat. Murat of Višegrad made himself famous all over Yugoslavia by carrying a sledge-hammer down to Mehmed Pasha's bridge and pounding apart a monument to the second famous son of the Drina River valley, the Nobel Prize–winning writer Ivo Andrić, who is unpopular with many Bosnian Muslims because of his portrayal of them in his many novels, including the famous *Bridge on the Drina*. Murat broke of the monument's marble relief of Andrić's head and dropped it into the Drina. It was apparently never seen again.

The Šabanović brothers became the men of action for the Višegrad chapter of Izetbegović's Party for Democratic Action. The Serbs knew that the Šabanović brothers were dealing and distributing guns to Muslims all over the district. They knew this because the Serbs were selling guns to the Šabanović brothers. The Serbs had lots of guns, as many as they wanted. Milošević's police and the Yugoslav army were sending them guns from Serbia in small trucks with canvas stretched over their cargo beds. The local Serb leaders sold the Muslims guns because there was a lot of money in it and because they coveted money more than they needed guns. They kept tabs on how many guns they had sold and to whom. The Šabanović brothers also got guns through the Party for Democratic Action. They had a secret compartment welded into the mixer on a cement truck and used it for transporting assault rifles and hand grenades.

The Serbs blamed the Šabanović brothers for starting all the trouble in Višegrad. The Šabanović brothers blamed Slobodan Milošević, Radovan Karadžić, the Yugoslav army, and the local leaders of Karadžić's party. In 1990, Serbs toting pictures of Milošević and double-eagle Chetnik flags rode into Višegrad on buses to demonstrate on Mehmed Pasha's bridge, at the very spot where Draža Mihailović's Chetniks had butchered Muslims in October 1943. The Serbs said Višegrad was Serbian. They called the bridge "Andrić's bridge." Murat Šabanović wouldn't stand for it. He grabbed one of the Chetnik flags and burned it in front of the hotel as bewildered policemen watched and several hundred onlookers whistled and guffawed. In September 1991, as the war in Croatia was gathering pace, groups of Serb irregulars began checking in at a Yugoslav army warehouse just below the hydroelectric dam in Višegrad. They were issued khaki uniforms and infantry weapons and drove off to join a drunken horde that was sacking the resort villages along Croatia's coastline south of Dubrovnik. One day, Avdija Šabanović set up a barricade and refused to let any more of these "volunteers" into the army's warehouse. After Avdija was taken away by the police, Murat and a group of his men secured his release by surrounding the police station and threatening to open fire.

The actual shooting started a few weeks later. Avdija and about fifty other Muslims set explosives in the highway tunnel near Dobrun and took up firing positions in the hills in order to prevent a column of Serb tanks and troop transporters from rolling through Višegrad on their way to Dubrovnik. The Serbs mortared the Muslims' positions. A gun battle erupted. The Serbian Democratic Party militia set up a barricade at a gas station in Dobrun after the column passed through. Avdija mustered a few men to force the Serbs from the road.

"If you don't get these guys out of there, we're going to attack them," he told Serb leaders. "Get them the fuck out of there."

Avdija called President Izetbegović in Sarajevo to see what he could do. But the president had enough problems dealing with Milošević without the Šabanović brothers shooting at Serbs next to the Serbian border. He told Avdija to go to the Višegrad police and have them deal with the barricade.

"Avdija," Izetbegović said, "these matters can be solved peacefully. Without arms. Without shooting. Without bloodshed. Just negotiate with them. Please, don't use force from your side. I will not agree to the use of force."

The Serbs refused to dismantle the barricade. Avdija decided on his own to attack. He went to the Serbs with an ultimatum: "If you don't have this road cleared by four o'clock, I'll break this barricade up by force."

That night the sound of gunshots echoed northward from terrace to terrace along Mount Zvijezda. Murat Šabanović and the Muslims fired down at the Serbs by the gas station in Dobrun. The battle lasted for a few hours before the Serbs pulled back.

❨   ❨   ❨

No one up in Kupusovići knew exactly what caused the battle until later. But all the men who had a pistol or a shotgun went out to the edge of the hamlet to stand guard. High school boys eager for excitement came down to smoke cigarettes and talk about guns. The men were afraid to light a fire and shivered in the cold all night. Nothing happened. They told tales and made up coded whistles. Paja had brought along Huso's pistol and a flashlight that he shone up onto the wall of the mountain. A day later, he heard a Serb on Višegrad's radio station announce that the Muslims had put guards around Kupusovići and that a mysterious signal light had appeared on the side of the mountain.

Paja's boyhood pal Senad Sućeska was with the men keeping watch over the Muslim houses in Odžak a few nights later when two Serbs happened along on foot. Senad raised his shotgun and ordered them to halt.

"Where're you boys going? You know no one is supposed to pass here this time of night."

Neither of the Serbs was armed. Senad knew them both; one of them worked with him filling propane tanks at the gas company down in Višegrad.

"Come on, man," he told Senad. "Quit screwing around."

"No one is supposed to be on this path after dark."

After a few minutes of more argument, Senad let the Serbs go on their way.

Paper notices appeared a day or so later, taped to tree trunks and fence posts all over Odžak, Kupusovići, and Žlijeb. A meeting would be held the next evening at the Odžak schoolhouse. It was high time to discuss the security situation.

A few dozen men, including Huso Čelik, showed up for the meeting. Their work boots thumped and scraped across the bare wooden floor of the main classroom, the first room to the left just inside the schoolhouse door. Some of the men leaned against the wall smoking cigarettes, others hovered around the woodstove Vitomir Janković had once tended. The men who crammed into the rickety school benches built for third-graders looked like giants.

One of the Serbs began the meeting. He said all the Serbs knew that the Muslims had armed themselves and that Behadil Kešmer did, in fact, have a cannon hidden somewhere. The Serb had been angry at Behadil ever since the day Behadil had gone down to his meadow and found the Serb's wife tending her sheep in it. Behadil had shooed them away and told her to stay out.

"Behadil has had that cannon stashed away since the war, *pička mu materina*," the Serb said.

Heads shook. There were incredulous groans. But the Serb was serious. And Behadil was still a little slow.

"Yes! I've got a cannon!" he sputtered. "Of course I've got a cannon!"

The Muslims smirked and sniggered like third-graders.

"And I've got a machine gun!" the Serb shot back in anger.

Now the Muslims grumbled and swore under their breath.

"Enough of this crap," one of the Serbs said. "Your guys were out on the road the other night and put a gun to two of our guys. This kind of shit has got to stop. And we can stop it if we guard the village together."

The Muslims bent their heads toward the floor and cast sidelong glances at each other. One of them finally spoke up.

"We'll have to think it over," he said.
And with that, the meeting ended.

❨   ❨   ❨

HAMED and I went to see his father at Vranica's brickyard in Sarajevo on the last Friday in February 1992, a month before the Bosnian war began. Huso was only fifty years old then; almost my height, almost six feet tall; balding worse than me, but not much grayer; he seemed depleted, though, and brooding, as if the cigarettes had sucked everything out of him except the angst. He led Hamed and me into an office whose interior resembled the construction-site trailers back in Cleveland, where I had delivered truck parts in a previous incarnation. The fraying carpet was full of dust; on the walls hung a cheesecake calendar or two, along with a black-and-white portrait of Tito in his prime. He quickly introduced us to the foreman, then ordered some coffees and glasses of juice. The workmen filled the room with cigarette smoke and chatter about a big referendum on Bosnia's independence that would take place over the weekend. Hamed and Huso were going to take the Friday afternoon bus together back to Višegrad. All the Muslims in Kupusovići would be there to line up inside the Odžak schoolhouse and cast their votes for independence. The government was holding the referendum to fulfill the last prerequisite the European Community countries had set for Bosnia's recognition as a sovereign state.

As we sipped our coffees and talked and joked in the brickyard office, the workmen tried to laugh off the portents of the approaching war and repeated the often repeated mantra about the unique "ethnic harmony" in Bosnia. "Look," one of the workers said, "this guy here is a Serb. We're friends. We always have been friends. Why would I want to fight against him?" The Serb workman smiled and nodded, and everyone else grinned.

I got up to leave a few minutes later, and Huso tried to persuade me to take the bus with him and Hamed up to Kupusovići. I had to stay in Sarajevo, I said, to report the news of the big referendum. He then insisted that Ljiljana and I had a standing invitation to visit.

IN mid-March 1992, Huso was walking along a sidewalk somewhere in Sarajevo when he collapsed with his second heart attack. Hamed took a bus from Belgrade to visit him in Koševo Hospital, and after a week, Huso went back to Kupusovići to recuperate at home. Talk of war was everywhere. Many of Višegrad's people and some of the folks from Mount Zvijezda were quietly departing the area. Sanela's boyfriend, Samir, had driven off to Germany. Drago the taxi driver left for Serbia. Hiba's father, Grandpa Avdija, went up to Austria to live with his son in Salzburg. Serb police officers had departed the Višegrad station and set up a police department of their own in a village near Dobrun. They were joined there by paramilitary units and "volunteers" from Serbia. But there still seemed to be no need for panic, and preparations had to be made for the spring planting.

Paja walked down the mountain to the main road and took an early bus to Višegrad on Wednesday, April 1. It was a sunny day. He had a chance to get in some time behind the wheel of a car before his driver's test that afternoon. One of his friends from Višegrad had to go to Žlijeb and had offered to let Paja drive his car up the mountain from town. Driving out of Višegrad, Paja spotted another one of his friends running along a street near the town's open-air market.

"What is it?" Paja said through the window.

"They're shooting up Dobrun again."

The driver's test would be at three-thirty that afternoon. Paja had no time for idle chatter about Dobrun. He maneuvered the automobile up the mountain, left his friend and the car in Žlijeb, then hiked down the mountain to catch the next bus back to town. The driving examiner had told Paja to wait for him by Višegrad's police station. Paja stood outside, smoking one cigarette after another and looking around. Murat Šabanović came by with some of his men. But the driving examiner never showed up. Paja wandered off and found him at the testing course near the town's soccer stadium.

"Can't do the test today, Paja. No more gas. We'll have to reschedule for sometime next week."

Paja turned over in his mind the names of his friends who had cars. There were not many, and none of them were around now. He would have to be patient for another week.

Paja walked to the gates of the gas company and waited until Senad's shift ended. Senad was dying for a cigarette when he got out of work, and they lit up together, walked to the center of town, and hung out in front of the post office.

Now Murat drove by in a large green automobile. Then he appeared again, this time on foot, striding along with half a dozen men carrying assault rifles. These were peasants mostly, lanky, sinewy, men with big, calloused hands and not much of a grasp on ideas. They had been transfigured, however, by the Islamic green bandanas they had tied around their heads and by their guns, as big and mean as Behadil's cannon. A sense of mission radiated from their eyes. They stomped by and headed off toward the police station.

Paja and Senad looked at each other. "That Murat," Paja said, "he's a legend."

Paja and Senad followed along to see what Murat and his men were up to. It was early evening. A crowd had assembled outside the police station, and in the middle of it a group of men huddled around Avdija Šabanović and a Serb whose name Paja did not know. Avdija denies it, but Paja said he heard him tell the Serb, "Look, we don't want this. Go to your people. Come to some agreement with them. And if there is something we can agree to, come back so we can sit together at a table and have a drink and something to eat. If not, remember this: There won't be a single Serbian ear left in Višegrad district."

If the Serb made any reply, Paja did not hear him. The man found his way out of the crowd, got into his automobile, and drove away. Paja and Senad walked to a taxi stand and caught a ride home.

Avdija Šabanović called in to report to the Bosnian police ministry what was going on in Višegrad. The Yugoslav army was amassing troops just across the border above Dobrun. A mobilization was under way in Bajina Bašta and other Serb towns on the other side of Mount Zvijezda. Višegrad's Serbs had been streaming out of the town for days, jamming their belongings into their compact cars and driving them up through Dobrun and into Serbia or across Mehmed Pasha's bridge and up into the Serb villages on the high plateau west of town. Avdija and Murat could muster about a hundred men in their home-spun militia. And there was Avdija bragging like Behadil about his cannon, making threats about Serb ears to a Serb leader who had an army with tanks and helicopters sitting just across the mountain.

8

HASIB KUPUS, Huso Čelik's cousin, had more ambition than most of the young men who made it down from Mount Zvijezda and set off into the wide world to find work. Hasib joined the Communist Party. He became a police officer. And he built himself a house in a town surrounded by rolling bot-tomland just inside Bosnia's northeastern border with Serbia. Bijeljina had changed radically since the winter of 1943, when Akja Čelik lived there in a Croat family's house with Huso, Latifa, and Salih. There were factories now, and asphalted streets, rows of private houses in various stages of completion, and a main highway—a four-lane, Interstate 90–style highway—just half an hour's drive away. Many of Bijeljina's townsmen had gone abroad to work, saved enough money to buy tractor-trailer rigs, and earned good livings by hauling goods all over Europe. Hasib had risen to become Bijeljina's police chief by the time he took early retirement. In 1992, he was devoting all of his attention to wood carving. Walnut gunstocks were his specialty; and he carved one for my brother-in-law, Milan. Hasib was a jovial, pudgy guy in retirement, and never had any problems with his Serb neighbors. He was about as pro-Yugoslav as they come. His teenage sons, Damir and Samir, were cadets at the Yugoslav army's military high school in Belgrade and visited Hamed on the weekends and dropped by to see Milan at my mother-in-law's apartment.

Bijeljina had put up with more than its share of the friction between Serb and Muslim troublemakers once the war in Croatia started. There were bar-room killings. The head of a Muslim party was assassinated. The Serbs in a precinct just up the main road toward the border had declared their independence from Bosnia in the fall of 1991, and by Christmas young Serb men there had begun illegally collecting tolls from all the cars passing through. There was a lot of money in the scam. The road was carrying more traffic than Bijeljina had ever seen. The fighting in Croatia had cut the big east–west highway, which had connected Zagreb and Belgrade, and the narrow, two-lane road through Bijeljina was the only exit route for the Serbs from most of the rebel-held districts in Croatia. Hasib had distanced himself from all of the turmoil and worked quietly at home on his gunstocks. He reckoned that there were only a few local hotheads and that they were not capable of causing serious trouble if left to their own devices. He would not have been in Bijeljina if he had known that the trouble would come from outside.

Hasib and his wife were at home when a gang of Serb gunmen led by a contract killer for Milošević's police ministry raced across the border from Serbia and attacked Bijeljina. The rattle of machine-gun fire sent the townspeople fleeing from the streets and into their houses. Burly gunmen in black balaclavas and jackboots stomped through Bijeljina's backyards and trashy alleyways. The gunmen made quick work of a small Muslim militia that had been organized by the Party for Democratic Action and a local Muslim named Hase Tirić. Once the Muslim militia had fled, the Serbs went from house to house, searching out and executing Muslims with education, influence, or money. Young Muslim men were dragged from their homes, shot in the head, and left to rot in the streets. Old women were killed inside their homes and left to rot there. A Serb government was then installed.

President Alija Izetbegović had little choice but to call on the Yugoslav army to intervene to stop the killing. The Bosnian government had no other means of restoring order. Even the American embassy in Belgrade was advising him to call on the army's commanders to uphold the Partisan tradition—

the tradition of defending all of the Yugoslavs, the tradition of Brotherhood and Unity. Instead of restoring order, the army units that ground into Bijeljina on April 3 secured the Serbs' theft of the town and allowed the gunmen to loot and kill Muslim civilians by night. Hasib and his wife, like almost everyone else in Bijeljina, stayed inside their house as the gunmen stalked the streets. But when the Yugoslav army arrived and announced that it had come to restore order, they peeked through their curtains and saw the neighbors beginning to reemerge from their homes. A day later, Hasib ventured down his street to the police station to arrange for the burial of a neighbor, a Muslim woman whose decomposing body had started to stink. Hasib never came back.

THE Serb gang that attacked Bijeljina was commanded by a pudgy-faced man who inhabits the darker realm of Serbia's police. His name is Željko Ražnatović; and at the time of his foray into Bijeljina, he was taking his orders from Franko Simatović, the man Milošević had appointed deputy commander for the special military units of the Serbian police ministry. As a child, Ražnatović was coddled by an overprotective mother and abused by his father, an alcoholic Yugoslav army colonel from Montenegro. Ražnatović began his criminal career in his early teens, snatching purses from women in central Belgrade's Tašmajdan park. By the mid-1970s, the Italian police were looking for him in connection with the murder of a restaurant owner. The Swedish police arrested Ražnatović for a bank robbery; but while he was on trial in Göteborg, members of his gang interspersed themselves among the courtroom spectators, produced concealed guns, and held security guards at bay long enough for him to make his escape. When Ražnatović got himself arrested in Yugoslavia, his father went to a friend, a Serb in the Yugoslav secret police, and asked him to get his son off the hook. He was in luck. Tito was dying. Croat and Albanian nationalists abroad were stirring. And Yugoslavia's secret police was stepping up the quiet campaign of political assassination it had been waging against them for years. The police needed men like Ražnatović, men who had been compromised by their criminal activities and were prepared to carry out any assignment to keep their freedom. Ražnatović was spared jail and sent to Western Europe with fake passports.

After Ražnatović had performed his services, the Yugoslav police ignored foreign warrants for his arrest. He settled down in Belgrade, opened a sweetshop, and built himself a house surrounded by an eight-foot wall and monitored by closed-circuit television cameras. He made the rounds of Belgrade's bars and casinos, cruising the town in a pink Cadillac, toting large-bore pistols, and boasting about how he had executed nationalist Albanian and Croat leaders, including one former executive of Croatia's oil company. In the late 1980s, the police gave Ražnatović control of the fan organization of Belgrade's Red Star soccer team, which had become a magnet for hoodlums and disgruntled, unemployed, and, very often, unemployable young men. From the worst of this raw material, Ražnatović formed a militia called the Tigers. Its members went on plundering and killing sprees during the war in Croatia, and Ražnatović eventually grabbed control of Croatia's oil fields and pocketed the profits. His attack on Bijeljina, which Serbian television described as a "rescue of innocent Serbs threatened with genocide," marked the beginning of the rape of eastern Bosnia.

(((

MY wife Ljiljana was off somewhere with our eight-month-old daughter, Sara, when I heard of the Bijeljina attack. I left a message on the kitchen table, met Jon Landay of the United Press at the airport, and boarded an airplane jammed with people going the wrong way. Sarajevo was quiet for a few days. The trams were running. Traffic was moving freely in the streets. Volleys of automatic-rifle fire were loosed into the sky every night, but this had been going on each night for months.

The face of Alija Izetbegović was more pallid than usual on Saturday afternoon, April 4, as he sat at a polished walnut table across from Landay and me during a brief interview in his office at the Bosnian presidency building. Izetbegović spoke in a calm and deliberate voice. He told us that the republic's presidency had just voted to order the mobilization of the national guard. An official announcement, which he was holding in his hand, would be made that evening on the television news. It was a precautionary measure, he explained, something that was not to be interpreted as a provocation. Besides, the national guard had hardly any weapons. The Yugoslav army had cleaned out most of the national guard's arsenals in the summer of 1990, before Izetbegović's party had even come to power. The interview turned to the question of outside military help. It was clear that recognition of Bosnia's independence, which was only two days away, meant war with the Serbs. Did any country offer to help Bosnia defend itself once it was recognized? Would the UN arms embargo be lifted? "We have had no assurances," he said. "But we know we have friends."

Izetbegović was leading Bosnia toward independence and war without knowing whether he had any allies who would help defend the republic once it had been recognized and without assurances that the UN Security Council would abide by the UN Charter and lift the arms embargo against the new member nation. The only real allies Izetbegović had were the party faithful, men like Avdija and Murat Šabanović, a few Muslim officers who had strayed away from the Yugoslav army, and a collection of Muslim criminal-gang leaders from Sarajevo—including Radovan Karadžić's former neighbor and would-be son-in-law, Juka Prazina—who knew how to use a gun and did not fear the Serb criminals Karadžić had recruited. Unlike Izetbegović, Karadžić knew his allies. He also knew what to do with the mobilization decision. He went on television and called the order a declaration of war against Bosnia's Serbs. He demanded that the Yugoslav army take action to defend them. And he knew he and Milošević had the pretext he needed to execute Bosnia's partition by force.

Overnight, Serb gunmen attacked a police academy on a key hilltop in Sarajevo, and the Serb leadership fled from the Holiday Inn to Pale, the ski resort in the mountains east of the city, where Karadžić and his partner, Krajišnik, had built themselves homes before their arrests for embezzlement. On Sunday afternoon, Serb snipers opened fire and killed unarmed peace demonstrators who had gathered in a plaza outside the parliament building. On Monday afternoon, the European Union countries recognized Bosnia as an independent country, Serb snipers perched in the Holiday Inn killed half a dozen peace demonstrators, and the shelling of the city began. On Tuesday, the United States granted Bosnia diplomatic recognition.

Ink-stained clouds gathered over Sarajevo late that afternoon. The air was heavy with chill. The *London Daily Telegraph*'s correspondent, Mike Montgomery, was holed up with Landay and me in an apartment on a hillside that overlooks most of Sarajevo's older neighborhoods. Mortar rounds began exploding outside, and for a better look we walked across the street to a cement stairway that led up to a cable car stop. A few men and boys were standing around up there, smoking cigarettes and keeping watch toward the east, toward a bald, rounded mountainside where the Serbs had set up their mortars. Montgomery chanced to spot a muzzle flash an instant before we heard the mortar discharge. A few seconds later, a round blew up in the city's center and lifted a plume of dust and smoke over some apartment buildings. We all saw the next bluish-white muzzle flash. Again, a round exploded in the city, and another exploded in an orange fireball in the yard of the old Austrian military fortress above the city's eastern edge. The men and boys gathered near the cable car stop began drifting back to their apartments when we heard the snap of sniper fire. The streets below were deserted now except for a few speeding cars. Back inside the apartment, we watched as Sarajevo television broadcast interviews with people from neighborhoods where the rounds had exploded. They were small bombs at first and did not cause much damage, as if Karadžić and the other Serb leaders were gambling that a few good bangs and a handful of civilian dead would so intimidate Izetbegović that he would accede to the country's partition. Montgomery ventured back outside on his own just before nightfall. He heard a bang below the cable car stop and spotted a lone man walking calmly along a sidewalk. He was lighting firecrackers.

THOUGH Sarajevo grabbed the headlines, it was clear from the first day of the war that eastern Bosnia, with its hydroelectric dams, highways, and Muslim-majority population, was the key to the Serb leaders' plans to partition Bosnia. Bijeljina was their prime objective because it controlled the east–west road across northern Bosnia linking Serbia with Serb-held areas of Croatia and western Bosnia.

The town of Zvornik was the second objective. It was home to 82,000 people, 60 percent of them Muslims, and controlled a hydroelectric dam, a huge alumina plant, rail and road bridges over the Drina to Serbia, as well as a main road between Sarajevo and Belgrade. The Serbs quit Zvornik's district government on April 6. Muslim leaders called for negotiations, appealed to the Yugoslav army for help, and threatened to blow up the hydroelectric dam and a protective wall around a chemical slime pit if the Serbs attacked. Two days later, Ražnatović marshaled his men on the Serbian side of the Drina. They were joined this time by the Yugoslav army and by Milošević's palace guard: the special commando units of Serbia's Ministry of Internal Affairs under Stamatović's command. An ultimatum was passed to the Muslims in Zvornik to give up their guns and surrender by the afternoon. The town's Muslim leaders let the deadline pass without a response, and Yugoslav army artillery opened fire on Zvornik from Serbia that evening. Milošević's police commando units and Ražnatović's men stormed into Zvornik the next day. They dispersed its token Muslim resistance and sent thousands of civilians fleeing into the mountains south of town. The bloodbath that followed went on for days. Ražnatović's gang and Milošević's commandos went on a house-by-house and apartment-by-apartment search, stealing money and jewelry and killing any Muslims they found. Stairwells in the dingy high-rises along the Drina were slippery with blood. The dead were stacked in the backs of trucks and dumped into the river. José Maria Mendiluce, the head of the UN High Commissioner for Refugees in Yugoslavia, happened to be passing through Zvornik that day and witnessed Serb gunmen putting children under the treads of tanks and running them over. Several thousand Muslims were killed in the assault on Zvornik; about 42,000 were driven from their homes. In Belgrade, President Milošević insisted to the world that he had no control over the Bosnian Serbs. But the operation to take Zvornik was planned in Belgrade by his police and executed by his police, Ražnatović's gang, and the Yugoslav army.

Their next stop would be another town with a bridge and a hydroelectric dam just up river: Višegrad.

9

PANOS is an unremarkable hump of rock capped by woods of pine and hardwood. It rises beside the southern edge of Mount Zvijezda, and from its top you can see most of Višegrad about three miles away. Serb mortars on Panos had fired the first rounds into Višegrad during World War I; Chetnik mortars on Panos began Draža Mihailović's attack on the town in October 1943; and on April 6, 1992, Serb mortars on Panos opened up again. The blasts blew out windows, and the shrapnel wounded a few townspeople. A couple of houses were set ablaze; the fire department managed to save one of them. The Šabanović brothers were warned that a column of Yugoslav army tanks and trucks pulling artillery pieces was grinding toward Višegrad from Serbia. Across the river, smoke rose from torched Muslim villages. Refugees streamed into town across Mehmed Pasha's bridge. But when they heard the army was coming at them from Serbia, they fled back over the bridge and headed up-river toward the next big town, Goražde.

The Šabanović brothers got together about a hundred Muslim men with automatic rifles and hunting weapons to fight off the army column approaching Višegrad. Avdija rigged up explosives in a tunnel below Dobrun to delay the advance, but the blast was too weak to knock down much of the roof. The Serb army commanders brought up bulldozers and cleared the debris in the tunnel overnight. Gunfights near Dobrun stalled the Serbs' advance, but the mortars on Panos continued to loft rounds into Višegrad. The Muslim resistance held out for three days before Avdija Sabanović decided to withdraw with Murat and sixty of their men to the new hydroelectric dam.

Trucks backed up to the dam's entrance all through the night. Men unloaded wooden boxes and carried them inside. Murat called Avdo Hebib, a deputy to the minister for internal security in Sarajevo, and Hebib put the word out that Murat was holding a dozen Serb hostages and had packed the heart of the dam with dynamite. Murat then got Sarajevo television on the phone and warned that if the army advanced any farther, he would blow the dam sky-high and create a forty-foot wave of water that would wash away the dams downriver at Bajina Bašta and Zvornik and unleash a torrent that would rupture the levees farther downstream.

Hebib was dressed in military fatigues and lounging in an armchair in his office the next morning, when Montgomery, Landay, and I went to the police ministry looking for a briefing on the fighting going on around the country. The building seemed oddly empty for a vital government ministry in a country on the brink of war, but it was only about nine o'clock in the morning and still in the early days of the war. Hebib told us about some shelling around Sarajevo and gunfire in half a dozen towns. He grinned when I brought up the situation at the Višegrad dam. Murat sounded like a lunatic on the television news the night before, I said, and I asked Hebib if he could get Murat on the phone. He quickly agreed, and held the receiver away from his ear when Murat came on the line and started ranting and raving.

Hebib said, "He's all yours," or something like it.

"Murat," I said, "tell me what's going on."

Murat swore at the Yugoslav army. He said he would flood half of Serbia if the army set foot in Višegrad. The curses were succulent and made me laugh, and I held my hand over the receiver so Murat wouldn't hear me. Even Hebib was chuckling as he took the phone and tried to get Murat to calm down. I decided I would write a story about it only if Murat blew up the dam, and I half wanted him to do it just to see what would happen.

Višegrad's streets were practically deserted that day. Thousands of the town's Muslims had fled in cars and buses to Goražde, while the remaining Serbs had high-tailed it to Serb villages across the Drina. The army stood in its tracks on the outskirts of town. Šabanović had the Serb hostages—including a Serb police officer, Sredoje Lukić, a distant cousin of Sead Čelik's old schoolmate Milan Lukić, and one of the Milicević boys from up above Odžak—confined to a room about three stories below the level of the water.

In the evening, the kitchen windows of the Čelik house and all the other houses on Mount Zvijezda flickered with the blue-gray light from the television sets. All across Bosnia people waited to see what would happen at the dam. They followed the reports of outbreaks of fighting all over the country. They watched live broadcasts with talk show hosts sitting between Izetbegović and Karadžić and shaming them into promising each other to call a cease-fire. Each evening, it seemed, the war was about to go away and Murat and his dam were about to become a bad joke. With each nightfall, however, new gunfire and explosions began, and each side blamed the other for starting it.

All the way in Kupusovići, the villagers could hear occasional detonations down near Višegrad. They could see the yellow flicker of houses burning across the valley. Each time the television reported on the situation at the dam, a fuzzy-focused tourist-brochure picture of Mehmed Pasha's bridge would pop up on the screen with a little white computer-style icon of a telephone with the receiver lifted. Through the speaker came the screaming voice of Murat Šabanović. On the third night, Murat spoke live with the commander of the Yugoslav army's garrison in Sarajevo, General Milutin Kukanjac.

"Murat, no one has to fire at that dam. And no one is firing at it," Kukanjac said.

Murat cut him off: "And no one should be firing on the town! They are firing on the town!"

"Murat, please. Please give it up. Many innocent people will suffer."

"Only the Muslims are suffering! And your Serbs are butchering them!"

"Everyone is suffering, unfortunately. Everyone is suffering and dying. Let's do what we can to keep as many as we can from suffering."

"I'm going to blow it!" Murat screamed. "And I'll become a war criminal. But you will be a bigger war criminal! Because you could have stopped this all three days ago!"

"I'm doing what I can to head off the conflicts. I'll see what I can do. . . . I'll check out what you're saying."

"There's nothing to check out. Thousands of people are watching it. That's the fact!"

"I'll do it immediately. But don't you let that dam go."

"I won't let it go so long as there is no more shelling. But if one soldier comes close, it's going up. There won't be any more of Alija's republic. It will be Murat's holy war, a fight to the last."

"Murat. Don't. Don't do it."

"Yes! Yes!"

"Don't do it. Don't do it. Don't do it, for the sake of the Muslims!"

"What's the difference? The Chetniks butcher us. The Drina washes us away. It's all the same."

"Okay. I'll look into it."

"You should be telling Arkan to stop butchering people and not be talking to Murat about blowing up some dam."

"I'll tell my people not to shoot."

"Fuck your mother!" Murat shouted.

Milošević's television was having a field day with Murat and his threats. Half of the grandmothers in Belgrade were sure they would be washed down the Danube once he blew up the dam. Downriver, the peasants living on the bottomland near Bajina Bašta and Bratunac packed up their valuables and headed for higher ground. The Yugoslav army stood by for days and let the television bring the hysteria to a boil. Now Serbs in Serbia were convinced there would be genocide against the Serbs in Bosnia. Up in Kupusovići, Paja was as wide-eyed with anticipation as I was down in Sarajevo. "If he lets that dam go, there will be chaos in Serbia," Paja thought. "Just imagine it. Just imagine the houses that will be washed away!"

On the night of April 12, Serbian army commandos rapelled from hovering helicopters and took up positions above the dam on the eastern side of the Drina canyon. One of the dam's technicians, following Avdija's orders, cranked open the floodgates as far as they would go. In less than an hour, rushing water carried off a small bridge below the dam. A dozen Muslim houses were flooded. Scaffolding that had been rigged up for restoration work on Mehmed Pasha's bridge was twisted around its stone buttresses and washed downstream.

Murat was sure there would be no way to close the floodgates once they were opened all the way. The force of the water would crack the next dam, at Bajina Bašta, he reckoned, and might even take out the dam above Zvornik. He told the Serbs that he and the sixty Muslim men inside were going to pull back from the dam and that if the Serbs fired off one round at them, they would kill all the Serb hostages. The Muslims moved out. They made their way upriver toward Goražde along the highway on the western bank of the Drina. From a bluff about a mile south of the dam, Murat looked back and saw the floodgates closing. He swore again. One of the Muslim technicians had stayed behind and stopped the flow of water. The great flood had been averted. There had never been any explosives in the dam, and the Serb army had known it all along. Avdija Šabanović released the hostages a few days later. He forced them to cut off their hair before he let them go.

ℂ ℂ ℂ

THE Yugoslav army entered the outskirts of Višegrad on Monday, April 13, along with Serbian police units, members of Ražnatović's gang, and several other paramilitary bands. They met no resistance. A day later, the Serb troops took over the town and its factories, the government buildings, and the hydroelectric dam; and all Muslim officials were dismissed from their posts in the local government and enterprises. Branimir Savović, the local strongman in the Serbian Democratic Party, was appointed district president. A general mobilization was decreed for all able-bodied Serb men, and Muslim workers were ordered to report to their jobs.

Paja and Senad were drinking with a neighbor in Kupusovići that Monday night. After downing two or three brandies, the men strayed outside. They heard voices in the woods about thirty yards away and crouched down behind a shack.

Shooting started. Phosphorescent tracer bullets burned giant pink crosses in the sky. The gunfire came from Odžak, from a bluff above Branko's house, from a thicket near the school, and from the rounded peaks along the crest of Mount Zvijezda. Bullets flew over Kupusovići, Žlijeb, and all the other nearby Muslim hamlets. Then the night sky went dark and silent. Perched high on Mount Zvijezda's peaks, unseen from below, were Yugoslav army units made up of Serbs mobilized from Bajina Bašta and nearby Serbian villages. They had been up there for days watching the border, guarding the Bajina Bašta dam, looking down with binoculars at Muslim peasants preparing their fields for the spring planting.

Paja and Senad went down to a meadow below the Čelik house. It was too dangerous to stay in Kupusovići or Odžak, they decided. So they moved their families, first to Žlijeb, then down into the empty meadow known as the Customs Area, and finally to Preseka, the next Muslim village down the mountain. The men stood guard all night. They filled empty glass brandy bottles with gasoline, plugged them shut with cloth wicks, and discussed whether or not to start burning the Serb houses.

AFTER daybreak, Paja hiked up to Odžak, to Branko Mitrašinović's house.

"Branko."

"Paja."

"Did you happen to see who was shooting up the place last night?"

"Don't know who it was, Paja. They scared the hell out of me, too." Branko said the Serbs had hidden in the woods the night before and were frightened. "We might all have to leave here," he added.

"I found a bunch of spent hunting cartridges on that bluff over there, Branko."

Paja pointed to a patch of meadow just below Branko's still and showed him a handful of spent shotgun shells and brass cartridges from a semiautomatic.

Branko shrugged.

"Don't know anything more, Paja."

"See you later, Branko."

Paja shuffled down to Dragoljub Radovanović's house, across from the school. Dragoljub was away getting treated for his glaucoma. But his brother Arsen was there. He looked haggard. "I've got no idea what this is all about," Arsen said.

Paja walked down to Kupusovići. He fed the oxen, cows, and chickens before fixing himself something to eat and heading back to Preseka to join Huso and the women. The Yugoslav army had set up camp in Prelovo, and local

Serb militias had erected roadblocks all along the main road to Višegrad. On the night of April 16, Paja and the other Muslims in Preseka decided to flee. They would cross over to Žepa the next morning.

Paja hiked home with Senad, Zlatija, and Sanela before dawn. They packed food and clothing, soap and laundry detergent, mattresses and bedding, pots and pans, and all the cigarettes they had. Paja fastened the oxen to his cart and started down the mountain. He did not think they would be gone long.

"Just enough for things to settle down," he thought. They brought along the electric coffee grinder, but left behind their winter clothing and the family photo album.

Snow and rain were falling together when they moved out of Preseka, two hundred people in a column about a quarter mile long. They spread out over the rocky road, the road the bulldozer had carved, the road that had replaced the trail Ajka Čelik had followed when she fled from home with Huso in her arms so many years before. The women walked behind as the men led the horses and oxen pulling the wagons laden with their belongings. Some families rode in carts pulled by two-wheeled tractors powered by lawn mower engines. Huso huddled inside Sead's army jacket. Paja had stretched a nylon tarp over his wagon to keep out the rain. But it was about a ten-mile walk down the mountain and north to the ferry crossing at Slap, and everything got soaked and splattered with mud. A cold drizzle was still falling when they reached the riverside and began hours of waiting for their turn on the ferry. Mirza whined. He walked around with no socks because he had pissed all over himself and Zlatija did not have a dry pair for him.

When the Čeliks' turn came, Paja led the oxen down the bank and paid his money to the ferrymen. The water and the rocking of the boat spooked the animals. He pulled Šaronja aboard one boat with the wagon. The ox bellowed. Then he tied Balja to the back of the boat, and the animal went into the river when the boat lurched toward forward.

From the fishing camp at the opposite bank, it took another few hours to get to Žepa. The oxen trudged on, and the wagon moved more and more slowly. Darkness had already fallen when they arrived in a hamlet known as Stop. They came across a man who said he had an empty house. His wife brought them coffee and took them over to look at the place. It was an old peasant house, but it was dry inside and not nearly so rickety as Saliha's old place had been. There was a woodstove, electric lights, and a washing machine that worked. A dozen people spread out over the floor.

Sunshine broke through the next day. The women packed loads of muddy laundry into the washing machine and hung the rain-soaked clothes out to dry. There was a bus stop about fifty yards from the house, and Paja and Huso watched as a dirty white bus bound for Sarajevo pulled away. One of the guys from Kupusovići had squeezed aboard.

"We should've gone, too," Huso said.

"There'll be more buses," Paja answered. "And we'll be going home in a few days anyway."

(((

I T was the officers of the Yugoslav army units occupying Višegrad and the Muslim members of the town council in Goražde who convinced the Muslim refugees from Višegrad that it was safe to go home. Višegrad radio broadcast the army's appeals. The refugees' security would be guaranteed, the reports said; they could return to their houses, their fields, and their jobs, collect their pensions, and resume normal lives. The Goražde council did not want to house and feed the twelve thousand refugees who had fled there from Višegrad. The seizure of the dam had ended. There was no fighting going on. The return proceeded in an organized fashion. The refugees who had cars drove home, and the ones who had walked to Goražde were returned in buses.

The refugees from Mount Zvijezda who had fled to Žepa heard there were Muslims going back to Višegrad. Some of the refugees in Žepa had gone back across the Drina to gather food, clothes, and other essentials from home and decided to stay.

"I'm going back, too," Paja told Huso two weeks after the Čeliks arrived in Žepa.

"You're out of your mind."

"I can't stand living like this. Everybody's going back."

"It's simply not safe back there."

Paja walked to Kupusovići the next day and stayed at home for two days. He talked a lot with the Serb neighbors. Branko told him he could come over and use his still whenever he was ready. Paja packed some jam and eggs and a tape player for music into his rucksack and carried it back to Žepa. Zlatija joined Paja on his second return trip to Kupusovići. They had to plant their fields. If they did not sow them soon, there would be nothing to eat after the summer. When they got home, they found the front door broken. Nothing had been taken from inside, but someone had stuck a knife into the family snapshots hanging on a wall in the kitchen, and the lock to the trunk had been shot off. A spent bullet cartridge lay on the kitchen floor. A gang of local Serbs under the command of Milan Lukić was searching the Muslim villages on the mountain for weapons. The Serbs in the Višegrad police had provided them a roster of all Muslims who had registered guns. They had come to the

Čelik house looking for Huso's pistol. Paja was carrying it in his waistband.

"We should all go home," Paja told Huso after he and Zlatija got back to Žepa. "Everyone's living normally up there. They're planting their fields. They're making brandy. Nothing is happening to anyone. And nothing is going to happen."

"I won't go. And I won't let Sanela go," Huso answered. "And you shouldn't go either."

Paja made his third return on May 8. This time he harnessed his oxen to the wagon and led them back across the river. Hiba, Zlatija, and Mirza went with him. Sanela and Huso stayed behind.

PAJA was all set to use Branko's still. He had barrels of plum mash that had been curing all winter long, waiting for the spring distilling. He loaded the mash onto his wagon, hitched up the oxen, and hauled the barrels up to Branko's house. It took three days for Paja to distill all the mash. Mile Janković came by on the first day and acted very friendly. It was as if he could smell the brandy distilling. Mile had been tall and well-built before the alcohol had gotten to him. Lukić's gang had assigned him to make the rounds through Odžak, Kupusovići, and Žlijeb to check up on the Muslims.

"Paja. Where've you been?" Mile asked innocently enough.

"Žepa."

"That so?"

"Yep."

"You shouldn't go away. They're going to burn the houses of anyone who leaves. Don't leave your home, and put a white flag up on the minaret. That way they'll know you aren't rebels against the government."

Mile looked good. Relaxed. But he needed a drink.

"Who was doing the shooting, Mile?" Paja asked.

"Don't know, Paja. Don't know. Where's your father anyway?"

"Caught the bus to Sarajevo from Žepa."

"Where's his pistol?"

"Huso took it with him. It's his pistol. He has it in Sarajevo now."

"That so?"

"Yep."

Mile seemed to believe it.

"Listen, Paja. If something happens, you guys can come to my house. My wife'll hide you somewhere. If the Muslim army comes, you can get Zlatija to give my wife a pair of *dimije*, and if the Serbs come I'll tell her to get Zlatija and Hiba skirts."

Mile slipped dried branches onto the fire beneath the kettle of bubbling plum mash. Branko's wife, Petra, made them all Turkish coffee. Mile sat and drank for a few hours. Then he stumbled home and came back a little while later when the urge to drink hit him again.

On the second day, Mile Janković came by in his army uniform. "May God fuck them all," he exclaimed, plopping himself down on a log beside the fire. "Someone shot at my uncle down by the mill. They want to make trouble for us."

"Mile, don't talk shit," Paja snapped. "It might not have been a Muslim at all. It might be some Serb who wants to create an excuse to get rid of all the Muslims around here."

"Wait, man. I never said it was a Muslim who did the shooting. I just said it was someone who shot at him. You know, Paja, my people were angry at me. When you were gone, the army came looking for you at my house because someone told them I was hiding you."

❨ ❨ ❨

OVER in Žepa, Sanela was getting on her father's nerves. She had wanted to return to Kupusovići with the rest of the family.

"We can get there in a few hours," she told Huso one night.

Huso said he was afraid for her.

Sanela scoffed.

"You think you know so much," Huso snapped. "You don't know so much. You don't know anything."

Huso continued. He said someone had passed him a message from Arsen Radovanović, Dragoljub's brother. "He said I should come back. He said he would take us over the mountain to Serbia. He said nothing would happen to us on the way and we would be safe over the border. We could go to Hamed's."

Huso paused. He may have remembered the word's *kad tad . . . kad tad.*

"You know why we can never do that? Because of that fight," he said, recalling the brawl in the Odžak school thirty-five years earlier and how he had lied at the court hearing and how Dragoljub's and Arsen's mother had warned of revenge, sooner or later. "We can't go, because memories have a long lifetime, and the evil memories have the longest lifetime of all."

❨ ❨ ❨

AT five in the morning on May 12, two mosques in Višegrad were set afire. When the blazes died down, the Serb militias blew up the minarets and the walls. Three days later, they trucked the stone away to a dump. An attack on Goražde did not go as expected. Members of the Yugoslav army returned to

Prelovo carrying the bodies of four dead comrades, and they burned twenty Muslim houses in retaliation. Seventy-year-old Fehrat Pirić was reportedly the first Muslim executed in the Višegrad district; witnesses said a Serb led him away from his burning house, put a gun into his mouth, blew out the back of his head, and left him there for his womenfolk to wash and bury.

Paja and Zlatija were asleep in the sitting room in Kupusovići that night. Hiba was with Mirza in the bedroom. She could not sleep. She sat by the window gazing down on the broad, dark expanse of the Drina valley. A light flickered over in Žlijeb. It was small at first, and Hiba thought it was the headlight of a parked car. Then she heard crying and shouting and livestock bellowing. A house was on fire.

She shuffled into the next room.

"Paja. Paja. Get up. Look outside. The village is burning."

Paja rolled back to sleep.

"Get up, man. There's a house on fire."

Paja got dressed and walked down the road to Žlijeb to see what had happened. A stall and a pair of houses were afire. One of them was Behadil's place, but he had escaped.

A man from the Hodžić family whom everyone called "Godfather" was over in Žlijeb that night helping a cow that was calving. The Serbs set the stall on fire and shot Godfather Hodžić when he tried to run into the stall to save the animals.

Paja went home. "Get out of the house," he told everyone. "You don't want to be in the house." Hiba, Zlatija, and Mirza spent the rest of the night at a house in Žlijeb, and Paja and other Muslim men stood guard all night by an outcropping of boulders. He went to see Mile Janković the next morning and told him about how Godfather Hodžić had been shot.

"I'm very sorry for Godfather," Mile said. "I was sleeping, and didn't go anywhere."

They sipped some brandy.

"You know, Mile," Paja said, "somebody called out, 'Godfather, Godfather,' just before he got shot. So the guy who shot him must have known him."

"I didn't go anywhere," Mile answered.

Paja turned away.

"Where are you going?" Mile called.

"Got to see what the women want to do."

Paja was light-headed from the brandy. He had not slept the night before. The women decided it was best not to stay in their house. There was shooting down the mountain all that day, and after nightfall they could see more houses going up in flames around the valley.

Hiba went to Odžak to see her friends and find out if anyone up there knew what was happening.

"We don't know what is going on," said Dragoljub. "Mercenaries must be doing this."

Dragoljub's wife, Zora, brought Hiba a glass of juice.

"Listen, Hiba. I don't know what this means. I can't sleep."

"We're afraid," Hiba told her.

"Whatever you do, don't listen to anything Mile Janković tells you," one of the other Serb women said. "He's no good. He isn't good even to his own child. And he will not be good to you. Don't believe anything he says. Don't send anyone to him asking for help. He's always drunk now . . ."

Hiba was sobbing.

". . . They're all drunk," the woman continued. "Your daughter-in-law is young, and they'll break Paja's bones. Hide. Whatever you do, don't roam around alone. And don't let your daughter-in-law or Paja roam around alone. Hide yourselves during the day, whatever you do."

"Come on," Dragoljub broke in. "Get out while you still can. I'll get you over to Serbia. All of you, one or two at a time. I'll get you to Hamed. I can't take you over all in one group. But one or two at a time we can make it. Huso can come back over. He can come as if he were my brother. I'll take care of it."

Hiba went home from Odžak. A cold rain was falling. She told Paja what Dragoljub had offered.

"It's some kind of ploy," he said.

BRANKO MITRAŠINOVIĆ'S wife, Petra, was Hiba Čelik's best friend. At dusk, Hiba went up to ask Petra what she thought. Petra was tending a cow in a meadow below her house. When Petra looked up and saw Hiba, she started to cry. They talked until it got dark.

"Look what has become of us," Hiba said.

"I don't know why this is happening or what kind of life awaits us living here alone. Where will you go?"

"Back over to Žepa."

"They should kill the ones who have stirred up this mess, the ones who send the young people to die for this."

"Can you store some dresses and bedding for me?" Hiba asked.

"I can't do anything until Branko comes with the sheep. Bring the things by, regardless . . . but only after it gets dark. I don't want anyone to see us together with anything."

Hiba took three quilts up to Petra's house later that evening, and the two women kissed each other good-bye.

"Hide everything, Hiba," Petra said. "Everything. I'll keep these for you as long as I live."

Paja loaded the wagon for the third time the next morning. Sacks of wheat flour went onto the bottom, and clothing and mattresses were stacked atop them. As he worked, Paja felt eyes following his every move. He hid his chain saws in a patch of deep grass by some rocks next to the house, but he felt that the eyes were noting every hiding place. So he decided to take the chain saw up to Branko's. Paja knew he would be back once the trouble passed. He was worried only that someone might steal his tools in the meantime. He figured no one would want the chickens, and he left the family photo album behind.

They set out at about eleven in the morning, May 20, 1992. The air was warm, the sky crystal blue. Huso's cousin Adem Kozić stayed behind. Adem lived in the poorest house in Kupusovići and always walked around wearing the same faded yellow shirt he had worn while working as a porter in a Sarajevo engine factory. "If the rest of them aren't going, I'm not going either," Adem told Paja. "I'll go when the rest go."

Three families joined the Čeliks on the way back to Žepa. They walked through Odžak and turned downhill toward the Drina. Quietly the men talked among themselves about where they might go. The road to Sarajevo was now cut off, and there would be no more buses from Žepa. The next nearest city was Tuzla. Maybe they could get to Tuzla.

Milojica Pepić, the adult son of an old Serb peasant named Petar, came out of his house and saw Paja and the rest of the Muslims heading toward the river.

"What're you doing? What're you leaving for, Paja?" Milojica said. "We're not going to do anything to you. Don't go."

"Everyone is going," Paja answered. "And we're going too."

"Whatever. But you can't take the path straight ahead. There's a guard up there. Go down the mountain and around through Blace."

This was not honest advice, and Paja sensed it. There had been trouble with the Serbs in Blace already. Petar had come out of the house in time to hear what his son had said.

"What the fuck are you butting in here for," Petar snarled at Milojica. "Get the fuck out of here."

Milojica slinked back to the house.

One of the Muslims asked Petar to lead them to the main road.

"If my army sees me, they'll kill me for sure," Petar said, but he agreed to do it anyway.

"Don't wait by the river," he warned. "The villages down there will be burned in two days. Don't stay in Žepa, either. There will be an attack on Žepa. Don't even go to Srebrenica."

"Where then?"

"Go to Tuzla," he said. "Tuzla will be yours."

10

In the forty-seven years after the end of World War II, Žepa's Muslims never tired of boasting that their isolated gorge had never fallen to the Germans, the Chetniks, or the Partisans. And Žepa's Muslims were not prepared to stand by idly and wait for Serbs loyal to Slobodan Milošević and Radovan Karadžić or anybody else to do to Žepa what they were doing to the rest of Bosnia.

By late May, the Serb nationalists had seized almost half of the country, and it seemed the Bosnian government would have to accept the reality of the country's partition within a matter of weeks. Sarajevo was practically cut off from the world. Brčko and other towns in the Sava River valley had fallen. The Serbs had leveled villages and set up concentration camps in western Bosnia. Trainloads of Muslims were being hauled into Serbia in boxcars, transported courtesy of the Serbia's state railroad company — another Milošević-controlled entity — and dumped out on the Hungarian border next to the barracks where Paja Čelik had once done his stint in the military. The city of Mostar was being pummeled by Momčilo Perišić, a Serb general who would soon be named chief of staff of the Yugoslav Army, Milošević's Army. The Serbian president was still claiming that he had no control over Karadžić and the other Bosnian Serbs, but his secret police, police commandos, and Yugoslav army paratroopers were showing up wherever there was trouble.

An eerie calm had descended over Žepa by the time Paja, Hiba, Zlatija, and Mirza had made their way back across the Drina. Huso quickly reminded them that they should have listened to him in the first place. Paja went to work chopping wood and took Šaronja and Balja out to plow fields for local peasants in exchange for flour, sugar, and other staples. About five thousand Muslims were crowded into the villages in the Žepa gorge by then, 70 percent of them refugees. It did not take long for jealousy to infect the place. The local women would whine when refugees came begging for food or a place to stay. "Oy, oy," they would say. "And what did you leave your village for? And why didn't you protect it?"

The Serbs did not cut the electricity or the phone line to Žepa until late May, and Huso managed one time to call Hamed in Belgrade from Žepa's post office. It was the first Hamed had heard from Huso since the war began. Huso told him where they were living, gave him the phone number of the post office, and said their food supply was dwindling. My wife Ljiljana phoned me in Sarajevo with the news and told me to try and reach Huso. I tried dialing the Žepa post office, but the line was busy all night. I went the next day to the Sarajevo office of the UN High Commissioner for Refugees and told the man in charge, Fabrizio Hochschield, that I had heard there were thousands of Muslim refugees in a village called Žepa. Neither of us had ever heard of the place. It took us fifteen minutes to find it on a map, which didn't show any paved road leading there.

Serb gunmen were hijacking UN convoys all over Bosnia during those early weeks of the war, dragging aid workers and drivers out of their trucks, sticking pistols to their heads, barking out that they were hostages, and threatening to kill them unless they gave up the food. It was clear from the map that Žepa lay far beyond the range of the UN aid trucks. The best thing to do seemed to be the thing everyone was doing: sitting tight, waiting for the storm to pass, assuming the worst had already passed, assuming all would go back to their homes and get on with life.

Then the phone and electricity lines in Žepa went dead.

ŽEPA'S leaders organized a crisis committee to deal with the emergency. Some meager emergency food supplies were distributed. A defense force was mustered. One afternoon, the Muslim men from Mount Zvijezda were ordered to form up in front of Žepa's mosque. They were instructed to return across the Drina and defend the village just above the ferry landing, which was coming under attack. The men were afraid; they mumbled and groaned and smiled nervously. One old-timer blurted out that he should be kept out of combat because his wife had once given birth to twins and he would be ideally suited for restoring the population. In the end, the village and the ferry landing were lost, but the Muslims who had fought for them drew Serb blood. Among the Serb dead was a jolly old peasant from Rujišta, one of the Lukić men, a guy everyone called Fat Milan, who was shot down while tending a cow in a field.

Crews of Muslims were press-ganged into digging trenches on mountainsides just west of Žepa, a few miles from an underground military base where the Bosnian Serbs' top general, Ratko Mladić, was setting up his military headquarters. The villagers there had come under attack once already. Guards were placed around the periphery of the gorge, and Muslim men with guns surrounded two dozen Serb soldiers and their captain in a communications bunker atop Zlovrh. If Mladić's troops succeeded in getting artillery to the summit of Zlovrh, it would hamstring all Muslim resistance in the area.

The first major Serb foray toward Žepa came on June 4, 1992. Ostensibly, it was to free the surrounded communications bunker. Serb commanders said someone on the Muslim side had given them assurances that they could pass. An alarm spread from one Muslim hamlet to the next early that morning. A column of trucks led by a tank and armored transporters was rolling eastward toward Žepa from the direction of the Mladić's headquarters. Inside the trucks were several hundred Serb soldiers, men and women. Muslim men grabbed their hunting rifles and automatics and ran through a forest toward a windy dirt road that leads to the top of Zlovrh. They dug in on the sides of a ravine through which the column would have to pass. The Serbs knew when they had entered Muslim-controlled territory. A loudspeaker mounted on one of the Serb vehicles issued warnings.

"Don't shoot at us. . . . We will not harm you."

Žepa was just over a hill. The lead Serb tank thundered and squeaked along the narrow dirt road hugging the side of the ravine. It was pulling into a curve when one of the Muslims cut down a thick pine tree with a chain saw. The tree fell across the road. The tank got hung up on the tree trunk and slid into a ditch. The rest of the column closed in behind it.

"This is a warning," the loudspeaker blared. "Don't shoot at us. . . . If anyone shoots at us, we will destroy the entire village."

The tank's turret could no longer rotate enough to fire its cannon at the hill where the Muslims were lying in wait. The diesel engines rumbled and belched exhaust smoke. The truck drivers in the column waited for the commander to give the order to back up. Then another tree fell behind the convoy.

The Muslims opened fire. Some Muslims say one of their men jumped from the woods onto the back of the lead tank, lit the wick on a Molotov cocktail, and threw it into an open hatch atop the turret; others say the men in the tank crew were shot down after they crawled outside and tried to escape. Either way, the crew members were screaming and burning as they struggled to climb out. At the same time, just above the column, the fuse was lit on explosives packed with nails and screws inside an old tire. The tire was sent rolling down to the road, where it blew up next to a truck loaded with soldiers and ammunition.

Soldiers scrambled out of the trucks and ran in every direction as the men on the hillside picked them off at close range. Muslim men threw hand bombs made from dynamite and screws packed inside tin cans. The column commander was pinned down under a truck. He pulled out a hand grenade, tossed it into the load of ammunition above him, and blew himself up with it.

Within the first hour, the Serbs seemed to regain their composure and began firing back, and the Muslim commanders fled to Žepa. The local villagers, however, kept firing, gunning down dozens of Serbs, including two women, nurses who came out of an ambulance with their hands over their heads. About five dozen Serbs were taken prisoner and held in a school. More than twice that many lay dead and dying in the forest and on the road next to the burning vehicles.

The gunfire became sporadic. Women and children from the nearest village combed the woods and the roadside, taking guns from the trucks and the Serb dead while there was still daylight. Some of the Serbs, afraid of being taken prisoner, threw away their identification cards and tried to mix in with the Muslims. As the day wound down, two Muslim men, both of them refugees, came across one tall soldier in a fresh khaki uniform who was crouching behind a tree trunk just off the road. He had big hands, broad shoulders, a clean-shaven face, and dark hair with a streaks of gray above each ear.

The Muslims pointed their guns at him.

"Don't shoot, man," he said calmly. "I'm a Muslim."

The Muslims drew nearer.

"Get your hands behind your head!"

"I'm a Muslim!" the man in the khaki uniform shouted. Then he lifted his arms.

"What do you call the top of the minaret, Muslim?"

"The crescent moon."

"Fuck your crescent moon. It's an *alem*, an *alem*, you fucking Chetnik."

"I'm no Chetnik. I'm no Chetnik. I'm a Muslim."

"Recite the Koran! Anything!"

"My parents were Communists."

"Take down your pants! Down!"

"My parents were Communists."

The soldier lowered his pants. His penis had not been circumcised.

"My parents were Communists."

He pulled up his khaki pants.

"Get your hands up!"

One of the Muslims approached the tall man and bound his huge hands behind his back with wire. They led him back toward the village and ran into a third Muslim refugee.

"What the fuck are we going to do with this one?"

"If his hands weren't tied, he'd beat the shit out of all of us."

The decision was taken in an instant. Without thought. Without debate. Without dissent.

"I know," the third man said. He pushed the soldier away from the road and into the woods. "Get going."

"I'm a Muslim!"

"Go!"

The man in khaki walked ahead. He ducked his head under tree branches and stepped carefully over roots and bushes. He did not try to escape. Dusk had already settled over the forest, and deep in the woods the leaves had turned shades of gray. The Muslims stopped. The soldier walked a few paces ahead.

"Stop, *u pičku materinu!* Don't turn around!"

The soldier halted.

"I'm a Muslim!"

The three Muslim men fired their guns into his back. The bullets came out through his chest, and he fell to the ground face down. The holes in his body seemed to gurgle and spit as his lungs filled with blood. He was still alive. One of the Muslims walked up, put his gun to the man's head and fired one bullet into it. The tall man's body jumped and stopped twitching a few seconds later. The Muslims scurried back to the road. They returned later and burned the body.

The fighting around the wreckage of the convoy died away after dark. A cool rain began to fall. The Serbs still hiding in the woods received no help until the next day, when a second column arrived with reinforcements. They freed the Serb prisoners, recovered some of the bodies and the vehicles, and pulled back. Serb artillery pounded Žepa and sent the Muslims running into the woods and caves on the steep sides of the gorge. Yugoslav army jet fighter planes bombarded Muslim hamlets and strafed the sides of the ravine where the column had been ambushed. The artillery attacks lasted for the next five days. Then the Žepa area went quiet again.

❦   ❦   ❦

PAJA had even less stomach for fighting than he had had for school. He befriended a man from Žepa whose father, Enver Štitkovac, was the commander of the local military police. This connection got Paja enlisted in the police. Walking around with a police patch on his shoulder was much better than digging or manning trenches. He was issued an automatic rifle. His first job was to go from house to house up and down the Žepa gorge and find men who refused to answer Alija Izetbegović's mobilization order. In Žepa, the men were required to spend one week a month in the trenches.

Paja's group arrested about two hundred draft dodgers a day. Some tried hiding behind kitchen doors. They snuck into cellars or ducked into the woods near the houses where their families had taken shelter. The police would escort them to the army's command center, and they would be taken into the trenches with their hands tied. Many men ran away again at the first opportunity. Paja's cousin Jusuf Čelik, Esad's son, was one of the men who did not show up for the mobilization. The police chief warned everyone that men who dodged the draft would be executed, and he asked Paja about Jusuf.

"Isn't he on the line?" Paja asked, as if he were surprised.

"He hasn't shown up a single day," the commander snapped. "You are to bring him in immediately. If he isn't at home, you are to wait there. All night if you have to."

The next morning, Paja went to the house where Jusuf was living with his mother and sister. Jusuf was not around.

Paja waited.

Jusuf's mother got angry with him, and he could not stand being there looking at her.

"Tell Jusuf when he comes home that he is not to go anywhere," Paja told her. "It's an order. There's nothing I can do about it."

Paja went back to the house the same night. Jusuf was there.

"You've got to come along."

Jusuf became angry. "How come you got into the police? I want into the police. It's not fair that you come to bring me in."

"You know what an order means."

"I want into the police, too."

"You have to obey. We both have to obey."

Jusuf refused to go. Paja went back to the commander without him.

There was a meeting of the military police that night. Paja raised his hand to speak.

"I have a suggestion. Don't send us to bring in anyone from our own families. My people won't listen to me. Send me to get the men I don't know."

The commander agreed. Four other men went off to get Jusuf. He was sent to dig trenches, and he was still angry at Paja when he got back.

LONG shadows fell across the road from Žepa to Slap on the morning in late June when Paja and Senad strode down to the riverbank. Their turn had come to pull a body from the river. It was nerve-racking work. The Serbs now controlled the entire right bank of the Drina along the foot of Mount Zvijezda, and they sometimes took pot shots at the Muslim men retrieving and burying bodies. Dozens of dead men and a few women and children had floated down from Višegrad that month.

The stench of rotting flesh hung in the air when Paja and Senad arrived in Slap. The Drina there forms the tail end of a lake held back by the hydro-electric dam downstream near Bajina Bašta. They could see the body. It was a yellow lump and floated in the placid water about a football field away. Senad sat down in the boat and grabbed the sides as Paja pushed off. Neither of them could swim, and Paja had never held an oar in his life. He fought to keep the boat from turning circles in the water, and men on the riverbank watched and laughed at him and at the terror in Senad's eyes.

Senad took hold of a rusty steel rod hooked at one end when they finally drew alongside the body. He tried to snag its yellow shirt; but on his first two attempts the hook tore through the cloth and the flesh beneath it and exposed some pale ribs. There was no blood.

"Hook it through the belt," Paja grumbled. The stench made him gag. "Let's get the fuck out of here."

Senad did as he said, and Paja turned the boat and rowed back as quickly as he could. After they reached the riverbank, Senad pulled the body out of the water, handed the metal rod to Paja, and walked into the woods with the dry heaves. Paja swore at him, then turned the corpse onto its back with his hands. He could not recognize the swollen face. The eyes were gone; the nose was bent to one side; and the lips were tumescent. The crown of the head had been crushed by a blow or a fall, and the brains had either been washed away or eaten by the trout. There were two bullet holes through the chest.

Paja stuck his fingers into the front pockets of the man's pants but found nothing. Then he rolled the body onto its stomach, slit one back pocket with a jackknife, and found a wallet. The men pressed closer as he opened it. There was no money, but he found a brown identity card and recognized the name and the face on the tiny black-and-white picture as soon as he peeled back the card's cover. It was Adem Kozić, Huso's second cousin, the man who always wore his yellow porter's shirt and said he would stay in Kupusovići so long as anyone else did.

Paja rolled Adem's body onto a gray army blanket and registered his name in a school notebook. The men helped Paja carry Adem to the end of a row of shallow graves. By the end of the month, there would be about two hundred of them.

11

A FEW survivors of the violence in Višegrad—men and women who had hidden away in attics, cellars, cattle stalls, or sewers—managed to escape across the Drina to Žepa and bear witness to what had been happening across the river.

At the behest of the United Nations, President Slobodan Milošević had the Yugoslav army withdraw most of its troops from Višegrad on May 18. These troops left Karadžić's loyalists with most of their artillery pieces and tanks, along with ammunition, light weapons, communications equipment, and other gear. The withdrawn Yugoslav army troops then encamped on the Serbian side of Mount Zvijezda, from where they could easily slide back and forth across the border undetected. Now the real trouble started for the Muslims who had returned to their homes from Goražde, trusting the guarantee of security given them by Milošević's army.

Early on May 20, cars mounted with loudspeakers began cruising Višegrad's streets. Chetnik songs filled the morning air. Voices blaring through the loudspeakers called on the town's Muslims to leave their homes: "Muslims, Muslims, you yellow ants, black days have come."

The first to be attacked were the wealthier Muslim families. Then came the Muslims with education and influence. Men in black wool caps and balaclavas burst into their homes. They demanded money and jewelry. They shot to death any men they found and killed women who were not cooperative. The Serb gunmen made off with whatever they could carry. Gold watches and rings. Cash. Washing machines. Televisions. Anything. Decomposing corpses littered the streets and yards. Dead bodies thrown into the Drina were snagged by downed trees or ran aground in the shallows along the riverside below Mehmed Pasha's bridge.

In all of the stories about Višegrad that were carried across the Drina to Žepa and beyond, one name is mentioned again and again and again. It is that of Milan Lukić, the same Milan Lukić from Rujišta who shared cheese pies in grade school with Huso Čelik's middle son, Sead; the same Milan Lukić who had the crush on Hasib Čavkušić's daughter Hadžira before going off to Serbia to find work.

A Serb military document says Lukić was back in Višegrad as a "volunteer" on April 26, 1992. He soon positioned himself at the center of a paramilitary gang, a ring of local Serbs and men from Serbia who were out to profit from the expulsion of all of the Muslims from Višegrad and Mount Zvijezda. In all likelihood, Lukić had become a force to reckon with because of his links with Milošević's army and police ministry. One of his distant cousins was a colonel in the Yugoslav army. Another distant cousin, Sreten Lukić, had risen to become a police commander in Belgrade. Sreten's brother, Mikailo Lukić, was the head of Serbia's secret police in the town of Bajina Bašta, just down the river from Višegrad. Mikailo reportedly played a role in a bid by Milošević to use Serbia's secret police to seize control of Bosnia's Communist-dominated government in 1989, and Serbs say Mikailo also profited by dealing guns in the Višegrad area in 1991 and 1992.

After the Yugoslav army's departure, Milan Lukić and his gang went from neighborhood to neighborhood emptying Višegrad of its Muslims. The gang marched unarmed Muslim men to Mehmed Pasha's bridge or the new highway bridge over the Drina, where they shot them, beat them, or cut their throats before pushing them into the river. The gang members occupied the hotel next to Mehmed Pasha's bridge and imprisoned and killed Muslims inside it. Young Muslim women were locked away in the new hotel at Višegrad's hot springs, the Hotel Vilina Vlas, and became sex slaves in a brothel run by Lukić's cousin Sredoje. On the night of June 11, witnesses reported seeing Milan and his men shoot and slaughter dozens of men on the new highway bridge over the Drina at Višegrad and dump their bodies into the river. Gang members tied one man's feet to a rope and dragged him behind a car to a sports center on the riverside before cutting his throat and throwing his body into the water. Over the next few weeks, women, children, and old people were herded aboard buses and driven westward toward central Bosnia or eastward into Serbia, and almost always through Bajina Bašta, the same town where Lukić's cousin was the police commander. If any Muslim men happened to make it aboard these buses in Višegrad, they were dragged off en route, shot, and dumped into ravines or forests.

Lukić warned other Serbs that they would be killed if they were caught helping their Muslim neighbors. From their windows or from in between the terra-cotta tiles of their roofs, however, many of Višegrad's Serbs watched members of Lukić's gang carry out the killings, and they have since spoken about what they saw. Some of these Serbs risked their lives to save Muslim families by hiding them in their houses or helping them escape over the border to Serbia or across the Drina to friendly territory.

❨ ❨ ❨

ADEM KOZIĆ, his wife, Hanifa, and two of their children, Munevera and Hasan, were at home in Kupusovići for two weeks after Paja, Hiba, and Zlatija left home for good. A dozen Serb men with guns, all of them peasants from nearby villages, came into the hamlet in a van. Here was Milojica Pepić, who had tried to lead Paja into a trap. Here, too, was Mile Janković, the brandy-addicted son of Vitomir, the man Uncle Avdo Čelik said could only have died like a dog.

"All you Muslims must leave," Mile and the other Serbs ordered. "You are to bring clothes and something to eat."

"Fuck your Alija," they snarled, cursing the name of Alija Izetbegović. "Why didn't you vote for Karadzić? . . . Now you have no future here."

They set an empty Muslim house on fire, then began driving off the Muslims' sheep and cattle.

"Now you must leave. Now!"

Adem and his wife and the other Muslims packed up what they could and fled down to the empty meadow below Žlijeb called the Customs Area. Some of them slept the night in the woods; others crowded into nearby houses.

The next morning, Hakija Sućeska, the uncle of Paja's friend Senad, walked back to his house in Odžak to get a razor and wristwatch he had inadvertently left behind. An hour or so later, the Muslims in the meadow heard gunshots from the direction of Odžak, then more gunfire from Kupusovići, from somewhere near Juz-bin's mosque. They were too afraid to venture back up the mountain to see what had happened. But there was a witness. Just before the gun blasts began, an old Serb who walked with a cane was hobbling through Odžak toward Kupusovići. He saw the Serb men who were beating up his friend Hakija. On his way back through Odžak, the old Serb saw his friend's dead body crumpled up on the road next to a stone wall a few yards from the Sućeska house.

Mile Janković came down into the meadow below Žlijeb at dusk. "Good evening, neighbors," he said. "Tomorrow you are to walk down to the main road and gather by the bus stop. There will be buses and trucks waiting for you."

The Muslims agreed to go.

"Hakija Sućeska is dead," Mile said. "There are two bodies up there. Somebody should come up to bury them."

Mile turned to Hakija's son: "Salko, how about you coming back up tomorrow morning and burying your father?"

"You bury him, Mile," Salko snapped. "Let the one who killed him bury him."

"Somebody should come up and bury him," Mile answered. Then he walked away.

Several hundred Muslims gathered in the Customs Area the next morning and set out for the main road on foot. Almost all of them were old people, women, or children. They, too, hiked down the mountain along the road that the bulldozer had carved out parallel to the stream with rocks worn smooth like pillows. When they reached the bus stop on the main road, Mile Janković was there with the other armed men who had come into Kupusovići. They surrounded the Muslims and waited until buses and vans arrived. The Muslims' names were scribbled on a piece of paper when they boarded. They were driven into the center of Višegrad, where Milan Lukić's men were waiting. They hustled the Muslims into the town's firehouse, a new stucco-covered building beside a railroad tunnel that used to carry the Ćiro into Višegrad station. The floor of the firehouse's garage was stained with blood. Someone had spread out over it books and tattered newspapers, and the women and children sat down on them.

"Bring all of your money and gold here to this bench," one of Lukić's men ordered. "If you do not hand everything over, we will butcher ten children."

The gunmen then led the women, four at a time, out of the garage and up a stairway to rooms on the fire station's second floor. The women were stripped and their bodies searched for money and jewelry before they were sent back to the garage. The shakedowns went on after nightfall.

Just before midnight, the garage plunged into darkness. Gunfire began an instant later at the firehouse door. The muzzle flash flickered like a strobe lamp. Screams of terror tore through the air. Then silence, and mumbles, and whimpers. Hanifa Kozić curled up on the floor next to Munevera and Adem. Now more gunfire. All over the garage, children were crying in panic. Then silence. Mothers clutched their children tightly. More gunshots.

Lukić's men stopped shooting altogether after twenty minutes. Then they began taking the men from the firehouse, one at a time. Out went Adem Kozić. Salko Sućeska was taken away. And another. And another. The women cried and shouted and banged on the metal door of the garage after the last of the men had gone. It was only a two- or three-minute walk down to Mehmed Pasha's bridge. There, on the *sofa*, they were shot in the back and dropped into the Drina. Gunfire on the bridge was heard from inside the firehouse. And Muslims and Serbs living near the riverbank could hear the screams in the darkness.

The next morning, Lukić's men brought breakfast for the women and children in the firehouse garage.

"Where are our men?"

"At the police station. All of them. They are awaiting interrogation, and they'll be back in two or three days."

"Where are they?"

"Don't complain."

"Where are they?"

"Don't shout."

The women and children were held in the firehouse for the next fifteen days. Lukić and his men took younger women to the upper rooms and raped them repeatedly. None of the men ever came back.

IT was a Thursday when seven buses pulled up in front of the firehouse.

"We need you for an exchange," one of Lukić's men said. They again scribbled down all of the Muslims' names on paper. Later in the day, workers from the International Red Cross arrived. They told the Muslim women they were going to be taken out of the country.

The buses moved out at five in the afternoon with no Red Cross escort. They crossed into Serbia and drove north over the mountains to a camp at Bajina Bašta where they spent two or three nights. From there, the old people, women, and children were driven southward, through the highlands of central Serbia, dumped out on Serbia's border with Macedonia, and herded into the no-man's land between the customs stations. The Macedonian border guards refused to let them enter their country; the Serbs refused to let them return to theirs. Albanians passing by in cars brought the Muslims food and eventually notified the Red Cross of their plight. Five months later, after two crossings through Bulgaria and Romania and one beating by Hungarian border police, Hanifa Kozić and her children found themselves in a refugee camp in Turkey.

‹ ‹ ‹

THIS was the end of the Muslims of Kupusovići and the rest of Mount Zvijezda. The killing in Višegrad went on for another two months. Flies swarmed over Mehmed Pasha's bridge and picked away at body parts and pools of drying blood. When the gore and the stench became unbearable, Mitar Vasiljević, the hotel waiter who had joined Lukić's gang, rousted out Muslim women prisoners and had them gather up the pieces of flesh and wash down the pools of blood on the stone. When bodies got hung up on gravel shoals or outcroppings of rock in midriver, Lukić ordered the floodgates of the hydroelectric dam to be opened so that the water would wash them down the Drina toward Slap and Bajina Bašta. So many rotting bodies came floating down the river that Serb men in Bajina Bašta gave up trout fishing in the river for the next three summers.

By the end of July 1992, the only Muslims left in the Višegrad district were the handful of people hidden away by friendly Serbs or those held for ransom by Lukić's gang. Some twelve thousand Muslim people had inhabited Višegrad before the war. About ten thousand of them had wound up in refugee camps throughout Europe and Turkey or were eking out an existence in Goražde, Žepa, Sarajevo, and other Bosnian towns and villages. The other two thousand were by now dead, and over one hundred of them had been crowded into houses and burned alive by Milan Lukić and his men.

12

THE UNITED NATIONS was organized in 1945 to promote world peace and the observance of international law. Its Security Council was created to deal with issues concerning international security and is dominated by its five permanent member nations, the core of the alliance that had emerged victorious from World War II: the United States, Russia, China, France, and Great Britain. These permanent members have the power to veto all Security Council decisions, which are known as resolutions. Under the UN Charter, the permanent members are obligated not to act solely in their national interest when dealing with cases of international aggression and threats to international security.

During the four decades of the Cold War, the Security Council managed on a number of occasions to assemble troops from a wide variety of nations, including Yugoslavia, to act as neutral peacekeepers in war-torn countries like Lebanon and Cyprus, where peace agreements or cease-fires had been hammered out. But many major diplomatic initiatives were steered clear of the Security Council because it was for so long hamstrung by U.S. or Russian vetoes. With the collapse of the Soviet bloc and the end of the Cold War, however, political leaders and thinkers in Western Europe and the United States were confident that the UN and its Security Council would emerge to play a new, pivotal role in maintaining international peace and security. The Security Council proved to be a major forum for decision making in the run-up to the Persian Gulf War.

Yugoslavia posed the organization's next big test. In a bid to keep the fighting in Croatia from escalating, the Security Council imposed an arms embargo on all the republics of Yugoslavia in September 1991. The war in Croatia ended in early 1992 with an agreement between the Croats and Serbs that was negotiated by a UN team led by Cyrus Vance, the U.S. secretary of state under President Jimmy Carter. The Security Council backed the Vance peace agreement by passing a resolution that created a neutral peacekeeping force, known as the UN Protection Force, or UNPROFOR, whose ten thousand troops from several dozen countries would be scattered over Serb-held areas of Croatia and headquartered in Sarajevo. Officials of the UN military force watched the bombardment of the Bosnian capital from the day it began. As one Bosnian town after another fell during the spring of 1992, calls went out for the governments of Western Europe and the United States to do something about the Serb campaign to grab territory and uproot Bosnia's Muslim population. These governments got their ambassadors together at the UN Security Council in May 1992 and imposed economic sanctions on Serbia and Montenegro, the only two republics left in the diminished Yugoslavia. But the Serbs did not stop the forcible expulsions in Bosnia, and the UN arms embargo barred the Muslim-dominated Bosnian government from obtaining weapons legally despite the fact that it was now a UN member nation and that members of the Security Council were characterizing the violence in Bosnia as aggression by Milošević's Serbia.

《　《　《

JUZ-BIN'S mosque, Saliha's new house, the Čelik place, and all the Muslim villages on Mount Zvijezda had been burned or dynamited into rubble by the time Western leaders finally met in London in August 1992 to discuss what to do about the Bosnian conflict. The American and European governments were happy to see legions of news reporters descend on the conference hall with their television cameras, microphones, and steno pads because the Western leaders had to create a strong impression that something was being done to stop the killing. A few weeks earlier, the British and French governments had appeared ready to appease the Serbs, and President George Bush was avoiding American involvement in Bosnia because he did not want to make it seem that, after the Persian Gulf War, the United States was willing to police Europe's backyard. Washington insiders saw the Yugoslav problem as a political "tar baby," a loser issue for the 1992 presidential election campaign then in full swing.

The London conference would probably not have been held at all if the world's television networks had not broadcast in early August footage of Bosnian Serb troops holding emaciated Muslims, most of them civilian men, in concentration camps. The prisoners in these camps were being starved and denied water and medical treatment, beaten to death, shot by firing squads, and made to mutilate and kill each other; witnesses described how one man went mad after being forced to take the penis of another into his mouth and bite it off. Reasonable estimates of the death toll in the concentration camps rose into the thousands. And then word got out that the Bosnian government and UN personnel in Bosnia and Croatia had informed senior UN officials, including

Secretary-General Boutros Boutros-Ghali, about the camps in the early summer and that they had said nothing, publicly anyway, about them. After the
television footage was broadcast, however, demands for international military
intervention in Bosnia came pouring in from across the political spectrum.

Several dozen countries and international organizations sent delegations to
the London conference. Prime Minister John Major of Great Britain presided.
Close by sat Lawrence Eagleburger, the U.S. deputy secretary of state, America's ambassador to Belgrade from 1977 to 1981, and the man reputed to be
Washington's most knowledgeable person on Yugoslavia and its affairs. There,
too, were the French, the Dutch, the Russians, Boutros-Ghali and the UN
team, and the Croats and the Bosnian government with its multiethnic delegation. And there, shoved off to one side, was one of Eagleburger's old acquaintances, a former official from a Belgrade bank: Slobodan Milošević.*

"Do you know why we're traveling to London?" the Serbian president
rhetorically asked his minister for information on the plane from Belgrade.
"Because we are the winning party. . . . We are the winners."†

At the time, Milošević had good reason to presume he had already won the
war. The Serb army, Milošević's special-police units, Ražnatović's gang, and
other paramilitary groups had overrun 60 percent of Bosnia by the time the
Serbian president's airplane took off for London. In a few weeks, it seemed, his
military would control all the territory Serb leaders wanted. Final victory
would be a matter of sitting tight and waiting for the rest of the world to accept a fait accompli and lift the economic sanctions the UN had imposed.

Balkan leaders understand the weakness of disunity because they have so
much practice dealing with it. And Slobodan Milošević certainly knew how to
recognize and take advantage of the divisions in the international community
on the question of Bosnia. None of the major Western governments had any
economic, strategic, or cultural interest in the country. None of them wanted
to intervene militarily. Most Western leaders were privately wishing the Bosnia
"tar baby" would just crawl away. Milošević knew Serbia could withstand the
economic sanctions for the short term, and for the time being they were not
without their silver lining. His propagandists cited the sanctions as more evi-

---

*According to the Congressional Record, after his stint as ambassador, Eagleburger became
president of Kissinger Associates and took positions on the boards of directors of a scandal-
ridden Yugoslav bank and an American corporation that imported into the United States
the ill-starred Yugo automobile, which was assembled in Serbia by Crvena Zastava, the enterprise that has been the heart and soul of the Yugoslav arms industry since before World
War I. President Reagan subsequently named Eagleburger assistant secretary of state for European affairs and, later, deputy undersecretary for political affairs.
†Siber and Little, *Yugoslavia*, p. 258.

dence of the international conspiracy against the Serbs. The sanctions gave Milošević a scapegoat for his own disastrous economic policies. He, his ministers, and criminal gang leaders like Ražnatović also exploited the shortages brought on by the sanctions. Milošević and his men squeezed billions of American dollars and German marks from ordinary Serbs by selling them smuggled gasoline and other imported goods at astronomical prices. And pyramid investment schemes run by Milošević's cronies bilked the gullible of millions of dollars in hard currency.

What Milošević wanted in London was an improvement in his public relations. He had somehow to deflect domestic dissatisfaction and Western criticism and recast himself as a peacemaker while his military mopped up the conquered swaths of Bosnia and emptied the pockets of Muslim refugees trapped in the Drina basin. The Muslims who were fighting to save themselves and take back their homes had to be portrayed as diehards and troublemakers. The war in Bosnia had to be presented as a civil war, an ethnic war, a religious war, the latest tremor along an unstable cultural fault line, an age-old struggle between Christianity and Islam, anything but what it was: a land grab managed from Belgrade with help from Zagreb.

The public-relations campaign began two months before Milošević's trip to the London conference. The Serbian president arranged for the appointment of two men, neither of them politicians, to fill the empty top offices of Yugoslavia's federal government. The clear goals in filling these positions were, first, to maintain the illusion that a Yugoslavia, however diminished, still existed in order to grab as much as possible of the defunct country's assets abroad and, second, to deflect attention from Milošević himself.

For Yugoslavia's president, Milošević chose seventy-two-year-old Dobrica Ćosić, a disheveled, ashen-haired ex-Communist who had for decades churned out tomes of romantic fiction glorifying Serbia's past. Ćosić knew exactly what was happening in Bosnia, but his vanity and longing to go down in history as a founding father of a Greater Serbian state would prevent him from even uttering a word in direct criticism of Milošević or the campaign of forced expulsions of Bosnia's Muslims. In the role of Ćosić's prime minister, Milošević cast Milan Panić, an ebullient, sixty-three-year-old Serbian-American who had defected from Tito's Yugoslavia in 1955 while competing in a bicycle race abroad and subsequently made himself a millionaire by marketing pharmaceuticals from California. Panić spoke Serbo-Croatian with an English accent and English with a Serbo-Croatian accent; he knew nothing about what was happening in Bosnia; and he rarely closed his mouth. This pair, Ćosić and Panić, led the Serbian delegation to the London conference. The members of the Bosnian Serb delegation, including Radovan Karadžić, whom Ćosić had handpicked and Panić had never met, were kept in the hallway outside the meeting room.

Prime Minister Major opened the London conference. He warned that Serbia would face isolation if it did not cooperate with the international community's efforts to end the war. Eagleburger chimed in, telling everyone how thousands of Muslims had been killed in a Serb camp in northern Bosnia, something anyone who read the newspapers already knew. Speaker after speaker took the floor and condemned the Serbs for international aggression. Milošević brooded in the second row of the Serb delegation and listened as Milan Panić did most of the talking. With an endearing, West Coast–style bubbliness, Panić proved capable of saying anything to stave off the faint chance that the assembled Western leaders would take action against Serbia for its role in Bosnia. Panić chided Milošević in public. He declared that Serbia would recognize the independence of Croatia, clearly without grasping that it would mean signing away the Serbs' territorial demands against Croatia. He agreed to a cease-fire in Bosnia. He promised that Muslim refugees would be allowed to return to their homes. He agreed to a ban on flights over Bosnia by Serb military aircraft and to support UN efforts to feed the hungry. And he agreed to stop the flow of artillery, tanks, and other weapons from Serbia to the Bosnian Serbs. When Panić was done, Eagleburger announced that Karadžić had agreed to withdraw Serb troops from some of the land they had seized and to allow the UN to monitor the Serb artillery around Sarajevo and other towns.

Western intelligence agencies and the embassies in Belgrade had advised their governments that Milošević and Karadžić were pathological liars and that Panić, who had been in Belgrade only a few weeks, had no means of keeping the promises he was making. But the Western leaders at London chose to play along with the Serbs' farce. The final declaration of principles adopted at the London conference contained no threat of military intervention if the Serbs did not keep Panić's promises. Nor was there any hint of convening the UN Security Council to lift the arms embargo for the Bosnian government. Instead, the conference appointed two negotiators, Cyrus Vance and a former British foreign secretary, David Owen, and charged them with formulating a plan to end the war. The Western leaders promised to provide, for the meantime, food and medicine to all sides in Bosnia. They pledged to get aid deliveries into hard-pressed areas by deploying to Bosnia military troops who would, under the direction of the UN's Department of Peacekeeping Operations, escort food convoys. The multinational military force in Bosnia, like the peacekeeping operation in Croatia, would be known as UNPROFOR, the UN Protection Force, but its only job would be to protect food, medicine, clothing, and other aid.

For the first time in its history, the UN Security Council was sending a neutral military force, a peacekeeping force, into a country where there was no peace to keep.

The television cameras whirred as the Western leaders filed out of the conference room. The Nikons clicked and whizzed as the leaders hailed their decisions as a watershed, and the stories the journalists dispatched created the impression that something was really being done to end the Bosnian horror. But the Serbs and Croats who mattered—Slobodan Milošević, Radovan Karadžić, and Croatia's president, Franjo Tudjman—flew away from London convinced that the international community had no backbone when it came to the Bosnian war. "I think the conference took a big step forward," Karadžić told reporters with staggering hypocrisy before he left London. "It is a triumph for the great tradition of British and European diplomacy, not to mention the United Nations."

Within days, it was clear that every promise Milan Panić had made in London was empty. Instead of taking immediate action, the leaders of the Western world allowed the conference to fade from sight. They deflected renewed criticism and pleas for action by appealing for time to see what would happen when the UN troops arrived and when the peace negotiators came up with their settlement plan. Within a few weeks, Franjo Tudjman's proxy army in southwestern Bosnia, the Croatian Defense Council, or HVO, slowed the trickle of arms that had been covertly getting to the Bosnian government's nascent army. An Italian cargo plane carrying food to Sarajevo was blown from the sky over Croat-controlled territory. The main Croat militia in Bosnia launched its own campaign of violence to uproot Muslim communities. The Serb carve-up of Bosnia had now overtly become the Serb and Croat carve-up of Bosnia.

Within a few weeks of the London conference, David Owen, the peace negotiator, had warned Muslim leaders in Sarajevo that there would be no lifting of the arms embargo and no outside military intervention. The Muslims' only option, he said, was to negotiate with the nationalist Serbs and Croats even as they were using their vast military superiority to occupy more territory, kill as many Muslim men as possible, rape Muslim women, uproot Muslim families from their homes, and herd them, sometimes barefoot, across front lines. Many Muslims initially welcomed the UN troops to Bosnia. They assumed the troops, and through them the rest of the world, would see the obvious. When it became clear that the world already knew the obvious and was not prepared to do anything about it, the Muslims came to regard the international peace effort as nothing more than a campaign to manage their capitulation. Muslim leaders redoubled their diplomatic effort to compel the West to intervene militarily or lift the arms embargo. The Sarajevo government had little choice but to continue its military effort to prevent the nationalist Serbs and Croats from solidifying their control of seized territories. And journalists in the capital writing stories about the bloodshed began referring to the Muslims as the "well-fed dead."

❨   ❨   ❨

AT the very hour that Milan Panić was making his promises to the London conference, Huso Čelik and his family were hunkering down in a cave on the side of a ravine above Žepa. Paja had just rejoined the family after a month of hauling food and wounded men and women through trenches dug into a hillside looking down on Višegrad and Mehmed Pasha's bridge. All of the refugee men from Višegrad had by now been conscripted into the Bosnian army. Most of them were angry. They did not want to die for some hilltop across the Drina from Mount Zvijezda. If they had to fight, they wanted to fight for their fields and their burned-out homes, which they could see on the other side of the valley. The men from Kupusovići, Odžak, and Žlijeb grumbled and bickered. Bosnia's army, if it could be called an army, was disorganized. No effective chain of command existed. The troops had few weapons, scant ammunition, and no decent food. Local Muslim peasants were bossing the refugees around as if they were slaves. Everyone, it seemed, was out for himself and his family.

One August morning at about eight o'clock, Paja, Senad, and a group of their boyhood friends packed up some food and walked away from the front line. They trudged northward into the mountains and joined their families in Žepa the next afternoon.

IT was a good cave. Dry inside, almost. Spacious enough for the ten people who sheltered inside it to stretch their legs comfortably on the sponge pads the women had laid out on the stone floor. Huso had discovered the cave and a nearby shack after word got around that Žepa's Muslims were planning an attack on a Serb antiaircraft installation atop a mountain just to the north. Any Muslim attack inevitably brought retaliatory Serb shelling and aerial bombing, and Huso figured it would be best to abandon the house where they had been living. About a week after the Čeliks moved out, the Muslims surrounded the antiaircraft installation. The Serb soldiers inside surrendered without firing a shot and were exchanged for fifty tons of wheat flour and twenty tons of diesel fuel within a few days. Fighter jets from Serbia bombarded the mountaintop installation the next day. Then, as Huso had foretold, they started in on Žepa. Serb MiGs attacked the hamlets clustered around

Žepa every hour or two from eight in the morning until seven or eight in the evening for days on end. The jets would roar just over the tops of the trees outside the mouth of the cave and drop cluster bombs and fire rockets. Serb soldiers hanging out the open doors of single-engine crop dusters dropped mortar rounds three and four at a time and rolled out homemade bombs fashioned from the tanks of hot-water heaters packed with nails, screws, and explosives. The shellfire was relentless. From across the Drina in Serbia—on the eastern flanks of Mount Zvijezda—the Yugoslav army pounded away with howitzers whose shells could blow apart an entire house. From Kamenica, Hiba Čelik's home village, and Rujišta, the home of Milan Lukić, came tank and mortar fire. The shells made a soft, tearing sound as they flew through the air above the Čeliks' cave and headed toward clusters of houses across the ravine.

The Čeliks slept in the shack during the quiet of the night and headed for the cave each day at the break of dawn. There was not much to do during the day. The men hauled up a wood stove to heat the cave and keep it dried out. They built a four-foot-high stone wall across its mouth to catch the shrapnel from any shell that happened to explode close by. The women baked bread and potato pies and boiled beans, and, when the sky went quiet, they ventured outside to water the oxen and fetch milk from a neighbor's cow. Filth and sweat covered everyone. Paja's son Mirza drove the women mad, gamboling about, tearing up his knees on the rocks, and trying to escape outside. When the bombs began to explode, adrenaline pulsed through their veins and frayed their nerves. Their muscles tightened. Their moods shifted unpredictably from uproarious laughter to fits of anger to silent depression. Hunger seemed to disappear. It was hard to fall asleep and easy to drum up excuses not to go outside even in the evening when the skies turned quiet. Hours of idleness and danger fed the imagination, and the mind conjured up ideal worlds and lives that would be lived once the shooting stopped.

In mid-September, word came that the Serbs were advancing. Paja and Senad were called to the front line and ordered to ambush an approaching tank. They carried forward two antitank rockets, a rocket-propelled grenade, and a pair of automatics and found a concealed spot near a dirt road. The men sat waiting until dark. No tank appeared. Serb soldiers approached to within a few hundred yards and stopped to burn a Muslim house. The Muslim commanders had told Paja and Senad to ignore any infantry and to withhold fire until the tank drew near. The night and the silence grew deeper. They watched the stars and listened to the Serbs joking and laughing.

A Muslim fighter came up from behind. "What the fuck are you guys still doing here? Everybody else has pulled back. All the men from Žepa are gone. You want to die? They're all back there having dinner."

A group of Muslims attacked the Serbs a few minutes later. When they struck back, the rest of the Muslims began running away.

"Let's get the fuck out of here," Senad said. By the time Paja and Senad reached Huso and the others in the cave, refugees were streaming into Žepa from the west. The Muslim trench lines across from Višegrad had long since given way. It seemed all of Žepa might fall. Word spread that an order had been issued for everyone to prepare for a general evacuation into the hills. Paja fetched his oxen, and by midnight the Čeliks were climbing northward through the forests between the Drina gorge and the summit of Zlovrh. They slept that night on the ground under a lean-to fashioned from branches and leaves, and stayed there for two days and two nights before deciding to leave Žepa for good and try their luck farther north. They waited until they found a group of local people who could guide them through the woods and keep them from wandering into any Serb villages.

As the sun set behind them the next evening, they were alone again. They turned from an asphalt road onto a dirt trail that ran downhill through a Muslim graveyard. They stopped at a trough fed by a spring next to a chestnut tree. Paja began watering the oxen. The place had the smell of wood burning. There were houses on a bluff nearby, and a town stretched out along the bottom of the ravine before them. Children were playing and giggling, but the air was eerily quiet except for the thud of axes chopping wood. A boy walked up to Paja.

"Where're you coming from?"

"Žepa."

"I've got some pears."

The boy handed around the fruit.

"Can we get a place anywhere around here?" Paja asked.

"Gimme a minute."

The boy ran off to get someone.

Sanela was too exhausted to think of where she might be. Her tired eyes focused on a house across from the trickling spring. The house had white walls, freshly stuccoed and trimmed with stained wood. Its yard was neatly kept. Sanela's mind drifted. For no reason, she wondered whether this white house had a balcony on its opposite side, the side facing the town. She wondered if the family who lived in the house could sit on that balcony and how fine it would be to observe everything going on in the town below. She could see the town through some trees. It stretched along both sides of an asphalt road that sloped downward from right to left along the bottom of the ravine. The hillsides were covered by pine, oak, and beech trees. The white bell tower of an Orthodox church stood across the way, and almost next to the church rose a white minaret beside a mosque. Just below them was the town's center. It had a government building or two built by the Austrians and, from the Communist era, a department store and clusters of drab, red-brick apartment blocks with crumbling concrete balconies. Farther up the asphalt road stood the older part of town, a string of private homes with terra-cotta roofs built atop foundations laid in Ottoman times. And above them were the crumbling walls of a stone fortress.

Sanela focused again on the white house. Then the boy returned with a woman.

"We're looking for an empty house, someplace to live," Paja told her. "Anything left around here?"

The woman pointed down toward an old place, a house with weather-beaten walls of pink stucco a few hundred yards away. "My sister's been living there, but she's just moved out. It's empty."

Paja thanked her, and the Čeliks descended the dirt road toward the house and the town just below it. The roof tiles were old and crusted with lichen, but they were all in place. The windows still had glass. The yard had an overgrown garden with an apple tree, and there was a cellar down below.

The date was September 19, 1992. The address of the house was no. 8 Rudarska Street, Srebrenica.

PART THREE

"KAD TAD, KAD TAD . . ."

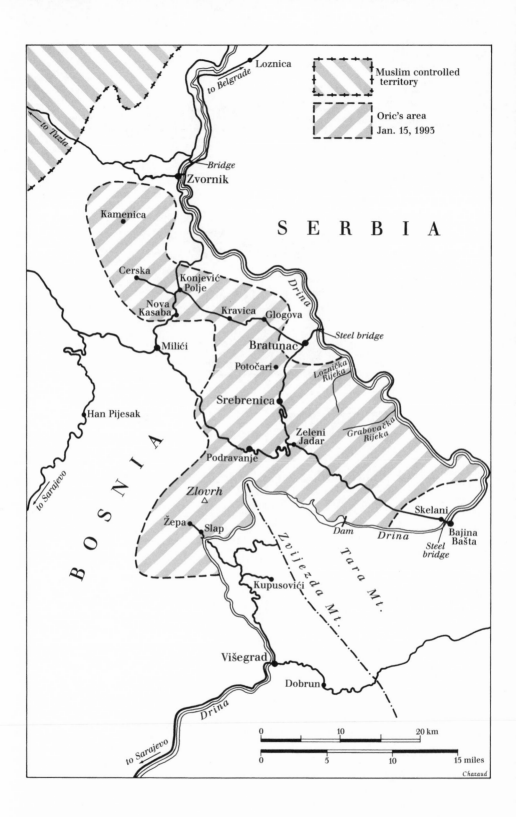

| | | Muslim controlled territory |
| | | Oric's area Jan. 15, 1993 |

Loznica

to Belgrade

to Tuzla

Bridge

Zvornik

S E R B I A

Kamenica

Cerska

Konjević Polje

Drina

Nova Kasaba

Kravica

Glogova

Milići

Steel bridge

Bratunac

Potočari

Loznička Rijeka

Srebrenica

Zeleni Jadar

Grabovačka Rijeka

Han Pijesak

B O S N I A

Podravanje

to Sarajevo

Zlovrh

Žepa

Slap

Dam

Drina

Skelani

Bajina Bašta

Steel bridge

Zvijezda Mt.

Tara Mt.

Kupusovići

Višegrad

Dobrun

0   10   20 km

0   5   10   15 miles

to Sarajevo

Drina

Chazaud

13

HIBA and Sanela wandered inside the vacant house and shuffled up a short, wide hallway. The floorboards squeaked underfoot and tilted toward the left like the floor of a dark passage in an amusement park funhouse. The walls were dry, but crumbling. There were four rooms, two on each side of the hall-way, each about twelve feet by twelve feet in size, each of them a mess. The women found a broken bed, some carpet, a kitchen cupboard, a woodstove, and a pile of dust-covered picture tubes and other components from canni-balized television sets. In the bathroom at the end of the hall were a toilet and a bathtub with running water and an electric water heater. Hiba switched it on, but there was no electricity. The house, like a lot of the other property in Bosnia, seemed to belong to no one any more. The television parts were pitched out the window immediately and later carted off to a dump.

Paja was tying the oxen inside the garage, when Sanela went to borrow a broom from a neighbor. She knocked at the first house. A woman came to the door. She was plump and cheery eyed and wore a skirt instead of *dimije*. Sanela looked at the skirt with surprise.

"Good day," she said.

"Good day."

"I've got to do a little cleaning up, and I haven't got a broom. Have you got one I can use?"

"No problem," the neighbor smiled. She disappeared into her house and came back with a broom.

"So you're from Višegrad," the woman guessed.

"How did you know?"

"Your accent. You sound like you're from Serbia."

"We're right on the border."

"I thought so. You can have the broom any time you'd like. My name is Dragica."

"Sanela."

AFTER a few weeks, Huso was dropping by Dragica's house. Dragica helped the Čeliks get on their feet, and within a few months Sanela was cutting Aun-tie Dragica's hair and telling her the stories from Višegrad and Žepa. Dragica knew Srebrenica well and told Sanela and the rest of the Čeliks a lot about what happened in the town before they arrived. First of all, she told them a

Serb had built the old house they were living in. But he had gone to jail long before the war. He had the place up for sale after his release but abandoned it when he went to Montenegro's seacoast and opened a café. His brother had tried to learn to repair television sets but gave it up and went off somewhere to find work and never came back.

Dragica's skirt had given away the fact that she was a Serb, too. She had been born and raised in Serbia, a few miles down the Drina in Banja Koviljača, a village with a spa and a hotel that had been a stopover for spies and secret agents during the years when the river formed Serbia's border with Austria. Veljko Vasić, the son of a Srebrenica shoemaker, had brought Dragica home as his bride in 1947. Veljko had fled to Banja Koviljača as a refugee during World War II and met Dragica there. He lost his family to the Ustaše, joined Tito's Partisan underground, and snuck back and forth between Banja Koviljača and Srebrenica during the German occupation. For a decade after the war, Veljko had been Srebrenica's district president. He took over one of the local enterprises after that, and the whole town turned out for his funeral a few years before the Communists lost control of Bosnia. It was this multiethnic Srebrenica, the Srebrenica of Muslims, Serbs, Croats, and Gypsies who showed up for Veljko's funeral, that Dragica had come to know and love during the years she and Veljko spent together there. But for many of Srebrenica's Muslims and Serbs, this Srebrenica of Brotherhood and Unity hid dark memories more fraught with violence and unsettled scores than even Mount Zvijezda's.

THE Čeliks and other refugees from Zvijezda who found their way into Srebrenica could readily sense the difference between their mountain and this valley town. The natives of Srebrenica spoke a different dialect. They were lowlanders compared with the Mount Zvijezda folk. They danced a *kolo* with different steps. They lived by different, less patient rhythms. In the time people from Srebrenica could hop into their beat-up compact cars and drive to Belgrade or Sarajevo, someone from Kupusovići would have still been crouching beside the gravel road, smoking a third cigarette, and waiting for Uncle Avdo's friend to come bouncing along the cinder road in his beat-up local bus bound for Višegrad. The thin soil and paucity of resources on Zvijezda had given the mountain's people little to choose from in life: they could emigrate to Sarajevo or Belgrade or Steyr or some place farther afield; or they could waste away in the poverty, ignorance, and alcoholism that gripped the mountain. The people of Srebrenica, however, had enjoyed opportunities for employment that kept them close to home.

The town of Srebrenica was the center of a developed mineral-mining region before the war. The wealth its mines and factories generated did not pave Srebrenica's streets with silver, but it was enough to keep the menfolk from leaving in droves for jobs abroad and enough to fuel old enmities between the area's Muslims and Serbs when decisions had to be made about how it would be divvied up. In May and June of 1992, as the Muslims of Mount Zvijezda were abandoning their homesteads or waiting to be butchered by Milan Lukić's gang, Muslims in the Srebrenica area, especially in its outlying villages, were laying down their lives to defend their homes and jobs. And they were succeeding.

☾   ☾   ☾

BATTLES for control of the Srebrenica area have always boiled down to fights over its mineral wealth, and these fights have been going on for centuries. In the fourteenth century, the feudal overlords of medieval Bosnia and merchants from the rich Adriatic city-state of Dubrovnik recruited German miners from Saxony to exploit the silver deposits around Srebrenica. Within a few decades, Srebrenica had become one of the biggest mining centers on the Balkan peninsula and its silver smelters were belching out so much soot and ash that the townspeople complained about the air pollution.

Srebrenica's silver underwrote the building of a chain of smaller trading towns and caravan stopovers along the Drina, including Višegrad and Zvornik. The Saxons taught the local Slavs mining engineering, and colonists from Dubrovnik, including silversmiths, sword makers, and other craftsmen, grew so numerous that they set up their own diplomatic consulate and courts. Troupes of traveling actors staged performances in the town. Franciscan friars arrived to extirpate the Bosnian Church's heretics, garner contributions, and minister to the area's majority Roman Catholics. Cloth merchants earned handsome profits in Srebrenica, and food had to be brought in to feed the population. The town's largest single import, however, was salt; the Srebrenica area had none. And its people also lacked a natural source of iodine in their diet and suffered the physical and psychological effects of thyroid malfunction. Folks for miles around came to call Srebrenica's townspeople *gušnje*, or goiters, and one family up the Drina valley even had Gušo as its surname.

The wealth pouring from Srebrenica's silver mines attracted the attention of covetous kings and feudal strongmen. Between the Ottoman Turk defeat of the Serbs at Kosovo in 1389 and the sultan's conquest of Bosnia in 1463, more than a dozen feudal overlords ruled Srebrenica from its hilltop fortress. Four of these overlords were Bosnian Slavs, three were Turks, one was Hungarian, and five were Serbs, including a despot named Djurdje Branković, whose ambitious, Greek-born wife was named Jerina. Legend has it that the fortress above Srebrenica was built by Jerina the Damned's soldier-slaves with stones held together by a sticky mortar made from milk and egg whites.

Centuries of Ottoman misrule gutted the mining community. The merchants from Dubrovnik wandered away. The German Saxons left behind only a word, Sasi, the name of a village they once inhabited. The Franciscan monastery fell into ruins, and the Roman Catholics either died off, emigrated, or converted to Islam. As the decades dragged on, Orthodox sharecroppers became the Srebrenica area's majority population. Under the leadership of a blacksmith named Kara Marko, or Black Marko, many Orthodox herdsmen and peasants in the Srebrenica area joined the Serbian uprising against the Ottoman Empire in 1804. After the uprising's collapse, Kara Marko fled across the Drina to Serbia and became an outlaw; but to this day, a swath of the Srebrenica district east of town is called Kara Marko's Territory.

Srebrenica's Serb majority shrank in the turmoil of the nineteenth century, when the only real law was the code of blood vengeance. Serbia had become independent of the Ottoman Empire, and Serbs from the Srebrenica area followed Kara Marko's example and emigrated to seek a better life east of the Drina. Many Muslims expelled from Serbia in the 1830s and 1860s migrated into the Srebrenica area and brought with them an animosity toward Serbs that infected many longtime Muslim inhabitants of the area.

❬ ❬ ❬

THE rebel tradition of Kara Marko was taken up in the mid-nineteenth century by Orthodox men whose ancestors had come to the Srebrenica area from Montenegro and settled in a cluster of hamlets that eventually became the Serb village of Kravica. It was a lowly place by any standard, and the century's migrations made Kravica a Serb islet in a Muslim sea. The area's Muslim authorities humiliated Kravica's Serbs by forbidding them to have an Orthodox church that amounted to anything more than a tiny chapel with a clapboard roof and by barring them from opening a school. The Serb sharecroppers in Kravica held on, though. They dreamed of a time when they would own the fields they were working for their Muslim landlords and merge the Srebrenica area into Serbia.

Vaso Erić, a man born into a family of sharecroppers in 1844, became a leader of the Serbs in Kravica after he taught himself to read and write the Cyrillic alphabet with a first-grade primer written by Vuk Karadžić. Vaso and other Serb men from Kravica joined the uprising against Bosnia's feudal landlords in 1875 and pledged their allegiance to Serbia during the war that broke out a year later. When Austria's troops marched into Bosnia in 1878, Vaso was living the life of an outlaw in the Srebrenica area's forests. He returned home to Kravica assuming that life would now improve, that Austria, one of the great, modern European powers, would quickly end Bosnia's obsolete feudal order and redistribute the feudal lands to the sharecroppers tilling them. Kravica's men built themselves a new Orthodox church of stone, brick, and stucco with a proud steeple and a bell. Next to it they built a boarding school, and Vaso enrolled his three sons—Jakov, Jovan, and Mikailo—in classes taught by a priest. Vaso and the other men of Kravica turned against the Austrian authorities when it became clear that there would be no land reform, and thereafter they had as little as possible to do with the Austrian administrators. The village's Serbs took part in uprisings that broke out when Austrian tax collectors showed up in the area. They sold tobacco and smuggled stock animals across the Drina from Serbia in an effort to improve their miserable living conditions. But the Austrians quickly cracked down on the cross-border livestock trade and ordered that all horses and cattle be branded. Border posts and customhouses popped up, and police officers were stationed in Kravica and other troublesome Serb villages.

At age sixty-four, Vaso Erić still had enough fight left in him to harangue against Austria when it annexed Bosnia on October 7, 1908. On that same day, he joined a delegation of Serbs that set out for Budapest to protest the annexation before Emperor Franz Josef. During a meeting with imperial officials in Budapest, Vaso stood up proudly and with a bumpkin's bluntness condemned the emperor's preservation of the rotten feudal order. He lashed out seditiously at Austria's annexation of Bosnia. Knowing that the police would try to arrest him before he left the city, he escaped by stowing away on a riverboat heading down the Danube to Belgrade.

Now a fugitive and unable to return home, Vaso went to work as a customs official at a ferry landing on the Serbian side of the Drina opposite Zvornik. There he met and began collaborating with a Serbian army officer, Captain Kosta Todorović, the man responsible for running networks of Serb secret agents across the border in Austrian-controlled Bosnia. The members of one network worked under the cover of a cultural organization called Narodna Odbrana, or the People's Defense, and their goal was to wrest Bosnia from Austria's control. Narodna Odbrana operated in Kravica through the Serb farmers' co-op. Vaso Erić's son Jakov became Narodna Odbrana's chief agent in the village, and his other sons, Jovan and Mikailo, were also involved. On May 31, 1914, Kosta Todorović's agents in the Narodna Odbrana organization helped smuggle Gavrilo Princip and his pistol across the Drina from Serbia.

The Serb societies Srebrenica and Kravica had made national pride a quasi-religious affair. On national holidays, they held romantic stage re-enactments of scenes from the Battle of Kosovo. Men in national costumes would recite epic poems about the battle as their *gusle* skirled and girls dressed as fairies held wreaths over their heads. On June 28, 1914, the Serbs of Srebrenica and Kravica were dancing the *kolo* in their churchyards, celebrating the Vidovdan anniversary of the battle. In the early afternoon, news arrived that Princip had assassinated Archduke Franz Ferdinand. The merrymaking ended. At about five o'clock, martial law was imposed. Villagers and townsfolk alike went inside their homes. Only policemen and soldiers were out, patrolling the villages, hauling in Serbs believed to be associated with Narodna Odbrana, and questioning them about the assassination.

The Great War began a month later. Even before the Austrian army crossed the Drina into Serbia just north of Srebrenica, Kosta Todorović, by now a major, had taken command of a group of several hundred volunteer soldiers. They crossed the Drina from Bajina Bašta and set about creating havoc for the Austrian army in the Srebrenica area. Major Todorović distributed guns to Serb families living in Kara Marko's Territory and in Kravica and other mountain hollows. His men attacked police stations and garrisons. They burned Muslim villages and killed Muslim civilians and Austrian conscripts, among them Huso Čelik's grandfather, Salih, who had been sent in to tame the area. Todorović captured Srebrenica and the nearby village of Bratunac and held them for a few weeks before the Austrians took him and a number of his men prisoner during a firefight in late September. Todorović, the story goes, was burned alive. The insurgency he organized collapsed. And many men from Kravica fled eastward over the river to join the Serbian army.

The Austrian army looked with suspicion and disdain upon the Serbs left behind in the Srebrenica area. A few dozen Serbs, including some women, were hung without trial. About a hundred more were summarily shot, others sent to concentration camps in Hungary, and entire families expelled across the Drina. The wartime authorities also looked the other way when Hungarian troops and Muslim and Catholic freebooters looted Serb-owned shops and homes and beat up, and sometimes murdered, their owners. Germany, Austria, and Bulgaria finally overwhelmed Serbia in 1915 and drove its army over the mountains of Albania in midwinter. Vaso Erić joined the long march and survived even as thousands of Serbian troops starved to death or died of exposure and attacks by Albanian clansmen. The Austrian military authorities discovered Major Todorović's diary when they occupied the town of Loznica, just downriver from Srebrenica. They deciphered the diary's secret code and arrested over 150 of Todorović's collaborators in Narodna Odbrana and tried them for treason. At age seventy-two, Vaso was sentenced to death in absentia. His three sons were arrested and perished in prison before the war came to an end.

Vaso returned to Kravica a few years after the Great War. He was convinced the Serbs had finally realized the great dream of Karadjordje and Kara Marko. The Ottoman Turks and the Austrians were gone. The entire Serb nation had been united in a single state under a Serbian king. Bosnia's old feudal order had been abolished. The estates of the Muslim landowners had been distributed among the former sharecroppers, though the Srebrenica area's Muslims would never forget it and stashed away Ottoman-era deeds for the fields, forests, and orchards they had once owned. For all its suffering, the Erić family of Kravica obtained a few acres of farmland they could call their own. Vaso's grandchildren, their widowed mothers, and a few of the other menfolk went to work on the land. The peasants, many of them crippled war veterans, struggled to rebuild their lives with few tools and livestock, and many women hiked over the mountain trails to Tuzla to buy salt and carry it home on their backs.

Vaso Erić died in 1932, nine years before Adolf Hitler swung the pendulum back again. A few weeks after the German invasion of Yugoslavia, German and Ustaše troops arrived in Kravica and Srebrenica, where they were welcomed by local Muslims. The Ustaše made their first priority the demolishing of Srebrenica's memorial to Major Kosta Todorović, though one Serb peasant managed to make off with its inscribed slabs of gray polished marble and hide them away somewhere in Kara Marko's Territory. Most of the area's Muslims subsequently enlisted in the Ustaše or the Croatian army, and the Ustaše began patrolling nearby villages, demanding that the Serbs surrender all their weapons and arresting Serb menfolk. The Ustaše closed Kravica's Orthodox church; its priest and schoolteacher were taken into the woods and shot; and its people were saved from a mass execution only when Muslims from a neighboring village intervened.

For the men of Kravica, resisting the Ustaše savagery was more than a matter of honor. On August 8, 1941, two of Vaso Erić's grandsons, Nego and Golub Erić, joined the other village men around the Orthodox church. They tolled its bell defiantly and proclaimed an uprising. Within two weeks, these Serb fighters had linked up with the Chetniks of General Draža Mihailović and taken control of the entire Srebrenica area. The Ustaše then set in motion a brutal cycle of violence by carrying out punitive raids on area Serb villages. In December 1941, Nego and Golub Erić and other Chetniks from Kravica took part in a retaliatory massacre of Muslims in the nearby village of Sopotnik. Some eighty-six people were beaten, knifed, and shot to death, and their bodies were burned up inside their houses. More Ustaše attacks and Chetnik reprisals followed.

From the spring of 1942 to the summer of 1943, there were no Serbs in Kravica. They came back only in June 1943 when Tito's Partisans took Srebrenica after a day-long battle during which the teenage cousin of the town's

Ustaše commander was killed. The Ustaše exacted blood vengeance when they returned three days later. Scores of people were massacred. Among the dead were Marta Vasić, the mother of Dragica Vasić's husband, Veljko, Marta's daughter, Zora, and her five children. Thereafter, the Ustaše went on killing sprees through nearby Serb villages, often in retaliation for acts of resistance by the Chetniks or Partisans. Kravica's turn came on July 3, 1944. At least a hundred Serb civilians were killed, about half of them burned to death in one house.

By then, it was clear that Tito's Communist Partisans of Josip Broz Tito were going to win the war in Yugoslavia. Nego and Golub Erić had abandoned the Chetnik forces and, like many Serbs and Muslims, joined the Partisans' ranks. When the war ended and Nego and Golub came home to Kravica, they buried their German-made machine guns instead of surrendering them to the authorities.

KRAVICA and the other villages in the Srebrenica area remained mired in backwardness for years after the war. The Communists were funneling scarce investment money into predominantly Partisan regions to create jobs for their families and supporters, and there had been too few Partisans from Srebrenica. The area's mines and forests were exploited, but the ores and lumber were hauled away to plants in Serbia and farther afield. Tito, who reveled in pageantry, never took the time to visit, and he clearly had difficulty finding loyalists to run the place. Veljko Vasić was only twenty-two years old when he was named district president a year before he married Dragica. They got to know Golub Erić after he, with his four years of primary schooling, displayed enough loyalty to the Partisan cause to become clerk of the local court. Golub had even gone to testify against General Mihailović before he was sentenced to death and shot by a firing squad. Golub's brother, Nego, stayed home to work the family land.

It was five years before Tito's secret police came to Kravica to arrest the Erić brothers. They confessed to having taken part in the Sopotnik massacre and claimed they had been acting under orders. A few weeks later, a court ordered that they be shot by a firing squad and that all of their family's property, including the land their grandfathers had fought to wrench from the Muslim feudal landlords, be expropriated. The Erić brothers' mother, Andjelija, went to Belgrade and obtained an audience with Tito. She begged him to spare the life of just one of her sons. He responded by asking her why she wanted to save only one of her sons and commuted both of their sentences to life imprisonment. For the next five years, Nego and Golub were held in chains and fed bread in water inside the same Bosnian jail where their uncles Jakov and

Jovan had been starved and beaten by Austrian guards during World War I. Thereafter, the brothers joined a prison work brigade, and Nego learned carpentry and Golub plumbing.

The brothers were pardoned in the mid-1960s, and they re-oiled and re-buried their German-made machine guns when they came home. They told their sons and grandsons they were sure Bosnia would see another war *kad tad*, "sooner or later." But they seemed to harbor no grudge against Tito or the Communists. Golub hung a portrait of Tito in his house just as Huso Čelik had done. At the same time, though, Golub cherished a picture of Grandpa Vaso with his war medals, and he began writing his memoirs and drawing up a family tree.

❨   ❨   ❨

UNTIL the 1970s, the Srebrenica area did not have a single factory for processing the lead, zinc, bauxite, limestone, and timber mined and cut in the surrounding hills. Dragica's husband, Veljko, had retired by the time the investment money started rolling in and Bosnia's Communists began gorging themselves on foreign credits and pouring the money into pork barrel projects run by large conglomerates in Sarajevo. In Potočari, a predominantly Muslim village along the main road between Bratunac and Srebrenica, the Communists built a workshop for refurbishing buses along with a battery factory, a metal-plating plant, and other, smaller enterprises that made use of the zinc and lead, and each year on May 25 the villagers there gathered to celebrate Tito's birthday with a horse race and dancing. Just south of Srebrenica, the village of Zeleni Jadar got itself a furniture factory and a stonecutting workshop. A weaving plant went up in Srebrenica itself. Construction crews built new schools, a hotel and spa, and a department store with a red-brick façade. They laid down an asphalt road that linked Srebrenica with Bratunac to the north and Skelani, a village to the southeast that had a steel-girder bridge over the Drina to Bajina Bašta.

All of the factories and mines overhired, and only some of them turned a profit. The people who lived in town and reaped most of the benefits from these investments—much of it by financial sleight of hand—got along well while the money was flowing. They stopped taking note of who was a Muslim or who was a Serb. Mixed marriages, like the one between Dragica's son, Boban, and his Muslim wife, Bera, became commonplace. Even in the outlying villages, people seemed to be getting along well despite the prevailing backwardness, especially among the Muslim peasants, some of whom were still refusing to send their daughters to school even into the 1980s. Most of the memories of World War II had been submerged, but outcroppings of the old enmities and the old jealousies surfaced during squabbles over who would be chosen to fill a sought-after job opening, which family would be allocated a new apartment in town, and whose teenage son or daughter would get a stipend to study at the university in Sarajevo.

With Yugoslavia's economic collapse and the end of the Communists' monopoly on political and economic power, most ordinary people in the Srebrenica area transferred their loyalty to the new Muslim and Serb nationalist parties in a desperate bid to safeguard their jobs and their futures. The Srebrenica area's predominantly Muslim population secured Alija Izetbegović's Party for Democratic Action majorities on local councils; the minority Serbs voted for Radovan Karadžić's Serbian Democratic Party. The local party leaders now struggled for control of the Srebrenica area's economic assets, and their struggle exacerbated relations between the Muslim and Serb communities.

The Serb party leaders immediately began complaining that their council representatives were being outvoted on all key political issues. But it was the economic questions that cut to the quick. With their majority in the local assemblies, the Muslim party leaders could, by law, begin interfering in the management of local enterprises just as the Communist Party bosses had always done. Redundant workers were going to be laid off, and it was easy for Serb party leaders to convince Serb workers that they would be getting pink slips from the mines and factories run by Muslim party loyalists. Since the courts were all corrupt and there were no other jobs anywhere for miles around, laid-off men would have no other option than to leave the area and abandon to their aged parents the homes in which many of them had invested their life savings. Moreover, capitalism would soon be replacing Tito's socialist economic system. Practically all of the socially owned property—the Srebrenica area's factories, mines, hotels, and apartments—would somehow be transformed into private property. Since the Muslim party controlled the government, the Serbs concluded that the Muslims would have the inside track on deciding who would get the deeds.

Muslim party leaders in Srebrenica and other area towns quickly started griping that the Serbs in the nearby village of Milići were hogging the profits from a huge open-pit bauxite mine. A bauxite company based in Milići and run by a Serb had made the lot of money exporting its output to Russia, Germany, and Czechoslovakia, and in the late 1970s its primary customer became the large alumina plant that had been built at Zvornik. The bauxite company had constructed more than a thousand apartments for its employees in Milići over the years, and almost all of them had gone to Serbs. The company had also built a cultural center in Milići, along with nurseries and schools and health care facilities and an outdoor swimming pool unmatched practically anywhere else in Bosnia, and these were being enjoyed almost exclusively by the Serbs of Milići. Now, the Muslims complained, the time had come for a change. Since World War II, the bauxite mine had been socially owned property, the property of every member of society, and, as Muslims tended to see it, most members of society for miles around Milići were Muslim. Muslim leaders demanded that Muslims now make up the majority of bauxite mine's workforce. They charged that the mine's director, Rajko Dukić, had embezzled company funds for personal gain. They alleged that Dukić had financed the entire Serbian Democratic Party to secure himself a top party position. The Serbs protested to the government and the Yugoslav army that Muslim party leaders were trying to use the tyranny of the majority to usurp control of the bauxite company and to deprive the Serbs of their livelihood and force them to abandon their homes.

❨   ❨   ❨

SREBRENICA'S Muslim and Serb communities had begun arming themselves by early 1991. When war broke out in Croatia that summer, Serbia imposed an economic blockade on Bosnia. Store shelves in the Srebrenica area emptied. The gas stations ran out of fuel. Raw-material deliveries to the factories were halted. Workers were laid off without pay. The news reports on Milošević's television whipped the Serbs of Srebrenica, Kravica, Milići, and the other area villages into fits of hysteria with footage of the Croatian World War II dictator Ante Pavelić and Adolf Hitler superimposed on pictures of Franjo Tudjman and Chancellor Helmut Kohl. Here were pictures of Serb soldiers and tank crews being cheered by frenzied crowds as they rolled through Belgrade on their way to bomb the Croatian town of Vukovar into oblivion. Srebrenica's Serbs, like anybody else driven by fear in uncertain times, saw what they wanted to see and believed what they wanted to believe. Before their eyes, Nego and Golub Erić and other Serb men saw a reborn Ustaše Croatia supported by a reborn Nazi Germany. The television imagery convinced them that another round of Ustaše butchery was just over the horizon.

The Yugoslav army was eager to mobilize Bosnian Serbs and Muslims and hustle them to the front lines in Croatia. In late August 1991, thirty soldiers arrived in Bratunac to take custody of the town's draft records. Local Muslim officials, following instructions from Izetbegović in Sarajevo, refused to hand them over. The Muslim men of Bratunac, they said, should not have to fight a war of conquest for Chetniks. This infuriated the local Serbs. The next evening, the leaders of the Serbian Democratic Party's chapter in Bratunac stomped into the town hall and demanded the draft files. The Muslim officials stood defiant. Several thousand Muslim men gathered outside the town hall and soon found themselves facing off against as many Serbs. Muslim police officers sided with the Muslim mob; Serb police officers sided with the Serb mob; and the Yugoslav army rushed in reinforcements. The two mobs exchanged curses and threats. They pointed guns at one another and fired into the air. The army's commanders backed down before a riot broke out. They withdrew their soldiers across the river and into Serbia. The draft records stayed with the Muslim authorities in Bratunac.

From that day on, Muslim and Serb peasants began standing guard around Kravica and the other villages near Srebrenica and Bratunac. Men from both communities left their jobs in Sarajevo, Serbia, and abroad to return home to take up arms and defend their families and protect their homes. Serbs were afraid to drive their cars through Muslim villages. Muslims knew to be especially careful when traveling through Kravica. By now, Nego and Golub Erić had already dug up their World War II–vintage machine guns.

Only four days after the draft-records incident, four Muslim men piled into a compact car and speeded through Kravica waving an Islamic green flag out the window. The car was sprayed with bullets, and two of the Muslims were killed. Another Muslim mob gathered outside the Bratunac police station. Hysteria gripped Kravica. The menfolk grabbed their guns, took up positions around the village, and sent their women and children fleeing along a goat path to the Drina and across the river to Serbia in boats. The Bosnian police quickly named two Serbs in connection with the killings, one from Kravica and the other from Serbia. Neither was arrested, but both admitted later that they had taken part in the ambush. Muslim and Serb politicians descended on Bratunac. Muslim leaders met with a crowd of their supporters at the town's football field and announced that they would dispatch police officers to reinforce the district police. The Serbs complained that the new police were all Muslims trained by the hated Croatian army; Radovan Karadžić declared that the Serbs would not allow the Muslim police to conduct any investigation in Kravica.

The Srebrenica area grew only more volatile near the end of March 1992 with the attack on Bijeljina by Ražnatović's gang and the declaration by Milići's leaders that they had formed an independent Serb district whose boundaries would encompass the bauxite pit and most of the mining company's other assets. The Drina River road from Srebrenica to Zvornik was still open on April 6, the day when Bosnia was recognized as an independent country. A vanload of Muslims who had undergone physical therapy at Srebrenica's health spa had to be driven home to Zvornik. Dragica Vasić's son, Boban, took on the task. He would have been home in two hours if Ražnatović's men had not pulled them over at a checkpoint. Dragica told the Čeliks that the gang members led away the Muslims and beat Boban. They held him for three days, questioning him why he had married a Muslim women and why he was transporting Muslim men wrapped in bandages. Finally sent across the Drina into Serbia, Boban phoned Dragica and his wife from his aunt's house. He told them to get out of Srebrenica.

WHEN word spread of the massacre of Muslims in Zvornik by Ražnatović's gang and police troops from Serbia, the Srebrenica area's Muslim and Serb peasants redoubled the guard around their villages. There was shooting into the air every night. Barricades were set up on the main roads.

On April 8, Serb party leaders demanded that the police forces in Srebrenica and Bratunac be divided along national lines. The local Muslim leaders agreed, and a Serb from Kravica became the chief of the Serb police in Bratunac. On April 12, Serb leaders demanded the creation of a Balkan-style apartheid: the partition of the Srebrenica district and the dividing up of all the assets of the local enterprises. Goran Zekić, the leader of the Serbian Democratic Party in Srebrenica, notified Muslim leaders that he had received instructions from Radovan Karadžić that the Serbs were to respect only the laws of the rebel "republic" Karadžić and other Serb leaders had declared in Bosnia. The Muslim leaders, in an effort to hold off an outbreak of open warfare, accepted the Serb leaders' demand for the district's division, including partition of the town of Srebrenica. A meeting of the local council was called for April 13 to vote on the matter. A working group of Muslim leaders was formed to draw boundary lines on the map. A crowd of ordinary people gathered outside Srebrenica's town hall just before the meeting was scheduled to begin. They cheered and applauded. They were ready to accept any deal that might forestall war. Zekić and the other Serb leaders did not show up.

Townspeople from Srebrenica, Muslims and Serbs alike, packed up and abandoned their homes in droves that day. In Bratunac, Yugoslav army tanks and armored transporters rumbled through the streets. Members of Ražnatović's gang and mobilized local Serbs began abducting Muslim men suspected of dealing guns and organizing a Muslim militia. One day a pharmacist disappeared. The next day, a police detective. Then a factory foreman. The former police chief. A mine manager. After dark, witnesses heard screams coming from a primary school in the center of town and from a garage on the school grounds. The Serbian Democratic Party's leaders had set up a drumhead court in the school and appointed a local doctor to preside over it. The pharmacist was found to have sent bandages and other medical supplies to Muslims in the hills; he was sentenced to death. The police chief and factory foreman had shown up on a video taken of the mob outside the town hall when the army came looking for the draft records; they were sentenced to death.

On April 17, Serbian Democratic Party leaders delivered an ultimatum to Srebrenica's Muslims. Now there would be no division of the town. Srebrenica had once had a Serb majority. Now it was going to be a Serb town. The Muslims were given until eight o'clock the next morning to hand over their weapons. The Muslim exodus from the town now turned into a panicked flight. Whole families crowded into cars and outbound buses and sped down the asphalt road to Bratunac and on to Sarajevo or Tuzla or, if they could, out of the country. Away ran the town's Muslim leadership, the district president, the head of the national guard, two parliamentary representatives, the head of the health clinic, the president of the local court, the enterprise directors. Dragica's daughter-in-law, Bera, packed up her kids and left to join Boban in Serbia. But Dragica refused to run. She did not want to abandon to fate the house Veljko had built her on the hillside overlooking Srebrenica. She had lived in this house alone since Veljko had died, and all the town had turned out for his funeral. She would stay in it now, alone, and wait out the storm.

AT ten o'clock in the morning on April 18, the nationalist Serbs took the town of Srebrenica without firing a shot. Goran Zekić drove in from Bratunac escorted by armed men, including members of Ražnatović's gang. Muslim peasants and townspeople on nearby hillsides watched through the trees as the Serbs set about looting and burning Muslim homes, stores, and workshops.

One of these Muslims was a burly, twenty-five-year-old man from Potočari. His name was Naser Orić, and surrender was the last thing on his mind. The Orić family had lived in the hills above Srebrenica for generations. Naser Orić's grandfather had been a member of the Ustaše during World War II, but the family stayed in Potočari when the Communists arrived. Orić had grown to be a brawny teenager. He enjoyed karate and weightlifting. When he graduated from high school with a certificate in metalworking, he realized that he had no employment prospects at home. So in 1988, after his stint in the Yugoslav army, he made the two-hour drive to Belgrade and found work as a bouncer in a disco.

Soon he enlisted in the special-police unit that Milošević had assembled to repress the Albanian majority in Kosovo. The young Muslim was in Milošević's bodyguard when the Serbian president warned of a coming war in his speech at the anniversary of the Battle of Kosovo in June 1989. When the war in Croatia erupted, Orić returned to Bosnia rather than join the Serbian paramilitary troops who took part in the destruction of Vukovar. He became a police officer in Ilidža, a suburb of Sarajevo. Within a few weeks, the Muslim police authorities had sent Orić home to Potočari to begin organizing a local militia that was kept a secret even from most Muslims. At first, it was not much of a military outfit, a few men armed with hunting rifles, some smuggled guns, and a number of automatics pilfered from Srebrenica's police arsenal. But Orić and his officers trained their men in some basics of guerrilla warfare: how to slit an unsuspecting soldier's throat, how to disable tanks with Molotov cocktails, how to lay an ambush.

Word of the disappearances of Muslims in Bratunac spread to the Muslim villagers around Srebrenica. Orić and the other men knew that if they did nothing, their expulsion would only be a matter of time. On the morning of April 20, members of Ražnatović's gang and local Serb gunmen invaded Muslim villages near Bratunac and demanded weapons. Orić got word that a group of Ražnatović's men had entered Srebrenica and begun a looting spree. At about one o'clock that afternoon, these gang members were speeding out of the town in a small convoy of police cars, a van, and a couple of Volkswagens. As they raced into Potočari, a truck trailer was backed across the narrow asphalt road in front of them. The lead car squeezed by. But the rest of the vehicles slammed on their brakes and skidded into one another nose to tail. A second truck pulled across the road behind them as the Muslims opened fire. Half a dozen of the Serb militiamen were killed.

Revenge was not long in coming. On May 2, Serb troops collected weapons in a Muslim village next to Glogova. The following day, they returned and burned forty-three Muslim houses, killed thirteen people, including a five-year-old girl, and sent the rest of the villagers fleeing through the woods toward Potočari and Tuzla. Four days later, the Muslims struck back. They demanded weapons from the Serb hamlet of Gniona and opened fire when the Serbs there took to the woods; one of them, an old peasant with bad eyesight who had gotten drunk at a party that day, was burned up in his house. Then, on the evening of May 8, a Muslim college student fired a bullet into Goran Zekić's head as he was being driven in a car through the mountains from Srebrenica to Bratunac. Not knowing that the Serb party leader was already dead, the Muslim student tried to toss a hand grenade through the window of his car. The grenade bounced off, exploded, and killed the Muslim. Zekić's assassination panicked the Serbs left in Srebrenica. Serb soldiers made a house-by-house search of the town, killing Muslim stragglers, setting fire to houses and stories, rousting out Serbs, and ordering them to flee to Bratunac. Dragica Vasić hid in her basement during the chaos. With her was her best friend, a Muslim woman named Fadila Omerović. By the end of the day, only a few dozen Serbs were left in the town.

The following morning, gangs of Serb militiamen and the Red Beret police troops from Serbia poured into Bosnia across the bridge over the Drina at Bajina Bašta and burned all the Muslim villages on the left bank of the river upstream as far as the hydroelectric dam. Serbs from Kravica marched into Glogova, herded away the women and children, and executed as many of the men as they could find; witnesses place Golub Erić among the Kravica Serbs who guarded Muslim prisoners taken from Glogova and later executed.

In Bratunac, where no Muslim had as yet fired a shot, Serb soldiers went through the streets with megaphones ordering the Muslims to come out of their homes. Columns of men, women, and children wound their way through the town and were herded into its soccer stadium. Babies cried. Guard dogs barked. There were explosions and gun bursts in the hills. Serbs in civilian dress worked their way through the crowd in the stadium for much of the day. They urged the people to be calm. They told them they would only be required to sign loyalty oaths. At five in the afternoon, men with megaphones ordered the Muslims to move out of the stadium through its main gate. Outside, the Muslim men were separated from their wives and children. The air became a din of voices calling out names. Women and children cried. Men who tried to linger with their families were beaten with clubs and metal bars. The women and children were packed aboard buses and trucks and driven over the mountains to Tišće, a mountain village where the Yugoslav army had set up a tank battalion. From there, they were forced to walk along an asphalt road to Muslim-controlled territory.

The Serbs ordered the 750 Muslim men left behind in Bratunac to line up in rows of four and march down the main street. One of these Muslims was Mustafa Mujkanović, the young father of two children and the cousin of two Muslim women who used to run around Belgrade with my wife, Ljiljana, when they were college students. Their grandfather had been the first district president of Bratunac after World War I; and in 1992, Mustafa was the *hodža* of the mosque in Bratunac. He walked out of the column as it was being marched down Bratunac's main street and approached Miroslav Deronjić, the head of the town's Serbian Democratic Party.

"What is going on here?" Mustafa asked. "Where are you leading us?"

The Serb leader glowered at the guards who had allowed the *hodža* to step from the column. "Don't worry, *hodža*," Deronjić said. "You're heading for a safe place."

The Muslims were marched to the yard of the primary school and told to kneel. Some of the men were beaten with wooden bats and electrical cables. Then they were lined up, two-by-two, and marched into the gymnasium. The nets were missing from the basketball hoops. On the parquet floor, the red paint of the out-of-bounds lines had worn away. Money and identity cards were collected, and then some more of the men were beaten.

"Why didn't you tell us you have a *hodža* among you?" one of the Serbs barked. "Give us the *hodža*! We want the *hodža*!"

Mustafa Mujkanović stood up. Mustafa had never really been a community leader. He was a village boy who wanted to live in town. He had enrolled in the Islamic religious school in Sarajevo only because his grandfather had promised to build him a house in town if he graduated. Mustafa did not want to be the *hodža* in Bratunac, either. He was shy and felt uncomfortable being an authority figure among people he had grown up with.

The prisoners cleared Mustafa a path as he walked forward. Everyone in the room saw what happened next, and the stories the survivors tell are virtually identical.

"Say something, *hodža*!" a guard barked. He grabbed one of the climbing ropes hanging from the ceiling and told Mustafa to climb. "Come on, *hodža*, up! Let's go!"

When Mustafa had pulled himself to the ceiling, the Serb yanked the rope back and forth as if he were ringing in a Christian victory over the Turks of old.

"Hey, *hodža*, you're swinging like a churchbell! You can swing like a churchbell! Hahaha!"

The other guards laughed as Mustafa eased himself down.

"Who told you to come down?"

The guard who had been swinging the rope let loose with the first blows. Two more soldiers rushed up to join in. Mustafa did not defend himself.

"Hey, *hodža*, fuck your wife!"

More blows fell. Mustafa raised his hand as if to straighten his dark-brown hair.

"Hey, *hodža*, drink!"

A guard handed him a bottle of beer.

"Drink!"

Mustafa clamped his lips shut as the guard began pouring the beer over his head. The beer streamed over his face and dripped from his chin onto the floor until he pushed the bottle away. It fell to the floor with a thud. Foam sloshed over the basketball court. Mustafa was beaten again, and a guard demanded that the clergyman raise the three fingers that pious Orthodox Christians use to make the sign of the cross.

"Three fingers, *hodža*!"

Mustafa raised his hand in the V sign. Five men went at him with clubs and metal bars.

Again, two fingers.

The hall was silent except for the screeches of the outraged Serbs and the thuds of their blows. A man with a blue beret and a police badge pulled a knife from his belt and thrust it into the back of Mustafa's neck. The *hodža* collapsed onto the parquet. A few seconds later his body twitched. A man in a black uniform approached the bleeding *hodža*. He drew a pistol, put it to Mustafa's head, and fired a shot. Witnesses identified the gunman as Brane Topalović, a Serb who still lives in a town northwest of Belgrade; he later told some of the other prisoners that he was being paid three hundred dollars for every Muslim he killed.*

Mustafa lay dead on the basketball court. Topalović and the other guards stepped to a corner of the gymnasium and guzzled beer. One of them ordered a prisoner to drag Mustafa's body out the door. The prisoner did so. In a garage behind the school, he saw stacks of corpses of Muslim men who had been abducted in Bratunac. Within three days, there would be 350 more. The dead were eventually loaded aboard trucks and dumped into the Drina.

Four hundred and two Muslims held in the school were released a week later. As they were being led into Muslim territory north of Sarajevo, the Serb authorities announced that these Muslims of Bratunac, men who had never fired a shot, were responsible for the deaths of two thousand Serbs. Radio Belgrade reported that dozens of corpses had floated down the Drina from Bratunac to the hydroelectric dam at Zvornik and that these were the bodies of dead Serbs.

It took only hours for the Muslims in Srebrenica to hear about the killings in the gymnasium in Bratunac. Witnesses came through the forests with stories of the executions in Glogova and the attack from Serbia on the Muslim villages below the Bajina Bašta dam. These attacks accelerated a cycle of violence that the Serbs were unable to control. Naser Orić and his men now knew they were practically surrounded. They saw what would await them if they ever surrendered.

Over the summer, Orić's militia grew into a fighting force of several hundred peasant men from the villages around Srebrenica as well as vengeance-driven refugees from Zvornik, Bratunac, Višegrad, and other districts. They were prepared to raid any village in the area. They attacked and ambushed without warning and killed without mercy whoever got between them and the weapons they needed to fight on. They took only a handful of prisoners and rarely made any distinction between combatants and civilians. Orić brooked no opposition. Martial law was declared in Srebrenica, and political life was suspended. Over the summer, the leader of a rival Muslim party,

*The account of the slaying of Mustafa Mujkanovic´ is drawn from the book *Satanski sinovi* by Sejo Omeragić. It was corroborated by interviews.

Nurif Rizvanović, infiltrated into Srebrenica from Tuzla with several hundred fighters; he was reportedly arrested and killed.

Many Serb villages in the Srebrenica area were protected by only a few young men and some elderly peasants who were not willing or able to fight for anything except their homes and fields. Some villages fell to the Muslims quickly. Others, like Kravica, held out. The Erić family had eighteen members when the war started, and all ten of the men went into the trenches. Golub Erić, the honorary commander of Kravica's fighters, died on May 29, 1992, with family members at his side, during a firefight with Muslims from the village whose menfolk had saved the Serbs of Kravica from the Ustaše during World War II. Golub's seventeen-year-old grandson, Mihailo, was wounded a few days later by a bullet that cut through his temple and came out the front of his head.

On July 12, the Muslims seized a hilltop north of Srebrenica from which the Serb spotters had gazed down into the town and hammered it with mortar fire. Srebrenica's eighty-bed health clinic reopened later that same day, and a team of doctors with no experience in surgery began operating on the wounded. Within weeks, the Muslims controlled half of the Srebrenica district. By the autumn, three or four hundred Serb soldiers and dozens of civilians had perished in the Muslim reprisals. Punitive Serb air attacks and bombardments by Yugoslav army howitzers set up on the western wall of Mount Zvijezda and other positions across the Drina only made the Muslims more desperate and determined.

Then came the Čeliks and thousands more refugees from Žepa, and with them came the hunger.

14

BY the time the Čeliks had trudged into Srebrenica, refugee men had to pay to enlist in Naser Orić's militia. Weapons were still scarce, and there was an overabundance of volunteers because soldiers got first pick of the food and the plunder from captured Serb villages.

Paja was drafted into a work brigade. He reported for duty every third night, rain or shine. Month after month, the men in the brigade toiled away at a network of trenches along the front line. They chopped down trees. They built earth, stone, and log bunkers. The workers were paid in food, but the rations shrank as winter drew closer. Even in peacetime, Srebrenica had never produced enough food to feed its people. Most of the district's fertile soil lies in a thin strip of bottomland beside the Drina, and in September 1992 the Serbs held it. Only some of the Muslim peasants at home in the hills above Srebrenica had been able to plant and harvest their gardens and fields. The refugees in town, who already outnumbered the original population, were left with next to nothing.

Western leaders had promised at the London conference that there would be deliveries of food and other aid to Bosnia's endangered people. But Serb commanders refused to grant aid convoys safe passage into Goražde, Žepa, or Srebrenica. The UN concentrated on feeding Sarajevo and other comparatively easy-to-reach areas within range of the television cameras. When Bosnia's government went public with complaints that no food was reaching the refugees in the Drina valley, UN officials and peace negotiators grumbled that the government was "exploiting" the food problem for military and political ends. Little improved even when the troops from France, Great Britain, and the other European countries showed up and began escorting the aid convoys.

A FEW hundred refugees from Mount Zvijezda had made it to Srebrenica. Aunt Latifa and Uncle Ismet Cavkusić were among them. Saliha and her son Avdo had come with the Čeliks. The Kozić boys—Deba, Bedzi, and Dzemal—found a place to live in a village down by the Drina and got themselves into Orić's army. Even Behadil had made it, and the mountain boys sometimes asked where he was keeping his cannon now.

The Čeliks were among the more fortunate refugees. They had at least something to start with when they moved into the house at no. 8 Rudarska. They brought with them ten blankets and a few sponge pads, some clothes, twenty pounds of wheat flour and forty-five pounds of unmilled corn, a wad of German marks worth about a $130, and Paja's pair of oxen. These assets were divided among ten people: Huso and Hiba; Sanela, Paja, Zlatija, and young Mirza; Saliha and her son Avdo; and Senad Sućeska and his mother, Dževahira. Since there were not enough sponge pads to go around, all of them crowded into one room. The women shared the housework and the cooking. Paja, Senad, and Avdo went in search of food. Huso and little Mirza stayed at home. Huso had long since run out of medicine for his heart condition. His calves swelled and turned purple, and a skin rash broke out on his legs. He spread boiled-down plum mash on it until Hiba came across a tube of some kind of ointment buried somewhere inside the house. Huso rubbed it into the rash, and it worked.

On most days, Paja and Senad chopped wood to lay in for the winter and took the oxen to graze in a meadow an hour's walk out of town. There was a lot of money to be made in firewood, and fights broke out between the refugees and local peasants over the right to cut trees in public forests around the town. Grazing also presented problems. The locals pointed out meadows that had belonged to the departed Serbs, but they were soon overgrazed. Srebrenica's locals grew angry because refugees were stealing whatever they could from whomever they could. Night after night, groups of refugees slipped through the porous Serb lines around the town and stole food from the Serbs' barns, corncribs, and cellars. One group had crawled into a wheat field just outside Bratunac in late summer. Quietly, these refugees used paper scissors to snip off all the spikes of grain, and the next morning the farmer awoke to find amber waves of beheaded stalks.

PAJA was grazing the oxen on the day Naser Orić discovered that he could exploit the desperation of Srebrenica's refugees to his military advantage. Orić knew that the Serb lines around the enclave were lightly manned and that the Serbs were depending on punitive artillery and air attacks to deter Muslim assaults. By September, his men had captured enough weapons to arm several thousand fighters, and he could pull away enough men from his perimeter defenses to muster a mobile attack force of about a thousand troops. Moreover, Orić could now count on a force that struck the fear of God into the Serb peasants living around the Srebrenica enclave: a horde of Muslim refugees, men and women, young and old, who were driven by hunger and, in many cases, a thirst for revenge. Thousands strong, these people would lurk behind the first wave of attacking soldiers and run amok when the defenses around Serb villages collapsed. Some of the refugees used pistols to do the killing; others used knives, bats, and hatchets. But most of them had nothing but their bare hands and the empty rucksacks and suitcases they strapped onto their backs. They came to be known as *torbari*, the bag people. And they were beyond Orić's control.

In late September, Orić and Žepa's commander, Avdo Palić, amassed their forces around Podravanje, a Serb village that controls a rich bauxite pit and straddles the ancient caravan route between Srebrenica and Žepa. Serb fighters in Podravanje had been drawing Muslim blood since the beginning of the war. They had not forgotten that the Austrian army, which included many local Muslims, had burned their village in 1914 and that the Ustaše, who also included many Muslims from neighboring villages, had killed over 250 Serbs and burned the place in 1942 and 1943. Podravanje's Serbs had been firing mortars and tank cannons into Srebrenica and nearby Muslim hamlets for months and had been ambushing Muslims hiking between Žepa and Srebrenica, just as their ancestors had done in the summer of 1943 when Naza Čelik, Huso's grandmother, was killed there. Now Orić wanted to drive the Serbs out and free the mountain trail between Srebrenica and Žepa.

At six o'clock in the morning on September 24, 1992, Muslim soldiers opened fire on Podravanje from three sides. The Serbs tried to defend the village but panicked and ran when they realized how grossly outnumbered they were and how quickly the Muslims were coming at them. The Serb fighters left behind men and women who had been wounded and killed by Muslim gunfire. Then the *torbari* rushed in. Muslim men shot the wounded. They fired their guns into the bodies of the Serb dead. They plunged knives into their stomachs and chests. They smashed their heads with axes and clubs, and they burned the bodies inside buildings. Orić's men grabbed half a dozen prisoners; one, a fighter from Serbia who had relatives in Podravanje, was beaten to death, and the others emerged bruised and battered when they were exchanged a month later. The Muslim forces also captured two tanks, infantry weapons, mortars, trucks, gasoline and diesel fuel, and enough livestock to start a small farm to produce meat for the troops. The *torbari* plundered everything else.

Paja grew angry at himself as he watched the men and women stream back into Srebrenica, bent over under the weight of rucksacks stuffed with meat, potatoes, flour, beans, and salt. Down the mountain into town came blankets, mattresses, clothing, canisters of gasoline, and farm tools. Paja had known that the attack was coming—everyone in Srebrenica had known the attack was coming—but he had been afraid to go. Paja had never before seen a Muslim attack that had ended in anything but retreat and confusion.

Srebrenica suffered days of rocket attacks from MiG fighter jets as punishment for the sacking of Podravanje. One rocket exploded below Dragica's place. The concussion shattered all the windows in the neighborhood and lifted the roof tiles from the Čeliks' house. The front door flew from its hinges and landed on top of Hiba and Mirza, and plaster dust from the ceiling turned their faces gray. From then on, Mirza could hear the engines of approaching fighter jets before anyone else in the family; his face would freeze, and he would run for cover, shouting, "*Ioni! Ioni!* Airpwains! Airpwains!"

The Čeliks' wheat flour and cornmeal gave out a few weeks after the plundering of Podravanje. Hiba picked the apples left on the tree in front of the house, carried them to the town market, and brought them back again because no one was willing to give anything for apples yet. Paja had little choice but to kill one of the oxen, Balja. It took a few hours to butcher the carcass. Balja gave the Čeliks more than 440 pounds of meat. There was no refrigerator or salt, so they roasted some of the meat right away, gave some to Dragica, and carried the rest to the center of town in pans Dragica had lent Hiba. They exchanged the meat for flour, sugar, beans, and washing powder. The last of the laundry detergent from Kupusovići had given out a few weeks before, and the women had returned to the age-old method of washing clothes using potash stirred into boiling water.

About twenty days later, nothing was left of the food. Soon there would be nowhere to graze Šaronja, so they slaughtered him as well. Again Hiba borrowed Dragica's pans and carried the meat from Šaronja down to the market to trade for flour and unmilled corn. Then Paja sold a hundred pounds of the corn for about $200 worth of German marks. His original plan was to hold the money in reserve in case he needed to buy food for Mirza. It was Huso who spotted the opportunity to speculate in tobacco. The peasants around Srebrenica had been growing tobacco for as long as anyone could remember, and practically every adult in eastern Bosnia is a chain-smoker. Huso heard that a peasant on a mountain about half a day's walk from town was selling seven pounds of his dried tobacco for about $200. Paja took his money, bought the tobacco, and carried it back to Srebrenica. He traded it for over eight hundred pounds of wheat flour, sold the flour for about $2,000, and went looking for more tobacco. Paja's career as an arbitrageur lasted only a few weeks, until the price differential closed and the cost of tobacco and flour shot up so high that he did not have enough to invest anymore.

ONLY a few weeks after the Podravanje attack, the refugees in Srebrenica were demanding that Naser Orić launch another attack. The *torbari* were risking their lives to infiltrate the Serb lines anyway. Serb peasants fighting to save their crops had begun ambushing them, laying mines in the cornfields, and booby-trapping the corncribs and potato cellars with hand grenades tied to trip wires. Military operations, attacking the Serbs with overwhelming numbers, reduced the risks the *torbari* were taking in their struggle to feed themselves and their families.

Orić's next big attack came on October 5 against the Serb villages in the Drina bottomland near a stream called Grabovačka Rijeka. Again the Muslims mustered overwhelming numbers of soldiers who were followed by the *torbari* horde. Again the Serbs panicked. Again the stragglers were killed and their bodies mutilated. Again Orić's men captured weapons, and the *torbari* streamed back to Srebrenica with bags stuffed with food. This time, Paja and Senad were among them.

IN the late fall, the Bosnian government began pressing the UN to get food convoys into eastern Bosnia. Weeks had passed since the arrival of the UN military force that was supposed to escort the food to keep the Bosnians alive until the peace negotiators could come up with some plan for settling the war. Negotiations to get regular food deliveries into eastern Bosnia went nowhere. Serb political and military leaders did not want to strengthen the Muslims they sought to drive from the Drina valley, and local Serbs around Srebrenica were furious at the plundering raids by Orić's troops and the *torbari*.

It took until November 28 for the first food shipment to reach Srebrenica. The Serb leadership gave the convoy permission to pass only after UN officials broke their own rules and threatened to cut off aid deliveries to Serb refugees elsewhere in Bosnia. Local Serbs from Bratunac and nearby villages blocked the convoy's progress for three more days before finally caving in. Serbs lined the asphalt road through Bratunac in silence as the convoy rolled toward Srebrenica. When the column of trucks crossed into Muslim-controlled territory, thousands of Muslims rushed to greet the trucks and the foreign reporters. Orić gave interviews and talked about a "dirty war." Local doctors said that more than three hundred people had died in the health clinic for lack of medicines and that over a hundred operations, including sixty amputations, had been performed without anesthetic. The hospital staff was stunned when they heard UN officials say the convoy did not include any medical supplies, because there had been an "oversight."

The forty tons of food brought on the convoy lasted a couple of weeks. Now the high command of the Bosnian army joined the *torbari* in calling on Naser Orić to mount more attacks. The *torbari* wanted food. Orić's superiors in Sarajevo wanted him to create havoc and tie down Serb forces while the Bosnian army launched an offensive north of Tuzla.

A freezing rain was falling on the Drina basin before dawn on December 14. Mist rose over the fields spread out on the bottomland. The Serb peasants in Loznička Rijeka, a cluster of riverside villages, assumed the weather would safeguard them for the day. They had not noticed the Muslim commandos who had infiltrated behind their defense lines and dug in along the Drina's banks. The attack came just after dawn along a line that meandered for twenty-five miles to the north. The Serbs, caught completely off guard, waged war from the windows of their houses. Women picked up automatics and blasted away. Villagers scurried toward the river and were pinned down on the bank. Muslims cut many of them down at almost point-blank range as they tried to cross the river in panic. About 130 Serbs had been living in Loznička Rijeka, and by midnight a quarter of them had been killed. Scores more Serbs had perished in the villages to the north. The Muslims had seized about forty square miles of territory and suddenly found themselves at the southern fringe of Bratunac itself. Paja and Senad were among the *torbari* at Loznička Rijeka. They got out quickly with bags stuffed with unshucked corn and had reached the safety of a woods before Serb crop dusters began dropping mortar rounds onto a trail choked with *torbari* moving in both directions, like regiments of worker ants.

The crop dusters dropped bombs on Srebrenica for the next four days. Dragica Vasić was at home and about to take an afternoon nap on the last day when her friend Fadila dropped by for coffee. The women sat in the warmth of a coal fire and chatted until about three o'clock, when Fadila got up to leave. As they were standing on a porch outside the house, Fadila heard the sound of an airplane engine. "Get down!" she shouted. The women jumped from the porch and dove into the basement of the next building. The crop duster dropped four mortar rounds. The first tore through the roof of Dragica's house, destroying everything in the room where Dragica and Fadila had been drinking coffee. Smoke and dust poured from the windows. Huso ran down the hill and stopped outside the house. "Auntie Dragica!" everyone shouted. "Auntie Dragica!" Huso started crying. Then he saw Dragica climb out of the basement. He grabbed her and hugged her as she cried for the house that Veljko had built her. "Thank God, I didn't take you into my home," she told Huso. "Thank God, I didn't take you in."

"Fuck that house," Huso said. "You're alive. You're alive."

Dragica went inside. Gray plaster dust covered a pile of rubble in the sitting room. They found a second bomb inside. It was Russian made and had bounced on the cushion of her couch and failed to explode. Dragica told Huso that she needed some place to store her furniture now that the house had a hole in its roof. She offered to give the Čeliks whatever they wanted. "Take it all," she said. "Take it all."

They took a set of shelves and a bed.

❨   ❨   ❨

THE Eastern Orthodox Serbs still use the Julian calendar to mark their holidays, and Orthodox Christmas Day in 1993 fell on January 7. Christmas is a high holy day for the Serbs, a national as much as a religious occasion. It is celebrated with customs that date back to the Serbs' pagan past and enhance the sense of uniqueness that they have fought for centuries to preserve. On the night of Orthodox Christmas Eve, Serb men in some areas sit outside, drink brandy, and tend a fire under the thick trunk of a felled tree. The next morning, the oldest son of each household waves a handful of oak branches and straw in each room of the house.

The few women left in Kravica in January 1993 had worked all of Christmas Eve preparing their cakes, salads, bread, and meat despite a sense of gloom that had settled over the village during the holiday season. Two weeks before

Christmas, Orić's men had recaptured neighboring Glogova, the overwhelmingly Muslim village that had been burned and emptied of its residents by Kravica's Serbs in the opening days of the war. The Muslims killed a number of Serb men when they returned to Glogova and critically wounded Kravica's military commander, Jovan Nikolić, a nephew of Nego Erić. The Muslim attack cut the asphalt road between Bratunac and Kravica, and the only way in and out of the village now was a dirt road the Serbs had built over a mountain to the Drina two years before the war began.

Kravica's Serbs were angry at their own people. The Serb army in Bratunac had done almost nothing to save Glogova. Serb soldiers sent into the Srebrenica area from other parts of Bosnia quickly got wind of the massacre of Muslims in Glogova and the Bratunac schoolhouse and became unwilling to risk their lives. They realized that the Muslims in Srebrenica, trapped, hungry, and vengeance-driven, were fighting with more ferocity than Muslims they had come up against elsewhere. Only about three hundred soldiers, most of them local men, were in Kravica to defend the village during the Christmas holiday. It seemed to them that no one outside of Kravica cared whether the place fell or not, and they were exhausted and complaining after weeks of serving eight-hour shifts on the front line each day.

Naser Orić had spent days preparing his attack. It came with anything but surprise. After dark on Christmas Eve, some three thousand Muslim troops assembled on the slushy hilltops around Kravica. Behind them lurked a host of *torbari* who lit campfires to warm themselves. At dawn they started clattering pots and pans. "*Allahu ekber!* God is great!" the men shouted. The women shrieked. Shooting began. The Serb men in Kravica scrambled into their trenches. They told their wives and mothers they would be home in a few hours.

The main Muslim thrust came from the direction of Orić's own village, Potočari. The Serbs resisted with a hail of gunfire from their trenches, but they could soon look up the mountain behind their lines and see houses burning in Serb hamlets above Kravica that had come under attack from Glogova. Muslim soldiers dressed in white uniforms blended in with the snow and fog and opened fire from unexpected directions.

Christmas morning passed with gunfire and grenade blasts. The village women, among them Nego's seventy-nine-year-old wife, Krstina, went on with their final preparations for the holiday dinner. They roasted pigs. They sliced off the steaming pork, wrapped it in foil, and placed it on their woodstoves to keep warm. They brought out fresh bread and pickled tomatoes, cucumbers and peppers. Then they sat together and listened to the explosions and the rattle of the machine guns a few hundred yards away.

In midafternoon, the Serb defense line collapsed. About thirty Serb men were already dead, among them fathers and sons and brothers who perished together in the trenches. By four o'clock, Serb soldiers were scurrying back into the center of Kravica, screaming for everyone to get out while they still could. Nego Erić and Krstina were still at home when the fleeing Serb soldiers tore into the village. In his eighty-one years, Nego had seen three wars. He was a toddler when World War I began. He had been a Chetnik during World War II. He had sat in jail for years. His brother Golub had died with a gun in his hand just down the hill; his nephew Jovan Nikolić, the commander of Kravica's fighters, had been wounded two weeks earlier. Now Nego refused to leave Kravica. "I built this house for myself," he told the soldiers. "I built it to live in, and to die here. I'll avenge my own death before they take me."

The Serb rear guard passed by the Erić house. The men again urged Nego to leave. A neighbor offered to carry Krstina to safety on his back. Nego refused to budge. He refused to let the Serb soldiers take his wife. The old woman was crying. The old man was crying.

"Nego, you can't stay here," his daughter-in-law urged.

"Kiss your grandpa good-bye," the old man told her. "I want to die in my house. I want us to die here . . ."

The Serb men gave Nego hand grenades and a machine gun before they withdrew a few miles up a dirt road and established a new firing line. From there, they listened as the old man blasted away. Nego caught about a dozen Muslims off guard and killed a few before Muslim soldiers surrounded his cinder block house sometime Christmas evening. The old man's machine gun fired all night long. The next day, the Muslims tried tossing hand grenades through the windows. Nego kept firing. One of the Muslims finally shot a rocket-propelled bomb into the upper floor of Nego's house. A fire started. The machine gun went silent. Nego went to the room where Krstina was lying in bed. He opened the door, pulled the pin on a hand grenade, and tossed it in. Then he took a pistol, stuck the barrel into his mouth and pulled the trigger. His brother Golub's memoirs, his family tree, and the picture of Vaso with his war medals all went up in smoke.

THE first of the *torbari* to arrive in Kravica found entire Christmas dinners that had been waiting to be eaten by Serb men who had gone off to fight that morning thinking they would be back by noon. Three Muslim soldiers barged into one home and stood there as if paralyzed at the sight of the pastries and the jelly, the bottles of brandy and the roast pork on the stove. They laughed and shouted and plunged into a cake. The ashes of burning houses and stalls fell like snow on the hillside. The pigs ran wild. Sheep were butchered and roasted on the spit or herded back to Srebrenica with the cows and oxen. The dead lay unburied, and within days the pigs, dogs, and wild animals had begun to tear away at the bodies.

The *torbari* combed the homes in Kravica for the next two weeks scavenging for food. There were firefights on the hill above the village when Paja, Zlatija, Sanela, and Senad went to Kravica four days after it fell. They had had hardly any food at home but did not join the initial wave of *torbari*, because they never thought the Serbs would give up Kravica; when word of its fall spread, they held back for fear that the Serbs would immediately fight their way back in. Paja walked past ten of the dead, all of them men, all lying in a row beside the asphalt road. Sanela saw only the blood on the snow. She found a stash of frozen potatoes and some pickled peppers in a cellar near the road. Paja scrounged up a sack of oats and a pair of bell-bottom pants.

They set off for home at dark. Sanela made it all the way back to the empty parking lot of Srebrenica's bus station before she had to sit down. Aunt Latifa and her family were by then living in a house just behind the station. Sanela thought about stopping there, but the sound of artillery fire scared her enough that she picked up the potatoes and trudged the rest of the way home.

With Kravica in his hands, Orić had military control over about 350 square miles of territory, stretching from the Drina's banks to a hilltop within five miles of the Bosnian army lines before Tuzla. He boasted that Bratunac would be his next objective, and he soon drew up plans for an attack. It would be a magnificent victory. It would be the first Bosnian town to be recaptured by the Muslims since the war began. It would be easy.

The refugee Serbs of Kravica had moved into the vacant Muslim houses in Bratunac. They found no honor living on someone else's property and sitting down to miserable meals at someone else's table. Mihailo Erić, the great-great-grandson of Vaso Erić and the nephew of Nego and Krstina, was in Bratunac by then. He was recuperating from the wound left by the bullet that tore into his temple and ripped apart the front of his head. He talked with the other men from Kravica that winter. They talked of going home. They talked of revenge. Forty-five Serbs had died in the Muslim assault on Kravica, thirty-five of them soldiers. Brothers had died beside brothers. Fathers had perished beside their sons.

"*Kad tad,*" the men swore to one another. "*Kad tad.* Sooner or later, we'll get our five minutes."

PART FOUR

THE
MAP
WAR

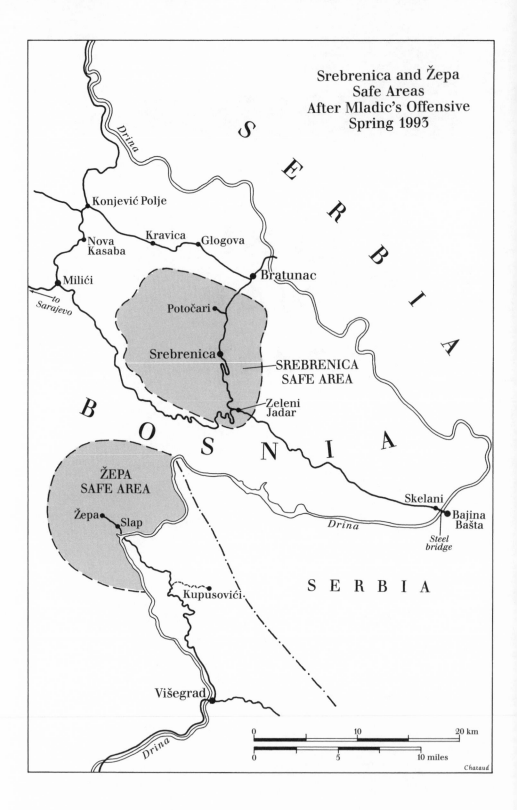

Srebrenica and Žepa
Safe Areas
After Mladic's Offensive
Spring 1993

SERBIA

Drina

Konjević Polje

Kravica

Nova
Kasaba

Glogova

Milići

Bratunac

to
Sarajevo

Potočari

Srebrenica

SREBRENICA
SAFE AREA

B

O

S

Zeleni
Jadar

N

I

A

ŽEPA
SAFE AREA

Žepa

Slap

Skelani

Bajina
Bašta

Drina

Steel
bridge

Kupusovići

SERBIA

Višegrad

Drina

0   10   20 km

0   5   10 miles

Chazaud

15

A FLEECY canopy of woodsmoke hung from the hillsides over Srebrenica. And as the dull, January days drew slowly by, the pinch-bellied refugees trapped in the town begged and pilfered food and fuel from the local peasants. They took up their gunnysacks and old suitcases and their firearms, clubs, and knives and snuck through the lines to plunder the corncribs and cellars and larders on Serb farmsteads farther afield than ever before. They ambushed Serbs traveling the back road between Zvornik and Pale. Some of them bundled up their families, summoned up their courage, and tried to escape the encirclement and the hunger by setting out across the thin stretch of Serb-controlled territory between Srebrenica and Tuzla.

By mid-month, the Čeliks had consumed all of the wizened potatoes Sanela had dug out of the cellar in Kravica, and the women were stirring a few tablespoons of flour or some raw oats into bubbling water and serving that up as a family meal. Sanela and Zlatija hiked to Žepa to trade a rug for food. After a family squabble, Paja bartered his gold wedding band for some flour and tramped from one village to another begging for more. Huso kept to the house. He manned the fire and massaged the rash on his legs with tiny dabs of the salve Hiba had found. He never offered to trade away the wristwatch he had brought back from Baghdad and still wore each day even after eight years. Probably no one in Srebrenica would have given anything for it anyway. The gold-colored plating had worn off to reveal the heavy stainless steel beneath; the dust of Vranica's brickyard had scratched its crystal; and its hands had frozen somewhere in time when the battery finally died.

Rumors around town, always riveted to the fighting and the struggle for food, began to play off word that the UN's peace negotiators, Cyrus Vance and David Owen, had proposed a plan for ending the war. News broadcasts from Serbia and Sarajevo, for the folks who still had batteries to power their transistor radios, announced that the plan would put Višegrad, Zvornik, Žepa, and Srebrenica under predominantly Muslim control and that all displaced persons would be able to return to their homes just as they had done after World War II. Vance and Owen had presented this plan to Bosnia's Muslim, Serb, and Croat leaders at the beginning of January. Formally anyway, the proposal would preserve Bosnia as an independent state within its original borders. But the central government in Sarajevo would be weak, and the country would be subdivided into ten autonomous provinces: three predominantly Muslim, three predominantly Serb, two predominantly Croat, and one evenly shared between Croats and Muslims. The peace negotiators themselves doubted that the plan would ever be implemented, because the major Western nations, and especially the United States, had demonstrated no willingness to send in the troops necessary to enforce the deal.

Bosnia's nationalist Croat, Muslim, and Serb leaders had predictable reactions to the peace proposal. The Croat leaders yammered and moaned for a day or two, then grabbed the deal because it would give them control of territory they had never expected to win. The Croat militia quickly relaunched its land grab at the Muslims' expense and ignited a Croat-Muslim war. Croat gunmen herded Muslim families from their homes in areas that the Vance-Owen plan had assigned to Croat-dominated provinces. Croat saboteurs blew up a bridge on the main supply road to Sarajevo. A few weeks later, Croat thugs were marching Muslim men from Mostar into concentration camps every bit as ghastly as the Serb camps had been in 1992.

Bosnia's Muslim leaders protested that the peace plan would condemn Bosnia to partition. But they accepted the deal a few weeks after President Bill Clinton's inauguration. President Izetbegović was convinced that the Serbs would never sign it, and he gambled that if the peace plan collapsed and the Serbs were held responsible for its failure, the UN Security Council, under American pressure, would lift the arms embargo against the Bosnian government and might even approve NATO air attacks against the Serbs.

The nationalist Serb leaders could not stomach the provisions of the Vance-Owen plan that provided for Bosnia's continued existence as an independent country within its original borders. Nor could they accept any possibility that the Muslims of eastern Bosnia, the region's majority population, would gain control of its local governments as well as its mines, factories, and road links with Serbia. Facing a threat of harsher international economic sanctions if they refused to accept the deal, the top Serb leaders on both sides of the Drina decided that the safest way to scuttle the plan was to stall, fill their public rhetoric with pleas for peace, and pave the way for unification of the Serb-controlled lands in Bosnia with Serbia by using their army to seize the rest of eastern Bosnia. After one concerted push with overwhelming military force, the Serb leaders calculated, the Muslims would be cast out of the Drina basin forever, Izetbegović and the other Muslim leaders would have to accept a fait accompli, and the world's powerful nations and their peace negotiators would accept the Muslim capitulation with tacit relief.

❮ ❮ ❮

THE man charged with executing the Serb strategy for undermining the peace plan and drawing the war to a close was the army officer whom Slobodan Milošević had handpicked in May 1992 to command the Bosnian Serb army: General Ratko Mladić. He was typical of the Yugoslav army colonels who, in the latter half of the 1980s and early 1990s, made a dramatic leap from the multiethnic, "Yugoslav" tradition of the Serbs who fought in Tito's Partisans to the "Greater Serbian" or Chetnik tradition. This shift in loyalties was often traumatic. Mladić himself was born into the Partisan tradition during World War II. He came from a tiny mountain village about thirty-five miles south of Sarajevo; and when he was only two years old, his father died fighting in Tito's ranks during a raid on nearby Bradina, the village where Ante Pavelić, the quisling leader of fascist Croatia, had been raised. Mladić went on to graduate from the Yugoslav army's military academy in Belgrade. He joined the Communist Party. And by 1991, he had risen to the rank of lieutenant colonel and was stationed in Kosovo, where the army was assisting Milošević's special police in their repression of ethnic Albanians. Mladić had clearly made his leap into the Chetnik tradition by the early summer of 1991; soon afterward, he was promoted to full colonel and took command of the Yugoslav army's barracks in Knin, the epicenter of the army-backed Serb uprising in Croatia.

Bullnecked and cobalt-eyed, Mladić enjoyed immense popularity among the Serbs in Bosnia. His troops hailed him in song as a *sokao*, a falcon, the South Slav totem for a warrior-hero. Here was a commander who personally directed the artillery pieces that fired into Sarajevo neighborhoods that were packed with civilians and bereft of military targets. Here was a commander who would be wounded at least once, who crawled into the trenches to sleep and slop down beans with the fighting men, and who laced his speech with peasant jargon and anti-Muslim epithets. Here was a man not afraid to chase down Serb war profiteers who made themselves rich while other men fought and died, a man who thumbed his nose at the international community, who loosed bombastic threats against London and Washington as if they were real bombs, who one morning stepped out onto the balcony of his headquarters in his underwear, glowered into the clouds, pounded his chest, and screamed for NATO to send down its fighter-bombers so that he could blow them from the sky. By January 1993, Mladić was itching to begin a new duel with the great powers, whose peace negotiators had just had the temerity to hand him a proposal that would require his men to surrender almost half of the territory they had seized and to leave their "Turk" enemies holding Srebrenica and other areas he had to capture if the Serbs' war aims were to be achieved.

❨   ❨   ❨

A FRENCHMAN emerged over the winter as the international community's most salient representative in Bosnia. He was the fifty-seven-year-old commander of the UN military force, General Philippe Morillon. The son of a French army officer who died during World War II, Morillon was, in his peace-keeping capacity, no military match for Mladić. Morillon had not come to Bosnia to command a fighting force equipped for waging war. He had been handed a few thousand troops with infantry weapons and blue berets and helmets, and a fleet of armored vehicles and helicopters painted glossy white. Their mission was not to make peace or save Bosnia or protect Bosnians; it was steer clear of harm's way while they escorted trucks delivering food, medicine, and clothing to people like the Čeliks who were trapped by the war. Their only weapon was the power of persuasion; their only defense, neutrality.

Morillon knew something of Yugoslavia and its army from a stint in the mid-1980s as president of a French-Yugoslav commission for armaments procurement. He also had a history of putting his career, and his life, on the line when he was convinced the politicians who were his ultimate superiors were in error. Born in the French colonial city of Casablanca, Morillon graduated from the French military academy, Saint-Cyr, as a lieutenant and took his first command in Algeria during its war of independence against France. In 1961, after six years of savagery, the president of France, Charles de Gaulle, ordered the French army to abandon Algeria. The order stunned Morillon and thousands of other French soldiers in Algeria. To them, the order was an act of treason. To them, Algeria was France, and it always would be France, and withdrawing from Algeria would be tantamount to abandoning thousands of Algerians who had been loyal to France and had fought with the French army. Morillon joined a group of French officers who rebelled against de Gaulle's pullout order. The putsch failed, and subsequently thousands of pro-French Algerians fled their native land or were killed. The purge of the rebels within the French army reached from the top echelons of the officers' corps to one level above the rank of lieutenant, sparing Morillon's military career. He went on to become a four-star general.

Throughout the fall and winter, Morillon insisted that the UN force under his command maintain a posture of steadfast neutrality. One humiliation followed another. Mladić and his men pounded Sarajevo's neighborhoods with artillery and shot down pedestrians on the city's streets, and the UN did nothing to stop it. Serb police murdered Muslim civilians and expelled Muslims and Croats from the town of Banja Luka. A Serb assassin shot to death a Bosnian government minister who was cowering inside a French armored vehicle guarded by French soldiers. Muslims fired on UN soldiers and aid convoys. Serb leaders refused to allow food trucks into Srebrenica and the other eastern enclaves. And all the while, Morillon remained unfazed and "even-handed," acting under the assumption that all sides in Bosnia were equally to blame for the violence. In effect, he undertook no action without the Serb leadership's approval . . . until one sunny winter afternoon, when he stood in some ankle-deep slush on the rooftop of a post office in the little town of Srebrenica.

16

IN mid-January, Naser Orić handed General Ratko Mladić an opening and a pretext to strike Srebrenica. Muslim soldiers and *torbari* attacked and practically overran the Serbs and some Ukrainian Cossack mercenaries in and around the riverside village of Skelani. Hundreds of Serb civilians fled eastward over the Drina on boats as the Muslims advanced to a bluff about a hundred yards above Skelani's steel-girder bridge, the only bridge over the river for miles and the only road link from Serbia to Srebrenica from the south. Orić's men fought desperately to reach the bridge and blow it up; they tried sneaking through the lines under the cover of darkness, and they sent down boats with men and explosives from upriver. Gunfire ripped back and forth across the river, but the Serbs held the Muslims off. During the gun battle, a Muslim machine gunner cut down panicked Serb villagers, including women and children, as they tried to scurry across the bridge to the safety of the Serbian side.

The stories of the fleeing civilians shot down on the Skelani bridge enraged all of Serbia, and General Mladić retaliated for it quickly. Paramilitary troops from Milošević's police ministry joined Bosnian Serb army troops and volunteers in a rush over the Skelani bridge behind several tanks. Howitzers, mortars, and rocket batteries on the Serbian side of the Drina blasted away at the Muslim positions on the Bosnian side. The artillery barrage and appearance of the tanks caught Orić's men completely off guard. They backed up toward Srebrenica, fighting off the advancing Serbs at every hillside. Dozens of Muslim soldiers perished as Mladić's men pushed northwest into the hills over the next ten days before drawing up on a hilltop in the middle of Kara Marko's Territory, about ten miles southwest of the town. The cannonade then slackened. The local commanders arranged a truce. And bodies and prisoners were exchanged.

❮   ❮   ❮

ONE morning soon after the Muslim soldiers battered at Skelani slogged and stumbled back into Srebrenica, Huso Čelik hurried to Fadila's apartment above the empty butcher shop in the center of town to visit Dragica Vasić. "Stay off the street," Huso cautioned his Serb friend. "Don't go out there at all. They're crazy out there." A double murder had been committed the night before in the apartment building just below the Čelik house. A Muslim soldier seeking revenge for the death of a relative, a military-police chief killed near Skelani, had used the butt of his revolver to smash the skulls of a Serb man and his elderly mother. Dragica had known both of the victims; Slobodan Zekić and his mother, Zagorka, were the second Serb family that Dragica had seen murdered since the war began. Zagorka, an elderly woman, had suffered a stroke and had been bedridden for years; and Slobodan, a middle-aged former factory worker, had stayed on in Srebrenica to care for her. Sanela had met Slobodan a few times, and he once offered to pay her to nurse his mother. Slobodan always showed up for his work detail and carried food to the Muslim soldiers in the trenches around Srebrenica. It was widely believed he had been a spy for the Muslim police during the three weeks that the Serbs had controlled Srebrenica in April and May of 1992; but even this did not save him or his mother.

Huso watched as the bodies of Zagorka and Slobodan were wrapped in blankets, carried out of their apartment building, and taken away toward Potočari to be buried before he rushed off to warn Dragica. And when his warning was delivered, he went home. It would be months before he would see Dragica again. She stayed inside, cowering in Fadila's apartment or in the nearest bomb shelter, as General Mladić and his men catapulted Srebrenica into newspaper headlines around the globe. Huso, Hiba, Sanela, and the other Čeliks spent most of their days hunkered down in the two shelters nearest their house: the basement of the Energoinvest mining company's building or in the cellar of the apartment house where Slobodan and Zagorka Zekić had lived and died. And there they waited as the Serbs closed in, as the shells rained from the sky, and as the world's most powerful men argued over what to do about it.

❮   ❮   ❮

EARLY February's snows blew into deep banks on the mountaintops of eastern Bosnia. They drifted against Jerina the Damned's fortress walls and settled inside the empty stone and brick shells of burned-out houses in Višegrad, Kupusovići, Odžak, Žlijeb, and scores of other villages in the Drina valley. In the lowlands, they blanketed the rooftops and the deserted roads and shrouded the earthen bunkers and the shallow graves and the unburied dead until the sun broke through and cleared the way for General Mladić to begin his offensive in earnest. With a local cease-fire in hand on the southwestern edge of the Srebrenica enclave, Mladić now shifted his forces to its northern edge. Serb commanders announced that any Muslim civilians who wished to leave the enclave could do so in safety along a corridor running westward through the war front to Tuzla. About five thousand people, most of them old men, women, and children trapped in outlying villages, trusted the Serbs enough to take up the offer before Orić's troops stemmed the outflow. The Muslim officers warned that Mladić's corridor was a ploy; and the Serbs complained that Muslim soldiers had attempted to improve their fighting positions by entering the corridor and that the Muslims fired on their own civilians fleeing toward Tuzla. The bodies of refugees who died in ambushes littered the escape route. The survivors who arrived in Tuzla were covered with lice, scabies, and frostbite, and UN officials in the city condemned the Serbs for launching a new wave of forced expulsions.

A full-scale Serb offensive was under way by February 9. UN refugee-relief officials in Geneva issued a warning that the outbreak in fighting threatened to uproot as many as fifty thousand people. Within five days, Mladic's forces had overrun much of Kamenica, the northernmost village in the Srebrenica enclave. Foreign journalists escorted to the Kamenica area by the Serb army were shown corpses that had been devoured by animals and other bodies that had been pulled from a pond and exhumed from three muddy graves on a forested ridge. The Serbs alleged that the bodies belonged to prisoners whom the Muslims had tortured and killed.

As Kamenica was burning, Bosnia's Muslim leaders grasped the fact that General Mladić had stymied any possibility that they had had of pushing a supply line from Tuzla to Srebrenica. The Muslim leaders also understood that Mladić had amassed enough tanks, artillery, and troops to wipe out Orić's forces. Sarajevo wasted no time in appealing to the outside world to come to the rescue. The new U.S. secretary of state, Warren Christopher, had hinted that the Clinton administration was considering more determined steps to deliver food and medicine to isolated Muslim pockets like Srebrenica, and the Muslim leaders decided to put the new administration to a test. They announced that they would not accept further deliveries of UN aid to Sarajevo until General Morillon and his troops succeeded in making deliveries of food and medicine to Srebrenica and the other eastern enclaves. The Muslim leadership charged that Morillon and the UN military force had breached their mandate by failing to use all the means at their disposal to deliver aid to the isolated Muslim pockets. A day later, the UN refugee-relief agency suspended the aid airlift that had sustained Sarajevo for eight months.

The squabble over aid deliveries aggravated Morillon because it put the spotlight on the failure of the UN mission. He condemned the Muslim aid boycott as a ploy to lure the Western nations into intervening militarily. He insinuated that UN relief officials and journalists were exaggerating their reports of the privation that the Muslims were suffering in eastern Bosnia. UN officials held urgent talks with the Bosnian government and appealed to Serb leaders to allow truck convoys into Srebrenica and Žepa. But General Mladić remained obdurate. His troops were shrinking the Srebrenica enclave, advancing toward the village of Cerska, the next Muslim stronghold south of Kamenica. Muslim ham radio operators in Cerska were calling in reports of heavy shelling and loss of life. The radio operators said starvation and disease had already killed hundreds of Muslims and were claiming twenty new victims each night. Morillon, desperate to save his mission, dismissed these reports as lies; but he had no observers in eastern Bosnia, and the screaming voices over the ham radios continued to paint a picture of starvation and unspeakable horrors that began a crescendo of press reaction.

It took fewer than nine days for the Muslims' aid boycott to succeed. In Washington, the White House announced that it would parachute food and medicine into Srebrenica and the other eastern Bosnian enclaves despite the objections of UN officials. The Clinton administration also hinted that it was contemplating a radical shift in American's policy toward the Bosnian war, a push to lift the UN arms embargo against the Bosnian government and launch air strikes against the Serbs. The Pentagon, along with France, Great Britain, and the other countries with troops on the ground in Bosnia, staunchly opposed each of these initiatives. Air strikes and a lifting of the arms embargo, they argued, were now impossible because they would compromise the neutrality of the UN troops in Bosnia and jeopardize their safety. General Morillon attacked even the airdrop plan as rash and unnecessary. "Overland aid deliveries are still possible," he insisted. "If the Americans start dropping supplies by parachute, there will be an explosion here. . . . In the current climate of paranoia, everybody will shoot at everything in the air."

(((

NOT a shot was fired from the ground on the night of February 27, when a pair of big-bellied U.S. Air Force C-130 cargo planes from Rhein-Main airbase in Frankfurt, Germany, crossed into Bosnia's airspace. They extinguished their running lights and scattered about a million leaflets notifying the Muslims trapped in Srebrenica, Žepa, and Goražde that food drops would soon begin. The next night, four C-130s parachuted supplies into a tight drop zone in the snow-covered hills around Cerska. The parachutes fell right into the targeted area, but it was too late to matter. The village's defense lines had already snapped, and the Serbs had already set to work burning and looting its houses. The Muslim ham radio operators screamed about massacres and shells falling into crowds of fleeing people. Over ten thousand civilians, most of them refugees who had been driven from their homes during the April 1992 Serb massacre in Zvornik, were now trudging southward into Konjević Polje, a cluster of hamlets in a narrow valley just ten miles northwest of the town of Srebrenica.

Each morning and afternoon during the Serb offensive, summaries of the frantic pleas by the ham radio operators in Cerska and other villages were collected by Anders Levinsen, a Dane who headed the Tuzla office of the UNHCR. Levinsen had been in Bosnia about as long as General Morillon, and the aid worker had been shaken by the absence of a robust international response to the Serb onslaught. On March 2, he sent his headquarters in Geneva a message that was passed on to Sadako Ogata, the United Nations High Commission for Refugees. Ogata immediately tore open a rift between the UN refugee-relief agency and General Morillon's military force by firing off a letter to Secretary-General Boutros Boutros-Ghali describing the horror of the situation. "Civilians, women, children and old people, are being killed, usually by having their throats cut," Ogata wrote, practically quoting verbatim from Levinsen's message. She cautioned Boutros-Ghali that her information had come from the ham radio operators and from Bosnian government officials who had an interest in exaggerating their reports of the suffering. But she threw her authority behind the accounts all the same. "If only ten percent of the information is true," Ogata continued, "we are witnessing a massacre in the enclaves without being able to do anything about it." She recommended that the UN refugee-relief organization abandon its long-standing policy of refusing to assist in the forced expulsion of civilians; she proposed that the UN save the lives of the Muslims by evacuating them from the Srebrenica enclave to Tulza even though it would effectively help the Serbs achieve their goal of violently clearing the Muslims out of the area.

Ogata's letter prompted the United States to call for an emergency meeting of the UN Security Council that afternoon, and the council responded by issuing a statement demanding an end to the wholesale killing in Cerska, blaming it squarely on Mladić's Serbs, and by requesting the secretary-general to pull UN troops from other parts of Bosnia and send them to the eastern enclaves. Kofi Annan, at the time the head of the UN's Department of Peacekeeping Operations, instructed General Morillon to take immediate action to get UN relief workers into Cerska and Srebrenica.

Morillon flew by helicopter from Sarajevo to Tuzla on Friday, March 5, believing he had negotiated an agreement between Serb and Muslim leaders for the evacuation of hundreds of wounded men and thousands of beleaguered civilians. By that evening, the French general had arrived in Konjević Polje with a unit of British soldiers and a team of relief workers, including a doctor from the World Health Organization named Simon Mardel, who left Morillon's party and hiked into the town of Srebrenica.

By Saturday morning, all the preparations for the evacuation were complete. In Tuzla, civil-defense reception teams and doctors and nurses stood by at a sports arena, waiting to receive the evacuees. Stretchers were laid out in rows to carry the wounded. Crews of men were ready to assist people unable to walk. Rows of sponge mattresses covered with gray blankets had been laid out on the parquet of the basketball court.

I remember that Saturday in Tuzla. It rained most of the day. The layer of snow on the airfield just outside of town had melted into a crunchy slush. Teams of newspaper and television reporters had gathered on the airport grounds by the time Morillon's armored vehicle pulled up in front of the command center of the British army unit stationed there. Morillon stopped and spoke to us before he boarded a waiting helicopter. He announced that no evacuation would take place. Serb commanders had demanded a population exchange: they would allow the Muslims to leave Konjević Polje only after the UN organized a transfer of some ten thousand Serb civilians from Tuzla and nearby towns under Bosnian government control. The Muslim commanders had also blocked the planned exodus, arguing that it would "undermine the morale" of Srebrenica's defenders and lead to the town's surrender; in other words, Naser Orić did not want to be deprived of the *torbari* who had once been his sword and were now his shield, and Alija Izetbegović did not want to have the UN helping the Serbs remove the Muslim majority population from territory that the UN's own peace proposal, the Vance-Owen peace plan, had earmarked to remain predominantly Muslim.

Morillon went on to tell the reporters that he had seen no fighting or starvation in Konjević Polje. The refugees there, he said, were living in trying conditions but far better than those described in the ham radio broadcasts. The displaced persons he saw had crammed themselves inside damaged homes heated with woodstoves. The 120 wounded and sick people, a tenth of what the ham radio operators had reported, were housed in several buildings, though they had no doctors, no medical equipment, and no medicines. Moreover, Morillon said he had seen no evidence of massive civilian casualties. "As a soldier, I, unfortunately, have the knack of smelling death. I didn't smell it," Morillon said that day. "I spent only one night there, and I can testify to only what I have seen. I did not see any trace of massacres. . . . That's very important because we have to calm the fears there. The most important thing at the present time is to break this vicious circle. . . . Srebrenica is in no danger."

17

AN inky fog descended on Tuzla late that afternoon as word spread through town that Morillon had canceled the evacuation and departed for Sarajevo. At Tuzla's sports arena, empty-faced doctors and nurses smoked cigarettes and waited for rides back to the local hospital. Relatives of Muslims caught in Konjević Polje maintained a vigil in the drizzle outside the arena even after nightfall, clinging to hope that they would soon be reunited with their loved ones. A gloom filled the offices of the UN refugee-relief agency. Morillon's pronouncements and the Serb demands had angered Anders Levinsen. It was one thing for the UN to retreat from its own policy by assisting in the evacuation of a civilian population under attack; it was quite another to accede to blackmail and broker an exchange of human beings. The Danish refugee worker, however, did not have to wait more than a few hours before he passed along some new information that would force Morillon to return to eastern Bosnia. Once again, the information came in a report over the ham radio from Srebrenica; but this time it came from a credible reporter: Simon Mardel, the WHO doctor who had hiked into the town.

"There is considerable weight loss," Mardel said. "Many pneumonia cases. Mortality rate twenty to thirty per day due to sickness. But hunger is contributing to this." The Muslim doctors in Srebrenica's hospital had been performing surgery without anesthetics for months, Mardel said. He appealed for an immediate airdrop of medicines and medical supplies into Srebrenica. Thousands of women, children, elderly people, and invalids were seeking evacuation, and new refugees were streaming in from Konjević Polje, sleeping on Srebrenica's wet streets, and eating roots, cornhusks, and buds picked from tree branches because they were not receiving any food from the airdrops.

Naser Orić had attempted to organize an equitable distribution of the food airdropped into Srebrenica. He had barred civilians from the drop zones. He had ordered work brigades to recover the sacks of wheat flour from the parachuted pallets and to transport them to the department store below the Čeliks' house for distribution. He had announced that each person would receive enough food for one meal each day.

Paja Čelik belonged to one of the work brigades that climbed the mountainsides above the town every night. The men waited in the snow-blanketed forest and lit fires to direct the airplanes toward their target. After the pallets snapped through the tree branches and crashed to the ground, the workers lugged the sacks of wheat flour to the nearest road and loaded them aboard a truck that was supposed to haul them to town. By the time the food arrived at the department store, however, there was never enough to go around. Soldiers, officers, and civilian members of the work brigades pilfered food for their own families, hiding sacks of flour in snow drifts and carrying them by night through the woods to their homes. Fist fights erupted outside the department store when the supplies ran out. Threats were exchanged. Weapons were brandished.

For ten days, Orić told everyone to remain calm. But when the situation failed to improve, he halted the distribution effort and announced that from then on it would be everyone for himself. The mountainsides above Srebrenica now flickered with the flames of a legion of torches each night as desperate people streamed through the forests to the drop areas. Few of the newly arriving refugees from Konjević Polje, many of them widows with children, got word of the drop locations or had the energy to make the journey and fight for the food. Word got back to Rhein-Main air base that the weakest refugees were still going hungry. Men were killing one another in the forests to get at the flour. Falling pallets, which were as big as two refrigerators and smashed into the ground at about eighty-five miles an hour, had crushed to death people who risked waiting inside the landing zones to improve their chances of reaching the food first. The Americans responded to the chaos by doubling the number of air-supply missions and by overflying the town at low altitude and dropping tens of thousands of individual meals in brown plastic wrappers that fell to the earth like vacuum-packed manna from heaven.

❨   ❨   ❨

GENERAL MORILLON set off from Tuzla for Srebrenica on Wednesday, March 10, in a convoy of mud-splattered white jeeps and armored vehicles whose personnel included two U.S. military men who maintained communications with the Pentagon. Morillon had met with General Mladić before departing and had received the Serb general's blessing for a food delivery to Srebrenica and an evacuation of wounded civilians from Konjević Polje. Mladić, however, gave notice that he would not permit any wounded Muslim combatants to be evacuated; he assured Morillon that the wounded Muslim soldiers could be treated in Serb hospitals.

In Zvornik, Morillon's convoy split. One segment, made up of British vehicles, crossed through the Serb lines and wound its way up a corpse-littered road to Konjević Polje, where the UN troops began preparing for the planned evacuation. Morillon and the other element of the convoy crossed the Drina into Serbia to negotiate a column of food trucks through army and police roadblocks on the Serbian side of the river. Despite Mladić's assurances and Morillon's insistence, however, the local Serb commanders refused to allow the food convoy to enter Srebrenica. After hours of argument, Morillon finally threw up his hands. He told the Serbs that he had to go to Srebrenica to evaluate the situation personally and that, if necessary, he would go there by himself and without the food convoy. The Serbs agreed to Morillon's trip. But they insisted that he travel into the town over a narrow mountain road that was covered in deep snow and mined. The French general headed out of Zvornik late that afternoon with two patrol cars and an armored vehicle followed by a truck loaded with medicines and sugar. His tiny convoy wound its way up the Drina to Bratunac before crawling into the mountains. At the front line, the truck hit a land mine and had to be abandoned. Darkness had already fallen on Srebrenica by the time the general and his men rode into town.

THE order to trap Morillon and the rest of the UN personnel in Srebrenica and Konjević Polje came to Naser Orić the next day in a coded transmission from the ham radio room in Bosnia's presidency building in Sarajevo. "Do it in a civilized way," the message said. "Use women and children." Orić instructed a local schoolteacher to mobilize Srebrenica's women. From house to house, the women organizers went, rousting out mothers and grandmothers and young girls and telling them to gather on the asphalt road down by the post office and block Morillon's vehicles so that he could not leave. When the French general climbed into his patrol car that afternoon to depart, the women sat down around it. Mothers slipped their children under its wheels so the car could not move. Someone managed to find cardboard and some crayons and draw up picket signs: "We are Hungry! Give us Bread!" "Don't Abandon Us!" "If You Leave, They Will Kill Us!"

Morillon strode back into the post office as if nothing unusual was happening. First, he tried smooth talking his way out. He assured the women that Srebrenica would not be abandoned. He appealed to Naser Orić for help, but Orić said he could do nothing and the women did not move. In the early evening, Morillon said he needed to get some sleep and went to bed. He awoke at about two o'clock in the morning and, together with his aide, slipped away on foot from the post office. They hiked about two miles down the asphalt road toward Potočari and waited for two hours in the frigid night air. Morillon's driver was supposed to attempt to deceive the women, take the general's car, and rendezvous with him. But the ploy failed, and Morillon returned to the post office on foot to find an even larger crowd blocking his car.

Sanela and Zlatija were among them; like all the other mothers and girls around the post office, they were frightened. They worried about being caught in the open if the Serbs directed artillery fire onto the crowd. They worried that the town's defenses would collapse. They feared having to flee in panic into the forests. Rumors spread through the gathering . . . a new attack was imminent . . . Naser Orić had been killed in action . . . the Serbs had broken through the lines. The women began standing guard around the clock in eight-hour shifts. Morillon got in touch with Lieutenant General Lars Eric Wahlgren of Sweden, the commander of the entire UN military mission in the former Yugoslavia. He told Wahlgren that he considered himself a hostage. He said he would not be allowed to leave Srebrenica until the UN deployed military observers along the Drina River, halted the Serb offensive, and gained access for aid convoys to the surrounded town.

THE British contingent in Konjević Polje had also been trapped by several thousand desperate women and children who had sprawled out on the ground in front of the caterpillar tracks of their armored vehicles. The British soldiers could see where the Serbs had felled trees and built gun positions on the hilltops around the valley. The local commander was furious that the UN had not begun the evacuation immediately and that it would not include his wounded soldiers. Early on Friday afternoon, March 12, the Serbs lofted mortar rounds onto the hillsides around Konjević Polje. A few hours later, at about 4:30 P.M., they fired from close range and without warning into the crowd surrounding the British vehicles. Sixteen people, five of them children, were blown to pieces, and dozens more were wounded. The women and children scrambled to take cover. A British army medic and Doctor Mardel operated on the injured without anesthetics before the British commander withdrew his men from Konjević Polje to Zvornik. During the mortar attack, the severed leg of a little boy, his shoe still laced up, had landed atop one British armored vehicle; the commander ordered the vehicle to stop when it reached the first Serb checkpoint on the road out of the valley. The engine idled. The hatch lifted. And the commander emerged. He took the child's leg and tossed it toward the Serbs. "Here," he said, "is your fucking war."

THE last of the Muslims who had been in Konjević Polje were by then fleeing for their lives through the snow-covered hills toward Srebrenica. They carried their wounded over the mountains and across swollen creeks on stretchers and in rattling oxcarts. The next day, the wounded who survived the journey found themselves in a hospital with no electricity or running water. Hundreds more homeless people were now living on the town's streets, warming themselves by burning trash and plastic that produced clouds of noxious fumes. Children wandered aimlessly about, shivering in their tattered sweaters and worn-out shoes, and smelling of shit and smoke and sweat. The tiny town of Srebrenica by now contained more than twenty thousand people, all but a handful of them refugees; spread out over the shrinking enclave, there were now just over forty thousand people, and well over half of them had been driven from their homes in Serb-occupied territory.

❨ ❨ ❨

PAJA ČELIK was lugging stretchers and emptying bedpans inside the hospital across the road from the post office on Saturday, March 13. There had been no shelling of the town since General Morillon's arrival, but the Serb offensive in the mountains had not abated and a bread truck continued to ferry wounded soldiers and civilians to the hospital's doors. The midafternoon sun was casting sharp shadows when Paja cast his eyes through the window of a hospital room and saw that the crowd on the asphalt road outside had grown. He spotted Morillon across the way. He was standing ankle-deep in slush on the roof of the post office. The general was grasping in his right hand a white pole, and on it flapped the powder-blue flag of the UN with its map of the world embraced by olive branches. Paja climbed through a window onto a balcony overlooking the post office, and from there he watched as Morillon smiled and gazed down into the faces of the bedraggled women and children who had blocked his departure for most of two days. The general waved his hands, and Paja listened as Morillon spoke.

"What did he say? What did he say?" Paja asked someone next to him.

"I think he just said he won't abandon us."

The crowd responded with a polite, muffled applause.

"*Živeo* Morillon! Long live Morillon!" people shouted. "Long live the United Nations!"

Morillon had sent the following message to the UN military headquarters in Sarajevo at about noon that day. He ordered that it be released to the press:

Last week it became clear that the Serbs were not stopping their offensive in eastern Bosnia-Herzegovina, not so much because they needed to capture the territory, but because they had become enraged after the discovery of a mass grave at Kamenica. I have tried to make them understand that justice for all war crimes should be dispensed once the fighting has ceased and peace has been established. But they did not want to listen. They have decided to take justice into their own hands. Fully conscious that a major tragedy was about to take place in Srebrenica I deliberately came here. And I have now decided to stay here in Srebrenica in order to calm the population's anguish, in order to try to save them.

Morillon demanded that General Mladić abandon the offensive. He called on the Serb and Bosnian commanders to issue a countrywide cease-fire. He also pressed for the UN to station military observers in Srebrenica permanently and for the Serbs to open a supply route into the town and an air corridor for a helicopter evacuation of the wounded. Morillon's demands enraged Mladić and the other Serb commanders and irked UN officials, including Secretary-General Boutros-Ghali. The UN's mandate to protect aid convoys was not, after all, a mandate to protect people, and UN headquarters immediately informed General Wahlgren that New York expected Morillon to leave Srebrenica as soon as a food convoy reached the town. Any UN personnel left in Srebrenica thereafter, New York said, would have to stick strictly to the mandate: protect aid deliveries and maintain strict neutrality. When Wahlgren advised Morillon to return to Sarajevo, the Frenchman replied that he would leave Srebrenica only by helicopter and only when the Serbs allowed the wounded Muslims to be airlifted out. Attack helicopters from the United States and France were poised on the Adriatic coast of Croatia to mount a commando raid to rescue Morillon; but the general himself called it off. When UN officials went to Pale from Sarajevo for discussions about Morillon's demands with Serb leaders, they were told that Mladić was away on vacation.

The Serb general's offensive was closing in inexorably on Srebrenica. His tanks had ground their way into Konjević Polje. And from there, five hours more was all it took for his fighters to push eastward and recapture Kravica. The bell atop the village's Orthodox church tolled for hours after the Serbs' return. The soldiers, many of them local men, found that the school, the church, and all of the houses and fruit cellars had been plundered. Nego Erić's home was a charred wreck; and Krstina's remains were discovered upstairs, still inside what was left of a bedroom. Somebody stumbled upon Nego's body in an ash heap behind the school; Muslim soldiers had bound the old man's legs with wire and apparently dragged his body outside and buried it in the soft ashes and cinders. Other bodies had been covered over with dirt and decomposing leaves and were easier to identify than the corpses that had been left in the open and consumed by the stray pigs and dogs and wild animals. The Serb villagers identified the remains of their relatives by the shreds of clothing the victims had been wearing, by the color and style of their shoes, by their eyeglasses, or by the places where they were found. One man packed his father's bones inside a nylon bag and carried them away to the cemetery next to the church for burial. Some of the graves there had been robbed.

Tombstones had been smashed. The lids of coffins had been pried open. And the dead, stripped of their jewelry, were glaring up from inside.

A joint funeral for the Serbs who died at Kravica was held in Bratunac a few days after the village was retaken. General Morillon attended the burial. The wooden coffins were lined up side by side. Beeswax candles splattered and hissed. The women wailed laments, and family members gathered around to drink brandy toasts, pour libations, and eat hunks of bread and spoonfuls of *žito*. When the dead were lowered into the earth, a line of mourners tossed handfuls of dirt atop the coffins. Then the gravediggers covered them over. They pounded wooden crosses into the loose soil. And family members and friends draped the crosses with towels.

AT midday on March 19, General Mladić unexpectedly allowed fourteen trucks loaded with medical supplies and food to enter Srebrenica. Cheering Muslim townspeople and refugees took to the streets and greeted the trucks when they arrived. Hordes of people waited outside the department store for their share of the food. "We brought the people life," Morillon told journalists in Sarajevo by radio, confident the convoy marked the beginning of the end of the horror. "I won't leave the people of Srebrenica while their security remains in doubt."

How General Morillon managed to persuade Ratko Mladić to allow the food convoy into Srebrenica mystified the UN's refugee-relief officials. It was the first food convoy to reach the town since before the New Year, and there was no sign that Mladić or the other Serbs had abandoned their campaign against the enclave. A few hours later, Morillon himself revealed that Mladić had allowed the convoy to pass because he and the French general had struck a deal. In exchange for the aid convoy and Mladić's agreement to a helicopter airlift of the wounded from Srebrenica, Morillon had pledged to organize an exodus of Serbs from the Tuzla area and promised to buy off the Serbs in Bratunac by giving them a portion of the aid meant for Srebrenica. Morillon's quid pro quo infuriated José Maria Mendiluce, the UNHCR's top official in the former Yugoslavia. Mendiluce shot off a letter to General Wahlgren blasting Morillon's deal making: "We have been placed in a position of asking Serbs to leave Tuzla in order to fulfill commitments made by General Morillon, thus becoming an active instrument of population exchange, against all the objectives of the Vance-Owen Plan." The departure of the trucks that made up the food convoy brought even more trouble. A panicked throng of women and children desperate to escape Srebrenica fought to get aboard the trucks even as they were pulling away from the town. General Morillon again calmed the people, assuring them that they would not be abandoned, assuring them he would stay with them even as General Mladić was shifting his troops to the south of town and renewing his attacks.

❮   ❮   ❮

MLADIĆ'S forces had pulled northward to within five miles of Srebrenica by March 23, and Naser Orić was mobilizing additional men to fight them off. Local leaders were screaming for international military intervention over the ham radio to officials and journalists in Sarajevo, calling the attack "unprecedented in human history" and saying they were unable to do anything to ease the suffering of the refugees. Despite the fighting on Srebrenica's southern fringe, however, the promised air evacuation of the wounded got under way the next morning, and Morillon departed Srebrenica. When he reached Bratunac, he found himself blocked by a group of Serb women complaining that no Serbs had been allowed to leave Tuzla. Mortar rounds exploded on the helicopter landing zone in Srebrenica minutes later, killing two Muslims and wounding a pair of Canadian soldiers. When British helicopters swooped in to rescue the Canadians, the mortar fire began anew and the aircraft, unable to land, had to hover above the ground and lift the wounded Canadians aboard by means of a winch.

Morillon was incensed. He rushed to Belgrade to appeal personally to President Milošević to put an end to the Serb offensive. Shells fired from Serbia, from territory Milošević controlled, were exploding in Srebrenica. Tanks, soldiers, and artillery from Serbia were continuing to cross the Drina over the bridges at Zvornik, Bratunac, and Skelani. Airplanes and helicopters were flying over Srebrenica from Serbian airspace, defying a UN ban on all flights over Bosnia. "Only you can now ward off an international catastrophe," Morillon told Milošević. "The Americans were ready to intervene yesterday, but I held them off. Now, perhaps, only hours are left for decisive action before armed intervention takes place."

"Action must be taken immediately and at the highest level," Morillon demanded. "The local Bosnian Serb commander, Colonel Ilić, is mad. And because of his desire for revenge, he is shelling and conducting ethnic cleansing. I have been insulted and betrayed by local Bosnian Serb commanders. Mladić is refusing to meet me. And, among the Bosnian Serbs, only Karadžić and Mladić can save the situation."

Milošević responded by putting on a conciliatory face. He stared at Morillon with eyes that might have been consoling a screaming child. He said, "I cannot give orders to the Bosnian Serb army."

But Morillon snapped at him. The offensive must stop, he demanded. The

Serbs had to stop attacking. They had to stop shelling. They should arrest Colonel Ilić. "You must tell Mladić to do these things, and to do so at once. . . . Only a few hours stand between Serbia and the Serbs and a catastrophe."

The next day, the man who could not give orders to the Bosnian Serb army gave General Morillon his cease-fire agreement. The truce would begin in two days, on Sunday at noon.

❨   ❨   ❨

A BLIZZARD was smothering Bosnia on the Saturday night before the cease-fire was scheduled to take effect, and all was quiet in Srebrenica when General Morillon arrived back at his headquarters in Sarajevo to the popping of corks and the clinking of champagne glasses. "Srebrenica is safe," Morillon assured his staff as the snow fell outside. "Everybody has to understand that the time of ethnic cleansing and the taking of hostages is finished." Mladić had promised him there would be no more attacks on Srebrenica; he had even pledged to court-martial a Serb commander who had ordered the latest assaults on the villages south of the town. And Morillon felt comfortable enough to assure everyone a second time: "Srebrenica is safe." The fate of the town was also out of his hands. General Wahlgren had informed Morillon that he could take no more independent decisions concerning the enclave.

18

IN Srebrenica the next morning, a blanket of fluffy snow muffled the thuds of axes chopping firewood, the cries and shouts of kids wandering about in the streets, and the singsong calls of women summoning their friends from the blasted-out windows of apartments and houses. The men on the front lines heard only scattered gunfire. Another truck convoy had arrived after nightfall with food, medicines, hospital supplies, and white plastic sheeting to cover the empty window frames.

During the night, thousands of women, children, and old people had gathered around the dozen or so UN trucks and watched as a work crew unloaded the sacks of flour. About a hundred Muslim soldiers stood guard around the trucks. The guards smoked cigarettes. They chatted with relatives in the crowd and loosed a warning shot or two into the air to keep people they did not know from drawing too close to the food. The local authorities had picked six hundred people to leave for Tuzla on the big Volvo trucks when the convoy departed the next morning. After midnight on March 29, however, as the last sack of flour was unloaded from the last of the trucks, a stampede of desperate people rushed past the guards. The people scrambled into the truck beds. The soldiers fired into the air, but no one took heed. Women and children swarmed over the trucks, climbing over each other like insects and elbowing and fighting for space. The soldiers swore and fired more bullets into the sky. They shouted for people to get off and pulled on legs and waistbands, and the people on the trucks pleaded for room. No one listened. More people jammed inside. The crush asphyxiated at least two children before the desperate ones still struggling to get aboard realized there was no more room. The people groaned and swore but refused to get down. And when the Danish truck drivers cranked up the diesel engines to depart the next morning, mothers waiting close by the trucks ran toward them and tossed their infant children aboard.

The Serbs kept the convoy waiting before allowing it to pass through their lines. A mile farther on, in the center of Bratunac, the trucks were halted again. A crowd of people had gathered. General Mladić stood to address them and told them the evacuation of these Muslim civilians was a sign of the Serbs' goodwill, a sign of their humanity. The people aboard the trucks stood in silence until the convoy moved out again. Along the road to Zvornik, the trucks bounced over potholes, throwing the human cargo off balance and jamming the people together even more tightly than before. Four other people, including a pair of children, were crushed to death. A few miles from Tuzla a tailgate broke open, and people tumbled onto the road. Another baby died.

On a crumbling cement step in front of Tuzla's sports arena, I stood with a steno pad and a pen in my hands and watched this convoy arrive. The headlights glistened in the gray evening air. The trucks stopped in the street a few hundred yards short of the sports arena before pulling up slowly one at a time. Their airbrakes hissed as they came to a stop, and when the engines were switched off, a cold hush hung in the air. Vomit oozed down the sides of the trucks. The limp bodies of old men and dead infants were handed down. Soldiers and hospital workers wept as they unloaded children with scab-covered faces. They carried the infirm, some on stretchers, some in their arms, into ambulances and cars or into the warmth of the arena, where they set them down under the basketball nets on sponge mattresses covered with gray woolen blankets. The natural reflex was to pitch in, to take someone's hand, and I thought about pitching in; but all I did was scribble some details into my notebook:

truck beds coated with filth and urine; people stinking of sweat, shit, woodsmoke, and death; someone said this; someone said that.

S UNNY weather returned on the Tuesday after the weekend's heavy snowfalls. The cease-fire had survived two nights. In Sarajevo, pedestrians were strolling streets that had been deserted for months because of sniper fire, and in Srebrenica workers were unloading sacks of wheat flour from another food convoy.

I strolled down to Tuzla's sports arena alone that Tuesday afternoon to scan the lists of refugees who had arrived the night before. Most of the refugees had already been relocated to schools and government buildings in the area, but some of the people still hanging around the arena said they knew a family of Čeliks in Srebrenica, though none of the first names they gave me matched up. Hamed had heard nothing but rumors about his family since Huso had telephoned him from the Žepa post office before the lines went dead. Hamed was in Austria by now. He had been living with Grandpa Avdija for eight months already, listening all the while to the rumors brought by refugees from the war. Huso was dead, they said; Paja had been killed in action; Sanela had taken a piece of shrapnel in her stomach; Hiba had made it to Srebrenica. I looked for the name Čelik on the list of refugees who had arrived at the sports hall, but did not expect to find it, and didn't. I did not know the names of anyone else from Kupusovići at the time and would not have recognized "Muratagić, Saliha" if I had seen it. But Saliha's name was there. She had walked right by me.

In the gray of that evening, thousands more people had gathered around another convoy of UN trucks in Srebrenica. The chaos was worse than that of two days earlier. One of Orić's commanders, Zulfo Tursunović, demanded that the first truck be reserved for people from his village, and his fighters climbed aboard and threw off the women and children who dared defy his instructions. Some of the refugees paid the local police the equivalent of $200 each in German marks to get aboard, and people who did not pay were thrown from the trucks. The convoy was halted on the way out of Srebrenica by Muslim soldiers furious that their family members had been left behind. They fired warning rounds into the air and threatened to blow up the lead truck with a grenade if it proceeded any farther. Once the convoy had cleared the enclave, Serb boys and women in Bratunac pelted the trucks with rocks and chunks of ice. And on the outskirts of Tuzla, Muslim soldiers set land mines across the road and halted the convoy to protest the pandemonium of the evacuation. The people jammed aboard the trucks waited for hours, squirming in place together with the dead while their own people ranted and raved at UN officials as if the UN, and not Naser Orić and his officers, were responsible for organizing the exodus.

❆ ❆ ❆

PRESIDENT Alija Izetbegović appeared distraught and powerless when José Maria Mendiluce met him at the presidency building in Sarajevo to discuss the evacuation. General Mladić, griping that Orić's men were provoking his troops, had announced that the Serbs would not allow any more food convoys into the enclave. He had instructed the UN to send in fleets of empty trucks to evacuate the civilians trapped in the town, and Orić responded by announcing that he would allow no more civilians to leave. Within a day, the Serb offensive was in full swing again, pressing Srebrenica from the south.

"Your dilemma is our dilemma," Izetbegović told Mendiluce after the UN official explained that a massive evacuation from Srebrenica would only do Mladić's bidding. Mendiluce waited as the Bosnian president left the room, phoned the commander of his army, a former Yugoslav army major named Sefer Halilović, and returned a few minutes later. "I have instructed the Srebrenica authorities to authorize an evacuation with three criteria: wounded civilians, elderly people, and women with small children," Izetbegović said. "The local authorities will take full responsibility for identifying those people who meet the criteria and ensuring an orderly boarding of the trucks." Mendiluce had the Bosnian president's approval to transfer about ten thousand people in an operation to begin on Tuesday, April 6. Later that night, Bosnia's prime minister, Haris Silajdžić, phoned Mendiluce's office and asked the UN to consider evacuating everyone from the enclave.

A convoy of twenty trucks entered Srebrenica as planned that Tuesday. But Orić barred the departure of any civilians until the UN evacuated his wounded soldiers by helicopter and deployed in Srebrenica a full team of military observers and a company of Canadian infantry. Mladić responded by pounding the town with artillery, cutting its water supply, and pressing ahead from the south. By now, the cease-fire had completely collapsed. In Sarajevo, Morillon pressed Wahlgren to allow him to return to Srebrenica, and the French general set off without the approval of the Serb authorities. He got as far as Sokolac, a village jammed with Serb refugees just above Sarajevo, before Serb soldiers blocked his progress and, after a stalemate lasting seven hours, forced three of the five vehicles in his convoy to turn back. Morillon pressed onward. At Zvornik, hundreds of women and children blocked the road. Young men climbed atop Morillon's armored car and ripped away its

UN flag, radio antennas, and metal canisters of diesel fuel. They spray-painted "Morillon-Hitler" on the white body of the vehicle. They pounded steel spikes into its bulletproof windows. They slashed its tires and tried to dismantle its machine gun. And at the side of the road, Serb policemen and soldiers looked on, smoking cigarettes and smiling.

BY that Friday, April 9, Morillon and Wahlgren were in Belgrade again, meeting with President Milošević and General Mladić and pressing for a cessation of hostilities. The Serbs were now obsessed with portents of American military intervention and a decision by the UN Security Council to send NATO war planes to enforce the UN's "no-fly zone." Mladić warned Wahlgren and Morillon that he would not tolerate any more international interference in eastern Bosnia. "Why is Srebrenica considered the center of the world?" Mladić asked.

"The United Nations doesn't want that to be the case," Wahlgren answered. "It is in your hands not to make it the center of the world."

The Serb general launched into a tirade about the Serb civilians killed near Srebrenica. "You must be neutral," he insisted, lashing out at Morillon. "The Serbs are doing their best to remain reasonable and objective. I am doing my best to make it possible to establish peace and to cooperate with UN-PROFOR, the UNHCR and other organizations. I have risked my life to protect Muslims, and in the final analysis I should not be deemed to be a war criminal." Mladić then repeated his offer to allow the UN to enter Srebrenica with empty trucks to evacuate the Muslims. He offered to open a corridor for all the Muslim civilians in Srebrenica to trek to Tuzla. He demanded that Orić and his men surrender to the Serbs or the UN.

"It will be a total catastrophe," Morillon interrupted.

Wahlgren broke in. He insisted that Mladić comply with a demand by the UN Security Council and allow the deployment of a company of Canadian soldiers in Srebrenica. "Neither you nor we have any option now," Wahlgren said. "You must decide, yes or no."

"What is the guarantee that the Muslims will surrender if the United Nations enters the town?"

"The demilitarization process will begin immediately," Wahlgren replied. "The Muslims must give up their weapons or leave the town. . . . Can you establish an absolute cease-fire in the Srebrenica pocket over a three day period?"

Mladić avoided giving a direct answer. He demanded instead that Sefer Halilović, the Bosnian army commander, meet him to hash out the terms of a surrender. "Halilović was a major until yesterday and couldn't even talk to generals. I am humiliated even to speak with him." Wahlgren arranged a meeting for April 12 in Sarajevo.

"Orić must be patient until we see the results of the meeting with Halilović," Mladić said. "If Halilović attends the meeting, the Serbs will not fire a single round even if the Muslims open fire."

Reporters accosted Mladić as he left the meeting. They asked him to comment on the Security Council's demand that 150 Canadian soldiers be deployed in Srebrenica. "Over my dead body, and the bodies of my family," he said.

AT about two o'clock on Monday afternoon, April 12, Mladić arrived at Sarajevo airport for the meeting with Halilović. Wahlgren and Morillon were already there, and the Serb general sat down and waited for the Bosnian commander to show up. Skirmishes were continuing along the front line south of Srebrenica. But the town was quiet enough for a group of young men to organize a soccer tournament on a paved playground just outside a white stucco school building where hundreds of refugee families from Konjević Polje and Cerska had taken shelter. Teenage girls had gathered on concrete bleachers to watch the boys play. Overhead came the reassuring roar of the NATO fighter aircraft on their first patrols to enforce the UN's no-fly zone.

Sefer Halilović never appeared for the meeting with General Mladić in Sarajevo, and as the Serb general sat there with the UN commanders, Wahlgren appealed again to Mladić to end the attacks on Srebrenica.

"I have two requests," Mladić answered. "First, a message should be sent to Izetbegović and Halilović. Tell them I came to this meeting to help the Muslims and to speak directly about the problem of Srebrenica. I am ready to attend another meeting. The Muslims should set the date, provided that I have notice three or four days in advance. If they fail to show up, it would mean that they have chosen to stay on the warpath. Second, please pass along my request that NATO planes not fly over the area of Republika Srpska. An incident can be staged to make it look like the Serbs have engaged NATO aircraft."

"I will continue to respect the March 28 cease-fire, as I have until now," Mladić continued. "But not in cases where Serbs suffer casualties or where the Muslims conduct strong offensive actions. There should be no more need to make war. It should be possible to negotiate and to solve issues peacefully."

"Will you take Srebrenica by force?" one of the UN officials asked.

"I could have taken it ten days ago," Mladić answered. "It was not politically expedient to do so." He stood up and assured Wahlgren that he would abide by the cease-fire. It was about 2:15 P.M. when the meeting adjourned.

Kuposovići in the 1980s: Hiba Čelik with Huso, wearing the gold watch he bought in Baghdad. Sitting in front of the wash-basin beside their house. (Courtesy of Avdo Čelik)

Ajka Čelik, Huso Čelik's mother.

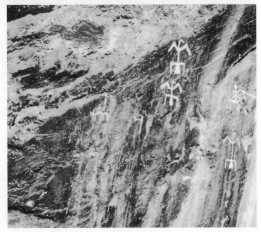

Above. Kupusovići in the 1960s. Against the backdrop of Mount Zvijezda, from the left in rear: Meho Sućeska, Huso Čelik (head above haypile), Esad Čelik, Saliha (Čelik) Murtagić, Zudija Sućeska, Ajkuna Čelik, and an unidentified woman. (Courtesy of Avdo Čelik)

Right. The Roman signs etched into the wall of Mount Zvijezda.

Along the road from Kupusovići to Odžak in the 1970s. From the left, Cousin Avdo Muratagić, Sanela Čelik (throwing a snowball), Behadil Kešmer (at the reins of the oxcart), unidentified boys in the rear. In the foreground: Avdo Čelik, Huso's older brother. In the background is the minaret of Juzbin's mosque. (Courtesy of Avdo Čelik)

Adem Kozić, Avdo Čelik, Huso Čelik, and a friend, posing with a portable radio in the 1970s. (Courtesy of Avdo Čelik)

The Čelik children in the early 1980s. Clockwise from the top: Paja, Hamed, Sanela, and Sead Čelik.

The Odžak school-house, 1997. Originally an Austrian custom-house. The precinct administration building between world wars. Detention site for the men killed at Zvekara in 1941. Burned in 1944. Remodeled as a school in the 1950s. Site of elections and referendums in the 1990s. Now vacant.

April 1992, a bluff over-looking Višeg-rad. Serb soldiers with antiaircraft guns trained on the town. (Miloš Cvetković)

Višegrad, April 1992. Serb army troops stand-ing before Mehmed Pasha Sokolović's bridge over the Drina River. (Miloš Cvetković)

Serb irregulars, or Chetniks, on patrol during the
operation to expel Muslim inhabitants of the Skelani
area in May 1992. (Miloš Cvetković)

Serbs fleeing across the Drina from Bosnia to Serbia
during a Muslim offensive on Skelani in January 1993.
(Miloš Cvetković)

A grieving Serb woman with the skull of her son, who was killed in a Muslim raid. (Miloš Cvetković)

Portrait of Naser Orić, the Muslim commander in Srebrenica. Taken in 1993.

The house at number 8,
Rudarska Street, the Čelik's
home in Srebrenica.

Paja Čelik, wearing Huso's
gold watch. (Rachel L.
Cobb)

General Philippe Morillon, commander of
the United Nations military force in Bosnia.
At the funeral for the victims of the Orthodox
Christmas attack on Kravica in January 1993.
(Miloš Cvetković)

The president of the Bosnian Serb republic,
Radovan Karadžić and Bosnian Serb gener-
al Ratko Mladić. Rogatica, April 1994.
(Srdjan Ilić)

Opposite above. A crying boy runs after a UN food truck jammed with Muslims fleeing Srebrenica in the spring of 1993. (Srdjan Ilić)

Opposite below. The hand of a dead boy hangs over the side of a UN food truck jammed with people fleeing Srebrenica in the evacuations in the spring of 1993. (Miloš Cvetković)

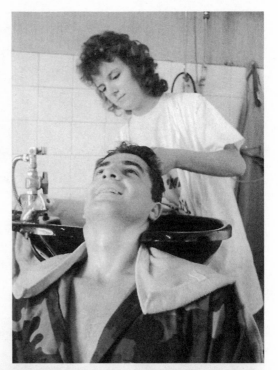

Right. Milan Lukić getting his hair trimmed in Višegrad in June 1992, the height of the ethnic cleansing of the town. (Miloš Cvetković)

The Čelik family at Šaban's farmhouse in Tuzla after the fall of Srebenica. From left rear: Zlatija, Paja, Hiba, Sanela, with children Edin, Mirza, and Nehrudin. (Rachel L. Cobb)

Sanela holding
a portrait of her
husband,
Mohamed
Halilović, and
nursing their son,
Nehrudin.
(Rachel L. Cobb)

Above. The tent city, Tuzla
airport, July 1995. Senad
Sućeska and Paja Čelik
holding Paja's sons Mirza
and Edin, born in Srebrenica in 1994.

Right. The leg bone of
a dead soldier sticking
from his boot. On a
trail above Nova Ksaba,
1996. (Courtesy of
Anna Husarska)

Kupusovići, 1997. Hiba Čelik sitting on the wash basin beside the ruins of her house.

Hiba Čelik with Dragoljub Radovanić, her former neighbor, during a visit to Odžak in 1997.

A few minutes ticked away before the first Serb mortar round detonated in the Srebrenica schoolyard where the boys were playing soccer. A plume of gray smoke and dust vaulted skyward, and bits of gravel pelted the ground. Shouts of frenzy blasted through the whistling scream that filled the ears of everyone caught by the thunderclap. Shrapnel had torn off legs and arms. Teeth had been ripped from mouths. Severed torsos squirted blood and oozed intestines. Hysterical children screamed and trembled. Parents inside the school rushed outside to the playground to look for their kids. A second shell hit. Flying shreds of flesh splattered onto the white wall of the school and got caught on the playground fence and on nearby trees and poles. Men and women rushed into the yard again to search for their children and help gather up the wounded. The bread truck arrived, and the handful of Canadian soldiers General Morillon had left in Srebrenica drove up and loaded injured and dying people into their armored personnel carrier. Muslim men piled bodies and body parts into oxcarts and wheelbarrows to carry them to the hospital.

The shellfire went on for the next hour. Three or four explosions. A few minutes of chaos. Three or four more explosions. People caught by surprise lay dead and dying in the streets and backyards.

PAJA Čelik was on duty in the hospital when he heard the first detonation from the schoolyard. The bread truck rumbled to the hospital entrance a few minutes later and spilled out the first of the mangled and dying. Paja helped haul them in. The Canadian armored vehicle pulled up with the second load. Then the bread truck returned again and again. The last hospital beds filled up. The orderlies laid the wounded in the hallways. The floor grew slippery, then sticky, with blood. The dying and wounded cried to be put out of their misery. Paja and another worker carried two mutilated youngsters directly into the morgue to live out the last few minutes of their lives. By early evening, weeping women were huddling together in front of the hospital longing to get inside to see their children. One woman from Mount Zvijezda spotted Paja. She asked him if he had seen her son, Jasmin.

"I haven't seen him, but you can come in and look for him yourself."

Paja led her inside. They walked along the sticky corridors and peeked inside the hospital rooms for half an hour before Paja scanned a list of the wounded and found Jasmin's name. He led the woman to a young man who was lying on the floor. They had looked him over once already. A deep gash ran across his face, and he had lost his right eye.

"This is Jasmin."

The woman gazed into the face.

"Jasmin has a mole on his back," she said.

Paja eased the young man onto his side. There was the mole. Paja summoned a doctor to calm the woman down and a nurse to bandage Jasmin's face. Then he slipped outside into the night air, rolled some tobacco into a shred of paper, and smoked it. Milošević's television was reporting that night that, in fact, there had been no shelling attack on any soccer game in any schoolyard in Srebrenica. The mutilated bodies that had shown up at the hospital were the remains of Serb prisoners who had been tortured to death, the television reporters said, and once again Serbs were the victims of flagrant Western propaganda.

❨   ❨   ❨

By the time of the Srebrenica schoolyard shelling, UN officials in Sarajevo and Zagreb had developed a knack for telling journalists and their superiors — sotto voce, of course — that they believed Muslim soldiers provoked the particularly bloody Serb attacks on Muslim civilians. This habit helped mute the calls for serious action that such horrors inevitably elicited. The schoolyard shelling was no exception. UN officials quickly fed journalists a story that one of Orić's two tanks had fired its cannon at the Serbs and that the Serbs had shot into the schoolyard only in retaliation. A UN spokesman later retracted this story, admitting that the UN military personnel on the ground in Srebrenica had no evidence to support it; someone had heard booms that sounded like a tank cannon firing but had never actually seen a tank, much less a tank shooting at anybody. An exasperated General Wahlgren, however, sent a message to UN headquarters in New York that was spread around the offices of Cyrus Vance and David Owen high over the East River in the Secretariat's skyscraper. One of the peace negotiator's staff members drew up a report citing Wahlgren's message. "The Force Commander believes that yesterday's shellings of Srebrenica and Sarajevo were provoked by the Muslim Forces," the report said. "Given the apparent Muslim determination to ensure that the cease-fire is not effective and to maintain Srebrenica in the world headlines, it is hard to see how the Force Commander can successfully bring the two sides together." The next day, Vance submitted his resignation as co-chairman of the international peace conference. He would be gone within a month.

Everything General Philippe Morillon had risked to save Srebrenica and its people seemed to have gone up in the spray of dust and blood that rose from the schoolyard during the soccer game. The morale in his headquarters slumped further with each new report that Mladić's troops had advanced north toward the edge of town after the playground attack. New villages were being burned. Newly displaced people were straggling into town and wandering the streets seeking refuge, food, and water. It was at this moment, on a night of chilly rain, that the government of France officially confirmed rumors that Morillon was being recalled from his post. Defense Minister François Léotard praised his general and denied that Paris was caving in to Serb demands for the general's removal. But no specific date was set for Morillon's departure, and no successor was named.

❮ ❮ ❮

GENERAL RATKO MLADIĆ maneuvered to blunt the international outrage over the schoolyard attack by allowing six UN trucks to carry food to Srebrenica and to evacuate about seventy-five wounded people, fifty of them stretcher-bound. About six hundred other women and children clambered aboard the trucks and escaped the encirclement. After the trucks had departed, Mladić's artillery batteries again opened fire on the outskirts of the town, killing another eight people and wounding a few dozen more. Orić's troops retreated from one fall-back position to the next before digging in about two miles from the town. By Wednesday, April 14, the Muslim defense lines appeared to be on the verge of collapse; and in a last-ditch effort to coax whatever international intervention it could, the Bosnian government announced it would withdraw its acceptance of the Vance-Owen peace plan if Srebrenica was allowed to fall into the Serbs' hands. Desperate to save the plan, David Owen went public with a warning that military action to rescue Srebrenica should not be ruled out; and, in private talks, the Clinton administration warned the Serbs that the United States would press for a lifting of the arms embargo if the onslaught did not stop. When Mladić's men recommenced the attack, Orić secretly informed the UN that he would surrender if the Serbs would permit an airlift of the wounded and an evacuation of all civilians by vehicle and guarantee the safe passage of Srebrenica's Muslim soldiers through Serb-held territory to Tuzla.

A surrender by Srebrenica's Muslims four or five months earlier would have been tacitly welcomed by the UN as well as by the governments in London, Paris, and, no doubt, Washington. No bells had tolled in any world capitals for the Bosnian towns and villages that had fallen to the Serbs in the late autumn after the London conference. If Srebrenica had been added to the list back then, it would have amounted to a partial reprieve from the criticism UN relief officials were taking for failing to deliver food to eastern Bosnia's hungry. By mid-April 1993, however, Srebrenica had become a nightmare for the diplomats and military officials working on the Bosnian problem. When UN civilian and military officials heard that Naser Orić had offered to surrender Srebrenica to General Mladić, they conjured up before their eyes a rerun of the massacre that followed the surrender of the Croatian town of Vukovar in 1991. They imagined television footage of refugees digging themselves out from under piles of rubble. They saw elderly people and women and children being separated from their menfolk, hauled away in buses, dumped out near battle fronts, and forced to walk across a no-man's-land. They saw hundreds of military-age men being shot on the spot or taken away in trucks and summarily executed in cornfields. If Srebrenica fell in a Vukovar-style massacre, the UN military mission would be exposed for what it had been all along, a fig leaf concealing an absence of Western backbone. The UN bureaucracy would be left devoid of credibility. The Vance-Owen peace plan would be dead. The UN Security Council would have to pass new resolutions even as its aid workers and military officials were searching for the bodies of the dead and administering the expulsion of forty thousand people. And worst of all for London, Paris, and Washington would be the deluge of public demands to know why a massacre had been allowed to occur in slow motion before the eyes of the world so many months after the London conference and its declaration of principles.

By Thursday, April 15, rumors were spreading through Sarajevo that Srebrenica would fall into Mladić's hands by noon on Friday. Doctors in Srebrenica's hospital were reporting that the wounded were dying at a rate of five a day because they could not be treated. Overnight, Mladić's artillery batteries pounded the town; and on Friday, Mladić's men made another thrust that brought them to less than a mile of its southern fringe. Shells rained from the sky. By the early afternoon, Srebrenica's post office, the base of the tiny UN contingent, had taken direct hits. Serb soldiers were climbing onto the ridges overlooking the town, and the Muslims could hear the whiz and pop of the first Serb sniper rounds. Soon after nightfall, an eerie quiet filled the air. Paja Čelik, who was sheltering with the rest of the family in the cellar of the apartment building just down the hill from the family's house, talked his friend Senad into climbing outside to get some air and fetch some water. They could hear the gnarl of chain saws clearing firing positions for machine guns and tanks on the hilltops around the town.

The pace of events in the diplomatic world had grown more frantic with Mladić's advance. In Washington, President Clinton made his strongest statement ever about the Bosnian war. He demanded that the attack on Srebrenica stop and called for the United States and its allies to consider taking actions that were, until then, "deemed unacceptable." This wording was a clear reference to air strikes and a lifting of the arms embargo. And with these words, Slobodan Milošević, Radovan Karadžić, and Ratko Mladić grasped that they had pushed as far as they could. During private meetings, they had been warned in no uncertain terms that Serbia would be hit with new economic sanctions. They had been made to understand that they were risking air attacks on the Drina River bridges linking Bosnia and Serbia. Both Milošević and Karadžić now assured American diplomats that the Serbs intended not to occupy Srebrenica but only "to pacify" it. And within hours of their meetings, Karadžić had announced this decision publicly. In talks with Morillon and Wahlgren the next day, Milošević and Karadžić pledged to guarantee the lives of all Muslim civilians and fighters in Srebrenica if Orić's men surrendered their weapons to UN troops.

As dawn broke over Bosnia on Saturday, April 17, Sarajevo radio's morning news bulletin reported that the UN Security Council in New York had just passed a resolution calling for the Serbs and the Muslims to treat Srebrenica as a UN "safe area." The choice of this term, "safe area," was a part of a diplomatic compromise. Led by Diego Arria of Venezuela, diplomats from countries that belonged to the Non-Aligned Movement and supported Bosnia's Muslim-dominated government, had summoned the Security Council members together at four o'clock Friday afternoon New York time and demanded that the UN military force in Bosnia be given a mandate to fight to protect Srebrenica's people. They wanted the council to put Srebrenica under UN protection. When France, Britain, and other European countries with troops in Bosnia inquired whether the countries of the Non-Aligned Movement would be willing to produce the soldiers and money needed to defend Srebrenica by force of arms, Arria and his colleagues agreed to scratch the words "protected area" from the draft resolution, and with them the demand for military action, and insert in their place the words "safe area."

The debate on this amended draft resolution dragged on for hours behind closed doors. The British and French delegations warned time and again that the UN Security Council should never make, or even seem to make, promises it could not keep; but the diplomats from the Non-Aligned Movement countries refused to withdraw the resolution or delay the vote until after negotiations on Srebrenica's demilitarization, which were set to begin Saturday afternoon in Sarajevo. The resolution was adopted just after eleven o'clock that Friday night, New York time. The diplomats who wrote and voted in favor of UN Security Council Resolution 819 did not bother to define the term "safe area" or identify just who was supposed to make it safe. The resolution did not delineate any territory. It did not hint at the duty the UN military force owed the safe area or the people inside it. And this vague wording allowed Bosnia's Muslim leaders, and many of their supporters abroad, to infer that the UN military force had some kind of obligation to rush to Srebrenica's rescue if the Serbs attacked again. On Saturday morning in Sarajevo,

Sefer Halilović knew he no longer had any reason to surrender Srebrenica when he sat down for talks that afternoon with Ratko Mladić.

Mladić's forces launched one final assault on the town early that morning. This time Naser Orić struck back with everything he had left in his arsenal. He fueled up one of his two T-55 tanks with transformer oil thinned with gasoline, packed aboard his last fifty tank shells, and hit the Serbs with a surprise cannonade. About three hundred of the Muslim commander's toughest fighters then drove Mladić's men back about half a mile toward the southeast and two miles toward the south before the Serb retreat stopped. Mladić showed up at the talks in Sarajevo half an hour late, and the discussions dragged on until the early hours of Sunday morning before he and Halilović agreed to a cease-fire around Srebrenica and a plan for the town's demilitarization. It was a hairbreadth shy of a surrender, but that hairbreadth meant there would be no mass exodus of Srebrenica's Muslim people. It meant Orić's soldiers would not have to hand themselves over to the Serbs, though they would have to surrender some weapons, ammunition, and other combat supplies to the UN.

Srebrenica was sunny and peaceful on the following morning, Sunday, April 18. It was Orthodox Easter. The company of Canadian soldiers entered the town within an hour of schedule to begin the demilitarization. By late afternoon, French and British helicopters had ferried over a hundred wounded people, including Muslim soldiers, to the Tuzla airport and on to the hospital.

19

EVEN with the arrival of the Canadian troops in Srebrenica, Naser Orić had scarce reason to trust General Mladić's cease-fire pledge or the UN Security Council and its safe-area resolution. Looking up into the hills around him, Orić found himself staring into the barrels of Mladić's tanks and artillery. Behind these weapons was a phalanx of battle-ready troops, including local Serbs aching to avenge the killing that had gone on in Skelani, Kravica, Loznička Rijeka, Grabovačka Rijeka, Podravanje, and other villages attacked by the Muslims earlier in the war. Mladić's men had broken scores of cease-fire agreements, and there was no hint that the Serb general had abandoned his goal to drive the Muslims out of eastern Bosnia forever.

From Orić's standpoint, the only factors keeping Mladić from sending his men swarming into Srebrenica were the 150 or so Canadians, who were armed with infantry weapons and four TOW antitank missile systems, and some vague talk from New York about air strikes. The Canadians' commanding officer, Lieutenant Colonel Thomas Geburt, presented Orić with a copy of the agreement requiring Srebrenica's Muslims to hand over, within three days, all of the weapons they had inside a "demilitarized zone" that had not yet been delineated or defined. Within the Serb ring around Srebrenica, an area of a little over fifty square miles, Orić had about forty thousand people and enough assault rifles, machine guns, and hunting weapons to arm about five thousand men. His two T-55 tanks and two dozen mortars and other small artillery pieces were worthless because the Muslims had run out of ammunition for them.

Orić's first decision was to announce that since Srebrenica was now a UN safe area there was no more reason to evacuate the thousands of Muslim civilians trapped in the town and nearby villages. Refugees like the Čeliks, the *torbari* who had been Orić's sword and shield, would be staying in Srebrenica regardless of what they thought about the matter. As far as Orić was concerned, it would be the UN's responsibility to feed, clothe, and shelter them. The Muslim-dominated Bosnian government also supported holding these refugees captive in Srebrenica. The presence of Muslim civilians underscored the government's territorial claim to the region, and it was a good bet that any renewed Serb attack on Srebrenica while it was still crowded with refugees would provoke the military intervention that the government had been seeking since the war began.

The disarmament process took a turn in Orić's favor. Colonel Geburt, who had orders to complete the disarmament and no means of carrying it out, expedited the handover process by unfolding a topographical map, drawing a circle around the town of Srebrenica, and declaring that to be the demilitarized zone. Orić surrendered a few hundred defective rifles and the worthless tanks and artillery pieces and ordered his men to stash the rest of their guns in villages like Potočari that were outside the demilitarized zone but inside the Serb ring. On Wednesday, April 21, the UN troops strolled through the town with some Serb observers. They spotted no weapons, and at the end of their tour the UN announced that the demilitarization had been completed on time.

Ratko Mladić was incensed. He had warned UN military commanders that if Orić's men did not hand over their weapons, he would consider the demilitarization agreement to be null and void. Now he demanded that the UN order the Canadians to step aside so that he could roll into Srebrenica and deal with Orić's Muslims on his own. The UN military commanders kept Mladić's demand a secret, but they stood firm. The demilitarization of the town was complete, they insisted, and the Canadians would not be going anywhere. The

Serbs sealed off all the roads into Srebrenica. They halted food and medicine deliveries. They held up teams of Western doctors and aid workers who were trying to enter the town. After a few days, General Wahlgren warned Serb leaders that the Canadians would fight if Mladić attacked the town. Colonel Geburt did not flinch at Mladić's threats, and the Canadian talked tough to the local Serb commanders, warning them that the safe area was now under his protection and that if the Serbs opened fire, the Canadians would shoot back. British diplomats notified Slobodan Milošević that if Mladić's forces attacked the Canadians, London would order its fighter aircraft to attack the Serb positions around Srebrenica.

Mladić held back. The standoff dragged on. And for the next six weeks, frantic politicians, diplomats, soldiers, and political analysts in New York and a dozen foreign capitals scribbled out cables, reports, resolutions, and press releases trying to calm the situation.

❲   ❲   ❲

WITH their campaign to overrun Srebrenica stymied, Milošević and the Bosnian Serb leaders now found themselves under intense international pressure to sign the peace plan they had been trying to defeat when they began the Srebrenica offensive in January. A day after declaring Srebrenica to be a safe area, the UN Security Council had passed a resolution that required automatic imposition of economic sanctions on Serbia if Milošević and the Bosnian Serbs did not sign the peace plan by April 26. These sanctions, if enforced, would hit Serbia and Montenegro hard. Ships would be banned from entering their territorial waters, and other countries would be barred from transporting goods across their borders. Any Serbian airliners, trucks, and cargo vessels caught outside the country were liable to be seized, and Serbia's foreign bank accounts and other financial assets would be frozen.

On April 25, as the midnight deadline neared, Milošević informed David Owen that he had agreed to the peace plan. He summoned Bosnian Serb leaders to Belgrade and demanded that they sign as well. He was clearly certain the signatures would amount to nothing more than an empty gesture that would ward off the sanctions. Members of the Clinton administration openly loathed the peace plan, and the Serbian president correctly reasoned that the U.S. government would never commit the troops necessary to implement the deal. Milošević told Radovan Karadžić and other Bosnian Serb leaders that without the American military there would be nothing to compel the Serbs to comply with provisions of the plan that called on them to withdraw from the territory they had conquered, to recognize the Drina as an international border, and to allow Muslim refugees to return to their homes. The Bosnian Serb leaders, however, refused to gamble on Milošević's assurances; and the sanctions deadline passed without their signature.

Milošević tried a second time to forestall the sanctions. On May 1, Vance and Owen brought him and all the major Bosnian leaders to a villa outside Athens for talks. Milošević again assured Karadžić that it was safe to sign the peace plan because it could never be implemented. But Karadžić still refused to go along. Milošević then threatened to isolate the Bosnian Serbs by imposing a sanctions regime of his own along the Bosnian-Serbian border, and he warned Karadžić about intelligence reports that Western fighter jets were standing by to begin bombing. Karadžić went to bed, still refusing to sign. The next morning, Vance racheted up the pressure. After he warned Karadžić that the U.S. Air Force was ready to bomb, the Serb leader slipped off into a corner with his old friends Momčilo Krajišnik and Nikola Koljević. When their huddle broke up, they announced that Karadžić would sign the peace plan, but only on the condition that his signature be ratified by the Bosnian Serbs' assembly.

On May 5, a fleet of sleek Mercedes-Benz saloon cars whisked the political elite of Serbia and Montenegro to Pale so that they could ply their powers of persuasion on the motley assortment of truck drivers, peasants, herdsmen, "businessmen," soldiers, teachers, and professionals who had walked out of Bosnia's republican assembly in 1991 and now called themselves the "parliament of Republika Srpska." Except for drawn-out cigarette and brandy breaks, the assemblymen remained in session in the meeting hall of a ski lodge until well after midnight. Dobrica Ćosić warned them of imminent air strikes on the Drina River bridges. Orthodox priests and metropolitans swished in and out of the meeting in their black robes. Foreign journalists buttonholed Serb leaders and quizzed their translators to find out what was happening. And from time to time, the jet engines of NATO fighter planes bellowed overhead. Milošević addressed the gathering twice, the second time behind closed doors. He reiterated his assurances that the peace plan would prove to be a nonstarter, and he appealed to the parliament to lift the burden of the latest sanctions from the shoulders of the entire Serbian nation by ratifying Karadžić's signature. "One can sacrifice for one's nation everything except the nation itself," Milošević said. "If you don't accept the Vance-Owen Plan you are going to sacrifice your people."

The parliamentarians, true believers in the quixotic idea that they were fighting to save their families and a sleeping Europe from a resurgent fascism and Islamic fundamentalism, stood firm. Then General Ratko Mladić took the floor, and the doors to the meeting hall were closed. Mladić bragged that he and his fighters had not been in the least intimidated by the recent threats of

NATO bombing. The Serbs, after all, had UN soldiers and officials practically in their clutches and could stop NATO in its tracks by seizing them as hostages. Mladić then pointed to a number of maps. He pointed out the highlands and valleys where the plan would leave Serbs vulnerable to attack. He pointed to Srebrenica and Zvornik and Žepa and Višegrad and the other districts that would remain in Muslim hands under the plan. And then he pointed to the river Drina. "For the Serbs living west of the Drina," Mladić would say later, "the river has never been a border. And it will never be a border. The Drina is our backbone. It flows through the middle of Serb territory. . . . For the Muslims, however, the Drina was always just a kind of symbol, something they needed to bridge in order to link up with the Islamic world stretching all the way to the Great Wall of China. The Drina has been for them a synonym for domination over the Serbs." When Mladić finished and the roll call was taken in the early morning of May 6, only two of the sixty-five delegates voted to accept the deal.

The Vance-Owen plan was dead at last. Western leaders were quick to cobble together stopgap measures to fill the diplomatic vacuum left by the collapse of the peace process they had initiated at the London conference. France had already seized upon the safe-area concept. And a few hours after the Bosnian Serb parliament adjourned, the UN Security Council passed a French-sponsored resolution declaring five more Bosnian enclaves—Žepa, Goražde, Bihać, Tuzla, and Sarajevo—to be safe areas. The countries of the Non-Aligned Movement seized the opportunity to renew their demand that the Security Council give the UN military force in Bosnia the mandate and the means to defend the safe areas if the Serbs attacked. This issue came to a head a month later, during the closed-door discussions preceding the passage of Resolution 836, the Security Council's most controversial decision concerning the Bosnian war.

The public debate on the resolution proved to be a mini-sequel to the London conference, a stage-managed effort to convince public opinion that the powerful nations of the world were finally doing something effective to staunch the bloodshed. The French ambassador, Jean-Bernard Merimée, lauded the resolution. He promised that it would ensure the survival of the civilians in the safe areas. "To carry out the new mandate," Merimée said, "*the draft resolution explicitly provides for the possibility of using force to respond to bombardments against the safe areas, to armed incursions into them* or to any deliberate obstacles to the freedom of movement of UNPROFOR or of protected humanitarian convoys. *It also provides for the use of air power within and around the safe areas in order to support UNPROFOR in the fulfillment of its mandate, if necessary.*" Russia's ambassador, Yuli Vorontsov, came out swinging a heftier stick. "Henceforth, *any attempted military attacks, shooting and shelling of the safe areas, any armed incursions into those areas, and any hindrance of the delivery of humanitarian assistance will be stopped by United Nations forces by using all necessary measures, including armed force."* (author's italics).

Lurking beneath all this reassuring rhetoric, however, was an uncertain reality. France, Russia, Great Britain, and Spain, the very countries whose ambassadors had given the firmest public assurances that Resolution 836 would guarantee the security of Srebrenica and the other safe areas, had inserted language into the resolution that hollowed out the apparent duty of the UN military force to protect them. The resolution was intentionally crafted to say that the UN military force would only "deter" attacks against the safe areas; and the wording says nothing explicit about fighting to protect or defend them. The resolution states that the UN troops in Srebrenica and the other safe areas would only apply military force "acting in self defense," a right peacekeepers everywhere enjoyed as a matter of course. The paragraph of the resolution providing for air strikes "in and around" the safe areas was left intentionally vague as to whether the air power would provide a security umbrella for the safe areas themselves or just for the UN troops inside them.

The frustrated diplomats from the Non-Aligned Movement countries understood that the resolution had no backbone. But they exacerbated the situation by demanding that, since the UN military force was not going to be required to defend the Security Council's safe areas, the council should at least require General Mladić to withdraw his forces from around the areas and allow Bosnia's army to maintain its presence inside them to provide a modicum of protection. The rest of the Security Council members accepted this compromise wording and thereby presented Muslim commanders with the opportunity to mount offensive operations from within the safe areas and leave it to the UN commanders on the ground to persuade Mladić that it was not a good idea to retaliate against the Muslims.

The UN's military commanders flew into fits of hysteria even before Resolution 836 was finally adopted. General Wahlgren fired off one cable after another to New York. He warned that the first NATO fighter jet to drop a bomb on the Serbs would create a de facto alliance between the UN and the Bosnian Muslim soldiers in Srebrenica and the other safe areas and invite Serb attacks on the poorly equipped UN troops. Moreover, he projected that the UN would have to deploy 34,000 troops in the safe areas before it would have a deterrent credible enough to ward off any attacks and prevent its troops within the areas from being veritable hostages. He estimated the annual cost of this force to be $1.7 billion, about $400 million more than the UN's entire regular yearly budget; and this did not include the cost of deployment, ammunition, or air support. Finally, he predicted that the Serbs would install air defense missile systems to deflect the threat of NATO air action.

The Security Council's permanent members would have none of Wahlgren's criticisms. A few weeks after Resolution 836's passage, the council voted to call on the UN member states to come up with 7,600 new troops. In the months that followed, not a single nation stepped forward to volunteer its forces for Srebrenica. The Canadian government, realizing that its troops in Srebrenica were now dealing with a situation Ottawa had never anticipated, immediately began lobbying to have them removed.

RESOLUTION 836 was never officially translated into the Serbo-Croatian language, and copies of it were never distributed in Srebrenica or any of the other safe areas. The only mass media available in the enclave, a Muslim FM radio station and Milošević's Radio-Television Serbia, spread only confusion, in no small part because Serbo-Croatian lacks a simple, accurate translation of the meaningless English phrase "safe area." "*Bezbedna zona*," or "security zone," was one common translation; another was "*zaštičena zona*," or "protected zone." These terms, always used in close proximity to the words "United Nations," clearly implied that the UN had a duty to protect the safe areas with military force if necessary. The inference drawn in Srebrenica was that if the place came under attack, NATO airplanes were going to bomb the attackers.

Whatever it was linguistically, after mid-June 1993 Srebrenica was little more than a concentration camp cut off from the world and soon almost forgotten, a place surrounded by an enemy hungry for revenge and watched over by foreigners who had no desire to be there. With no advance notice, Secretary-General Boutros-Ghali dealt with General Wahlgren and his complaints about the safe-areas mandate by sacking him as the commander of the UN military force in the former Yugoslavia. A week or so later, General Morillon was sent away from Bosnia. One sunny summer's day before departing, he flew back to Srebrenica in a helicopter. Thousands of refugees, townspeople, and local peasants turned out to greet him. The same women who had surrounded his car and kept him from leaving Srebrenica in March now presented him bouquets of flowers. And Naser Orić announced that one stretch of the asphalt road running through town would from that day forth carry the name Morillonova Ulica, the rue Morillon.

PART FIVE

A
SAFE
PLACE

20

HUSO and I had our ham radio conversation on a drizzly evening late that June. After we signed off, he returned to the house on Rudarska Street and told Hiba and the rest of the family that he was certain I would find a way to visit them. He was sure I would bring money and, especially, cigarettes. He went to bed that evening cheery and relaxed.

I had been careful not to promise Huso that I would come to Srebrenica. I had told him I would try but knew that I would never make it, at least not while the war was on. The Serb army was keeping journalists out of Srebrenica. And it had expelled me the previous summer from all the territory it had seized in Bosnia. I received notice of my expulsion at the army's press center in the town of Banja Luka during August 1992 while writing stories about the Muslims being held in Serb concentration camps. I had gone with some friends—once with permission, and once without—to a nearby town named Čelinac, whose Muslims were living under legal restrictions similar to the Jewish laws the Nazis had imposed all over occupied Europe during World War II. I interviewed one terrified Muslim family in the town, talked to Muslim men forced to sweep its streets, and heard the Serb town fathers explain that they had imposed the restrictions in order "to safeguard" the Muslims. The town's police took us in on the same day that Serb soldiers came into Čelinac seeking Muslims to kill in retaliation for the deaths of Serb soldiers who were fighting along a front line just up the road. The next morning a colonel from the Bosnian Serb army ordered me to leave Serb-held territory immediately; he said the army would no longer guarantee my safety at any of its checkpoints. My wife, Ljiljana, and I had received about half a dozen anonymous death threats already that spring and summer. But this was a threat from an army colonel glowering at me from across a table.

I phoned Karadžić in Pale to try and smooth out the problem, but he never picked up the line or returned my calls. And I never forgot, and will never forget, the threats I subsequently received from his press office or the calls to my home number in Belgrade with male and female voices on the other end of the line warning me that the teeth would be ripped from the mouth of my daughter, a two-year-old girl whose great-great-grandfather had died in 1912 fighting with the Serbian army that "liberated" Kosovo from the Turks and whose Serbian grandmother had lost her entire family to the Ustaše in World War II.

HUSO sent off his first Red Cross letter a few days after our radio conversation. He wrote it on a single sheet of the standard Red Cross letter paper, about six inches wide and eight inches long and perforated along the left side. His name and address and the name and address of the recipient were filled in on the front of the sheet; on the back were twenty-three dotted lines for a message that had to be innocuous enough to pass a military censor. Huso managed to squeeze in about six words on each line and didn't get much beyond listing the names of the children, grandchildren, in-laws, and aunts and everyone else he was greeting. He described life as difficult and did not elaborate. He asked for letters and money. He wished everyone well. He wished everyone's neighbors well. Then the dotted lines ran out. Huso sent the first letter to Salzburg. Hamed, Gordana, and the kids had already departed for Canada by the time it arrived.

Canada was a godsend. I had told Hamed and Gordana not to bother trying to emigrate to the United States, because it would be much easier to begin life anew in Canada. The Canadians really wanted, and needed, people willing to work. They had job-training programs for immigrants. They offered language programs, a state medical system, and well-run public schools in their inner cities. The visa procedure took a few months. There were documents to obtain in Austria and Serbia. There were physical examinations to take, diplomas to be translated and notarized, and interviews with consular officers. Muhamed had been in Salzburg almost a year before he met Gordana and his kids at the airport in Budapest for their flight to Toronto. He hardly knew his own children.

About twelve hours after their plane took off, they moved into a motel room somewhere in Toronto. A few months later, they were living in a state-subsidized apartment with parquet floors, a shower that gushed hot water, a twenty-foot balcony, and a parking place. Their elder son and daughter started primary school, and Hamed and Gordana started English lessons. Hamed found a job baking doughnuts that winter. And when we spoke on the phone, I told him not to look back, not to fill up his mind with stories of the war or the videotapes of the violence that were circulating through the Bosnian émigré community. "Don't think about it, and don't think about your family. They are not in your hands. There is nothing you can do for them now. Just live for your children and get ready to bring the rest of the family to Canada when the war is over." In a few years, the kids would be speaking English. In a few years, they would be able to go to college. And in a generation it might be safe to look back.

Hamed tried to hide German marks inside Polaroid snapshots enclosed in the Red Cross letters he sent Huso and Paja. None of the money was ever delivered. It would not have stretched very far anyway. Cigarettes were the accepted currency in Srebrenica then. When Huso and I spoke, Marlboros cost fifty dollars a pack, and even paper for rolling cigarettes was difficult to obtain. Paja and Senad started cutting up the Red Cross stationery and tearing out the pages of old books to roll cigarettes filled with pumpkin leaves. Huso could never find enough to smoke, and when he didn't have enough to smoke, he would pace the hollow floor of the house searching, as the Bosnians say, for hair on eggs to bitch about.

Huso also wrote a Red Cross letter that summer to his brother, Uncle Avdo, up in Mölln, Austria. He begged Avdo to send money, and not to put it off. But Avdo was not much of a correspondent. He says he sent a few letters but never had any money to send. He never let Huso know that after a dozen or so years he had finally received a reply to the card he had sent exulting in the death, "like a dog," of Vitomir Janković. The message came from Odžak. A family of Serbs who were Avdo's neighbors in Mölln had gone back for a visit to their home village just below Odžak. They brought the message back to Avdo personally. It was stark. Just two benign words and a name, and the neighbors had no idea of the malicious glee they dripped. "Best Regards" was all the message said. It was from Mile Janković, Vitomir's son.

$$\text{❝ \quad ❝ \quad ❝}$$

NOT even the silver rush of the Middle Ages had brought so many people to Srebrenica: twenty thousand of them, four times more than the town's prewar population, and in the surrounding villages lived some twenty thousand more. The artillery shells stopped falling into the town when the Canadians arrived and the safe area was declared. The front-line gunfire was far enough away to allow people to spend most of their time outdoors. Old men in navy-blue felt berets huddled in conversation on the streets. Hordes of people descended like flies on the piles of garbage from the Canadians' mess. Men and women hauled firewood on their backs. They stood in long lines to receive their food rations. They wandered around and went nowhere. Refugee families filled up all the rooms of the hotel. They moved into the basements beneath dilapidated houses. They squatted inside office buildings like the Energoinvest mining company's headquarters, just below the Čeliks' house. Stacks of logs and clotheslines hung with the refugees' ragged laundry made labyrinths of all the yards. Stove pipes were stuck through sheets of plastic covering the windows. A few refugee families moved into Dragica Vasić's house after someone climbed onto the roof and stretched plastic tarps over the hole left by the mortar shells that had nearly killed her.

The sun burned high in an azure, cloudless sky for days on end. The roar of NATO fighter jets patrolling overhead drew the small boys' faces skyward, and their eyes searched for the flash of a wing reflecting the sunlight. Packs of children chased after Canadian soldiers when they rolled by like blue-helmeted Pied Pipers in white jeeps and trucks.

"*Bonbon! Bonbon!*" the boys demanded. On good days, the back hatch of a fat white armored vehicle would fling open. A hand would emerge from the darkness inside and toss into the air a small cloud of candies wrapped in shiny colored plastic or foil. The kids would swarm over the candies, shouting and grabbing and laughing. The hatch would close, and the vehicle would try to trundle away. But other children, and more of them than before, would give chase.

"*Još bonbon! Još bonbon!* More *bonbon!* More *bonbon. . . .*" And on the best of days the hatch would open again, and the hand from inside would send up another cloud of candies before the Canadians could finally escape.

❆ ❆ ❆

A CORSO began that summer in the tree-shaded park in the center of Sre-brenica. The promenade of young people starving for a social life after a year of fighting and weeks of living underground got started every afternoon at about four o'clock, right after the girls finished washing the dishes from the afternoon meal. Young people came from all over the enclave to escape the boredom of the villages and the tiny rooms jammed with nagging parents and aunts and uncles and cousins who were driving themselves and everyone else mad. The girls, some in ragged *dimije*, sweaters, and tennis shoes, others in tight pants and spiked heels, strolled arm in arm with their kindred spirits. They snickered and sneered, whispered secrets, and cast sidelong glances at the young men hanging around in their blue jeans, silk-screened sweatshirts, and, if they had them, black loafers or athletic shoes. The air hummed with voices. Young men whistled and shouted. They cracked sunflower seeds between their teeth and talked about the war, and where to get cigarettes, and the results of big soccer games they had heard about.

Sanela had found herself a new boyfriend by the time Srebrenica's young people had begun gathering regularly for the corso. She had met Nijaz during the winter. He was a few years older than Sanela, a soldier from a village just outside of town. She fell for him because he was a clown and more than slightly mad. Before the Canadians arrived, Nijaz had a habit of coming back from the front line late at night, climbing the hill to no. 8 Rudarska, and waking up Sanela and the rest of the family.

"Tell that guy not to come around here any more at three in the morning," Huso commanded.

"Right. Right. Okay. Okay."

Sanela did tell Nijaz not to come late at night. But each time he trudged home from the front line pumped up with the adrenaline of survival, he would reappear, calling through the window for Sanela to come outside, and waking everyone up in the process.

Sanela could have left Srebrenica on one of the UN trucks that evacuated the thousands of women and children to Tuzla in March and April. Saliha had gone. So had a few other Muslims from Mount Zvijezda. But Sanela stayed behind to be near Nijaz as much as for anything else. After the Canadians came, Nijaz's platoon no longer did a shift on the front line, and Sanela started working at a food distribution center. She assumed there would be more time for them to spend together, but Nijaz seemed never to be around when Sanela was not working. He spent his time down near a base the Canadians had set up in the gloomy knitting mill on the main road into town. The UN troops eventually called the place Camp Bravo. Nijaz got to know the Canadians. He hung around outside the camp's front gates and tried to communicate with the guards. He spoke a language every one of the soldiers understood. Nijaz had found half a dozen women and started arranging for them to sell themselves to the Canadian soldiers and other UN personnel. Five packs of cigarettes a shot; four packs for the woman, one for Nijaz. The price fell as more women offered themselves. The Canadians were soon talking about a Srebrenica "mafia" and a Potočari "mafia." The local police arrested some of the prostitutes and shaved their heads. And any Muslim woman who went to work for the UN was assumed to be a whore.

Sanela found out about what Nijaz was doing. It seemed to her that there was something wrong about it, but she overlooked it for a while. Huso's outrage settled the matter and suffocated whatever was left of Sanela's relationship with Nijaz. Sanela had been thinking a lot about getting married, not necessarily to Nijaz, but thinking about it just the same. Most girls her age were married or getting married, and many of them already had children. Women in eastern Bosnia are generally married by their late teens; if they are not married by their mid-twenties, they probably will not get married at all. The taxi driver from Žlijeb whom she had been going out with since the sixth grade had run off to Germany because of the war, and she heard he had gotten married to another girl. Huso kept telling her not to think about getting married until the war ended, and Sanela feared that it might cost her years more of waiting and uncertainty. She had had two guys propose to her before she was eighteen, and Huso had put an end to it. And now Nijaz was gone.

THE UN negotiated only a few food convoys into Srebrenica that summer, but American, French, and German flight crews parachuted enough supplies into the enclave to feed the population. The Čeliks and almost everyone else in Srebrenica lived off humanitarian aid. Huso and Paja traded some of the food for tobacco. There was no more need for Sanela, Paja, or anyone else to pick up their empty bags, sneak through the front lines, and raid nearby Serb farms. General Mladić kept the safe area surrounded by about nine hundred of his men, most of them Serbs driven from their homes in Srebrenica. He equipped them with tanks, artillery, and mortars. The Serb troops did not occupy the strip of land to the south between Srebrenica and Žepa. But they mined the road over Mount Zlovrh, set up ambushes in the forests, and from time to time mounted small offensives to flush the Muslims out of the area. Over the summer, three hundred Canadian soldiers were stationed in Srebrenica, along with an eight-member team of UN military observers and a few UN civilian police observers. Just as General Wahlgren had warned, the UNPROFOR contingent was neither strong enough to keep the Serbs from attacking nor numerous enough to keep Naser Orić from using the demilitarized town as a rest area for his troops. The Serbs and Muslims were still exchanging fire along the ring around the town, but military activity gradually fell off as General Mladić turned his attention to other battlefronts. UN observers tallied "only" sixty-five hundred cease-fire violations for the month of June, about one every seven minutes.

The Serb commanders were still irked that Orić had not surrendered all of his weapons to the UN or allowed a massive evacuation of Srebrenica's civilians. The Serbs refused to permit the Canadian soldiers to repair the town's water-filtration plant, which was sitting just inside the front line at Zeleni Jadar. At one morning press briefing in Sarajevo, an UNPROFOR spokesman, a jovial Canadian colonel named Barry Frewer, said that the Serbs had let the Canadians visit the filtration plant but that they did not go inside, because the door was locked and they had no key. A day or so later, the Serbs blew the filters up. For the next year, everyone in the town of Srebrenica had to wait in line for water. It took the Čeliks three or four hours to fill their plastic bottles at the spring across the dirt road from the white stucco house with the neatly kept yard that Sanela had gazed at when the family first arrived in Srebrenica.

The Bosnian government complained that Srebrenica was threatened with outbreaks of contagious disease because there was not enough water to flush out the sewage. Personal hygiene became impossible for many old people and refugees crowded together in close quarters. Packs of dogs wandered free. Within a few weeks, fleas had infested the town. Everyone was scratching the bites and picking at the tiny, blood-sucking bugs as they jumped onto light-colored parts of their clothing. Shooting the dogs did not require the permission of a Serb commander, and the Canadians handled it because they were the only ones in town who were supposed to have guns. The Red Cross mounted a fumigation campaign that got rid of the fleas, but the water shortage punished the town like an Oriental form of torture. UN military officers, anxious not to look feckless or put themselves (or their governments) in a position of having to take action against the Serbs, blamed it on both sides.

"It must be realised that it is not in either side's interest for the water situation to improve," reported Brigadier Guy de Vere Hayes, the British deputy to General Morillon's successor, Lieutenant General Francis Briquemont of Belgium. "The Serbs see it as a form of pressure for the evacuation of the area. The Bosnians see it as a way to keep international attention focused on Srebrenica. Whilst this may seem inhuman and the worst kind of cynical manipulation of the suffering of the ordinary people, it is regrettably the reality of the situation."

Friction between Srebrenica's original inhabitants and the refugees increased as the danger of the common enemy receded. Over 80 percent of the people in Srebrenica were refugees, and they knew that Naser Orić and his commanders, who made all the key local decisions for the army, police, and government, were using them as human shields to protect their homes and property. Many of the refugees had expected to be evacuated when Morillon arrived in Srebrenica in March, and since then they had shown no interest in working to improve their living conditions. Apathy and a sense of betrayal set in after they realized they were trapped by the Serb soldiers surrounding the enclave and by Orić's troops just inside the ring, who were arresting any Muslims caught attempting to make a break through the lines and sneak across Serb territory to Tuzla.

Orić and the other Muslim commanders ran the distribution of the food and other aid materials brought in by the UN. The refugee-relief agency calculated the amount of food necessary to feed the population by multiplying the number of people in the enclave by a standard daily minimum of food required to keep each person alive and reasonably healthy. The Muslim leaders overstated the number of people in the enclave by at least four thousand in Srebrenica and another ten thousand in Žepa in order to boost the amount of food and other items the UN would have to deliver. In Srebrenica, the local authorities distributed only minimal food items to about ten thousand peasants who were counted in the population figures but who lived in villages outside of town and grew their own food. Some of the excess food was squirreled away in a secret reserve; the rest was given to the officers' families or sold for profit in the crowded town market.

Struggles to control the trade in pilfered aid set the various commanders against the refugees. Gunshots sometimes erupted around the department store where the food was warehoused. Gangs of refugees marched on the department store at least twice demanding to be fed. One night Orić lost his temper, rousted out all of the people working in the building, threw open the doors, and dared anyone to go in and take whatever he or she wanted of the meager supplies that were there. No one stepped forward. One morning, a man named Bilal, a refugee from Cerska responsible for distributing food to the people from his area, was in front of the town hall when a group of women held a demonstration complaining about the food handouts. The police broke up the demonstration. They questioned Bilal and allegedly beat him with a club in a bathroom at the town hall. He was found dead nearby a few hours later; he had been shot.

(((

BY the autumn, an eerie gloom had settled over Srebrenica. Cold evening breezes blew down from the mountains, fanning the tree branches and tearing at the plastic stretched over windows all over town. Most people crawled into bed just after dark. It was impossible to work or read by the firelight or the glow from animal fat burning in homemade lamps. But younger people still hung around in the park in the gray early evenings and sometimes sat up late at night smoking cigarettes and telling stories in the dark to entertain one another and relieve the stress and depression.

One evening, Sanela was walking in the park with a friend named Dževad, a pious young man from a village near Srebrenica. Dževad needed to talk with someone that evening. He looked deathly pale and afraid. He told Sanela he had walked alone through the school playground after twelve the night before. He said he had heard the crying of children coming from the spot where so many young people were blown to pieces during the soccer game in April.

"There were screams," Dževad told her. Sanela knew Dževad was not one to lie or tell tales. "Children were calling for help. I'm sure I heard them. They followed me until I got beyond the playground. Then I froze up in fear. When I came to myself again I was down by the bus station."

Sanela told Dževad she was afraid of the schoolyard, too. She said she knew other people in Srebrenica who claimed they had heard crying around the schoolyard. Sanela started having nightmares during the late winter after she went into a garage to look at the body of a young mother whose head had been blown apart by a mortar shell. She went to Šemsa Kozić, the woman from Kupusovići who had driven away the hex on Saliha's cow. Šemsa prayed over Sanela, and she felt better right away.

HUSO grew more obsessed than ever with news of the war and each day walked down to listen to news programs broadcast over loudspeakers set up near the Energoinvest building. There was no relief in sight. Mladić's offensives had tightened the Serbs' stranglehold on Sarajevo and severed the mountain trail the Muslims from Goražde were using to carry in food from central Bosnia. Croat artillery and rockets were pummeling Muslims herded into the eastern side of Mostar. For months, UN officials had tried to negotiate with the Serbs and Croats to hold off the attacks and allow aid convoys to pass, but by now the Muslim army had become better organized and was launching attacks of its own that were drawing retaliation. General Jean Cot, the Frenchman who replaced Wahlgren as commander of UNPROFOR in the former Yugoslavia, had NATO carry out a few mock bombing runs, figuring they might deter General Mladić from attacking the safe areas. But these were soon halted by the top UN civilian official in the former Yugoslavia, Yasushi Akashi, a Japanese diplomat who found a home in the UN bureaucracy and had been appointed "special representative" of Secretary-General Boutros-Ghali. Akashi considered the mock air attacks provocative.

General Cot needed all the deterrent he could muster by October 1. The Canadian government finally withdrew half of the Canadian contingent in Srebrenica. "The forces left in Srebrenica are insufficient to guarantee the conditions of safety in this safe area," Cot wrote in a communiqué to his UN superiors. He had ordered a Swedish military unit attached to UNPROFOR in Bosnia to replace the Canadians, but the Swedish government, irked by the dismissal of General Wahlgren and wary of getting involved in Srebrenica, had overridden the order. "The refusal of the Swedish Government to deploy one unit to this area prevents me from fulfilling the mission I have been given," Cot wrote. "Therefore, I am asking you to convey this information to the Secretary-General."

Cot was still irritated two weeks later. "Briquemont and I are military men," he reminded his political chiefs in New York. "I leave it up to you to ensure that governments commit themselves to observe the rules of employment of any military force. . . . The first rule of employment is that orders given are carried out. If a contingent is unable to carry out these orders, do not send them here. . . . This is not an incident, but a fundamental question of principle. I will react in the same way when faced with any refusal to carry out orders, wherever it may come from. There cannot be two types of contingents: those on whom I can rely . . . and those who do not follow orders."

New York advised General Cot to settle down. He did not need to be reminded that France and Britain and the other main backers of Resolution 836 had refused to send any troops to Srebrenica. Except for the Netherlands, only one other country had stepped forward with an offer to deploy troops in the safe area. It was a tempting offer indeed, and painful for the UN head-quarters to reject: ten thousand troops, many of them combat experienced and prepared to assert themselves to protect the beleaguered Muslims if needs be. With the troops would come a fully equipped medical unit and an engineer-ing unit capable of building houses and installing a water plant and electrical generators. The offer, unfortunately for General Cot and UN headquarters, had come from Iran.

21

IN early January 1994, Zlatija was struggling through the last few weeks of pregnancy. Hundreds of women had given birth in Srebrenica already that winter, and perhaps hundreds more had their pregnancies terminated by a local doctor who had gotten his surgical experience sewing up battle wounds and found he could profit by selling abortions for the equivalent in German marks of thirty-five dollars each. Zlatija and Paja had discussed having a sec-ond child even before the war. They wanted Mirza to have a sister and did not want him to be too much older than her. A few weeks after the airdrops began providing Srebrenica with a regular food supply, Paja and Zlatija decided to make an attempt at having another baby. "If you are living well, there are never enough children," Paja told her. "*Inshallah*. God can take care of the future."

Zlatija vomited up most of her food for the first sixteen weeks and had dif-ficulty eating the rest of the time. Her weight dropped, and she feared she might lose the baby because of it. She felt no pain, but standing up and mov-ing around for more than ten minutes at a time became a test of endurance. Mirza seemed anemic, too. He had eaten not much more than cornbread and soup for the first year of the war. Like all of the children in Srebrenica, he grew slowly and put on no bulk. Zlatija worried that the poor diet might affect his mind, and the signs of even a common cold or other childhood illnesses brought fear of pneumonia or some other disease that might get out of control. She took Mirza to the hospital a few times. The doctors grumbled about all the children in town having bronchitis and handed her packets of some kind of antibiotic without ever looking the boy over.

During the winter, Paja took some of the household items and clothing dis-tributed by the UN and traded them for potatoes to supplement the wheat flour and canned food they were receiving from the airdrops and convoys. He and Sanela went out with Senad and other young people from the neighborhood to gather what they could from the air-dropped food. Huso never went. He complained about his health and his lack of money and slumped into fear and self-centeredness, taking whatever he could and giving only when it brought immediate returns. This behavior was endemic. Almost no one in Srebrenica wanted to work. Almost no one would do anything unless it was absolutely necessary or unless he was paid. Huso also dictated more strictly than ever where Sanela could go, with whom, and when. There would be words and door-slamming whenever she started to go out with a young man. And he would explode in anger if she happened to come home late.

❨   ❨   ❨

ONE January afternoon, Huso saw Sanela and Zlatija preparing a potato pie for dinner and lost his temper. "Why don't you cover your hair when you cook. It isn't healthy."

He demanded that the young women start covering their heads with kerchiefs whenever they cooked the meals.

"I've never covered my head. And I won't do it now," Sanela insisted. "Have you ever found a hair in the food I've made for you?"

"Never. But I don't care. Now you must do it. You must cover your head."

Sanela refused to give in or let Zlatija go along.

"If you don't cover your head, then I won't eat it," Huso barked.

Paja came in to eat when they brought the pie out of the oven. Huso refused to join in, and Paja knew why.

"Why aren't you eating?"

"They didn't cover their heads when they made this," Huso moaned. "I want them to cover their heads."

Paja would have none of this.

"My wife isn't ever going to cover herself. Ever. I'm not going to allow her to wear a kerchief on her head. You can't continue to have it the way it always was. Who are you to give orders like this in wartime? Who are you to make demands? Sanela can do what she wants, but Zlatija's not going to wear anything on her head."

Hiba, who had covered her head all her life, sat to the side silently until Huso told her to make him something to eat. He refused to speak to Zlatija and again ordered Sanela to wear a kerchief.

Later that evening Huso was sitting near the front of the house when a young man, a family friend from a village near Kupusovići, came to get Sanela. They were going to climb into the mountains to wait for an airdrop.

He and Sanela had already left the yard when Senad opened a window and shouted out that there would be no parachutes that night.

"How do you know?" Sanela asked.

Senad had no good answer. But it was enough for Huso to order Sanela to go back into the house.

"What's with you?" Sanela shouted back at him.

"Get back into the house."

She started to cry and was stepping into the house as Paja came out of their room and into the hallway. "What happened?" he asked. Sanela told him.

"Why don't you let her go?" he told Huso. "She's grown up. Let her go out."

"You have nothing to say about her. I'm her commander. If I think it's right to cut her throat, I'll cut her throat. She's my child, not yours."

Huso slapped Sanela, and Paja stepped in and wrestled him back. Huso screamed in outrage. He accused Paja of hoarding food. He said he would go for his own food from then on. "You go on your own, and I'll go on my own, and that's that."

There was no rest in the thick silence in the room that night. The tension dragged on for days. Hiba took over all the cooking for her husband. The younger women and Paja kept to themselves. Whenever Paja came back from collecting food, Huso would refuse to take it and Paja would hand it over to his mother. After a few weeks, Sanela started to cover her head and help Hiba cook for Huso just to lift the burden from her mother. But Paja remained obdurate when it came to Zlatija. She was now trapped between father and son. She would remain silent or speak in a soft voice to the others when Huso was in the room. If guests dropped by, Hiba would fix coffee, while Zlatija, the daughter-in-law who would normally be responsible for showing hospitality to guests, looked on and felt ashamed.

Zlatija told Paja that she could no longer stand the tension in the room. "I can't live like this any more," she said. A few days later, they took some of the sponge pads, blankets, and pots and moved into the vacant room across the hall.

ON February 11, Zlatija walked down the hill to the hospital to have the baby. The labor was not difficult. It lasted from about four o'clock in the afternoon until about nine that night, and the result was a baby boy, Edin. The midwife rousted Zlatija out of the hospital bed an hour or so after she gave birth and sat her down on a chair to make room for another woman who had just come from Potočari. Zlatija sat up all night without sleeping. Paja showed up the next morning, and they walked home. There was no celebration. Huso crossed the hall to see his new grandson. After that, he did not come back. He never spoke with Zlatija. If they found themselves sitting somewhere close together, Huso would turn his head and look away.

(((

THE beginning of the end for Bosnia's safe areas came six days before Edin's birthday, at thirty-seven minutes after noon on Saturday, February 5, 1994. At that moment, a single mortar round hit an open-air market in Sarajevo. It exploded among market stalls packed with peddlers and shoppers. Its shrapnel tore into the heads and brains and torsos and limbs of the sixty-nine people it killed and the two hundred it wounded. Camera crews rushed to the scene and captured images of men and women sliding through pools of blood as they carried dismembered bodies into cars and vans.

Never had any one of the half million shells fired into Sarajevo inflicted such mayhem or elicited such outrage from abroad. Bombs that killed half a dozen or a dozen civilians had become commonplace in Bosnia during the months after the UN Security Council adopted its resolutions declaring Sarajevo, Srebrenica, and the other Muslim enclaves to be safe areas. The war in Bosnia had slipped from the headlines in these months of senseless killing. Western governments had turned their attention to other crises. Somalia gripped the attention of policymakers in Washington after eighteen U.S. soldiers attached to a UN military force were killed in Mogadishu during a botched effort to impose a peace settlement. The UN and European Community peace negotiators, Thorvald Stoltenberg and David Owen, appeared to be on the verge of persuading Muslim leaders in Bosnia to accept the creation of an unviable Muslim statelet wedged between Slobodan Milošević's Greater Serbia and Franjo Tudjman's Greater Croatia.

The video footage from the marketplace massacre, however, riveted the attention of American and European opinion makers to the Bosnian horror just as the footage of the Serb concentration camps had done prior to the London conference of 1992 and just as the stories of Mladić's offensive against Srebrenica had done before passage of the safe-areas resolutions in 1993. Within hours of the marketplace bombing on that February 5, Western governments understood that they had to come up with something dramatic if they were going to preempt demands for answers to some embarrassing questions and make it seem that the political will had been mustered to stop the killing. This time around, the Western leaders turned to the North Atlantic Treaty Organization. The mighty defense alliance built by the United States and its allies to defend Western Europe against Soviet Russia had won the Cold War without firing a shot. Like the old Austrian Empire, which came apart at the seams when the Ottoman threat had disappeared, NATO had lost its enemy, Communist Russia, and in 1994 was seeking to redefine itself.

NATO's involvement in Bosnia began as part of an elaborate diplomatic game of good cop, bad cop. Citing the UN Security Council's safe-areas resolutions as its authority, the bad cop, NATO, handed Mladić an ultimatum on February 9. The Serb general was given ten days to remove or place under UN control all of his hundreds of artillery pieces and tanks around Sarajevo. If he failed to comply, NATO would bomb his big guns out of existence. The siege lines around Sarajevo had already fallen silent by the time the ultimatum was issued. NATO fighter jets were growling in the skies over Bosnia. NATO generals and admirals were assuming menacing poses. Western political leaders were talking tough. But Mladić and the other Serb leaders were standing defiant.

Four days before the ultimatum was to expire, the good cop took over. Prime Minister John Major of Great Britain, the host of the long-forgotten London conference and leader of the only NATO member state to oppose issuing the ultimatum, flew to Moscow to meet with Russia's president, Boris Yeltsin. The Russians came out of their meeting railing against NATO for taking unilateral action without Russia's participation, and a Russian diplomat called the ultimatum "illegal." Yeltsin said he and the British prime minister had agreed that NATO should take no action in the Balkans without Russia's consent. In Sarajevo, the new commander of the UN military force in Bosnia, Lieutenant General Sir Michael Rose, the former leader of the British army's most elite commando unit, the SAS, engaged Serb leaders in negotiations seeking some way for them to back down without losing face. Rose coerced Muslim officials into taking part in cease-fire talks with Serb leaders by informing the Muslims that he had scientific evidence that the marketplace bomb had been fired from a Muslim-controlled part of the city. He threatened to release the evidence to the public if the Muslims did not cooperate with him. The evidence was later shown to be erroneous.

A day after Major's visit to Moscow, Yeltsin suddenly announced that he would transfer Russian troops to Bosnia to secure Serb-held neighborhoods in Sarajevo from which Mladić had been persuaded to remove artillery pieces and tanks. Rose also persuaded Mladić to deposit the rest of his heavy weapons around Sarajevo in "collection areas" that would be set up on Serb-held territory in the city and watched over by lightly armed French, Russian, and Ukrainian soldiers attached to the UN military force. As the deadline neared, UN officials announced that the Serbs had complied with NATO's ultimatum. When the deadline passed, the leaders of the NATO alliance clearly understood that the crisis had reduced the leverage they could now apply in

Bosnia. How could NATO drop bombs on Serb lines in Sarajevo where Russian troops were hanging around? How could NATO launch air strikes when General Rose had served up to General Mladić ready-made hostages, the UN troops in the weapons-collection areas? In the final analysis, the marketplace bomb and the NATO ultimatum had actually strengthened the hand of General Mladić.

Still, for a few weeks, the good-cop, bad-cop routine appeared to have succeeded. The Sarajevo safe area became safer than it had been at any time since the beginning of the war. The danger of Serb shelling receded. A cease-fire was declared, and the sniper fire dropped off. The city's residents swept up the glass and rubble from streets that had been deserted for two years. Cafés and pizzerias threw open their doors and began serving customers. A road out of the city opened. Soon the trams began running. UN forklifts removed the shipping containers that had been set up to protect pedestrians from the snipers.

General Rose took advantage of the calm on Bosnia's battlefronts in early March to send to Srebrenica 570 Dutch troops to relieve the 150 or so Canadians who had been kept there for months because Serb leaders had refused to allow their replacements access to the enclave. The Serbs took advantage of the Canadians' departure to reoccupy four villages around Srebrenica, including parts of Podravanje, which had remained in Muslim hands after the enclave was declared a safe area. A temporary Serb foray into Srebrenica on March 5 sent hundreds of Muslim refugees fleeing from a housing settlement built by the governments of Sweden and Norway. The UN military force quietly protested, but did nothing. Srebrenica was far from the television cameras. Rose said he had no obligation to fight for ground around Srebrenica, because no one knew where the boundary of the safe area actually was; the UN Security Council members had never taken the time to delineate the "area" they had created. UNPROFOR officials were clearly content to wait for a joint commission made up of Muslim and Serb military officials to draw the line.

❮   ❮   ❮

MLADIĆ had no trouble finding a use for the artillery, tanks, and other weapons he had withdrawn from around Sarajevo. In early April, ten days after the funeral of his daughter, Ana, a twenty-three-year-old medical student who had committed suicide, he rushed to relaunch his campaign to drive the Muslims from eastern Bosnia and force Muslim leaders in Sarajevo to capitulate. Mladić knew he needed to hurry. The United States had a month earlier patched together an uneasy peace between Bosnia's Muslims and Croats as well as a military alliance between Sarajevo and Zagreb. Washington soon rewarded the Muslims by tacitly agreeing, among other things, to allow the transfer of Iranian weapons through Croatia and into Bosnia, in violation of the UN arms embargo. The Muslims now had less reason than ever to settle for Bosnia's division. Mladić clearly knew this and understood that the longer he waited to strike, the stronger and better organized his Muslim foes would become and the less likely Muslim leaders would be to accept anything close to the peace terms Serb leaders were demanding.

Cocksure that the threat of NATO air strikes had disappeared over the horizon, Mladić initiated an offensive to overrun another UN safe area, Goražde, the only Muslim enclave in the Drina valley whose military had not been neutralized. The Serb forces advanced quickly toward the town of Goražde, driving before them thousands of refugees and leaving in their wake one burning Muslim village after another. The offensive was clearly an attack on a safe area; but in an effort to head off calls for air strikes that might escalate into the military intervention Muslim political leaders desired, General Rose publicly downplayed the severity of the Serb attack. On one day, Rose characterized Mladić's offensive as a "tactical operation"; the next day, he said Mladić had attacked "to relieve pressure" and "gain some sort of political advantage." But on April 6, Rose sent to Goražde a team of his own British SAS commandos to act as target spotters for NATO fighter jets; this move would preempt NATO from picking its own targets, allow Rose to micromanage any bombing, and thereby minimize the chance that NATO would be drawn into the conflict on the side of the Muslims. Significantly, the UN took no measures to extract any of its personnel—all of them potential hostages—from Serb-held territory.

A crescendo of demands for air strikes began the next day, after the *New York Times* published the contents of confidential reports from the UN military observers in Goražde. These documents, which were leaked by a UN official in Sarajevo who was no friend of General Rose, described massive shelling barrages and hundreds of dead and wounded civilians and showed clearly that Rose had been informed from the outset that the Serbs were intending to overrun the safe area. In a message to UN headquarters in New York on April 8, Rose's superior in the UN military chain of command, General Bertrand de Lapresle of France, responded to the press reports and argued in no uncertain terms that action had to be taken in Goražde.

"A safe area is represented by population centres, regardless of their size," de Lapresle wrote, defining for the first time what safe area actually meant:

> Whilst not wishing to establish a checklist, in order to meet the UNPROFOR definition of an attack against a safe area the following criteria would have to be met: a. The attack must be deliberately targeted against a civilian population. . . . An at-

tack against [Bosnian army, or Muslim] soldiers defending a confrontation line would not meet this criteria; b. The attack must be unprovoked; and c. Given the propensity of arms in the region, an attack would have to be of sufficient intensity and duration to separate it from everyday skirmishing or exchanges of fire. . . . When these outlined criteria are applied to the situation in Goražde, one can draw the following [conclusion]: . . . *The shelling of Goražde and other population centres and the burning of villages south of the Drina, are, in our view, attacks on a safe area* (author's italics).

When Mladić launched fierce attacks on April 10 and April 11, Rose decided to play the air strike and hostage cards, once again reasoning, in complete accord with British government policy, that he was forestalling broader intervention that might spin out of control and make UNPROFOR a military ally of the Muslims. He requested small-scale air attacks; and NATO fighter planes dropped six bombs on a tank, three armored vehicles, a truck, and, without Rose's approval, a command center coordinating Serb artillery attacks on Goražde. Western commentators cried foul and said NATO's first air attack in history had made the alliance look like the proverbial elephant that gave birth to a mouse. Predictably, Mladić called Rose and threatened the lives of all the UN officials on Serb-held territory. Serb soldiers took hostage hundreds of UN troops and observers, including soldiers in the weapons-collection areas near Sarajevo.

Mladić waited for four days to see what else NATO might have up its sleeve. On April 15, he ordered the offensive to begin again. In one day, Serb troops captured the high ground overlooking the town of Goražde and drew within a few hundred yards of a Muslim munitions plant on the Drina's banks. Rose called twice more for limited air attacks. The first request came after the Serbs had wounded two of his own SAS commandos, one of them mortally; but Yasushi Akashi, Boutros-Ghali's personal representative in Yugoslavia, effectively denied the request by insisting he could negotiate an end to the Serb attack. Rose's second air strike call came a day later, amid continued fighting; this time Akashi approved it, and the Serbs blew a British Sea Harrier fighter out of the sky with a surface-to-air missile. A Russian diplomat, Vitaly Churkin, held off further NATO action for a day by claiming Serb leaders had given him a pledge to stop the attack and withdraw from Goražde. Mladić's offensive went forward anyway.

The good-cop, bad-cop routine played out in Sarajevo in February had by now deteriorated into a feud within NATO over what should or could be done to protect the Goražde safe area. Resolution 836 called on the UN military force "to deter" attacks on the "safe areas" and provided authority for air strikes. But clearly the pinprick air attacks launched by General Rose had proven to be no deterrent. The United States and NATO's secretary-general, Manfred Wörner, were pounding tables demanding more robust air strikes to stop Mladić in his tracks and hammer out the dents he had knocked in NATO's prestige. Great Britain, once again, opposed escalated air action, arguing that it would exceed the provisions of Resolution 836, jeopardize the UN troops on the ground, and hamper the "peace negotiations." The British scolded the Americans for not being willing to send troops to bolster the moribund UN military mission in Bosnia.

As American and British diplomats squabbled, Mladić launched fresh infantry assaults into Goražde and blanketed the town with artillery fire. One tank shell slammed into a makeshift first-aid station and killed twenty-eight people who had already been wounded; another shell killed ten people collecting water at a spring; seven more people were blown up in a riverside neighborhood, six more on a bridge about a football field away from the local UN offices, five more near a mosque in Goražde's old town. Finally, on April 20, President Clinton demanded that NATO get busy, and two days later NATO issued a second ultimatum, again over British objections. Mladić was given twenty-four hours to stop shooting and back his men away from the town. For good measure, NATO also added a paragraph to the ultimatum, a threat its leaders were clearly attempting to use to deter future Serb assaults on safe areas:

> If any Bosnian Serb attacks involving heavy weapons are carried out on the UN-designated safe areas of Goražde, Bihać, Srebrenica, Tuzla and Žepa, these weapons and other Bosnian Serb military assets, as well as their direct and essential military support facilities, including but not limited to fuel installations and munitions sites, will be subject to NATO air strikes, in accordance with the procedural arrangements worked out between NATO and UNPROFOR.

A few hours before the deadline expired, the UN military observers in Goražde reported that Mladić had pressed ahead with his offensive.

"Team leader's assessment: These guys have balls," says one of the observers' reports, adding that the observer team had tallied fifty-five shell explosions on Goražde in one ten-minute period. "They have blatantly increased their aggressive activities in the face of the NATO ultimatum. . . . At this moment a heavy Bosnian Serb army infantry attack is being conducted into the north side of the right bank of the city."

Gun battles continued after the ultimatum deadline passed. But General Rose's headquarters announced that a Serb withdrawal had begun and explained away the artillery barrages by asserting that Mladić was using them to cover the pullback of his infantry. NATO's commander in southern Europe,

Admiral Leighton Smith of the United States, called Akashi and requested clearance to begin bombing the Serbs. Akashi balked. Smith complained to NATO Secretary-General Wörner, and Wörner tried to contact Akashi. The UN diplomat, who was meeting in Belgrade with Milošević and the other Serb leaders, refused to pick up the phone. Whether this was another round of good cop, bad cop may never be known. But the Serbs were convinced they had pushed into Goražde as far as they could without provoking a NATO response that would debilitate their army. Mladić agreed to withdraw his troops and artillery from the town and soon released his hostages.

Goražde survived. Barely. But the credibility of the UN safe areas had again taken a beating. It would be another six months before the nightmare scenario that General Wahlgren had predicted came to life. In the late fall of 1994, Muslim forces inside the Bihać safe area launched a full-scale offensive that drew a massive Serb counterattack. Serb fighters blasted away at a contingent of Bangladeshi soldiers attached to the UN in Bihać, killing peacekeepers who were so desperately needed as a "deterrent" that UN commanders had rushed them into the safe area with no weapons or winter clothing. NATO undertook limited bombing missions around Bihać. But as soon as the air action began, the Serbs took hostage hundreds of UN personnel. Then Mladić upped the ante and began blasting away at NATO aircraft with newly installed anti-aircraft missiles that were transported into Bosnia from Serbia and directed to their targets by means of a radar system located in Serbia.

Great Britain and France now warned that they were ready to withdraw their troops from Bosnia. UN military force officials drew up elaborate plans for a "fighting withdrawal" by the peacekeepers that would require 75,000 additional soldiers and could be undertaken only if the United States agreed to come to the rescue. To everyone's relief, on New Year's Day, 1995, the Serbs and Muslims agreed to begin a cease-fire that was supposed to last four months. They would use the respite to oil their guns, sharpen their troops, and plan one last season of killing.

22

BEYOND the afternoon corso at the park, Srebrenica offered few diversions from the idleness, the incessant gossip, the nagging hunger, and the uncertainty grinding away at everyone's nerves. Packs of kids were still nagging Dutch soldiers for *bonboni*, and a few of the Dutch began complaining about it as harassment. Young people danced to blaring music at a disco near the market on Wednesday and Sunday nights. Horse races, like the ones once held each year on Tito's birthday, were organized down in Potočari from time to time, and Orić's men conducted military maneuvers, made forays behind Serb lines, and kept watch on the Serbs and the UN troops along the en-clave's perimeter. A brothel and a handful of cafés threw open their doors. And a few families operated cinemas in their homes and charged admission for showings of videotapes.

Paja and Cousin Avdo, Saliha's son, started taking in the movies at the house just across the dirt road from the spring where the Čeliks paused on their way into Srebrenica; it was the same white house Sanela was gazing at when she daydreamed about how fine it would be if the place had a balcony over-looking the town. Admission for the movies cost four cigarettes, and at the door sat the owner's eldest son, Muhamed Halilović. He and his brothers set up benches in a sitting room with a television at one end. To the audience's right was a wooden wheel about three feet in diameter that was connected by a belt to a pulley and a generator. Members of the Halilović household took turns spinning the wheel by hand to power the VCR and the television set; if some-one wandered in with no cigarettes, he could spin the wheel and thereby earn the right to watch the spaghetti westerns, the kung fu movies with Bruce Lee and Jean-Claude van Damme, and old Yugoslav slapstick.

SANELA fetched water at the spring next to the Halilović house almost every day. She was topping off two plastic jugs one afternoon in May 1994 when Muhamed stepped from the door and approached her. "Let me take this one for you," he said, picking up the larger jug.

"No. You take this one," Sanela answered, handing him the smaller one.

"Whatever."

They walked down the dirt road together toward the Čelik house. Muhamed was about six feet tall, a head and a shoulder taller than Sanela. He was thin and had light hair and a mole on his right cheek. Cousin Avdo and Muhamed hung around a lot together, drinking brandy, smoking cigarettes, playing cards, and, of course, eyeballing the girls at the corso. "You know," Muhamed said as he and Sanela approached the Čelik house, "there are three girls in this town I'd like to get to know. . . . One of them lives over there by the church. She's your cousin. The other one is that Aida. You know her, too."

"Who's the third?"

Muhamed paused. "I'll tell you later." Then he walked off to town alone.

During the corso a few days later, Sanela was standing in the park with two of her girlfriends when Muhamed strolled by with a group of his friends. One of the girls blurted out, "Hey Sanela, there's the guy who asked about going out with you. My, he has pretty eyes. And if you don't want him, I'm going to take him." The boys kept moving, but the next time Muhamed and his friends passed by it was Sanela who spoke up: "Hey, Muhamed, which one of us do you like best?" The girls giggled. Muhamed blushed and walked off. And that night Sanela started keeping a diary of everything Muhamed said to her in the park.

Her diary entry for May 24, 1994, says it was a sunny Tuesday. Sanela hurried through the dinner dishes so that she could get to the corso, and the minute she arrived in the park she walked up to one of Muhamed's friends. "I want to start seeing Muhamed," she confided, fully expecting the message to be conveyed immediately. He grinned and walked away, and Sanela watched as he approached Muhamed and started talking. Her eyes followed the two young men as they meandered through the park and disappeared behind some trees. She was looking in the wrong direction half an hour later when Muhamed's friend sidled up: "He wants to start seeing you, too."

"Tell me everything."

"He wants you to meet him in the park tomorrow. That's all."

For the next day's corso, Sanela dressed in the best clothes she had: a maroon-colored silk blouse and a pair of heeled shoes that she had tucked away and carried in her rucksack all the way from Kupusovići. After a few circling maneuvers, she and Muhamed strolled away together from the murmur of voices in the park and sat down on a stone wall in a dull, uncomfortable silence. Sanela took the initiative to ask the mundane questions. Muhamed was twenty-one. He had three younger brothers and no sisters. His father, Smail, used to work as a technician in a mine. His mother, Naza, kept house. Muhamed had finished high school a few weeks before Yugoslavia fell apart. He played goalie for a local soccer team, studied the Koran with a *hodža*, and thought about becoming a math teacher.

Muhamed and Smail were members of a commando unit that was led by a *hodža*, and they shared one German-made submachine gun that couldn't hit a house from more than fifty yards away. Smail's second son had escaped to Germany just before the war; the third was a soldier in the same outfit; and the youngest had been in the seventh grade when the school closed down. Muhamed spoke very little about what he did in the army. He told Sanela that he carried the wounded and had not killed anyone; and she believed him. He was lucky to be alive, even by Srebrenica standards: he was riding in the back of a truck loaded with soldiers in October 1992 when the Serbs sprang an ambush; twenty men, including Naser Orić's deputy commander, Akif Ustić, were killed; a bullet tore through Muhamed's jacket sleeve as he climbed down from the truck; he ran into a woods and back to town; only one other man survived.

SANELA and Muhamed began meeting every afternoon, but as the afternoons passed it seemed to Sanela that Muhamed was contributing little to their conversations, and this irritated her. He was not aggressive like other young men she had dated, men who wanted to show intimacy as soon as possible. "I can't stand him any more," she told one of her friends. "He says nothing and just sits there." She decided to give him ten more days; and whether he knew about the deadline or not, he somehow beat it. He started opening up. He started cracking jokes. And Sanela never found out why. They began taking strolls and sat among the ruins of the fortress that Jerina the Damned had built from cut stone and mortar mixed with milk and egg yolks. They perched each day on an old radiator that had been dumped out on a hillside next to an A-frame building, a restaurant that had become a refugee shelter. There, Sanela told Muhamed about Kupusovići, about life on the mountain, and its breezes, and its snows, and its views of the Drina valley, and the long walks to school. She told him about smoking cigarettes and staying up late in Saliha's new house. And Muhamed told her about how he liked to draw and how he learned to read the Arabic of the Koran. Sanela could scarcely believe he didn't ask her the first question young men had always asked when they took an interest in her; Muhamed had never asked whether she was a virgin. He did not seem to care. Sitting on that radiator beside the refugee shelter, Muhamed kissed her for the first time.

"I want to move to Germany when I get out of here," he said. "My brother is there. He's working as a carpenter. I know how to work as a carpenter. I can make a life there." Sanela talked of going to Canada. Her brother Hamed was getting along a lot better in Canada than Muhamed's brother in Germany. Perched on the hillside, Sanela and Muhamed could see only the bleak landscape of dingy apartment blocks, the walls blackened by the smoke of wood stoves, the windows covered in white plastic, the washed-out clothing, and towels hanging from every balcony. The smell of wood fires drifted in the summer air and commingled with the scent of the evergreens from the forests. They would walk home after dark. On clear nights, a sea of stars filled the sky and seemed to pour down the mountainsides and wash away the gloom, the trash, the broken-down cars, the empty shells of buildings, the shoes cobbled out of wood and shreds of old carpet, the uncertainty, the gossip. All of it.

THE idea to get married surfaced that July. Sanela and Muhamed were watching a movie in an apartment somewhere in town. She was bored. "Come on," she joked. "Don't make it so I have to ask you to marry me."

"I'll be ashamed if you have to ask," he answered. Muhamed studied Sanela's eyes. "Do you want to marry me?"

"What's with you?" she laughed. And they laughed again as they left the movie and walked out into the darkness. At the Energoinvest building, just below the Čeliks' place, Muhamed turned to her. "I was serious about what I asked you," he said. "You can give me an answer tomorrow morning." Sanela did not say anything more, and she hardly slept that night. She found something comforting, something promising, in the thought of getting married. Sanela was obsessed with Muhamed. She was not getting along with Huso. She knew her girlfriends were jealous of how well Muhamed treated her. The Halilović family was respected all over town and lived better than refugees. Their house was still intact. They still had all of their possessions.

Sanela left to fetch water from the spring at about eight o'clock the next morning determined to give Muhamed an answer, but she didn't know what it would be. He came out of the house as she filled her jugs: "We're going into the woods to cut some wood. Have you made up your mind?"

"I thought about it all night long. I haven't decided."

"I knew it would take time. I'll be at the park this afternoon. You can tell me then." The topic seemed to drop from the agenda after that. Muhamed did not bring it up that afternoon, or the next, or the next. One Saturday evening, they were sitting together on a bench in the yard of Srebrenica's oldest mosque. Muhamed was stripping away shells from chestnuts he had taken from the tree near the spring beside his house. He handed one to Sanela and told her he had tried to contact his brother in Germany by ham radio but had been cut off. "I wanted him to send me some money," he said.

They sat quietly for a few minutes as Muhamed picked at more chestnuts. "Sanela, it isn't worth waiting any more for a convoy or for money to get in here. What we've got, we've got here, here and now."

"What are you talking about?"

"You know what I'm talking about."

"We should go," he said. They got up, walked from the yard, and strolled through the crowded marketplace.

"When will you come for me?" Sanela asked.

"Saturday. The eighth."

Sanela never gave a positive answer to Muhamed's proposal. Her legs were shaking as he walked her home. It was October 1. One week.

A food convoy arrived in Srebrenica a day or two later, and flour and other supplies were distributed to everyone. "Set the sugar aside," Sanela told Hiba as they put away their supplies. "I'm going to go with Muhamed."

"Don't talk foolishness," her mother said. "Don't go with him. There's a war on."

"Listen," Sanela answered, "you let one go by. Then you let the second go by. You let the third go by. And the years go by. We've been here two years already." Sanela left Hiba in the room and walked outside.

"She's crazy," Hiba said aloud. "There's a war on."

Huso wasn't around to hear her, and Hiba told him nothing when he came home.

☾ ☾ ☾

DURING 1994, Sanela went to visit Dragica Vasić three or four times. Dragica was still living in an apartment above a butcher store with her friend Fadila, and still keeping off the streets. Sanela cut Dragica's hair from time to time, and Huso brought her potatoes from the garden and apples from the tree in the front yard. Dragica had fallen ill over the winter. She had been bedridden with chronic bronchitis for nine months already. Her body had wasted away. She had weighed a plump 130 pounds before the war, but had shrunk to barely 90 pounds when Sanela dropped by and told her she was getting married to Muhamed.

"Don't get married," Dragica advised. "Wait. Be patient." Dragica had waited during World War II when Veljko was in Tito's Partisan underground and crossing back and forth over the Drina between Serbia and Srebrenica. They enjoyed many years together after the war, and this war would certainly not last forever.

A few days later, the Red Cross evacuated Dragica to Serbia. Sanela and Huso went down to say good-bye. They walked together down the asphalt road from Fadila's apartment in the center of town to the hospital where the Red Cross jeep would come to pick her up. Dragica said her sickness was forcing her to leave, but she knew there had been threats to her life because she was a Serb. She sobbed as she wished everyone good-bye. She said, "Now I know who my true friends are."

A Red Cross jeep drove up, and Dragica climbed inside with one small brown suitcase. She left everything else behind when the jeep turned away down the asphalt road toward Bratunac. The Serbs took her to her sister's apartment across the river in Loznica. Dragica spent the next ten months in the town's hospital before moving in with her widowed sister. Dragica repeated time and again what she had seen in Srebrenica. She told her sister how the airplane had dropped the Russian-made mortar rounds on her house. She told them how the bombs had exploded in the schoolyard during the soccer game, and her sister shook her head. She told Dragica that she understood and that it was best for her to rest. She told her that she had been a victim of Muslim propaganda. "The schoolyard attack never happened," she said. "That schoolyard was filled with the bodies of dead Serbs. . . . Serbs could never have carried out such an attack."

Dragica soon began making plans to move away, to Holland, where she could live with her son Boban, and her Muslim daughter-in-law.

❲   ❲   ❲

ON Friday night, Muhamed told Sanela that she should be waiting for him outside her house at exactly five after six the next evening: "I'll walk up the hill on the road and whistle as I pass by."

Sanela could not sleep again that night. Her neck ached, and her nerves tingled with excitement. All the next day, she went through the normal routine of household chores while secretly preparing to leave. She bathed. She trimmed her long nails, knowing she would soon be preparing food in a new home for a new family. At about ten minutes before six that evening, she took her clothes and her diary and her other possessions down from a shelf inside the room and packed them into a bag, then she slid some of her parents things onto the shelf in their place so that Huso would not notice anything was missing. The daylight was fading into gray as she carried her bag down the hall to Cousin Avdo's room. She was changing into her best skirt and blouse when Hiba knocked at the door.

"Let's go to sleep," Hiba said.

"I'll be there in a few minutes."

A whistle came from outside the window as Hiba walked back to their room. Then Sanela quietly opened the door and made her way down the wooden hallway in her bare feet so that her heels would not thump on the floor and attract Huso's attention. Muhamed was waiting when she got outside. They walked up the dirt road alone and joined the rest of the men in the wedding party by the chestnut tree near the spring. Sanela was afraid and felt her knees weaken as she approached the Halilović house. Still outside, one of Muhamed's aunts tried to put a veil over her head. "Get that thing away," Muhamed snapped; but the aunt persisted and flung the veil over Sanela's head and slipped a volume of the Koran under her left arm. Muhamed then stretched his right arm over the threshold to the house and Sanela walked under it and into the sitting room, which was jammed with relatives and friends. The women of the family skittered up to her. The singing began. There was drinking and dancing. And the only vows Muhamed and Sanela ever exchanged that night remained in the realm of an unarticulated agreement that they were indeed man and wife. They moved into the pantry of the Halilović house after the party and slept on a sponge pad spread out on the floor under a window whose glass was somehow still intact.

The marriage brought Sanela creature comforts she had not enjoyed since the war began. The white house did, in fact, have the balcony Sanela had daydreamed about. She hung the family laundry there to dry. And sometimes she sat out there with Muhamed and looked down into the streets and yards of the town below. Muhamed's father, Smail, had built a dam across a creek below the house and rigged up a waterwheel, a generator, and cables that powered their refrigerator, water heater, and television. The house also had running water from the spring, and Sanela now took hot showers. She pressed clothes with an electric iron and watched television and listened to the radio whenever she pleased. Huso and Hiba took to Muhamed and quickly reconciled themselves to the wartime marriage. Paja pitched in to help Muhamed and Smail build a new, more ambitious hydroelectric dam. They used a handsaw and an ax to bring down a thick walnut tree across the creekbed below the house. For four days, they packed rocks, sand, and dirt behind the log; then they dug a channel for a spillway and set up a waterwheel connected by rubber belts and pulleys to a generator pinched from the furniture factory in Zeleni Jadar. Protected by a locked shed next to the dam, the generator churned out a steady flow of three and a half kilowatts of power. Huso, Paja, and Muhamed strung an uninsulated cable down to the Čelik house so the power could not be stolen without the thief's getting himself shocked. And now the Čeliks' water heater worked, and they had lights and electricity for their iron.

IT was Sanela who insisted on having a baby right away. "Children give meaning to life," she told Muhamed. "I want that reason to live."

The thrill of discovering she was pregnant came in late November, and it overjoyed her. She knew that many couples had to wait years to have children and that some of them never succeeded. Now, somehow, her life seemed no longer to be held in abeyance by the incessant gossip, the sense of confinement, the lethargy, the nagging hunger, and uncertainty that was eroding the spirit of her father and practically everyone else around them.

The child was due July 17, 1995.

23

THE fact that folks in the Drina valley had for generations nicknamed the people of Srebrenica "goiters" did not go unnoticed by Serb military commanders. Nor did the story passed down by parents and grandparents that the "goiters" were so desperate for salt during and after World War I that women had hiked all the way to the salt mines in Tuzla and hauled it home on their backs. At about the time that Sanela and Muhamed got married, the Sarajevo government leaked a copy of a Yugoslav army document pertaining to the lack of salt in the Srebrenica area. The document was allegedly written in March 1992, two weeks before the Bosnian war began, by General Kukanjac, the commander of the Yugoslav army's Sarajevo corps. If it is authentic (and I have seen no reason to presume it is not), this document shows that Serb commanders foresaw a long-term siege developing around Srebrenica and planned to exploit the area's lack of salt and iodine to their military advantage:

> A finalized program for the planned encirclement of the non-Serb population in the Drina valley . . . has been completed. The findings of the military scientific research team have arrived. The team tested and analyzed the drinking water and natural springs in the Drina valley, and the results show that the water has a low iodine content. Thus, the deprivation of salt from the diet will lead to a number of malfunctions in the so-called endocrine organs and, in the psychological area, will lead persons to experience confusion, instability, and aggressiveness; an inclination toward anarchy and panic; and a susceptibility to psychological manipulation. The analysis shows that the Srebrenica and Žepa regions are especially interesting in this regard.

The Serb soldiers who inspected the UN aid shipments to Srebrenica restricted deliveries of table salt. Thyroid complications aside, the paucity of salt prevented Srebrenica's Muslims from preserving their meat, cabbage, peppers, and other vegetables for the winter, and without food reserves they were more susceptible to hunger and boredom and pressure to leave the enclave.

Desperation and the scarcity of salt and other goods produced astronomical prices. During late 1992 and early 1993, a pound of iodized table salt cost about fifty dollars in Srebrenica. Prices dropped and stabilized after the enclave became a safe area, but a pound of salt still cost about ten dollars. The profit opportunity spawned a lucrative trade between Muslims and Serbs. The salt shortage persisted even after the UN refugee-relief agency managed to deliver extra salt to Srebrenica. Muslims complained that Orić's officers were selling aid items and hoarding salt to keep prices artificially high and reward their most loyal soldiers. Sometime in 1994, Orić learned that a group of his men had arranged to buy salt from Serbs on the front line above Kravica; under his orders, the Serbs were trapped in an ambush and gunned down by the kind of Rambo-style machine gun Orić liked to pose with in photographs.

Caravans of pack horses and men plied the ancient trade route over Zlovrh and imported into Srebrenica salt, cigarettes, razor blades, wheat flour, gasoline, toothpaste, diesel fuel, and other goods available in Žepa. Orić's officers exploited the men in their work brigades as burden bearers. Paja and Senad made the journey lugging ten-gallon containers of gasoline and other goods over the mountain on their backs. The men were paid in wheat flour and tobacco. In Žepa, Paja's former military-police commander, Enver Štitkovac, had developed trade links with Serbs across the front line who were eager to get their hands on easy money. About eighty-five Ukrainian soldiers, who were deployed in the Žepa safe area by the UN and who received miserable salaries from their own government, earned money by transporting goods from the Serbs to Štitkovac.

❨ ❨ ❨

As the months wore on, even UN officials sympathetic to the plight of the Muslims grew fed up with the whining of Srebrenica's local leaders and their unwillingness to undertake any initiatives to improve the lives of their people, especially the refugees, unless it brought the leaders personal profit. When the town's sewer system needed to be flushed out, local leaders not only asked the Dutch military contingent in Srebrenica for materials to unclog the lines; they expected the Dutch troops to do the work for them. Srebrenica's officials made public appeals over the ham radio to draw attention to the plight of its people and exaggerated the level of suffering. They claimed people had starved to death. They complained of epidemics, including hundreds of cases of yellow fever, 3,150 cases of intestinal disease, 14,553 cases of scabies, and 26,530 cases of lice infestation. Some 80 cases of tuberculosis, including 42 deaths from the disease, were reported. A UN field officer made a trip to Srebrenica in September 1994 to investigate these claims and found no evidence to support them. "The mayor has been one of the most vocal when describing the substandard conditions of the enclave," the field officer reported. "I asked him two main questions: How many people have starved in Srebrenica in the last six months and what have you and your predecessors done to improve conditions within the enclave? His answers were 'none' and 'not too much,' respectively."

The staff of the Médecins sans Frontières (MSF), a French aid organization that sends doctors to treat people in war zones, threatened to leave the safe area. The director of the hospital, Doctor Avdo Hasanović, was giving MSF's physicians trouble because he wanted to take control of their pharmacy and use it to earn money. "I advised them to document any and all problems and incidents, and if Dr. Hasanović again suggests they should leave, ask for it in writing, and leave," the UN field officer wrote.

"All aspects of life are controlled by Naser Orić, . . . head of the local 'mafia,' " he continued.

> Orić controls the civilian authorities and the government and, in spite of appearances to the contrary, he approves every major decision they make. Only one other individual is powerful enough to stand up to Orić, and that is Zulfo Tursunović, Commander of the 281st Brigade, who is also Orić's main competition in the "mafia." . . . The Chief of Police for Srebrenica is Mr. Hakija Meholjić, who, like other key persons in the enclave, is also alleged to have some involvement with the black market.

Meholjić's police had no jurisdiction over any of Orić's soldiers. Meholjić complained to the UN official that whenever a soldier committed a crime, the army blocked investigations and arrests. Srebrenica's three judges had a backlog of over three hundred cases and refused to preside over serious cases because of death threats. One Muslim officer in particular, Ejub Golić, was suspected by the Muslim authorities in Sarajevo of having taken part in as many as a dozen murders, including killings of other Muslims; and one Serb family was killed allegedly because another Muslim officer wanted its house for his family. In April 1994, three teenage Muslim girls ran away from Srebrenica; after passing through a minefield, they threw themselves at the mercy of the Serbs and told the Serb police vivid stories of how Muslim soldiers had gang-raped them and how Srebrenica's police had done nothing.

(((

ABOUT thirty-five months had passed since my friends and I had stood on the steps of the cablecar station in Sarajevo and watched the muzzle flash of the mortars that began the wanton destruction of the city's multiethnic heart. These months of fear and stress and loathing had damaged the soul of practically everyone I knew in the city, including many of the foreigners, myself among them. A depression and a resignation settled over the mind like a thin fog shrouding the entire broad frontier between the obvious and the irrational.

Still under siege after more than two years, still shelled and sniped at every day after more than ten thousand of its people had been killed and buried, Sarajevo had by then been overrun by rural Bosnia, lumpen Bosnia . . . the Swedes. The urban population—the doctors, the engineers, the educated and the streetwise and the motivated—had to a great extent fled in search of new lives abroad. Waves of refugee Muslim peasants, most of them survivors of the rape of eastern Bosnia, had moved into the city's neighborhoods. Desperate for shelter, they forced their way into abandoned apartments and homes. They harassed many of the city's Serbs, many of them people who chose to remain loyal to the Bosnian government, which still had non-Muslim members. They massed around distribution centers each morning to collect their food and clothing. They stole what they could, and they nursed a grudge that the city and its people owed them something. Their highland accents, their archaisms, their *dimije*, their apparent identification with Islam, and their blind deference to the Muslim nationalist party were greeted with a contemptuous glare from many of the remaining city people, who grumbled to each other about these Swedes and the Ćiro that could never take them away. But the drift into the irrational caught up everybody, country and city folks alike, and the depression and resignation driving it were nothing like the acute fear and exhilaration and urgency to save Bosnia as a multiethnic land that had inspired the city's people and so many of the journalists working there in the early months of the war.

During the last few months of 1994, my last months in wartime Bosnia, I watched this drift into the irrational taking place in the street below my fourth-floor window at the Holiday Inn. Back then, this street, Sarajevo's main thoroughfare, was still named after Vojvoda Radomir Putnik, a Serbian army general during World War I. It is a broad street with a median strip and tram tracks and wide sidewalks. Each day, thousands of pedestrians used Putnik Street's sidewalk opposite the front of the Holiday Inn. Back and forth they would go, hiking to and from the city's center and the apartment blocks built on the western end of town. Soldiers trudged home from their trenches. Women lugged market baskets. Old men pulled cartloads of firewood. Mothers walked with their kids in tow. Directly across from the hotel were two crosswalks, two twenty-yard stretches of asphalt, where all the pedestrians passed in plain sight of Serb snipers. The bullets struck with no warning, in ones and in twos and, on rarer occasions, in threes, pop . . . pop . . . . pop, the third aimed to kill the first person foolhardy or unlucky enough to assume that the shooting was over. Whenever I heard the sound of gunfire bounce off the walls of the nearby buildings, I would scurry to my window to see if someone had been shot. Most often the sniper had missed—many times, I'm sure, on purpose—and four stories below there would be a group of pedestrians crouching behind some UN armored vehicles for protection. About once or twice a day, some wounded soul would be lying in the street, and about once every second or third day one or two people would be killed.

The UN "anti-sniping squad" began taking up positions on that stretch of Putnik Street each morning after the death toll started to mount. The UN soldiers would sometimes park their armored personnel carriers in the crosswalks to provide the pedestrians some cover, and these French and Russian soldiers would try and pinpoint the sniper's perch amid the rubble of the homes and apartment buildings across the front line. The UN soldiers would gather up any wounded or dead and truck them off to the hospital or the morgue. Television crews always set up on the sidewalk before lunch. Some of them would focus their cameras on the crosswalks and keep the tape running so they might catch some man or woman at the moment he or she was shot. The photographers' cameras would click and whiz. Reporters would jot down quotes from the survivors. Announcers would string together a few sound bites in English, French, Spanish, German, and Italian. And that day's horror from Bosnia would soon be packaged and beamed to millions of viewers and readers, complete with pools of blood; the faces of one more bereaved friend, one more bitter comrade, one more childless mother or motherless child; and a smattering of "political analysis" for garnish.

Missing from the reports, however, was the horror the Putnik Street killings revealed more clearly than anything else: the numb, irrational disregard for self-preservation into which Bosnia had descended. These deaths, unlike the sniping deaths early in the war, were practically suicides. Except for the youngest children, all the people who walked through the crosswalks and the crosshairs opposite the Holiday Inn knew the risk they were assuming. And they knew they were assuming it for the sake of a shortcut and nothing more. The street running parallel to Putnik Street, about a hundred yards behind the Holiday Inn, had crosswalks shielded from the snipers by tall buildings and shipping containers placed there by UN soldiers with front-end loaders. The Sarajevo government, the Muslim leadership, had not seen fit to rig up so much as a clothesline hung with bedsheets to keep the snipers from targeting the pedestrians walking in front of the Holiday Inn. And the city's police officers stationed at each end of this shooting gallery did not bother to direct people away.

I spent a few rainy afternoons on Putnik Street and asked the pedestrians why they chose to wager their lives by walking there. About an hour after a man had been gunned down, I watched a group of teenage girls flitting back and forth across the danger zone to flirt with the French and Russian soldiers on each side. A woman shouldering a bag of food said it was much longer to walk behind the Holiday Inn. A Bosnian army soldier answered this way: "This is my street. I will always use this street. And it makes no difference to me if they shoot or not. This will always be my street. And the Chetniks are not going to take it away." He went on to say that it was the responsibility of the UN to protect the people walking along Putnik Street: "If they can't, they should leave."

The UN troops assigned to Putnik Street had no authority to close the street or even warn people away, and they were relieved they did not have this authority. A captain in a French army airborne unit that fired back at the Serb snipers from time to time pointed out to me a Bosnian army soldier strolling through the firing range as if his uniform made him invisible to the Serbs just a few hundred yards away. "Just look at this idiot," he said. "If you were a Serb soldier on the other side and saw him walking there, what do you think you'd do? You'd shoot, that's what you'd do. . . . I don't know whether it's laziness or hopelessness or what, but we've asked the city authorities to put up barricades, and they have done nothing." He grew silent and glanced heavenward when I asked him to draw the obvious conclusions: that somebody, somewhere in the government did not want the shooting gallery to shut down. That somebody, somewhere, knew that the broadcasting of pictures of dead children and grieving mothers kept the Bosnian genocide from disappearing from the evening news in the powerful countries of the world. That civilian deaths meant nothing to Bosnia's leadership if that was the price for winning international intervention and keeping or retaking territory. The UN had proven earlier that autumn that Muslim soldiers had intentionally fired at least one mortar round into a Sarajevo neighborhood and that Muslim snipers had shot at people walking along Putnik Street, and it was impossible not to draw the inference that these acts were committed in a conscious effort to garner sympathy and drag the international community toward military intervention.

(((

THIS was the pathetic, irrational desperation that Bosnia had sunk into when I asked my bosses to bring me home that autumn. They had already given me a full-time job and a salary that meant I no longer got paid by the story. And without the incentive of piecemeal work, I found myself having trouble getting excited about the hunt for stories. A simple tale about people coming under fire each night on the road into Sarajevo over Mount Igman took me days and days to write, and I never did finish it. I was prone to superstition. Back in Cleveland, in the years during and after college when I was delivering spare auto parts to body shops and construction companies and waiting tables and mopping floors and selling flowers, I had joked incessantly about the Indians and predicted that I'd be dead before they ever won a World Series;

and here I was in Bosnia and the Indians were about to go into postseason play for the first time since 1954.

In mid-December, I filed my last story—a piece about the Putnik Street killings that never ran, because I did not want to strike the words "genocide" and "irrational"—and I left Sarajevo for the last time during the war. I told myself I would never go back to Bosnia, and I left without saying good-bye to too many of my friends and without thinking twice about the Čeliks in Srebrenica. I took a long train ride by myself to Scotland and inquired about doctoral programs in the history of science before I went home to Belgrade. Ljiljana and I packed up for a few weeks and told our daughters about how we would soon be living in America in a city by an ocean. We had a Christmas party. And my mother-in-law, Mara, came over for New Year's Eve and drank sparkling wine with Ljiljana and me beside a glowing wood fire. On January 3, we took a plane to Zurich; and the next day we flew to Cleveland. I rented an oceanfront apartment in Brighton Beach, Brooklyn, a few weeks later and found myself assigned to the *New York Times* bureau at the headquarters of NYPD. It was the best place my boss could have sent me, but I knew in my heart the minute I opened the door that, despite the fear, the exhaustion, and the snipers and Swedes, leaving Bosnia behind for a secure career in big-city journalism had been a terrible mistake.

PART SIX

"DON'T SHOOT THE PIANO PLAYER"

MUSLIM TERRITORY

to Tuzla

Kalesija

Baljkovici
Breakout

Križevačke
Njive
Execution

Zvornik

Ambush
Snagovo

*Path of
column*

S E R B I A

Drina

Udrč △

*Ambush
areas*

Konjević Polje
Football field
Nova Kasaba

Kravica   Glogova

Milići

Bratunac

Buljim
Jaglići
Sušnjari

Potočari   □ UN BASE

SREBRENICA
SAFE AREA

Path of refugees

*Camp
Bravo*   Srebrenica

*Dutch original
defense line*

OP. blown up

B O S N I A

Zlovrh
△

ŽEPA
SAFE AREA

*Mladic's Attack
July 1995*

Skelani

Bajina
Bašta

Drina

*Steel
bridge*

S E R B I A

Drina

| 0 | 10 | 20 | 30 km |

| 0 | 5 | 10 | 15 miles |

Chazaud

24

THE Serbs win in war and lose in peace. Or so goes an old Serb saying. It punctuated the cheerless café talk in Belgrade and Pale in early 1995 as the final hands in the poker game over Bosnia were about to be played.

The UN economic sanctions had hobbled Serbia's economy. President Slobodan Milošević, the man who had first stirred the fears and bloodlust that fueled the Serbs' nationalist passions, was more annoyed than ever at the Bosnian Serb leaders. They had failed to deliver him the quick victory he had bragged about as he was flying to the London conference in 1992. They had refused to pay even lip service to the Vance-Owen peace plan in 1993. They had rejected a second peace plan cobbled together by the United States, Russia, France, Great Britain, and Germany in 1994. Milošević´, now anxious to make any gesture that might lead to an easing of the UN economic sanctions, announced that he would not permit anything except food, medicine, and clothing to cross the Drina from Serbia to the Bosnian Serbs. In spite of his rhetoric, fuel and weapons still found their way across the border from Serbia into Bosnia.

General Mladić and Serb military and political leaders from both sides of the Drina met in Pale in early March 1995 to plot out their endgame. They pored over topographical maps, weighed their strengths and weaknesses, and assessed their enemy. The morale of Mladić's troops had slumped over the winter. The police in Serbia had to be called upon to round up Bosnian Serb draft dodgers and send them back across the Drina to patrol thousands of miles of winding front line, to guard vast, desolate tracts of conquered territory, and to fence in the Muslims caught in Srebrenica, Žepa, Goražde, and Bihać. While Mladić had already exhausted much of his potential for launching offensive operations, the Muslims had grown stronger. They had rearmed and reorganized. They had gotten their hands on American-made M-16 assault rifles, M-60 machine guns, antitank weapons, and American communications gear delivered by air and overland through Croatia. They had assembled refugees and orphans in their late teens and early twenties into a mobile attack force known as the Black Swans, which had begun hacking away at the front line. The Muslims still lacked the heavy artillery, tanks, and command skills necessary to mount large offensives, but their Croat allies had them and seemed ready to put them to use.

The strategy Mladić and the other Serb leaders decided upon was a return to their original war aims. The first goal was to create hardship in Sarajevo in a bid to convince Muslim leaders that further resistance was futile; the second was to overrun the Srebrenica, Žepa, Goražde, and Bihać safe areas in order to make possible the eventual merger of the Serb-held land in Bosnia and Croatia with Serbia. To achieve these aims, Mladić had to first neutralize the UN and NATO. All of his earlier efforts to force an end to the war had failed because intervention by the UN and NATO, however meager, had forced him to fold his hand. His bombardment of Sarajevo had failed to bring Muslim leaders to their knees, largely thanks to the UN military and refugee-relief missions. The Muslims were still hanging on to Srebrenica and Žepa, thanks to General Morillon and the UN. The attack on Goražde had been stymied by NATO. As Mladić drew up his plans in March 1995, however, he reckoned that after the hostage taking following NATO's air strikes around Bihać and the Serbs' deployment of a surface-to-air missile network, Yasushi Akashi and the new UN military commander in the former Yugoslavia, Lieutenant General Bernard Janvier of France, would not dare summon NATO to stop him.

(((

GENERAL JANVIER was considered a rising star in the French army, and tipped to become commander of the army's land forces, when he was named to lead the UN military force in Yugoslavia. He seemed perfectly suited for the UN post. He had experience in dealing with evacuations and massacres and was regarded a strictly-by-the-book officer. In 1982, he commanded a French Foreign Legion unit that helped remove thousands of Palestinian Liberation Organization guerrillas from Beirut after Israeli army soldiers had surrounded them; a month later, the Israelis gave Lebanese Christians carte blanche to carry out the wholesale murder of Palestinian civilians whom the guerrillas had left behind in the Sabra and Chatila refugee camps. Janvier had also led the French Daguet Division in a cautious advance into Iraq on the opening day of the Persian Gulf War in 1991. With an hour of daylight left on the day of the invasion, the French soldiers had started pitching their tents across the Iraqi desert. "To avoid mistakes," he told his staff, "it's better to delay."

Janvier learned of Bosnia in briefing papers that blamed the Muslims as much as the Serbs for the war. Upon arrival at the Zagreb headquarters of the UN military force, he insisted that the force had to remain strictly neutral, at least until it could be reorganized. The mission's personnel had to be made less vulnerable to hostage takings. Despite the provisions in Resolution 836 authorizing NATO to launch air attacks to protect the safe areas, Janvier decided he would under no circumstances let the military force in Bosnia be drawn across the "Mogadishu line," the thin frontier between peacekeeping and peacemaking that the UN force in Somalia had stepped over with such tragic results for the U.S. soldiers in 1993.

Janvier, like Wahlgren and Cot, was no friend to the safe-areas mandate with which the Security Council had saddled the UN military mission. Dealing with the safe areas had become a logistical nightmare. The Serbs had effectively made hostages of the Dutch troops in Srebrenica by restricting their movements in and out of the safe area and by cutting off their supply convoys at will simply by denying them permission to pass. The Muslims in Srebrenica, who were slowly starving, came to resent the Dutch because they were the most salient representatives of the UN, and the UN was failing to deliver food and failing to stop Serb attacks on the fringes of the enclave. Janvier and his new top officer in Bosnia, Lieutenant General Rupert Smith of Great Britain, proposed solving the problem of the safe areas by withdrawing the UN troops from them and leaving behind only a handful of military observers and target spotters for NATO fighter bombers. The generals reasonably argued that this token UN presence would provide the same deterrent as hundreds of soldiers who needed to be fed and supplied. Janvier presented the withdrawal scheme personally to the Security Council and to the ambassadors of the countries that had troops deployed in the UN military force in Bosnia.

"The situation in Bosnia is unmanageable," Janvier told the council members, explaining that the four hundred or so Dutch troops in Srebrenica, for example, could neither defend the enclave's forty thousand people nor deter attacks against them, especially since Muslim soldiers were operating out of the safe area. "Missions that put UNPROFOR's troops at great risk, such as deployment to the eastern enclaves . . . should be dropped."

Council members viewed this suggestion as a sellout even before Janvier blurted out that he thought the same Muslims who had retreated in panic before Mladić's onslaught against Srebrenica in 1993 were now fully capable of defending the enclave by themselves.

"The eastern safe areas were created to defend the population from Serbian attack," Janvier told the council. "Now the government of Bosnia has the resources to defend them." The diplomats shook their heads in disbelief, and Janvier flew away from New York knowing that he would have to carry the safe-areas burden for the foreseeable future. He was not happy about it.

For General Smith, to be neutral was one thing, but to be a supplicant was something else entirely, something not acceptable. He saw that the policy of acting only with the daily approval of General Mladić and his men had sucked the life out of the UN military force in Bosnia. Smith concluded that the UN force could succeed in delivering aid and protecting the safe areas only if it could forecast how the war would develop and prepare in advance for the anticipated conditions.

Smith grasped that Mladić's time was running out. He forecast that Mladić would go on the offensive to conclude the war during 1995 and that heavy fighting would break out around Sarajevo and the safe areas in the Drina valley. Smith anticipated that NATO air attacks would be needed to protect the safe areas and shore up the UN's and NATO's credibility, and he foresaw that the Serbs would seize UN personnel as hostages. But, unlike Janvier or Akashi, he carried his planning one step further. He reckoned that Mladić would find himself at a dead end as soon as he had seized the hostages; the Serbian general would not be willing to kill his captives, because he knew it would only outrage the international community and bring massive intervention that would lead to the Serbs' final defeat. Smith calculated that the UN could force Mladić to back down quickly by applying more military pressure, including more air strikes, after the Serbs had taken UN hostages. Once Mladić had been forced to yield, the UN's credibility would be restored. Its troops could deliver food and protect safe areas as it saw fit. And international peace negotiators would have a foundation on which to build a real peace. Smith's reasoning even changed the minds of some members of the Conservative government in London, who had until then been opposed to any possibly inflammatory action by the UN military mission. Smith did not have to wait long to see the first parts of his scenario played out.

❨ ❨ ❨

MLADIĆ had begun tightening the noose around Srebrenica in early 1995. The UN military force relieved the original Dutch contingent in the enclave with a second Dutch battalion in January. Once again the Serbs, this time a Red Beret unit under the command of a captain from the Yugoslav army, MILOŠEVIĆ's army, took advantage of the handover to grab land. Naser Orić had warned the Dutch that this might happen. He and Zulfo Tursunović, the Muslim commander in the area of the Serb incursion, were incensed when the Dutch let it happen. Orić and Tursunović instructed the new Dutch commander, Lieutenant Colonel Ton Karremans, to keep Dutch troops out of areas under Tursunović's control, clearly because the men there were armed and because Tursunović felt they could take care of their own security. When Karremans defied the ban, Tursunović seized a hundred Dutch soldiers and held them captive for four days. Now the Dutch were incensed at the Muslim leaders.

By March 1995, Mladić had halted fuel shipments and fresh-food deliveries to the Dutch. By April, his commanders were denying access to all supply convoys bound for Srebrenica and complaining that the Dutch were failing to stop Muslim *torbari* from venturing out of Srebrenica and plundering Serb farms. Relations between the Dutch and local Muslim leaders worsened as the food reserves in the enclave ran out. Muslim officials demanded assurances from Karremans that Srebrenica would be defended if attacked, and no guarantee was given. Dutch troops with night-vision goggles reported seeing Muslim soldiers sneak through the perimeter around Srebrenica and open fire on Dutch observation posts, or OPs, to make it seem that the Serbs were attacking them.

From Yasushi Akashi on down, UN military and refugee-relief personnel had by now had enough of Naser Orić. Akashi personally viewed the senior Muslim commanders in Srebrenica as criminal gang leaders, pimps, and black marketeers. Muslim army commanders in Sarajevo, clearly with some goading from the UN, finally took the decision to remove most of them from the safe area. In late March, Orić, Tursunović, Ejub Golić, and a dozen of Srebrenica's other top officers received orders to leave Srebrenica for "consultations and training." They hiked southward out of Srebrenica and waited night after night at a rendezvous point known as Orlov Kamen, or Eagle Rock, a peak a few miles north of Zlovrh. After almost two weeks, a Bosnian army helicopter plucked them from the mountainside and flew them out to Tuzla.

Orić met with Alija Izetbegović about five days later at the headquarters of the Black Swans in the central Bosnian town of Kakanj. Orić assured the Bosnian president that the Muslim military forces in Srebrenica could defend the enclave from a Serb attack, but only if they seized the mortars, antitank rockets, and other weapons that the Dutch had brought into the safe area. Orić's absence, however, weakened the mesh of loyalties among the fighters in Srebrenica. The Muslims' morale sank. Inside the enclave, rumors spread that the Tuzla corps would mount an invasion to liberate Srebrenica; other rumors held that the Muslim leaders in Sarajevo had done a territorial swap and that the people of Srebrenica would soon receive houses in suburbs of Sarajevo that the Serbs would abandon. People were willing to believe anything, and the vast majority of them just wanted to leave. Mladić's spies did not have to go farther than a pizza joint in Tuzla to spot Orić hanging out and trying in vain to recruit men to go back into Srebrenica.

In early May, after two small advances led by the Black Swans in central Bosnia and east of Tuzla, Mladić moved to close down the last entry points into Sarajevo. Serb gunmen hijacked UN aid trucks and closed the city's airport. Serb gunners blasted away at anything that moved along the narrow road over Mount Igman that linked up with the tunnel into Sarajevo. On May 7, a mortar round hit the tunnel entrance and killed ten civilians and Muslim soldiers.

Artillery duels and exchanges of gunfire made a dead letter of the deal the Serbs had made with the UN to comply with the NATO ultimatum issued after the marketplace shelling in February 1994. But when General Smith requested air strikes, Akashi, Janvier, and Boutros-Ghali turned him down.

Within days, Mladić was pumped up enough to transport artillery, tanks, and rocket launchers into the Sarajevo area and start pounding the city with mortars located inside the very weapons-collection areas that were supposed to be guarded by UN troops. This was a slap in the face NATO could not ignore. On May 24, General Smith issued the Serbs an ultimatum to pull back their weapons. The Serbs ignored the demand, and on May 25 NATO caught Mladić off guard by dropping bombs on two ammunition bunkers in Pale. The Serb general retaliated by shelling the safe areas. Half a dozen shells fell into the center of Srebrenica, breaking two years of relative quiet; in Tuzla, a mortar round killed seventy-one young people crowded into a cobblestone street a few steps from the pizza joint where Orić and the other officers from Srebrenica were regularly hanging out. Smith repeated his ultimatum, and another NATO air strike destroyed four more ammunition dumps on May 26. Now Mladić's men seized 324 UN soldiers and personnel as hostages. Television cameramen sent out pictures of hostages chained to hangars, ammunition depots, and other potential targets all over Serb-held areas of Bosnia.

The UN military force stopped dead in its tracks as Mladić began his move against the safe areas in the Drina valley. On May 28, the Serbs seized thirty British soldiers from UN observation posts around Goražde. Two days later, the Serbs demanded that the UN in Srebrenica abandon a key observation post, OP Echo, which overlooked the softest stretch of the safe area's defense line south of town. The demand came while the Muslim military in Srebrenica was in a state of disarray. A helicopter peppered with ground fire had crashed while trying to ferry Srebrenica's officer corps back into the enclave. Everyone in town had assumed Naser Orić would be aboard. When word of the crash reached Srebrenica, the local Muslim leaders feared that Orić had fallen into Serb hands. The Muslims mustered a hundred armed men to mount a rescue operation. They found the crash site on Muslim-controlled territory. Nine passengers, including four doctors, were dead. Three of Orić's officers—Zulfo Tursunović, Ramiz Bećirović, formally Orić's second in command, and Ejub Golić—had been injured. Orić had not been allowed to return; he said later that he had already been relieved of his command.

On June 2, Mladić again turned up the pressure on the UN to eliminate any threat of NATO air attacks. A Serb surface-to-air missile shot down an American fighter plane on patrol over Bosnia. NATO had long known that the Bosnian Serbs could detect the takeoffs and flight paths of the NATO aircraft patrolling Bosnian air space and soon concluded that the American fighter had been caught in a deliberate trap involving radar in Serbia. Janvier immediately instructed General Smith in Sarajevo to avoid all actions that might lead toward a confrontation with the Serbs. The next day, the Serbs attacked OP Echo, the Dutch abandoned it without firing a shot, and no air attack was ordered. The surrender of the observation post angered the Muslim commanders in Srebrenica. Muslim soldiers had brandished an antitank rocket in a vain attempt to stop the Dutch soldiers from fleeing the observation post. Now Muslim soldiers threatened to shoot if any more Dutch soldiers pulled away from the line. Colonel Karremans was not unsympathetic to concerns of the Muslim commanders. He soon set up two new OPs on the southern tip of the safe area and advised Ramiz Bećirović that Muslim soldiers could now establish defensive positions beside and behind all the Dutch observation posts, so long as the Muslims remained out of sight of the Serbs.

(((

THE hostage taking had elicited calls by world leaders for restraint, but General Smith stuck to his strategy and argued for military action by the UN to break the tightening Serb blockade of Sarajevo before the Muslims were forced to try and break it themselves. Smith opposed holding any talks with Bosnian Serb leaders until they released the hostages. He called for the deployment of a rapid-reaction ground force to break through the Serb lines around Sarajevo and break the siege of the city once and for all. Despite tough public demands that the hostages be freed without conditions, however, Yasushi Akashi, General Janvier, UN headquarters in New York, and the new French government of President Jacques Chirac had agreed to negotiate the hostages' release. Janvier met secretly with Mladić near Zvornik on June 4. The French general opened the meeting by appealing to Mladić's sense of honor as a military officer. He told Mladić that taking hostages was not worthy of a soldier. He appealed to him to behave like a gentleman.

"Your attitude has made you outlaws in the eyes of the international community," Janvier said. "Some governments, humiliated by your actions and their exploitation in the media, will not tolerate this situation much longer. They will take risks regardless of the consequences. Political leaders have already said the present situation is intolerable."

Janvier tried to convince Mladić that the air strikes against Pale had paradoxically opened a window of opportunity for the Serbs. They could grab the diplomatic high ground by releasing the hostages and allowing the UN to resupply Srebrenica and the other enclaves. "If you really have the will to move toward peace, do not ignore this opportunity," Janvier advised. "It can enable you to reemerge as a credible interlocutor with the international community."

"The eastern enclaves are in urgent need of resupply," Janvier pleaded. "The situation is unbearable. The soldiers there need food and fuel. If you continue to block resupply convoys, we will be obliged to carry out a resupply with helicopters. You can easily imagine the risk of provocations and escalation that this could entail."

An incredulous Mladić stared at Janvier from across the table. When his turn came to talk, he cut to the heart of the matter and played on Janvier's anxieties by referring to the UN hostages as "prisoners of war."

"The Serbs are waiting for an immediate guarantee that air strikes will not take place in the future," Mladić demanded. "The release of the prisoners of war is directly linked with this guarantee." He pulled from his papers the text of deal he wanted Janvier to sign. The paper said General Janvier, the commander of the UN military force in the former Yugoslavia, and General Mladić, the commander of the army of Republika Srpksa, the Bosnian Serbs' self-declared state, had agreed to the following: "1. The Army of the Republika Srpska will not threaten the lives and security of UNPROFOR members by the use of force. 2. UNPROFOR will not use force in any way or apply air strikes on targets in the territory of the Republika Srpska. 3. The signature on this document will lead to the freeing of all prisoners of war."

The minutes of the meeting do not indicate that Janvier signed the agreement. It clearly would have been foolish to sign it. The wink of an eye would have sufficed to communicate agreement to the Serb general's demands. The wink of an eye leaves no paper trail. But Janvier had no reason even to wink his eye. Janvier, like Akashi, now opposed the UN military force's using any force in Bosnia, including air action, except in the most extreme cases of self-defense. All he had to do was persuade Mladić to believe this. And he apparently did. Three days after the secret meeting, and after a theatrical display of "good will" by Milošević clearly aimed at getting the UN to lift the economic sanctions against Serbia, Mladić freed about half of the UN hostages.

ɕ   ɕ   ɕ

YASUSHI AKASHI and General Janvier clipped General Smith's wings at a meeting in the Croatian city of Split on June 9. They had already informed Smith that Boutros-Ghali had demanded a personal veto on all NATO air attacks, even in cases where UN troops needed to be defended. But Akashi and Janvier wanted to hear nothing more of Smith's calls for military action. Akashi spoke first and immediately tutored the British general on how to square circles. "I understand why you have taken the position of no negotiations with the Serbs until all hostages are released," Akashi said. "However, Zagreb and New York believe that some discussions should take place. But this is not contradictory. We can have firmness on the ground while exploiting opportunities to talk with political and military leaders."

Smith, who was not about to concede his views without an argument, introduced his case by outlining the mess the UN military mission was facing in Bosnia because of the decision to back down in the face of the hostage crisis.

"There is still a hard core of hostages held by the BSA," Smith said, referring to the Bosnian Serb army. "The eastern enclaves are also to be considered hostages in that we cannot feed them. In Žepa and Srebrenica we have OPs that could be overrun and captured. We also have a large number of camps at risk of artillery attack: the eastern enclaves, Sarajevo, Tuzla, Visoko and others. . . . To all intents and purposes we have been neutralized. . . . The safe areas are under increasing threat. . . . The Serbs continue to squeeze us, and I do not believe that they want a cease-fire. I believe that they want to continue to remove UNPROFOR from their affairs and to continue to neutralize NATO. This analysis is supported by the facts. Being more speculative, I believe that the BSA will continue to engage the international community to show that they cannot be controlled. This will lead to a further squeezing of Sarajevo or an attack in the eastern enclaves, creating a crisis that, short of air attacks, we will have a great difficulty responding to."

Smith indicated that the air strikes on the Pale ammunition depots had failed to achieve his goal, because there had been no follow-up. No one had called Mladić's bluff after he seized the hostages and reached his dead end.

"We are much worse off than we were when I started," Smith insisted. "We have neutralized air power and further marginalized ourselves. The parties and events are moving at a speed much greater than we have proven able to keep up with."

"Neutralized" and "marginalized" were just the words the French general wanted to hear. Further military action by the UN, Janvier told Smith, was out of the question. It was too risky. Mladić's bluff could not be called. The Serbs were in control of the situation, and therefore it was necessary to talk with Mladić, to educate the Serbs. "We discuss with them, demonstrate to them the situation, enlighten them on a path that might be followed. It is not easy. It is not enjoyable to ask Mladić for permission for convoys. But it is something that I had to do. And I did it. . . . Our first objective is the release of the hostages, and we must also resupply our soldiers in the enclaves. . . . If no crisis comes to modify the situation, if the hostages are liberated, and if we are able to resupply the enclaves, we can maintain this pause until political negotiations resume. . . . Another point to underline is that the BSA considers UNPROFOR as an enemy. This is clear. Their behavior reflects this. Mladić said that he would not fire on our positions. He knows that it is not in his interest to do so."

General Smith broke in: ". . . If we bring force behind us, he will make concessions. But if we do things on his terms, he will succeed in neutralizing us."

"We are a peacekeeping force, whether we want it or not," Janvier interjected. "What is essential is to allow for political progress to begin. As long as the situation is such, we cannot go toward confrontation. *What would be most acceptable to the Serbs would be to leave the enclaves. It is the most realistic approach, and it makes sense from the military point of view. But it is impossible for the international community to accept*" (author's italics).

Smith retorted, "I remain convinced that the Serbs want to conclude this year and will take every risk to accomplish this."

Janvier said the international community could help the UN military force out of its mess by offering Bosnian Serb leaders concessions. "The Serbs need two things: international recognition and a softening of the blockade on the Drina. I hope that these conditions will be met quickly, given the urgent situation. I think the Serbs are aware of how favorable the situation is to them. I don't think that they want to go to an extreme crisis. On the contrary, they want to modify their behavior, to be good interlocutors. It is for this that we must speak to them. Not to negotiate, but to show them how important it is to have a normal attitude."

"We need to do more than stabilize the situation," Smith objected. "We are in danger of reverting to the status quo minus, of operating in the mode of a supplicant. . . . We need to be prepared to fight across a whole range of threats. If we are not prepared to fight, we will always be stared down by the BSA. We are already over the 'Mogadishu line.' The Serbs do not view us as peacekeepers."

"Can we return?" asked Akashi.

"Only by doing nothing or by showing an absolute readiness to fight, including going over the top," Smith argued.

"I insist that we will never have the possibility of combat, of imposing our will on the Serbs," Janvier persisted. "The only possible way is to go through political negotiations."

Smith again cautioned Janvier that it was folly to expect that the Serbs would hold back around Sarajevo and the safe areas. "I anticipate actions that will lead our political masters by the nose. I can easily see a situation arising where we will be forced to request air power."

"It is just for this that we must establish contact with the Serbs, to show, to explain to them that there are just some things they cannot do," Janvier said.

"My judgment is that they will not listen," Smith answered. He warned Janvier in no uncertain terms that he and Akashi were destroying whatever credibility the UN military force in Bosnia had left.

"As long as the enclaves continue to exist," Janvier said, *"we will be neutralized to an extent"* (author's italics).

AFTER the meeting, the UN military force declared publicly that from that day forth it would abide by "peacekeeping rules." This sent a clear signal that the military force would remain strictly neutral, that it would not invoke Resolution 836 and use force to deter attacks on the safe areas. The declaration was a clear message to Mladić that the possibility of air attacks had dropped off the agenda except in extreme cases of self-defense. On June 17, Akashi and Janvier went back to the Serbs to work out the final release of the last hostages. Akashi flew to Belgrade to talk with Slobodan Milošević; Janvier traveled from Sarajevo to Pale to see Mladić. Janvier began the meeting by proposing initiatives the Serbs could undertake to create conditions that would lead to a negotiated settlement of the war. He advised Mladić not to attack civilian targets and counseled him to respond to Muslim military attacks by retaliating against military targets.

"Events are dictating behavior instead of the other way around," Janvier said. "This might lead to a still more serious crisis. There is only one offensive the Bosnian Serbs can undertake, the diplomatic offensive."

Janvier again pleaded with Mladić to allow for the resupply of the UN troops and the beleaguered Muslims in the eastern enclaves. He told Mladić this would be in the Serbs' long-term interests. "No one is going to recognize you as an equal partner if you do not actively participate in advancing yourselves in the eyes of the international community," Janvier said.

Mladić sat quietly taking notes for the thirty minutes that Janvier spoke. Then he blew up. He ranted about a large Muslim offensive that had been aimed at breaking the siege of Sarajevo. He raged about weapons getting into the safe areas. He roared about how the enclaves in the Drina valley were being used for black market activities.

"Unlike the Muslims, we are not looking for anyone to come here and fight for us," Mladić said. "All we want is equal treatment. If Serb forces carried out an attack similar to the one that the Muslims have undertaken now, we would have long ago found ourselves under air attack by NATO, not to mention condemned by the UN Security Council."

The Serbs freed the last hostages the next day. Nikola Koljević, a Bosnian Serb leader, bragged that the release had come as part of a deal with the French government. In Moscow, President Yeltsin said he, too, had been assured by President Chirac of France that air strikes in Bosnia were finished. And on June 19, Akashi sent a cable to UN headquarters in New York that included these words: "Milošević stated that he had been advised by President

Chirac of President Clinton's agreement that air strikes should not occur if unacceptable to Chirac." When the cable was made public a year later, the White House denied that any such assurances were made.

❮   ❮   ❮

A DAY after the hostages' release, NATO tested the waters. NATO jets were being locked on by Serb radar and had spotted Serb military jets in the air over Bosnia. The alliance requested that General Janvier allow NATO to respond by knocking out the Serbs' airfield at Banja Luka as well as their surface-to-air missile system. Janvier denied the request and sent a message to New York: "Such a proposal appears to me out of proportion and self-defeating in the present political and military environment. Conducting such disproportionate action would immediately affect any ongoing diplomatic process and precipitate reprisal attacks against United Nations personnel. . . . I have no intention of debating with the media on this question."

NATO fired back a request for an assurance from the UN that Janvier and Akashi had not played fast and loose with NATO's credibility by making a deal linking the use of NATO air power with the release of the UN hostages. This time Akashi answered: "I can state emphatically that neither I nor General Janvier have given any such assurances, nor could we condone any such assurances; we have always maintained that the release of the hostages must be, and was, unconditional."

Akashi failed to mention that he and Janvier did not have to rule out air strikes in deference to Mladić's precondition for the hostages' release. Akashi and Janvier had ruled out air strikes in principle, and Janvier had simply communicated that decision to Mladić. NATO clearly drew the same conclusion that Mladić did, and NATO commanders were no longer willing to have their pilots and aircraft exposing themselves to the Serb antiaircraft missile threat if Akashi and Janvier were only going to use them as noisemakers in the skies over Bosnia. NATO slashed the number of fighter-jet patrols over Bosnia. From now on, if Mladić chose to attack the Dutch troops in Srebrenica, the Dutch might have to wait four hours for NATO to mount an air attack to defend them. Janvier cabled New York and said he was satisfied that NATO's air cover was sufficient. All the hostages were free now. There was no reason to invite another hostage crisis.

With the poker game drawing to its climax, Akashi and Janvier had forced General Smith in Sarajevo to throw in his cards and emasculated the entire UN mission in Bosnia in the process. NATO had asked to be dealt in, but Akashi and Janvier had kept it out of the game. Now it was General Ratko Mladić's turn to play out his hand.

25

SANELA had been pulling her hair out every night since the beginning of her eighth month of pregnancy. She felt no unusual pains. But by mid-June the tingling of her nerves gave her no rest even in the silence that settled over Srebrenica during the tiresome hours after midnight. She would lie awake, drift away into dreams, and find herself gazing out the window or staring at the ceiling as Muhamed lay motionless next to her on the sponge pad. There was a lot to think about, a lot to prepare. She had sewn together some diapers and bibs from an old bedsheet, and she had knitted two pairs of wool socks and a hat. Hiba had given her a bar of soap as a gift. From this realm of planning and wondering and inventory taking and gazing into the ceiling, Sanela awoke one night to the popping of gunfire outside. She lifted herself from the sponge pad. The clock read two. Muhamed was still sleeping soundly. Again, pop, pop. She plodded over to the window. A flash of blue light hit the trees. There was a boom, then more pop . . . pop . . . pop . . . pop . . . pop. Pink tracer bullets crisscrossed the darkness.

"Muhamed. Muhamed, there's shooting."

He jumped up, wide-eyed, hurried to the window, and looked outside. More pops and explosions. Muhamed woke up the rest of the family, and all of them scrambled down into the cellar. After ten minutes, the commotion ended. Muhamed's father, Smail, wandered outside to see what had happened. Sanela, Muhamed, and his brother, Hajrudin, got dressed and lit cigarettes and waited to see if they were going to have to run.

Smail returned a while later. A Serb commando squad had infiltrated the town, he told them. The Serbs had come through an abandoned mine tunnel that runs for miles under a mountain to an opening near the soccer field. The Muslims had blown up the tunnel three years earlier, but the demolition job had been poorly done, and Mladić's men had burrowed through. The gunfire had erupted just above the hospital and the post office, the residence of the team of UN military observers in the enclave. The monitors had rushed to the scene in minutes and found scattered over the ground a few dozen spent grenade tubes, scores of brass bullet cartridges, and blotches of blood. A Muslim couple had been walking home from somewhere with their son when they stumbled upon the Serbs. Gunfire cut the woman in half and wounded her husband and child before the commandos backtracked to the tunnel entrance, scattering behind them land mines strung with trip wires.

The Dutch, whose compound in the town, Camp Bravo, was a few hundred yards away from the hospital, did not show up for five or six hours. Ramiz Bećirović, the Muslim commander who had formally replaced Naser Orić, was fuming about the Dutch response to the attack. The Dutch commander, Lieutenant Colonel Ton Karremans, told Bećirović that he assumed the gunfire was a shoot-out between rival Muslim gangs. There was no proof the Serbs had even carried out an attack, Karremans said; the whole thing might have been staged.

General Mladić had administered a test.

MEMBERS of a Muslim raiding party returned to Srebrenica the next day. Whether it was true or not, they boasted about how they had ambushed a truck and killed some thirty Serbs. Before dawn on June 26, during their trek back into the enclave, the raiders plundered what food they could from a Serb hamlet called VIŠNJICA. They shot into the air and set fire to a house to scare off the defenseless villagers. Then the Muslims drove off the Serbs' cattle and torched a dozen homes. A gunfight began when Serb soldiers rushed to the rescue; one of the Serb soldiers was killed and three more were wounded. Zulfo Tursunović had organized the raiding party. A Bosnian army officer in Tuzla had ordered the military commanders in Srebrenica to launch raids that would harass and tie down Serb forces during the Muslim offensive to break the siege of Sarajevo. There had been a few ambushes around Srebrenica after the order was given. Muslim soldiers had carried out a few plundering raids after the Serbs had cut off food convoys to Srebrenica, and *torbari* were slipping out of the enclave to steal what they could. But no one had paid much attention to them. Within hours of the Višnjica incident, however, Mladić's press officer had organized a trip to the village for foreign journalists. Some of these journalists presented the Višnjica incident, as a failure by the UN troops in Srebrenica to protect the Serbs outside the safe area from the Muslims inside. Serbs complained that the UN had taken sides with the Muslims.

General Mladić was handed his pretext.

❦   ❦   ❦

IN the blackness and silence after midnight, July 6, Sanela felt a prickle creeping along her spine. It edged its way through her arms and legs and into her fingers and toes. She lay half-awake on the sponge pad spread over the pantry floor. She studied the blank ceiling and the window frame and tried to squirm herself into a position comfortable enough to fall asleep. It was a Thursday. Six from seventeen is eleven. Eleven more days and nights and the waiting would be over. Eleven days from Thursday would make it a Sunday. The more she thought about it and counted down, the more time seemed to stand still and the more deliberately the prickle seemed to edge down her spine and radiate into her legs and arms.

Sanela had been ready for a week. The baby had turned downward and was thrashing about so much that it had to be a boy. A list of male names ran through her head. But she felt nothing for any of them. He could not be named Muhamed. This was the Muslim custom, anyway. Sons could not be named after their fathers.

Outside the window, Sanela heard the hollow pounding of artillery and the clatter of machine-gun fire coming from the hills south of town. Then shells began crashing into the houses and yards of the town itself. One mortar round blew up in the park. The prickle running along her spine found itself crowded out by the movements she made as she climbed to her feet and got dressed. Everyone in the Halilović house awoke and took cover in the cellar. In these same minutes, Hiba and Zlatija grabbed Mirza and Edin and followed Huso to a basement shelter in the apartment building down the hill from the Čelik home. The shelter was already stuffed with people. The women spread out their sponge pads and blankets on the cement floor. The sleepy children whined and fussed, and the men filled the musty air with cigarette smoke and mumbles.

Mladić's men had begun softening up the dugouts and trenches that the Muslims had built between the UN observation posts along the southern fringe of the Srebrenica safe area. Serb howitzers, mortars, and tank cannons blasted away throughout the morning. Shells blew up all over town. Cannon fire from a pair of tanks tore into the lookout tower of a Dutch observation post (OP) that had a clear view of the only road running into the enclave from the south. It is an asphalt road. It begins in Serbia and crosses the metal bridge over the Drina at Bajina Bašta. Then it climbs northward through the mountains before coasting down a steep grade into the town of Srebrenica and sloping gradually through Potočari and on to Bratunac. The lookout tower of the Dutch OP had been outfitted with a TOW antitank rocket system. Mladić wanted to advance his tanks northward along the asphalt road. He had to eliminate any possibility that the Dutch troops in the OP, or the Muslim men around it, could use the antitank rockets to block the road.

Lieutenant Colonel Karremans contacted his UN superior in Sarajevo, Brigadier General Cees Nicolai of the Netherlands, and discussed air support to defend the Dutch soldiers who were coming under fire. Nicolai reminded him of General Janvier's new restrictions on the use of force and said Janvier and Akashi did not want to create complications for the European Union's new peace negotiator, Carl Bildt, who would soon be meeting with Slobodan Milošević in an effort to restart the stalled peace process. The conclusion Nicolai drew was that the risks of air support outweighed the advantages.

PAJA and Senad were in Žepa on the morning the Serbs began their attack. They had gone there to beg and buy cornmeal and beans and were resting for the hike home when they heard the far-off thuds of the artillery to the north. They packed the food in their rucksacks and left Žepa before dawn. Climbing over Zlovrh, they could hear the gunfire and the explosions, sometimes to the right, sometimes straight ahead. They wondered whether the trail back to town would still be open. They feared trigger-happy Muslims who would be on the lookout for any movement in the forest just outside the southern edge of the enclave. Clouds darkened the sky as they approached Srebrenica's defense line in the early evening. Wind gusts buffeted the trees. Lightning flashed. Torrents of rain began to fall. Mladić's artillery crews stopped firing and took shelter. The Muslim soldiers, still inside their earth-and-log dugouts, could not see very far in front of them, and Paja and Senad crossed back into Srebrenica unnoticed. The town was quiet except for the thunder and the beating of the rain. The two friends slogged home with the flour and the beans, changed into some dry clothes, headed down to the shelter to see the rest of the family, and went home to sleep in their beds.

❮   ❮   ❮

FOG shrouded the hillsides around Srebrenica at daybreak on Friday. Mladić's artillerymen lobbed a few shells into the forests near the intersection of the asphalt road and the southern edge of the enclave. Bursts of gunfire resounded from the woods from time to time. But nothing moved among the trees and the mist. Paja slept late into the morning. Hiba went up to the Ćelik house to boil a pot of beans. She saw people scurrying through the streets, carrying blankets and suitcases and rucksacks with food. Sanela and Muhamed climbed out of their cellar for a while, too. They showered, changed clothes, and fixed something to eat. Sanela packed the baby clothes, the bibs, and the diapers into a bag with her album of family snapshots, her diary, and the bar of soap Hiba had given her. She squeezed in a couple pairs of jeans for herself, some T-shirts, some underwear, a towel, a rag, a sweatshirt, and some clothes for Muhamed. He laughed when he saw her packing. He asked where she was planning to go.

A DUTCH liaison officer in Srebrenica told local Muslim leaders on Friday afternoon that Lieutenant Colonel Karremans's call for air strikes had been denied.

"No NATO aircraft were available," the liaison officer lied. Nothing in the UN military observers' report on the meeting indicates that the liaison officer even hinted that Janvier had issued orders restricting the use of force or that the general had recommended a withdrawal of the UN troops from the safe areas.

Srebrenica's district president, Osman Suljić, told the liaison officer that the defense of the enclave would be the UN's responsibility. Srebrenica was its safe area, he said; the Muslims would not resist an offensive, because they did not have enough weapons and ammunition. The military observers' report noted that they had not seen the Muslims take any retaliation for the Serb attacks.

Karremans advised his superiors that he considered the Serb attacks to be nothing more than harassment and that he did not expect Mladić to seize any UN OPs. Despite the rocket attacks, the heaviest shelling of the town in two years, and the approach of tanks up the asphalt road from Bajina Bašta, Karremans had reasonable grounds to support his assessment. His commanders in Sarajevo, Zagreb, and the Netherlands respected it, and the Muslim commanders in Srebrenica concurred.

Muslim scouts had spotted Mladić bringing up some of his forces across the Bajina Bašta bridge on July 5, but he had mustered only about two thousand fresh soldiers around Srebrenica. This is far fewer than the number a prudent commander would throw into a battle against five thousand men, the number of Muslims estimated to have guns in the safe area. Mladić concentrated most of his men to the south, between Srebrenica and Bajina Bašta. Members of Željko Ražnatović's gang, the Tigers, were on hand, as were the Drina Wolves, a militia group from Zvornik, and a menagerie of criminals and irregulars from Serbia and mercenaries from Greece, Germany, and Russia. Milošević's special paramilitary police were also summoned from their base in a hotel in Serbia just north of Mount Zvijezda. The Serbs were backed up by fifteen to twenty tanks and armored vehicles and about fifty artillery pieces, including the howitzers on the Serbian side of Mount Zvijezda. The UN had border monitors stationed along the Drina at the time of the attack. Witnesses say the monitor in Bajina Bašta had been spending his days getting drunk with the Serbs.

❨   ❨   ❨

SHELLS and rockets were again jolting the center of town and exploding near the Dutch troops in Camp Bravo by Friday evening. The Čeliks curled up on their sponge pads in the basement shelter for a second night. Edin had a stuffed-up nose but romped around the room getting on everyone's nerves until Hiba delivered a solid swat to his butt; he cried and pouted for a few minutes, then dozed off as his grandmother rocked him back and forth with her legs. Mirza was running a temperature and refusing to eat. He lay next to Zlatija and kept his eyes shut even while he was awake, and he listened to everything around him. Huso also refused to eat. He smoked his cigarettes, scarcely spoke with Paja, and still ignored Zlatija except when he wanted something. He hunted around until he found someone who would listen and then launched into outbursts of pessimism and complaints about the aching in his legs.

"They're going to get us," he said. "We're trapped. It's over. This is the end."

"Mama," Mirza repeated. "Mama, they're going to slit our throats. They're going to kill us all."

The explosions came at irregular intervals after midnight, but at least one bomb fell for every two minutes. In the cellar beneath the Halilović house, Sanela lay awake, smoking cigarettes, too frightened even to go upstairs to the bathroom alone. She listened for the dull thumps of the bombs that exploded miles away, and she flinched when the shells falling nearby ripped the silence like thunderclaps that seemed to pound back and forth between the tall apartment buildings before rumbling over the horizon. The night dragged on. Muscles tightened and ached. Moods shifted from fits of anger to outbursts of cynical laughter. Practically everyone wanted nothing more than to leave, to escape. Sanela counted down. Nine more days.

The world beyond the cellar was quiet when she opened her eyes on Saturday morning. A gray mist hung over the town and hid the hillsides around it. Hiba and Paja left Huso, Zlatija, and the boys in the shelter and ventured up to the house. They lit a fire in the stove. Paja brought in some vegetables from the garden and smoked cigarettes as Hiba baked bread.

❊   ❊   ❊

A LITTLE past noon, the Dutch sergeant commanding the UN observation post overlooking the asphalt road radioed in. Bombs were exploding just outside the OP's sandbags. Within minutes gunfire and artillery barrages had begun all along the southern edge of the enclave. Mladić's infantry advanced for the first time.

A tank shell blasted away a section of the OP's protective wall an hour later. The same tank then scored two more direct hits into the sandbags. The Dutch soldiers inside had taken cover in their armored vehicle. The sergeant radioed in again and received permission to abandon the post. The armored vehicle's diesel engine revved, but a gun battle between the Muslims and Serbs pinned down the Dutch troops. Ten Serb soldiers rushed into the OP. They disarmed the Dutch troops and ordered them to withdraw into Serb-held territory. The sergeant balked. He argued with the Serbs and persuaded them to let the Dutch withdraw toward Srebrenica. The white armored vehicle rumbled away from the post a few minutes later. It zigzagged down a twisting dirt trail to the asphalt road and turned north toward town. A Muslim soldier and three civilians halted the armored vehicle at a makeshift roadblock. They did not want the Dutch leaving them in the lurch. The sergeant checked to make sure the Muslims had no antitank weapons, then ordered his driver to move on without their permission. A Dutch soldier, Private First Class Raviv Van Renssen, was lowering himself into the hatch atop the armored vehicle as it lurched forward. An angry Muslim loosed a grenade that exploded before Van Renssen could shut the hatch. A bullet or a piece of shrapnel tore into the private's head. His body sagged, then dropped into the vehicle. The Dutch soldiers radioed for help and administered first aid as they drove toward their field hospital at Potočari. Van Renssen died about an hour later.

Now the Dutch had seen one of their own killed by one of the Muslims they had been sent to Srebrenica to protect. Now the Muslims seemed to pose more of a threat than the Serbs.

Mladić's infantry and tanks pressed ahead toward the last two Dutch OPs controlling the asphalt road into Srebrenica. The Muslims mounted resistance from positions behind the Dutch to keep them from retreating. Three hours later, however, the Serbs drove the Muslims from a ridge behind the first of the two OPs, and two dozen Serbs stormed inside it. The Dutch surrendered their weapons and, knowing what had happened to Van Renssen, chose to put themselves in the custody of the Serbs. They allowed the Dutch troops to drive their white armored vehicle out of the OP. They were escorted over the mountains to Bratunac, and they used their two-way radio to tell their comrades in the other OPs that they were on their way to a hotel and that the Serbs would soon let them leave for Holland.

Karremans and the Muslim commanders were still not convinced Mladić wanted to seize the entire Srebrenica enclave. Karremans reported to his superiors that he considered the capture of the two OPs to be part of a limited Serb operation to seize only the southern tip of the enclave. He forecast that Mladić had almost achieved his goal. Serb leaders had been complaining for two years that they wanted control of the southern edge of the safe area. It would give them access to the bauxite mines and the furniture factory and enable them to sever the Muslim lifeline between Žepa and Srebrenica. The Dutch liaison officer, however, told Ramiz Bećirović that Karremans had warned UN headquarters that the crisis was deepening. Bećirović apologized to the liaison officer for the killing of Private Van Renssen. But he called the UN's response to the Serb offensive shameful. He demanded that the Dutch find the means of "preventing a total massacre" and call on NATO for air strikes. The Dutch officer advised Bećirović to let the Dutch "do the job their way."

❮ ❮ ❮

MLADIĆ'S men and tanks crashed through the UN's southern gates into Srebrenica on Sunday, July 9, and took over two more OPs near the asphalt road. The Dutch troops inside them were also escorted to the hotel in Bratunac in their armored vehicles. Along the way, the Dutch soldiers radioed Karremans and told him they had spotted Serb artillery pieces set up on most of the hills along the eastern edge of the enclave. Here was an obvious sign that Mladić was going for much more than the safe area's southern tip. But Karremans again told his commanders that he did not think the Serbs would try to take the enclave because they lacked the necessary manpower for house-to-house fighting against the more numerous Muslims. He warned that any pinprick NATO air strikes against the Serbs would provoke a massive artillery retaliation on the town as well as the UN bases. He clearly indicated to his UN superiors that such an artillery attack could be prevented only by larger-scale NATO air strikes. Karremans passed his superiors the map coordinates of fifteen targets, including Serb tanks and artillery pieces. The target list reached NATO, but no request for air action came from Janvier.

The Serb advance sent hundreds of Muslim refugees fleeing north into the town of Srebrenica. The refugee shelter built by the Swedish government had been bombarded and abandoned. By noon, the Serbs were setting fire to houses in Pusmulići, a hamlet two miles south of Srebrenica, and their tanks were grinding farther north toward town along the asphalt road. Mladić's forces had grabbed another OP and were holding over twenty Dutch soldiers hostage. Furious Muslim soldiers were blocking the withdrawal of an armored vehicle with Dutch troops who had abandoned their OP after it had come under attack.

INSIDE the shelter, the Čeliks played rummy and smoked cigarettes. There were about fifty people in the basement of the apartment building. They would go home to use the bathroom, and sometimes to cook food. Few people inside believed the town would fall. Paja thought to himself that when the war ended he would be able to walk home. The short way, southward over the mountains to Skelani, across the steel-girder bridge to Serbia, and up over the back of Mount Zvijezda to Kupusovići.

"It took me nine hours that way once," Huso said. "I walked over to Srebrenica to play for a wedding. One guy got drunk and requested a song, and when I played it he gave me enough money to buy an ox. His wife came by a little while later. She was crying and said her kids would go hungry without the money. So I gave it back to her."

Huso's words broke the year and a half of silence between them.

❦   ❦   ❦

LATE Sunday night, Yasushi Akashi and General Janvier sent General Mladić a message. They called it a warning and informed him that his forces would face pinprick NATO air attacks if the Serbs opened fire on a Dutch defense line that would be set up on Monday morning on each side of the asphalt road just south of the town of Srebrenica. They also demanded that he withdraw his forces from the Srebrenica safe area and release the Dutch hostages.

"The BSA is reminded of the grave consequences of ignoring this warning," the message read, referring to the Bosnian Serb army.

General Nicolai called Mladić's headquarters from the UN base in Sarajevo to deliver the message. Mladić's deputy, General Zdravko Tolimir, picked up the phone. When Nicolai came to the part of the message demanding that the Serbs withdraw from the safe area, Tolimir cut him off.

"What are you talking about?" Tolimir demanded. "There are no Serbs in the enclave. General, you should not blindly trust Muslim propaganda."*

Janvier had already issued Karremans an order to create the defense line.

"Take up blocking positions using all means available to you in order to prevent the further penetration and advance of BSA units in the direction of Srebrenica," the order read. "Every possible measure must be taken to reinforce these positions, including measures relating to weapons."

Janvier promised Karremans that if the Serbs attacked the Dutch defense line, the Dutch would receive limited air support from NATO. Karremans was apprehensive. Four dozen Dutch soldiers spread out to the right and left of six armored vehicles painted iceberg white and sitting in plain view of Mladić's men could not fight to repel a Serb attack. If NATO launched pinprick air attacks, Mladić would call down his rockets and heavy artillery to punish the entire town and the UN bases. What Karremans knew he needed was the only deterrence against attack that Srebrenica had ever had, the deterrence of

*See Honig and Both, *Srebrenica*, p. 15, citing Frank Westerman, NRC/Handelsblad, October 14, 1995.

large-scale air strikes that NATO was clearly ready to provide if Janvier gave the word.

By 5:00 A.M. on Monday, July 10, Karremans had obediently deployed his men onto an exposed defense line perpendicular to the asphalt road south of town. The Dutch troops were given permission to open fire under two conditions: they could shoot over the Serbs' heads if the Serbs advanced toward them; and they could shoot at the Serbs if the Serbs attacked the Dutch on the defense line.

Mladić had no trouble seeing that Akashi and Janvier's message did not contain any threat of military retaliation if he ignored their demand for a withdrawal. Nor had Akashi and Janvier threatened to take any military action if Mladić continued the attack on the safe area, so long as the Serb troops left the Dutch defense line untouched. Mladić clearly knew that General Smith, the man who had ordered the air strikes in May, had been sidelined by Akashi and Janvier; Smith himself, obviously not wanting to have his name associated with the unfolding debacle in Srebrenica, now left Bosnia for rest and relaxation at the seaside villa Fitzroy Maclean had received from Tito after World War II. The Serb general, having had long experience dealing with Akashi, knew he would be loath to approve air attacks even in cases of self-defense. Mladić had also clearly measured the length and breadth of Janvier's resolve during their secret negotiations for the release of the hostages in June. There had to be no question in Mladić's mind about what to do next.

26

THE Serb attack began Monday, July 10, at dawn. Mladić mounted the most furious artillery barrage Srebrenica had ever seen. His infantry sidestepped the ends of the Dutch defense line and battered the Muslims deployed there. Gunfire zinged past Dutch soldiers tucked inside one armored vehicle on the defense line. A Serb tank opened fire on another Dutch vehicle. The Dutch had requested a NATO air attack by 9:00 A.M. NATO planes took to the air and circled over the Adriatic; they remained aloft for the next three hours; and they attacked nothing. General Janvier had held them back. He decided that air attacks were not warranted, because the fighting on the ground had involved only an infantry assault. The Serbs had indeed shot at the Dutch, but in Janvier's mind the defense line had not really been attacked.

Mladić's infantry took a breather at noon to wait for the NATO fighters to run low on fuel and clear out. In the meantime, his artillery brought the center of Srebrenica under a second heavy bombardment. Some two thousand refugees with no shelter had gathered near the hospital during the morning hours, gambling that it might not be shelled. The hospital, however, was just fifty steps from the Muslim army's military headquarters, the post office, the same building where General Morillon had pledged in the name of the UN never to abandon Srebrenica and its refugees. The Serbs blasted away. The bombs blew out the hospital's windows. Shrapnel and glass shards buried themselves in the operating room's walls. Panicked refugees scrambled in every direction to save themselves. By the early afternoon, UN refugee-relief workers had tallied up six civilian dead and twenty-three wounded, but many of the dead and injured could not be counted because they could not get to the hospital. The artillery fire into the population center of the safe area went on hour after hour. The smoke from burning villages wafted into the sky south of town.

In their situation report, the UN military observers in Srebrenica warned of a possible massacre. But Janvier and Akashi paid the warning no heed. Despite the Serbs' vendetta against Srebrenica's Muslim men, the drive for vengeance that had prompted Morillon to take his stand in the town, the two highest-ranking UN officials in Yugoslavia were making their decisions as if it did not exist. Akashi, in fact, behaved as if nothing extraordinary were happening in Srebrenica. On that morning, he saw fit to go ahead with a planned day trip to the Croatian resort of Dubrovnik. Janvier was given the authority to call in limited air support without Akashi's approval in order to protect the Dutch troops; but Akashi retained his veto power over any call for the only action that would have made a difference: a large-scale air strike at the Serb artillery and tanks.

❮   ❮   ❮

IN the late afternoon, Mladić resumed his infantry advance.

The Dutch officer commanding the defense line, Captain Jelte Groen, ordered his men to shoot warning flares with their mortars and open fire over the Serbs' heads.

Mladić's men pressed ahead.

The Dutch officer saw the Serbs outflanking the Dutch soldiers. He ordered them to withdraw to a new defense line across the center of town. The Dutch came under attack. They opened fire on the Serbs and joined the Muslims in mounting armed resistance.

By dusk, Mladić's men had advanced farther along the asphalt road. They pulled up onto a bluff at a hairpin turn three hundred feet above the market square. The bluff was within shouting distance of the tidy white house where Sanela and Muhamed were sheltering in the cellar with the rest of the Halilović family.

Everyone in the Halilović household had been in the cellar all day except for Muhamed's father, Smail. He came down from time to time to make small talk but otherwise stayed upstairs. The hydroelectric generator was working fine. He was watching television, listening to the radio news, and kneeling in prayer. The women had fixed beans for the evening meal. They had just put their dishes away when a flurry of gunfire erupted. Muhamed peeked outside and spotted the Serbs up on the hairpin turn.

"Smail, get some bread in a bag, get your shoes on, and let's go," Muhamed shouted.

Sanela grabbed her rucksack. Muhamed brought her an athletic suit and told her to slip it on.

"It will be easier to run in this," he said.

Sanela was already wearing a pair of Muhamed's undershorts and some tennis shoes, and she quickly slipped on the athletic suit and tied the pull string across her belly. Muhamed slipped a brown jacket over a white shirt with Marco Polo silk-screened across the back. He helped Sanela climb through a window on the side of the house facing away from the Serb soldiers on the bluff.

"Go ahead of me, fast," Muhamed ordered her as he looked after his grandmother.

"We'll go together," Sanela snapped.

She waited for him next to the house, and after Muhamed climbed outside she waddled along next to him. Bullets whizzed through the air over their heads. Sanela glanced back and saw the Serbs a few hundred yards above them, still on the bluff by the hairpin turn. She kept moving forward, northward, away from the gunbursts. After half an hour the shooting stopped, and they rested. Sanela plopped herself down on a felled tree. She and Muhamed lit up cigarettes and looked around at the chaos of fleeing humanity. The men talked among themselves and quickly decided that the women should go down toward Camp Bravo and wait in the apartment of one of Muhamed's relatives. Muhamed, Smail, and Hajrudin would go back up and fight.

The good-byes took only a few seconds. Muhamed said farewell to his mother and grandmother, a neighbor, and then Sanela. He asked Sanela for her snapshot. She pulled it from her photo album, and he slipped it into his pocket before he kissed her good-bye. He was crying.

INSIDE the apartment-building basement where the Čeliks were sheltering, a woman who had given birth to a baby just two days before ventured upstairs and peeked out a window to see what was going on.

"People!" she shouted to the others in the basement. "Come look! The road is full of people! The people are leaving their houses!"

Everyone inside the shelter leapt up and scrambled to pack their belongings. Huso picked up the blankets and some food and was the first to pull out. The Čeliks joined the thousands of people hustling north down the asphalt road toward Camp Bravo. The Serb soldiers looking down from the hairpin turn could see the bedlam in the streets below. Families had fled their houses in the old town. They carried with them suitcases, duffel bags, rucksacks, and their children. They pushed the lame and the aged in wheelbarrows. Some had cattle and horses and sheep. The wave of refugees burst through the gates of Camp Bravo and people poured in seeking protection from the shelling. The Dutch offered to begin transporting the refugees to the main UN base in Potočari, and a wave of Muslims headed north on foot. But Srebrenica's Muslim authorities did not want the town to be emptied. They wanted the UN to take action.

Muslim soldiers brandishing guns blocked the asphalt road toward Potočari.

"Go on back. Go on back," a Muslim soldier cried out to a crowd of people. The Čeliks were among them. They were itching to leave. Everyone wanted nothing more than to leave.

"This is just propaganda," the Muslim soldier said. "Our guys won't let the Chetniks enter the town."

Paja, Huso, and the rest of the family turned back. The air went quiet for minutes at a time. The Serbs on the hairpin withdrew, and disappeared toward the south.

The night sky was clear when Paja and his parents left the children and Zlatija with friends near Camp Bravo and walked back up to the house to get the flour he had lugged from Žepa. Hiba pulled up onions from the garden, and Huso picked up the photo album from inside the house and packed it in a rucksack. Rifle fire popped around the valley. Tracer bullets scratched red lines over the hills south of the town and sometimes ricocheted upward in clean obtuse angles before burning out in the blackness. A shell whistled over the Čelik house and blew up a few dozen yards away. Hiba dove onto the floor.

"It's over for us," Huso told her. "We've got nowhere to go. They're going to catch us. But if we do somehow get out of here, I want to move to Sarajevo. I don't ever want to go back to Kupusovići. I knew what they did to us before, and I stayed. Now they have done it again. I don't ever want to go back there."

OSMAN SULJIĆ, the Srebrenica district president, spoke with President Izetbegović on a Muslim army radio link. Suljić described the situation. Izetbegović, who was staying in the headquarters of the Black Swans in Kakanj, told him there was nothing he could do for Srebrenica. Everything depended on the UN. The Muslim army's commander, Rasim Delić, and the commander of the army's Tuzla corps, Sead Delić, ordered no action to draw away Mladić's forces. The Sarajevo government of Haris Silajdžić made statements condemning the attack on Srebrenica and the lack of an international response. Silajdžić reportedly assured Bećirović by radio that the UN would defend Srebrenica. The government made no contingency plans to deal with the enclave's people in the event that the UN failed to protect them.

By the early evening, Lieutenant Colonel Karremans had fallen ill. And at 7:15 P.M., his deputy, Major Rob Franken, requested an air attack to protect his men on the blocking positions who were coming under fire and shooting back. He faxed off the coordinates of forty potential targets: the artillery pieces, the multiple rocket launchers, and the tanks Mladić had used to pummel the safe area and attack the UN forces within it. If NATO could destroy these weapons, Mladić would not be able to threaten an artillery blitz against the crowds of civilians on the streets or the UN bases. If the weapons were destroyed, the safe area of Srebrenica would not fall.

General Janvier received the request at about seven-thirty. He delayed making a decision even though Akashi had given him the power to authorize NATO air support without him. Janvier clearly saw no reason to decide in a rush. Now the man who had told the UN Security Council that Srebrenica's Muslims could defend themselves was worrying about "escalating" the violence. He summoned his top advisers for a meeting at his headquarters in Zagreb at about 8:00 P.M. Each of the advisers supported a small-scale air attack because Mladić's men had attacked the Dutch defense line. But Janvier had a different criterion. He said he still could not believe that Mladić actually wanted to take Srebrenica. He told his advisers that he could not understand why Mladić would want to complicate matters when the new peace negotiator, Carl Bildt, was about to get the peace process restarted. Janvier announced that he needed more information. He sent off some aides to fetch it. The discussions dragged on. After 9:00 P.M., Janvier stopped the meeting, left the room, and got Akashi on the phone. When he returned, Janvier told his staff that he had made personal contact with Mladić's deputy, the same General Tolimir who, not twenty-four hours earlier, had said there were no Serb troops attacking the Srebrenica enclave. Janvier said Tolimir had assured him that the attack on Srebrenica was being mounted by renegade militias and that Serb commanders needed more time to get them under control. Janvier said Tolimir had issued orders for the Serb troops to stop firing and not to attack the UN forces. This order, Janvier said, would take some time to reach the Serb troops on the ground. At 10:00 P.M., NATO air activity was suspended for the night. Janvier reissued the "warning" he had sent Mladić the night before.

The Serbs sent the UN military force in Srebrenica a message of their own that night. The Dutch were instructed to begin withdrawing from the safe area by 6:00 A.M. the next day. The Serbs said they would guarantee safe passage for the Muslim civilians.

Now it was clear even to Karremans that the Serbs wanted to seize the entire enclave. At about midnight, he told Srebrenica's Muslim political leaders and commanders that NATO would launch massive air strikes against Mladić's men if they did not withdraw from the enclave by six the next morning. Karremans pointed out to the Muslim leaders an array of Serb weaponry that would be wiped out in the air strikes. He said NATO would make a "death zone" out of the asphalt road south of town. The Muslims were incredulous. They queried Karremans. They asked him if he was certain there would be an air attack.

"I can't read the future," Karremans answered. "Don't shoot the piano player."

The Muslims asked again.

"Don't shoot the piano player."

Karremans's translator, Hasan Nuhanović, did not know what Karremans was talking about. Janvier and Akashi would not have known what he meant either. They had not issued any ultimatum or ordered any massive air strikes. On the basis of Karremans's assurances, however, Srebrenica's Muslim commander, Ramiz Bećirović, withdrew his men from areas where Karremans said NATO would bomb. Bećirović shifted his forces westward, removing all but a token resistance force, led by Ejub Golić, from the eastern side of the enclave. There was no more reason for the Muslims to fight along the front lines. If the air strikes came, the Serbs would be forced to withdraw; if the air attacks did not come and the Muslims stayed, they would be doomed to die beside their families in an orgy of hellfire and house-to-house fighting. The carnage would be worse than the violence at Vukovar. Bećirović made the shift toward the west in preparation for a withdrawal, a march across Serb-held territory by the military-age Muslim men, men who knew that the Serbs would show them no mercy if they were captured.

❨   ❨   ❨

WHEN Karremans was promising the Muslim leaders that NATO would blast the Serbs from the face of the earth, the Čeliks were sheltering inside Aunt Latifa and Uncle Ismet's house behind Srebrenica's bus station. The night sky was quiet except for the sounds of the crowd spread out on the ground around the station and the people milling about in front of it on the asphalt road. Body odor fouled the darkness inside Aunt Latifa's kitchen. Huso sat wide awake at a table in the center of the room, smoking cigarettes and muttering disjointed words of complaint and anxiety. Edin slept on a folded wool blanket on the floor next to Zlatija and Hiba. Paja had dozed off. Senad had crawled under a table next to one wall and stretched his legs across the floor. He twitched in a nervous sleep.

Soon after midnight, men broke into a food warehouse a few yards from Aunt Latifa's front door. Ismet stomped into the kitchen from the front stoop of the house.

"What're you boys lying around for? They're making off with all the flour."

Paja got up and bent toward the kitchen door. He had no store of food at home. "Srebrenica isn't going to fall," he thought.

Paja started to go. Huso stopped him.

"Don't go. Stay here. The police will come around later. They'll confiscate the flour and take you away with it."

Paja glanced at his father. Then he walked out to the front stoop. Huso followed him. In the moonlight, they could see a churning crowd of men across the way and dark figures making off with sacks of flour.

"I'm going. The police can do whatever they want."

Huso watched Paja shuffle over to the warehouse. It was a one-story building that stood on the asphalt road and adjacent to the bus station. Hundreds of men had jammed together outside the building. They pushed each other toward the open door, as men on the inside, bent over by the sacks of flour on their backs, fought to squeeze their way out. Paja pressed through the warehouse door and into the blackness of the building. The men inside jostled each other. They argued and cursed each other's mothers. Men atop the piled sacks of flour stooped and lifted and shouted down to their relatives below. Men pried away the bars over the windows and started dropping flour sacks outside. Paja lifted a sack onto his back. He pointed toward the door and moved forward, headfirst. His heart pounded as he nudged ahead. His fingers ached. It took twenty minutes to get outside. In a few more minutes, he had lugged the sack over to Aunt Latifa's house.

Uncle Ismet was now afraid that the police would come. "What are you bringing into my house?"

"I'll get this stuff out of here right after daybreak. Keep it inside. I'm going back for more."

Paja forced his way into the warehouse again and hauled out another sack of flour. This time a group of soldiers was waiting by the road when he emerged. "Give us the flour," one soldier ordered. "Men on the front line need this."

Paja handed over the sack, and the soldiers disappeared up the road toward the center of town. He went back inside and brought out another sack and carried it to Aunt Latifa's. Again Huso warned him not to take any more.

"Don't go back. The police will come."

"I won't," Paja promised. "No more."

A few minutes later, Paja turned and hurried again to the warehouse to grab a fourth sack. He felt happy. He was sure the town was not going to fall. He loaded cans of peas, sacks of beans, and a couple of red tins of Moroccan sardines into his rucksack. He went into the cellar of the warehouse and spotted boxes of unassembled wooden bed frames and headboards. Paja had not slept in a bed since the family had left Kupusovići. He began carrying them out one at a time to Latifa's house.

Now Uncle Ismet was excited. "Are there more of these?"

"Yes. I'm going to get more."

"Yeah," Huso agreed. "Absolutely. Get more beds."

Paja went back again and made off with a large pan, a knife, and another bed frame. Word came from the center of town that men were plundering the aid supplies kept in the department store. To the east, the black of night was softening into a leaden gray that was dissolving the stars. A man came by the house carrying a bag filled with canned sardines and exchanged a dozen of them for half a sack of wheat flour.

Huso had slipped back into pessimism.

"This is what we'll need," Huso said as he grabbed the canned sardines. "We're going to have to run for it. This town is going to fall, and the people here are all done for."

❲ ❲ ❲

SANELA had spent the night in the apartment near Camp Bravo. She was too worried to sleep. Again she thought about what to name the baby. She dozed off and heard Muhamed's voice.

"Where is Sanela?"

She got up immediately and ran out. Muhamed was standing at the door. She hugged him and started to cry.

"It will be all right," he said. "It will be all right."

Muhamed handed her a plastic packet of orange marmalade, the first marmalade she had tasted in three years. Muhamed said some neighbor kids had given it to him.

"You know," Sanela said, "I've decided what to name the baby. If it's a boy, he'll be Muhamed."

"You're crazy," he said. "And you'll never change."

❮ ❮ ❮

AS dawn approached, Lieutenant Colonel Karremans contacted the Dutch command center at a UN base just outside of Tuzla. The Serbs had not pulled out of the safe area. Karremans was sure the air strikes would commence at 7:00 A.M. The Dutch officers in Tuzla were sure of the same thing. Karremans had sent out a revised list of targets. A new defense line had been deployed. The target spotters were in place. NATO fighters were taking to the air. The radar screens in Serbia showed the planes taking off from Italy. They tracked the aircraft as they approached and circled.

Nothing happened at 7:00 A.M. By 8:00 A.M., the ground fog in Srebrenica had cleared.

Karremans again called for an air strike. Nothing happened.

❮ ❮ ❮

SANELA guessed that the Čeliks would be at Aunt Latifa's house, and she and Muhamed went over to see if they could get something to eat. Paja had walked home, pulled up some onions from the family garden, and brought them back down to Latifa's. He and Muhamed ate the onions raw and picked at some Moroccan sardines with a fork. They tasted bitter, as if they had been soaking in Moroccan motor oil. Paja and Muhamed filled their mouths with fresh bread to soak up the flavor. The air was quiet. Huso ate nothing and pulled the last of his cigarettes from one of the deep pockets in his jacket, Sead's army jacket. Huso and Ismet sat inside the house listening to the local radio news.

"NATO planes will attack at eight-thirty," the announcer promised. "There is no reason for panic. . . . Srebrenica has been declared a 'death zone.' . . . NATO will deal with the Serbs. . . . The town will not fall."

A few minutes later, a single white UN jeep sped by Aunt Latifa's house down the asphalt road toward Potočari. The people near the road looked through the windshield.

"It was Morillon!" one of the men shouted. "Morillon! Morillon has come back!"

"No, it was Mladić! Mladić himself!" another voice shouted. "Inside the car. It was Mladić. I saw him!"

Rumors spread through the neighborhood behind the bus station. Something big would have to be going on if Morillon or Mladić was speeding toward Potočari in a UN jeep. The sky was still quiet. The Serbs had not attacked. Aunt Latifa's house relaxed. Uncle Ismet now started complaining that Sanela and Hiba were using up all of his firewood to bake their bread. Ismet was getting on Huso nerves, and he was ready to lose his temper.

"Let's get out of here," Huso snapped to Paja.

"You can go. But we won't go," Paja answered. "Where are we going to go? We can't all go back up to the house. There's been shooting all over up there."

❮ ❮ ❮

LIEUTENANT COLONEL KARREMANS called for an immediate air attack again at 10:00 A.M. Serb tanks had just ground toward the southern edge of town. Karremans wanted them destroyed. Again, nothing happened.

❮ ❮ ❮

HIBA dropped a few more pieces of Uncle Ismet's wood onto the fire burning in Aunt Latifa's stove and slid fresh mounds of dough into the oven to bake. A man skilled at cutting tobacco dropped by the house. He was Ismet's neighbor. Huso offered to trade him a few tins of sardines if he would cut some of Huso's raw tobacco. It seems a simple task to roll up some tobacco and hack away at it with a knife. But Ismet's friend had a special skill. He could take a single tobacco leaf and from it shred enough to roll ten cigarettes. He curled the leaves crosswise and pulled out the razor-sharp knife and tiny wooden cutting block he always carried with him. The knife-edge diced the tobacco at a forty-five-degree angle, shaving it into a mass that smelled of glory and seemed miraculously larger than the leaf he had started out with. In ten minutes, Ismet's friend had cut enough for Huso to roll a hundred cigarettes. Paja watched the tobacco cutter in fascination, but when he tried to cut some for himself he came up with crumbs and dust. He shook his head and stuffed his raw tobacco into his rucksack. Huso packed his tobacco into a pouch and happily surrendered the red tins of the Moroccan sardines packed in motor oil.

❮ ❮ ❮

MUHAMED led Sanela back down to his relatives' apartment near Camp Bravo. When they reached the door to the apartment building, he told Sanela to go inside and wait. He said he was going to take a walk to find out what was happening. Sanela took one slow step into the building and looked back. Muhamed was still standing there. He was watching her. They gazed at each other for a few seconds but said nothing before he turned away. Sanela climbed the stairs inside the building. She went into the apartment and sat down on the floor of a room that was crowded with relatives and neighbors, bags of food, stacks of blankets, sponge pads, and suitcases full of clothing.

Somewhere on a radar screen in Serbia, the blips of the NATO aircraft over Bosnia began to curl away and head toward their bases in Italy. The fighter jets had circled over the Adriatic since six o'clock in the morning. In those five hours, they received no orders from General Janvier or Yasushi Akashi to attack. Now they had to refuel. The radar operator in Serbia watched them as they disappeared from his screen. There were no blips from any fighter jets taking off to replace them.

Mladić began the final assault on Srebrenica at about 11:00 A.M., as the NATO jets were turning away. The Serbs' tanks opened fire on positions held by the UN target spotters. Shells exploded near the refugees jammed together around Camp Bravo. Serb soldiers returned to the hairpin turn above the town to the west, and from a bluff to the east, above Jerina the Damned's fortress, they opened fire down into the streets and the market square. Serb tanks blasted away at the Dutch defense line and chased retreating Dutch armored vehicles with their cannon fire. More Muslim soldiers retreated, but Ejub Golić's men continued to mount resistance to the east of town. The Dutch pulled back to the market square. Inside their headquarters in the post office, Srebrenica's Muslim leaders panicked. They knew that the UN and NATO were going to do nothing to protect them. And they knew what would happen if the military-age men fell into the Serbs' hands.

Sanela heard the shooting and explosions and the panicked shouts of the people outside the window. Then she heard Muhamed call up though the stairwell for his father.

"Smail. Let's go. Let's go. The army's moving out." Smail rushed out of the apartment.

A minute later, Sanela ran down the stairs to catch Muhamed before he left. He had already hustled outside. She lifted herself back up the stairs as fast as she could go. She walked through the apartment door, pushed between her relatives and the neighbors, stepped around the suitcases, the bundles of blankets and sponge pads, and the rucksacks packed with food, and rushed out onto the balcony. A mob was hustling down the asphalt road toward Camp Bravo. She searched for Muhamed's brown jacket in the crowd. She looked toward the north. He was gone. Soldiers were moving down the road, and he had left with them. He had given one painful good-bye the night before and returned, Sanela thought to herself. He did not want to endure another farewell and find himself back together with Sanela a few hours later.

❨   ❨   ❨

THE pounding of the guns sent the Čeliks and Aunt Latifa and Uncle Ismet scurrying out of the house, through the bus station, and down the asphalt road. Huso was sweating in his heavy army jacket. He struggled under the rucksack with the cans of food and the picture album. Hiba lugged potatoes and blankets. Paja had Mirza in his arms and a pack slung across his back. Zlatija carried Edin, and Senad led his mother and carried a bag of his own. Shells blew up behind them. The Dutch were pulling back from their defense line. A torrent of people rushed down the narrow asphalt road, indifferent to the bodies of the dead along the way.

The flood of humanity ran into the crowd of people and suitcases and wheelbarrows and cattle logjammed around Camp Bravo. The Čeliks pressed together among them. They waited to see what would happen. There was nowhere to sit down and nowhere to run. More bombs exploded behind them, onto the center of town and onto the ridges to the south, the east, and the west. The menfolk swore as they waited. They turned on one another. The women cried to go on. The children cried for fear. Serb soldiers could see the roofs of Camp Bravo with the initials UN painted in ten-foot-long white letters. They could see the white shipping containers and the UN flags.

The Čeliks wound their way out of the crowd and gathered under a first-floor balcony outside the apartment building where Sanela was waiting with her in-laws. Paja and Senad watched as retreating Muslim soldiers and other men climbed the hillside across the road and made their way westward out of the town. Paja was not convinced that taking to the woods was the right thing to do. There was safety in numbers.

A soldier with an automatic called to Senad. "Hey man, what are you waiting here for? You want these Chetniks to grab you alive."

The soldier kept going.

"Let's go, Paja," Senad urged. "Let's go too."

Paja handed Mirza over to Zlatija.

"Take the sugar and salt. You'll need them," Huso said, stooping to open his pack. "*Allah Imanet.* May God keep you. And stay together."

Paja stooped over and packed his rucksack with sugar and salt, but it became too heavy to carry. He then repacked the bag in slow movements, still unsure that running from town was necessary, or even wise.

"Come on, man," Senad urged. "The sooner we get out of here the better. Come on."

"Allah keep you," Senad told Zlatija. She gazed at him with a face twitching and wet. Huso lifted his hand and waved as the two friends cast off. Hiba's throat burned.

"Papa, where are you going? Paja, where are you going?" Mirza cried out. The little boy ran after his father. "I'm coming with you."

Paja looked down at his son. His thick, calloused hand reached down and closed around the boy's tiny palm. He led Mirza back under the balcony.

"Listen," he told him, "don't you worry about me. Papa will be back. You understand?" He led Mirza back to Zlatija's grasp. "Take care of these kids."

Paja turned away, walked up a dirt track, and rejoined Senad. At a bend a few hundred yards away, he looked back. Zlatija was looking upward, waving and pointed up at Paja. She lifted Edin and moved his arm back and forth in a wave. Paja waved back, then turned out of sight. He was sure they would be back together in Srebrenica that evening.

❨ ❨ ❨

HUSO, Hiba, Zlatija, and the boys had been crouching under the apartment balcony with Ismet and Latifa for about twenty minutes when the UN safe area of Srebrenica ceased to exist even as a fiction.

By about 11:30 A.M., the mortar rounds had advanced northward down the asphalt road from the center of town. The bombs detonated around Camp Bravo and spread a panic that broke up the logjam of people gathered there. Fleeing civilians rushed headlong down the asphalt road toward Potočari. The shell explosions pulled away from Camp Bravo and began climbing the hill toward the west, following the dirt track Paja, Senad, and the other military-age men had taken. In this momentary calm, Huso decided it was safe enough to leave and too dangerous to stay. The Čeliks picked up the children and rucksacks and set off down the asphalt road. Sanela waddled along just behind them with her mother-in-law. The moving mass of people took no heed of the dying and the dead they passed. Some old men rode horses. One old woman crawled. Children lost in the chaos wandered along, crying for their parents. Mothers held out their infants to Dutch soldiers driving by and pleaded with them to take their children.

At about one-thirty, there were still some four thousand people seeking protection in and around Camp Bravo. Serb artillerymen directed two mortar shells into the crowd just inside the camp gates. The shrieks of women and children pierced the whistle scream in the ears of the people caught close to the detonations. Beams of sunlight cut through the clouds of dust, smoke, and debris. The Dutch soldiers there had never seen anything like this, bombs fired into a crowd of civilians huddling in plain sight around UN vehicles.

Dutch troops scrambled to load the wounded and the dying into trucks so that they could be taken to the field hospital at the main UN base in Potočari. Frantic people scrambled aboard the UN trucks packed with the wounded. People clung to the hoods, the roofs, the fenders, the mirrors, and the tailgates, and they refused to move when soldiers tried to pry them off. The trucks pulled out at about 2:30 P.M., and more people tried to clamber aboard.

It had been two and a half hours since Yasushi Akashi and General Janvier had finally called on NATO to conduct a pinprick air strike. After having assumed all night long that NATO's bombs were going to reduce the Serb artillery and tanks near Srebrenica to slag, Karremans had requested an air attack at 8:00 A.M.; it, however, had been turned down, ostensibly for being filed on an improper form. He had resubmitted his request at 10:00 A.M., and, if the Dutch army is to be believed, it took an hour for the paperwork to reach Zagreb, because a fax machine was not working properly and because the request did not include proper targeting information. Only after the Dutch officers asked their own government to intervene did the request finally get through to Janvier and Akashi, and they sat on it for an hour before giving their approval at about noon. By then, the NATO jets had already landed at their bases in Italy to refuel. When Janvier's request for air support was passed along, eighteen fighters and escort aircraft began taking off for Srebrenica. Akashi gave his approval minutes later. It would take them another two hours to reach Srebrenica.

(((

PAJA and Senad took cover in a house, with dozens of other men, after the salvos started climbing the hillside behind them. Paja sat under a cement staircase smoking one of his last cigarettes. The shellfire drifted by. He and Senad sprinted to the next house and waited. They were still unsure whether Srebrenica had fallen, or even would fall. They were still not convinced that fleeing into the woods made any sense.

"We've got to go back and see if something's happened to them," Senad said.

Paja mulled it over. "Let's go to the next house."

"Let's go back. We've got to see that they're all right."

"Don't go," Paja said. "You won't get through."

A shell blew up outside.

They waited a few minutes more, then glanced out the door. Men were emerging from other nearby houses and drifting farther westward.

Soldiers came by. They said everyone had been ordered to meet in Borkovići, a village about a mile away.

"Don't go to Žepa," one of them warned. "Žepa has already fallen."

Paja and Senad now joined a great herd of men, some fifteen thousand of them, scattered in the hills west of the asphalt road. They bushwhacked and followed logging trails and goat paths. As they moved across a rise on a hillside, Paja and Senad looked south and saw flames and muzzle flash. Serb soldiers had advanced onto the bluff next to the Halilović house. They had set fire to the homes around it. They were shooting down into the town from between the trees.

It was now about 2:40 P.M. Paja and Senad and all the other Muslim men on the hillside heard the crescendo of an approaching jet engine. Their eyes scanned the sky for a metallic flash of a wing, but they saw nothing. The roar of the plane rolled over the horizon like far-off thunder. Another skirling crescendo began. It came from behind them, from the north. Antiaircraft guns and small arms on the ground opened fire. An explosion rocked a hillside above the hairpin turn from where a tank had been firing. Another crescendo. Another bomb was dropped on the same hillside. Columns of smoke and dust swirled upward among the trees and meadows. The men cheered and shook their heads in relief.

The air attack had finally taken place. It had come at 2:45 P.M. and was carried out by two Dutch fighters, one of which was piloted by a woman. Two Serb tanks had been targeted. Within minutes, the muzzle of a tank cannon flashed on the hillside and a shell had exploded somewhere in the town below. At least one of the tanks was still intact.

❦ ❦ ❦

MLADIĆ passed a message to the UN base in Potočari. He demanded an immediate end to the air attack. He threatened to have the Dutch hostages executed and to begin shelling the refugees crowding into Potočari. Mortar rounds began hitting the hillsides around the UN base at Potočari. Women and children and old people at the entrance to the base screamed in terror. The roar of the jet engines had already dissipated over the horizon, and on the radar screens in Serbia the blips curled westward and out over the Adriatic. When Dutch defense minister, Joris Voorhoeve, heard of Mladić's threats, he personally called the NATO air command center in Vicenza, Italy, and further air operations were halted.

Serb soldiers penetrated the outskirts of the town from the south. They crept from house to house, wary of Muslim snipers. The Serb soldiers kicked in doors. They threw hand grenades into kitchen windows. They shouted and flushed Muslim men and women out of hiding and executed them on the spot. And Muslim men hiding among the gardens and woodpiles in the town listened to the Serbs approaching and calling for people to give themselves up and come outside. They heard the gunshots, and the cries for mercy, and the silence. Then they heard the smashing and the shouts of the soldiers beginning to loot.

The sun beat down on the people streaming into Potočari. Shell and rocket detonations fluttered the leaves on the trees. Gunfire cracked. Huso's legs had swelled. He stopped to rest next to the rusting shell of an old truck beside the road.

"Wait," he ordered Hiba. "We'll wait until Sanela comes by."

Hiba crossed the road to pick apples from a tree in someone's front yard. A woman stormed out of the house and swore at her for stealing her fruit. Hiba scurried back across the road and tried to get Huso to eat.

Sanela caught up a few minutes later. She said nothing and pushed ahead. Her face was wet. Her stomach throbbed. Her body shook. She thought she would go into labor. The baby did not move.

❬   ❬   ❬

PAJA and Senad waited for half an hour in Borkovići before one of the commanders called for the men's attention and began to speak.

"We've tried to get in touch with Sarajevo," he said. "We've gotten no answer."

The commander kicked a radio transmitter. Then he ordered the men to line up and move out.

The column set out and moved in slow motion. When one man stumbled, the men behind him bunched up and stopped in their tracks. When a creek or a fence had to be crossed, the men jammed together and waited their turn. The column snaked slowly around a hill called Babuljica and curled to the north. In the distance, from the direction of Bratunac, began the long, muffled rumble of launching rockets. The roar grew louder, then louder still. The men ran in every direction. They ducked behind trees and rocks. The roar tore over their heads. With lightning flashes, the rockets exploded a few hundred yards downrange, missing everyone. The men waited. There was silence. Then they moved on.

By late afternoon, Paja and Senad had sat down to rest in a meadow beside Šušnjari, a village just inside the northwestern edge of the Srebrenica enclave. The men argued and picked through their packs for something to eat. More men arrived and found places to sit and to wait. Dozens of horses grazed and whinnied in the soccer field next to them. The stallions bucked and kicked at each other and copulated with the mares.

And the men sat and watched and waited.

SOME twenty thousand Muslim women, children, and old people had by now washed over the UN base in Potočari. An explosion jarred the hillside just above the base as the Čeliks and Latifa and Ismet arrived. Sanela and her mother-in-law ducked through one hole cut in the metal fence around the base. Huso, Hiba, Zlatija, and the boys split off and ran through another hole in the fence before a guard prodded them back outside. They hurried into the grounds of a neighboring factory and settled down on coarse, dry grass in a meadow. The ground was dusty. Hiba and Zlatija pulled up clumps of grass, laid them down across the ground like a mattress, and spread a blanket out over them. Huso sat still, mumbling about how he would never see his children again.

"My Paja," he said. "My Paja."

He got up and walked over to the fence around the UN base to look for Sanela. "Sanoooooo! Sanoooooo!" he called.

Sanela caught sight of Huso in his old army jacket. His eyes were confused and wet. He stepped toward her, but she could not talk. She held up one hand and waved him off as if nothing was wrong. He turned away.

A Dutch guard led Sanela into a room jammed with wounded men. She sat on a metal bed with no mattress. People swarmed through the building. More shell blasts resounded from the hillsides. Children screamed. Sanela's eyes burned in the ammonia stench of a latrine a few feet away. She sat there alone, smoking one cigarette after another and wondering what had become of Muhamed. Long after nightfall, numb to the world, she lay down on the metal bed, looked up into the ceiling, and tried to sleep.

27

THE men sat waiting for hours in the woods and meadows around Šušnjari. They followed the shadows as the sun slowly descended toward the western horizon. They griped. They made threats. There was too much waiting. Too many men grouped together. Too little time left. They wanted to move out. To move now. To use the cover of darkness to escape. Some individuals and small groups headed back toward Srebrenica. They had decided to try to make it to Žepa or to swim the Drina and hike to Muslim villages twenty miles inside Serbia.

Ramiz Bećirović was still, formally anyway, overall commander of the Muslim brigades in Srebrenica. He told the men to be patient. The officers huddled. They decided to organize the men into a single column. They would hike toward the northwest and try to cross the twenty-five miles of Serb-held land between them and Muslim territory. They would have to skirt Kravica, cross the main road at Konjević Polje, and climb through a belt of burned-out Muslim villages before they could get to the front line near Tuzla and either negotiate or fight their way across. General Mladić had offered the Muslims safe passage along this same route before he launched the offensive against Srebrenica in January 1993. Naser Orić had declined the offer; his troops blocked the Muslim civilians who tried to take it.

The officers ordered the soldiers to form up by brigade. The soldiers with guns were told to position themselves at the front and rear of each brigade; the unarmed men and the few women and children among them were tucked in the middle of each brigade. All were instructed to tie strips of white cloth around their heads or arms so they could tell the difference between members of the column and any Serbs who might try to infiltrate it.

The vanguard moved out at midnight. Paja, Senad, Deba Kozić, and half a dozen of their friends from Mount Zvijezda joined the 282nd Brigade, and they set off from Šušnjari about an hour after the first group. They were gambling on the brigade's commander, Ibro Dudić; they respected him as a fighter and as an officer who would not take unnecessary risks. They stumbled along a dirt road. It was a pitch-black night, and they feared becoming separated in the darkness. They stopped and tied their belt loops together with a white nylon string before pushing on. They were sure the string would keep them from losing one another. The rope tugged and sagged. Paja's belt loop held him back when he wanted to move forward quickly. And the men ahead complained that Paja was holding them up. "This is stupid," he thought. But he walked on and said nothing, not wanting to be the first to complain, not wanting the others to call him stupid. Senad finally ripped the nylon string away, and the rest of them did the same.

They moved on in slow motion, about a thousand yards in one hour. Again, they were ordered to sit and wait in a meadow. A commando unit had to go ahead and clear a path through a minefield on the edge of the enclave. The process would take hours. Paja searched for a house in which to bake some bread, but the officers ordered the men to extinguish all their fires. Paja pulled up onions from a garden, brought them back to the meadow, and stuffed them into his rucksack. He repacked his raw tobacco; then he stretched out on the ground and watched the stars. The men moved forward again at dawn, another thousand yards or so, to Buljim, a hill just before the front line.

The commando squad had marked a path across the minefield and pushed ahead to secure the Konjević Polje road. Srebrenica's military and political leaders, the hospital staff, and the wounded left at dawn; Zulfo Tursunović rode with them on horseback. The rest of the men were ordered to stay in Buljim until the rear guard, Ejub Golić and his fighters, arrived from Srebrenica. The men obeyed, but for four hours they bitched and argued and muttered threats. Golić and his men did not arrive until about ten o'clock in the morning. When the first brigade moved out half an hour later, the men jammed together in line waiting to clear a bottleneck at the entrance to a trench. They moved across the minefield two by two, each man stepping into the footsteps of the man ahead of him.

Another hour passed. Paja and Senad waited for their turn. Paja pulled out some tobacco leaves and his knife and started cutting.

❮   ❮   ❮

GENERAL RATKO MLADIĆ called Lieutenant Colonel Ton Karremans to the hotel in Bratunac. He instructed Karremans that the evacuation from Potočari would begin at 1:00 P.M. He demanded that the refugees be split into groups: the wounded, the sick, and the infirm; the women and children; the elderly; and the military-age men. The latter would be screened, and "war criminals" would be removed. Karremans objected to the screening and insisted that the Dutch be allowed to escort the departing refugees. Mladić ignored him. Everything would be done his way.

❮   ❮   ❮

HIBA had boiled some potatoes that morning in the meadow at Potočari. Huso sat on the blanket, tucked inside Sead's army jacket. The field had already begun to stink of the shit and urine left on the ground by people who had nowhere else to relieve themselves.

"Eat some potatoes," Hiba told him.

"I can't."

"Take some. Eat."

He turned them away.

SERB soldiers began arriving in the field at about noon, just five or six at first, then dozens more. They were mostly clean-shaven men, middle-aged or younger. They wore army and police uniforms. Dutch troops had formed a cordon around the Muslims, but after Serb soldiers threatened to use force, the gates to the UN base were opened and the Dutch troops allowed the Serbs to take their weapons and roam freely. Some Serb soldiers mounted horses set loose by the Muslims who had ridden them to Potočari. The Serbs used the horses to patrol the fringes of the crowd and herd the Muslims together. German shepherd dogs chased down Muslim men who tried to bolt from the crowd.

Women cried. Soldiers drunk on plum brandy belched out songs with crude lyrics. They fired bullets into the air and began leading the menfolk away.

A woman came back from fetching water at a nearby stream and started talking to Hiba. "Come this way, look. There are five bodies over there. Dead. Their heads are turned downward. I couldn't see who they were."

"Quiet you," Huso snapped. "Don't say anything about this to anyone. Don't go over there. What are you doing over there? Do you want somebody asking you questions later on?"

He told Hiba not to go near the water. She avoided looking at the Serb soldiers. She patted down the grass, straightened her blanket on the ground, and waited. The sun beat down on their heads. Huso turned red in the face. He complained about his legs. He refused again to eat. He never took off the army jacket.

The Serbs now brought up a van loaded with bread and a fire truck with water. They offered cookies and candy to the Muslim children and flirted with Muslim girls. Some told stories of how they had snuck into Srebrenica and watched movies at the cinema. Then General Mladić arrived with his bodyguards and a journalist from Belgrade who was taping the scene with a video camera.

"You have no reason to be afraid," Mladić assured the refugees as he spoke to the camera. "Anyone who wants to stay here can stay. If you want to go, you can go. First we will evacuate the women, children, and elderly people, and all those who want to leave this combat area, without forcing them. Slowly. Let the women and children go first, please."

He turned into the camera lens. "Srebrenica is now liberated. But there are still small groups putting up resistance."

The minds of people in the crowd began to crack. One man hung himself inside the factory building next to the meadow. A woman whose husband had disappeared tried to hang herself. Dutch soldiers led away a man who was beating his head with a stone.

The first buses to arrive were stormed by panic-stricken refugees. The Dutch then formed an orderly pathway to the buses, and the Serbs began the organized separation of the men.

PAJA was chopping at his tobacco leaves when the 282nd Brigade got its turn to leave the Srebrenica enclave. He packed up in haste and began walking with Senad and Deba. It was just before noon.

They moved a few steps before stopping. They waited for the men ahead to clear the bottleneck before the trench. They stood still, stepped forward, and stood still again and again as they proceeded through the trench and down a hillside. In a creek bed, Paja passed the bodies of half a dozen men killed days earlier trying to escape Srebrenica. Men in the column who had no water bottles cupped their hands and drank from the creek before climbing out on the other side.

They entered the minefield two by two, and accelerated their pace when they came out on the other side a minute later. The forest was silent as they walked on. Half an hour passed.

The gunfire came by surprise. The bullets tore into the men from the left, and the column broke apart. Paja sprinted forward and became separated from his friends. Senad helped three other men roll a wounded man onto a heavy jacket and carry him forward. There were shouts in the woods, screams of pain, and more gunfire. Paja ran until he had left the pandemonium hundreds of yards behind him. The shooting stopped. An officer ordered the men to wait so that he could reorganize the column. He ordered the wounded brought forward, and Senad caught up.

"Paja, help grab one of the wounded," he said. "You'll be at the front, Paja. It'll be safer up there. Grab one of the wounded."

Senad moved farther ahead. Paja refused his advice and stayed behind with the bulk of the men. They lined up and waited. The woods in front of them were quiet, and the men wanted to push on. More gunfire erupted to the rear. Ejub Golić's men bringing up the end of the column silenced the Serb ambush with blasts from an antiaircraft gun they had taken from Camp Bravo and strapped to the back of a horse.

Again there was silence in the woods, and the column was moving on. The men angled toward the northwest. Senad was nowhere to be seen, but Paja spotted Muhamed in front of him. His shoulder was propping up a wounded man, one of his neighbors.

"Paja, what are you running ahead for?" Muhamed asked.

"Why are you going so slowly?" Paja answered.

Muhamed handed him a cigarette. After a few words, Paja set out again.

The second ambush came at midafternoon. Mortar rounds crashed through the forest canopy onto the rear of the column, as if the Serbs were goading the men to advance more quickly. They fled in every direction. They dove for cover or crouched behind trees. Rocket-propelled grenades hissed between the tree trunks and exploded. Muslim men shot at each other in panic until Ejub

Golić came forward and got them to stop firing and shut up. The sound of the last gunblasts soon faded over the mountains. Golić ordered the men to form a new single-file line and carry the wounded to the front. In order to keep the men in a single line, he deceived them. He said there were land mines on each side of the trail. Cries for help from just off the path went unheeded.

Half a mile ahead, Paja crouched in the tall grass of a meadow with hundreds of other men waiting for Golić and the rear of the column to catch up. Paja grew anxious and walked forward into a woods and sat down on the rocky ground to suck on a stem of grass and roll cigarettes.

"What are these people doing?" he thought. "We're waiting, and they're going to get us killed. We could have made it across the road last night."

Paja lifted himself up. He walked among the trees searching for someone to travel with—Senad or Deba or someone else he could trust. He strolled down a hillside and came to the edge of the woods. Below him from right to left stretched the road that runs between Bratunac and Konjević Polje. The Muslim column was moving parallel to this road. Just to the right, Paja could see Kravica. He spotted Serb armored vehicles below, and he followed the progress of a convoy of buses that came down the road from Bratunac and moved out of sight. Paja climbed back to the top of the hill. He found Deba and sat down next to him to wait some more. Senad and the other men carrying the wounded had pushed even farther ahead. They had caught up with the commanders and the medical staff from the hospital on a wooded hillside just above the road the column had to cross, the main road through Konjević Polje. And there they waited. And waited.

28

HUSO ČELIK had known Jusuf and Mujo Kapetanović all his life. Mujo had been the postmaster in Prelovo, and he was the one who picked through the mail sack when Huso came looking for the greeting card Uncle Avdo had sent to Mile Janković on the occasion of his father's "death like a dog." Mujo's brother Jusuf was a peasant, and like all the other peasants on Mount Zvijezda, he had a big, dirt-stained, woody grasp, and if you met him while he was working, he would offer you his forearm instead of his hand to shake. But in centuries past the Kapetanović clan had not been lowly peasants at all. They had been one of the mountain's most notable Muslim families. The Kapetanović men had been beys. One of their ancestors had been an Ottoman army officer, and their surname derives from the Turkish word *kapetan*, which has the same Latin root as the English word "captain." The story goes that the sultan granted the Kapetanović family land on Mount Zvijezda after the advancing Austrian army drove their *kapetan* from Budapest in 1686. The Kapetanović beys subsequently recruited Serb peasants from Montenegro to come and work their land. The wars, the collapse of the Ottoman Empire, and the Serbian king's land reforms took their toll on the Kapetanović family's wealth and prestige, and by early this century the family had sunk into poverty. World War II claimed the lives of thirty-eight Kapetanović family members living in a village just below Kupusovići; twenty of them were women and children killed by Serb Chetniks, including members of the Lukić clan.

Jusuf had fled with his family to Žepa and to Srebrenica in 1992, just as Huso and the Čeliks had done. In the late afternoon of July 12, 1995, Mujo was in the woods above Srebrenica and Jusuf was near Huso in the mass of Muslims gathered inside the fence of the battery factory the Communists had built in Potočari. A group of Serb militiamen from Mount Zvijezda had come to Potočari in a white truck. They recognized Jusuf and his teenage grandson, Meho, in the crowd. The Serbs called them over. The men chatted with Jusuf for a few minutes, then led his grandson away toward some houses behind a second factory building across the asphalt road. The Serbs sent Jusuf back into the crowd with a message for the Muslims from Mount Zvijezda.

"They want us by the gate," Jusuf told Huso, Uncle Ismet, and other men. "They want everyone from Višegrad by the gate. Milan Lukić has come. He said we'll be the first to get to Tuzla."

Jusuf pointed out the Serb men milling around on the asphalt road outside the gate of the battery factory. And they recognized Milan Lukić, the man who had shared cheese pies and played soccer in junior high with Huso Čelik's son Sead; the same man who had led the death squad in Višegrad in 1992. Lukić's men were wearing clean uniforms, so they probably had not taken part in the actual "fight" for Srebrenica. Their arrival gave credence to rumors spreading around Serbia that General Mladić went looking for militia units from up and down the Drina valley that wanted to take part in settling scores with Srebrenica's Muslims. Lukić was wearing a black T-shirt and khaki pants when he arrived in Potočari. He carried an automatic with a metal stock that folded up. A long bayonet dangled in a sheath from his waist. Serbs say he and his men were angry that a young Serb police officer had been shot dead as a group of Muslim men was coming out of a nearby forest to surrender in Potočari. But Lukić clearly had not appeared too angry to Jusuf.

"It should be fine," Jusuf told Huso and the others. "I trust them. They swore on the cross that they would bring back my grandson."

More Muslims from Mount Zvijezda gathered around to hear Jusuf. They, too, recognized the Serbs. They were the sons and grandsons of Serbs knew who had been the Muslims' neighbors. A Muslim named Adem Šeta recognized one of the Serbs standing with Lukić on the road. "Whatever you do, don't tell that one I'm here," Adem told the rest of his friends. "They'll kill me for sure. His house was right behind mine."

Adem did not join the rest of the Muslims from Mount Zvijezda, about thirty of them in all, who walked over to the factory gate beside the asphalt road. They waited there for about an hour before Lukić approached with three of his men.

"Sit down," one of the Serbs said. "Is everyone here?"

"Not yet."

"Get them together."

Lukić began to chat with the women: "There will be a special bus to take everyone from Višegrad to Tuzla. You will have priority. You must be here to get your tickets."

Jusuf Kapetanović's wife, Kada, was upset because her grandson had been taken away. She approached Lukić. "Oh, my brother," she implored, "bring back my child."

"Don't worry about anything. He'll be right back. There'll be as much wrong with him as there is with me."

The elated woman tried to hug Lukić and kiss his hand. He slapped her away. "Back off," he shouted. "Don't come near me." The woman started to cry.

"Bring me back my grandson," Jusuf said.

"He's been taken to Bratunac for interrogation. He'll be back in about fifteen minutes," Lukić said. He added that the Muslim men would have their hands chemically tested to determine whether any of them had fired a gun. Jusuf quieted down and waited.

Lukić then asked for Hadžira Čavkušić, his puppy love from the eighth grade, the brown-haired little girl with the ebony eyes. The Muslims told him that Hadžira was in Sarajevo. She had gotten married. Then he asked for her sister Biba, but she did not step forward. He turned and grabbed the jacket of a fourteen-year-old Muslim boy.

"How old are you?" he snapped.

"I'm twelve."

"Oh, you little Ustaša, you'll do well to be twelve years old and remain alive."

The boy's chin quivered. One of the other Serbs told Lukić to let the boy go, and he released the boy's jacket. His mother led him back into the crowd and put a shawl over his head to make him look like a girl.

One of the Serbs recognized Uncle Ismet and cracked a joke. Then Lukić turned to a man standing beside Ismet.

"What's your name?"

"Hasib Čavkušić." Hasib was Hadžira's and Biba's father. He was considered a wealthy man on Mount Zvijezda. He had worked long enough in that Austrian sawmill to qualify for a government disability pension and had returned home from Steyr a few weeks before the fighting broke out in Bosnia. Hasib had planned on spending only the Bairam holiday with his wife and family, and Milan Lukić's own uncle, Rale Lukić, who was Hasib's friend in Steyr, had advised him not to go at all. It would be dangerous, Rale said. There would be a war. He cautioned Hasib just as Rale's relatives had warned Hasib's father, Nurko, to get out of Rujišta before the Chetniks killed Nurko's first wife and all of their children. Now, after the Bosnian war had cut Hasib off from the world for three years, there were three years' worth of Austrian pension checks coming to him.

"When were you born?" Milan Lukić asked.

Hasib answered, "In 1944." He was still of military age. "I have a disability pension. I haven't been able to cut wood in ten years. How could I have been in some trench?"

"Oh, Hasib, your disability isn't so bad that you couldn't have been in the trenches shooting at me. We're going to test your hands. If we find you didn't shoot, we'll give you a ticket for the bus and you can leave tomorrow."

The Serbs picked out three other Muslims and turned to lead them away toward the factory building across the road.

Huso called to Lukić, "Do you need anyone else for that bus?" He gazed at the Serb with his one straight eye. "I'll go with you. I'm ready to go right now."

"Sit down," the Serb ordered. "God threw up his hands when he made you. There's nothing you can do for me."

Huso fell back into silence. He slumped onto the ground beside Hiba, Zlatija, and the boys and curled up in the army jacket. They waited for the Muslim men to bring back the bus tickets. But none of them returned. They heard shouts and cries for help from the direction of the houses behind the factory across the road.

At dusk, one of the Serbs appeared near the factory gate again. He called out for the people from Višegrad.

"Over here," Zlatija answered. "Over here."

The Serb approached.

"Where is Hajra Čavkušić?" he asked. Hajra was Hasib's wife. She did not want the Serb to see her.

"She's not here," Zlatija lied. "I don't know where she is."

"Her husband is asking for her."

The Serb turned toward Hasib's daughter Biba. He knew her and recognized Hasib's four-year-old granddaughter. "My, my, she's gotten big," he said. "They grow up so quickly."

They chatted for a few minutes more. "You know, Alija Izetbegović is responsible for all this," the Serb said. "And Karadžić is responsible for all this. But we're not to blame. . . . We're not going to be taking any more of you tonight. It's getting dark. . . . You can go back and find somewhere to rest."

Within a few hours, Lukić and his men had left Potočari. Hasib and the other Muslim men who had gone off for the bus tickets had still not returned. None of the other Muslims had seen them alive, and none had seen them dead. The Čavkušić and Kapetanović women would wait another two years before they would hear from Milan Lukić again.

29

PAJA'S friend Senad slouched against a tree and waited as darkness descended on the evening of July 12. The director of the aid warehouse at Srebrenica's department store was lounging on the ground nearby. He was spreading orange marmalade onto cookies and eating them. The marmalade came in plastic packets. The warehouse director looked up and noticed Senad and the other men staring at him. He asked the men for some water. One of them poured him some from a bottle. Then the warehouse director looked away and took another bite from one of his cookies.

Commandos just ahead of Senad at the front of the column of Muslim men crept into the thick underbrush beside the main road through Konjević Polje. This was the road the column had to cross. The soldiers crouched in firing positions near a Serb armored vehicle parked on the asphalt and keeping watch over the road. Half a dozen commandos scurried across the asphalt unnoticed. They hid in a cornfield and set up a heavy-caliber machine gun. The road was now covered. But the Serb armored vehicle was still there. Senad was close enough to hear the commando leader shout down to the Serbs.

"Pull back now! Let us pass!"

Senad heard no answer.

"If you don't pull back from this road, I'll bring ten thousand men down on your heads."

The armored vehicle started up and rumbled around a bend to the north.

The commando leader radioed in that the main road was now clear. The column could proceed. Bećirović and the other officers did not want to wait any longer. They ordered the men carrying the wounded to cross the road. Senad and three other men grabbed the corners of the jacket on which their wounded man was lying. The jacket swished over the low undergrowth as they descended the steep hillside through the trees.

In an instant, a fusillade of machine-gun fire tore into the side of the hill. Senad and the other men slid the jacket with the wounded man behind a bush and crouched against the trunks of trees.

Four miles behind them, on the wooded hillsides above the new farmers' co-op building in Kravica, mortars pounded the men who had been waiting in rows to march. Muhamed and his brother, Hajrudin, pressed their faces to the dirt. A detonation three arm lengths away blasted their ears and made them dizzy. A few hundred yards ahead of them, Paja, Deba, and thousands more men were sprawled out on the ground. The shellfire stopped for an instant. Paja heard angry German shepherds barking down on the road near Kravica. He had been a border guard and knew what the dogs could do.

"The bitches are going to eat us alive," he told Deba. "Let's get the fuck out of here. Go to the right."

A hail of bullets and antiaircraft rounds pelted the hillside as Paja and Deba got up. They hurdled down the hill in a mindless herd caught in the line of fire. Rocket-propelled grenades tore into the woods, and a bomb exploded at the trunk of a beech tree. It crashed down in front of them, but the mass of men stampeded forward. Deba tripped just before the tree. He pulled his arms over his head as men trampled over him. Bullets zipped through the air. Men fell wounded, but no one stopped for them. Paja scrambled over the trunk of the fallen tree. His shoes pressed down on the squirming bodies of the men caught beneath it. He ran on, leaped over an embankment, and turned somersaults over thorn bushes and waist-high stems of grass and daisies. As bullets whizzed overhead, he crawled back up to the embankment for cover.

Paja shouted for Deba. He shouted for Muhamed and Senad. He heard the bursts of gunfire and the moans of men near the fallen beech tree, calling for their friends and their mothers.

"Deba! Deba!" Paja called.

"Here. Paja. Here." The guns continued to blast away. Deba crept up to the embankment from the brambles. "I lost my backpack," he said.

In the chaos of the gunfire, Ibro Dudić screamed over a walkie-talkie to the other commanders.

"Where are you? Where are you?"

"Up ahead. Come ahead!" the voice on the radio said. "Come ahead! Now!"

"We can't. We can't get there. I will never get there."

NIGHT had fallen. The Serb guns on the road had stopped firing, but gun-blasts continued in the woods near the beech tree. An officer lowered his gun on Paja and the other men crouching along the embankment.

"No one moves from here until all the wounded are brought down," the of-ficer ordered. A few guys started back. Paja grabbed his ankle and grimaced. He bent down to Deba.

"Take me by the arm. I'll pretend I've got a sprained ankle."

The officer came over. "You, get up."

"I can't. My ankle is sprained."

"Take off your shoe."

The officer took Paja's right foot in his hands and moved his ankle from right to left, pushing down on his bones with his thumb. Paja grimaced again.

"How's that?"

"A little better. . . . Yes, it's a little better."

The officer moved away. Paja squeezed his shoe back onto his foot. Voices called for help in the woods behind. The men by the embankment breathed silently and mumbled. One man started lashing out at the others with his fists before someone punched him in the face a few times and left him dazed on the ground.

Paja lifted himself gingerly, as if his ankle were in pain. "Carry me," he told Deba. "If we have to go back up there, we're dead."

Deba propped Paja up with his shoulder, and Paja hobbled down the hill-side away from gunshots, the barking of the dogs, and the voices of the men calling for their mothers. The shadows of the trees in the woods squeezed all the light out of the air. The psyches of the men ruptured. Muslims mistook other Muslims for Serb infiltrators. They threw hand grenades and fired their automatics at one another.

It was a bullet shot by a Muslim that tore through Muhamed's right leg and lodged in his left calf. By now, only relatives were extending a helping hand to the wounded. Muhamed had his father, Smail, and brother, Hajrudin. They stumbled forward in the darkness together.

"I can walk," Muhamed told his father. "Slowly."

Sporadic shooting again broke the silence. Muhamed, Smail, and Hajrudin found themselves at the edge of a woods where a thousand Muslims, half of them armed, had taken cover. The soldiers' silhouettes huddled together and meandered through shadows cut by moonlight. The men here were strangers to one another, men who had lived in different villages in the Srebrenica enclave and who had broken away from their units in the chaos. Distrust spread like an infection. One Muslim soldier in a camouflage uniform let rip a spray of bullets and threw a hand grenade at a group of Muslim men; another man shot a bazooka and killed ten of his comrades.

The Serbs on the road below heard the commotion and lobbed in shells that shrouded the woods in smoke and dust. Wide-eyed men hallucinated: they fired gunshots at the moon. They saw figures in white uniforms march in single file down the mountainside and dissolve into silvery moonlight. They saw plumes of pink and purple smoke rise from shell blasts and drift through the woods. They saw enemy soldiers appear from nowhere, administer injections and pills to the wounded, then vanish.

Profiles in the blackness wept aloud: "We must surrender! We must surrender!"

Soldiers threw down their guns and stripped off their uniforms. Men shot themselves hoping the Serbs would show the wounded mercy. One man pulled a Skorpion automatic from its holster, slipped the barrel into his mouth and pulled the trigger. Another unclipped a hand grenade from his belt, pressed it to his Adam's apple, and yanked the pin.

Muhamed, Smail, and Hajrudin were still caught somewhere in this pandemonium on the hillside above Kravica when Paja and Deba finally headed away, toward the south, sometime around midnight. They had tagged along with two dozen armed men who had decided to break away from the column and make their way alone. The group grew into the hundreds as the hours passed. Gunshots crackled all over the hillsides. The men moved slowly. They exchanged gunfire with other Muslims holed up in a village. At about three o'clock in the morning, they stumbled upon a trail that sloped downward toward the main highway. The men were unsure whether to head down or not. They did not know whether the Serbs would be waiting on the road below.

Deba spotted his brother Bedži. "Where've you been? When did you get here?"

Bedži lifted his pants leg and showed Deba a hole in his calf about the diameter of a dime. The jagged lump of shrapnel that had punctured his leg was still inside. Blood was streaming down his leg and filling his shoe.

They decided to move down the trail. Bedži hobbled along with a crutch. Other men carried the wounded on stretchers made from blankets and tree branches.

From around a curve in the trail ahead someone shouted, but quietly so that he could not be heard from far away.

"Chetnik! Chetnik!"

Bedži bolted into the woods.

"Bedži. Bedži," Deba called in a whisper.

There was no answer.

"Here's a Chetnik! I've got a Chetnik! What the fuck are you doing up here?"

The Muslim had an automatic pointing at a freshly washed young man dressed in a clean athletic suit. He had been carrying a pistol. None of the men on the trail knew him. He had walked alone up the hill in the dead of night from the direction of the main road.

"Shoot him!" one of the men said.

"No. No. Listen, I'm a Muslim," the young man answered.

"Fuck you! Fuck you!"

"Shoot him! Right now! Before he can shout. Kill him."

"No. No. I'm a Muslim. No. No. I'm a Muslim."

"Down with your pants. Let's see your cock."

The soldier lowered his automatic to the man's stomach. The young man pulled down his pants, then stuck his thumb under the waistband of his underwear and slid it down. The tip of his penis had been circumcised.

"You see."

His waistband snapped back up. The men around him grumbled threats for a few minutes more before a Muslim walked up and recognized the young man. He really *was* a Muslim. He had snuck out of Srebrenica after an argument with his parents; the Serbs had let him stay in Milići. He had risked his life to climb the hill to tell the men that the Serbs had two or three armored vehicles on the main road below and how to avoid them.

The soldier with the automatic returned the young man's pistol. He slipped it into his waistband and led them down the hill.

Paja moved farther down the hill while Deba lagged behind, looking for Bedži.

Warnings were passed from the front to watch for mines—someone had hit one. Paja came upon the body a few minutes later. The man was barely alive. The mine had been rigged with a trip wire, and when he hit the wire, the mine sprang a few feet into the air and exploded. The shrapnel tore into his chest and split his head open. Paja did not recognize him at first, but he looked more closely when he heard the body gurgle. The man could not talk, and was shaking. It was Uncle Ismet's neighbor, the man who could cut ten cigarettes from a leaf of tobacco. He was left to die.

Paja moved more quickly now. His legs stepped easily downhill. Near the bottom of the valley, the men passed into the morning fog. Paja sprinted across the road. He passed under a tree and followed the men ahead onto the wet grass of a soccer field. Coming out of the fog to his right, he heard a bleating sound, like the sound of a goat in pain. A man knelt there in the grass. The skin of his face had been stripped away, leaving a crusty black pulp of coagulated blood and muscle. His lips had been cut away, and from the cavern of his mouth he bleated again. His index finger sliced across his throat.

Paja's steps slowed as he turned all the way around and looked back at that face. He stopped long enough for the man to climb to his feet. Another bleating cry. Another appeal to cut his throat. Paja moved on.

Deba got across the road a few minutes later and ran inside a burned-out house to wait for Bedži to come limping across the road. Wave upon wave of dark profiles appeared from the trees and darted over the asphalt. After a few minutes, a silver Volkswagen appeared on the road. The driver spotted the stream of men, threw the car into reverse, and pulled away before anyone got off a shot. Deba made for the back of the house and the river beyond it.

Paja had already stepped into the swollen river. The current pulled at his legs as he slid his arm through the arm of the man ahead and waited a second for the next man to link up with him. The water pushed up against his stomach, and he stumbled on the rocks. As the men at the front of the chain reached the river bank, they broke free and ran for the woods.

Paja dashed toward the woods beyond the river. One of the men began screaming.

"Fuck Karadžić! Fuck Karadžić's mother! Fuck the Serbs! Fuck their Chetnik mothers!"

He was tackled to the ground, tied up, and gagged, but within a few minutes a Serb armored vehicle appeared on the road and opened fire on the men on the path coming down from the hills. It cut them off. Bedži had not made it across.

Paja shuffled through the woods and climbed the flanks of a hill. He moved automatically. His pants were wet and his legs tight, but his groin tingled with fear. Half an hour passed. He kept climbing. The sun was overhead before he noticed it, and the road and the river and the gunfire were far behind and below him. He felt safe enough to rest. He told himself he had to take a break. He did not remember the last time he had slept. He lay down in some tall grass beside a dirt road. He put his hands behind his head and closed his eyes. He felt the sun warm his face, and he drifted into a deep sleep.

"Paja."

Paja opened his eyes and squinted. It was Deba.

"Where is Bedži?" Paja asked.

"They put him on a horse," Deba answered. "Over there. He's on the horse."

Paja looked around. There was no horse, and no Bedži. There was no one. Paja gave Deba a swallow of water, slapped more water onto his face, and fed him a handful of cookie crumbs.

Deba never saw Bedži again.

30

THE women were still wailing in the meadow next to the UN base in Potočari after sunrise on Thursday, July 13. Serb soldiers had wandered through the crowd with flashlights most of the night, shining them into the wizened faces of the aged women, the pale faces of the sleeping children, and the eyes of the men they picked out. Gunshots popped on the surrounding hillsides. German shepherds barked. Huso had not slept at all. He complained about pain in his legs and in his chest.

Before the ground fog burned off, he reached into his rucksack and pulled out his photo album. Here were the family snapshots: the house in Kupuso-vići; Sanela as a young girl; Hamed, Gordana, and the kids; my daughter Sara in a diaper. They were all photos sent to Srebrenica in Red Cross letters from Hamed in Toronto and from men Huso once worked with in Vranica's brick-yard back in Sarajevo. Hiba saw Huso handing her the album.

"Take these pictures and put them somewhere," Huso told her. "We're never going to see each other again."

Hiba was ashamed. She was afraid the women nearby might notice her husband's fear.

"Put those back," Hiba scolded. "Don't be like this. You aren't the only one here. Look around. There's a whole crowd of people. Let whatever happens to all of them go for us too. We're all in this together."

Huso offered the photo album one more time. Hiba refused to take it.

He pulled out her eyeglasses from the rucksack and set them on the blanket. Then he slipped from his wrist the gold watch he had bought in Baghdad and never let any of the boys touch. The hands were still frozen in time.

"Give this to Paja."

"You'll see him again, don't worry. This is going to pass. The men are going to come back. They're going to get through somehow. It's not as if he's going to get killed."

Huso fingered the watch.

"We're dead," Huso said. "They've cut our throats already."

He handed his wife the watch.

"Give this to Paja."

Hiba took it. She folded it into her hair and tied her scarf over her head. Huso slipped the photo album back into his bag.

TRUCKS and buses arrived at about six o'clock in the morning for the second day of evacuations. Anxious people started to gather near them. Dutch troops set up a cordon to prevent a stampede. The peacekeepers stood inches away from the Serb soldiers who were separating the Muslim men, one by one, from their families as they were allowed to pass and climb aboard.

Zlatija held Edin in one arm and clutched Mirza's right arm. Huso's hand was locked around the boy's other arm. Hiba followed behind.

Zlatija passed through the Dutch cordon first. Then Mirza. When Huso stepped through, a Serb shoved him back and told him to stay behind. Zlatija climbed into a truck with the boys and looked back. Huso and Hiba had dissolved into the crowd of blank faces.

It took a few minutes more for Huso and Hiba to work their way to the front of the crowd again. A Dutch soldier in short pants waved them through. It was just a few steps to the truck. Huso lifted himself over the tailgate and turned back to give Hiba a boost.

A Serb soldier, fat, dark skinned, about six feet tall, and clean shaven, ordered Huso to get down. "Fuck your mother," the soldier shouted. He pushed Huso off to the side of the truck and ordered him to throw his rucksack with the photo album onto a pile of suitcases, bags, and blankets. By the time Hiba climbed aboard and looked back, Huso had disappeared from sight.

The trucks drove off in a convoy. It passed through the deserted UN checkpoint before Bratunac, then entered the town.

The trucks stopped. A Serb soldier leered into the back of Hiba's truck.

"Hand over all of your money."

Hiba had her wedding band in her socks and Huso's wristwatch folded in her hair under her kerchief. She said nothing. One woman pulled out a wad of German marks, but the Serb did not see her.

"We don't have anything," a woman shouted.

Someone else handed over about thirty-five dollars worth of German currency. The driver got angry. He wanted to move on, and the truck lurched ahead. In the center of Bratunac, they turned left. Again they were stopped at a checkpoint. Again Serb soldiers demanded valuables. Again a few women handed money over before they drove on and approached Kravica.

Hiba saw three bodies beside the road, face down. She saw shirtless men being marched down the road, two by two, holding their hands over their heads. They were young and old. She looked for Paja among them. She did not recognize any of them. The truck moved on.

❨   ❨   ❨

THE Serbs had been calling out for hours with megaphones for the Muslim men to walk down from the woods on the hillside above Kravica where Muhamed and his father and brother had taken cover. The Serb women, children, and old people had been evacuated from Kravica the night before, after word was spread that a huge column of Muslims was headed in their direction. White UN armored personnel carriers appeared on the road down near the farmers' co-op.

"Surrender," the megaphones blasted. "Your own commanders have betrayed you."

"Surrender. We will dress your wounds."

"We have your women and children here. We will kill them if you do not surrender."

"Surrender and you will be able to go wherever you wish."

Thousands of Muslim men descended the hillside and surrendered. On the roads below, they found Serbs sitting atop the UN vehicles. Serb soldiers immediately shot some of the men; others were forced into nearby fields, where their throats were slit. Several hundred prisoners were marched into the new warehouse of the farmers' co-op in Kravica; and after some Muslims overpowered and killed one of the Serb police guards and wounded another, the rest of the Serbs outside the warehouse opened up on the unarmed Muslims inside with machine guns and bombs. Other prisoners were marched and trucked to Bratunac, where they were cut down by machine guns. Prisoners were herded into the soccer field in the village of Nova Kasaba, where Paja had seen the man with the skin peeled from his face; their hands were bound behind their backs, and they sat on the grass in the sun.

General Ratko Mladić appeared. "Nothing will happen to you," he said. But when he left, the men were marched away in groups, shot in cold blood, and dumped into mass graves.

EUPHORIA spread through Bratunac after the fall of Srebrenica. Mihailo Erić, the great-great-grandson of the Serb sharecropper who taught himself to read and fought against two empires to become the owner of the land he had worked as a sharecropper, was in town on the day the executions began. A few of Mihailo's friends approached him. They were excited.

"Come on," they said. They told Mihailo to grab his gun. They told him to get on down to the soccer field in Bratunac. Military-age men from Kravica, including Mihailo's father, Zoran Erić, had been summoned to Bratunac for "obligatory work details." After two years of waiting, they said, their five minutes had finally come. If they dealt with the Muslims from Srebrenica now, they would never be back.

Mihailo, who had gone to war at age seventeen and had his head torn open by a bullet, refused to budge.

"I don't shoot prisoners," he said. Then he went home.

❨   ❨   ❨

HIBA ČELIK'S truck stopped at a crossroads she did not know. The women and children dropped down from the tailgate. She recognized no one. A Serb soldier pointed down a crumbling asphalt road, ordered them to walk, and warned them that there were mines on each side. The women and children started off.

To the side of the road was a patch of rhubarb, and beneath the broad leaves Hiba saw a dead body. The women walked on. No one spoke. In a creek bed they saw a dying man, moaning, stretching his arms and hands as if reaching for something. The women went on.

Hiba came to a beech tree blocking the road. She climbed over and kept walking. When she reached a tunnel, a group of men told her she was in Muslim territory. She still had the gold watch in her hair and the wedding band inside one of her socks. Zlatija and the boys were nowhere to be seen.

HUSO ČELIK disappeared behind the truck parked on the asphalt road in Potočari in the same way that Hurem Suljić, a fifty-two-year-old carpenter from a village near Srebrenica, and about seventeen hundred men were separated from their families. Suljić walked away from the trucks with a limp and was taken with some two hundred other men to an unfinished house across the asphalt road and held there. The men inside whispered to one another. Serb soldiers stood around the doors and talked.

"I need medicine for my heart. I've got a weak heart," one of the Muslims complained.

"You'll get medicine," a guard answered quietly.

Prisoners near the house were told to stop praying.

At about six o'clock that evening, General Mladić walked into the doorway of the house. He was dressed in a camouflage uniform with rolled-up sleeves. Three men with automatics stood behind him.

"Neighbors," his voice boomed, "if you have never seen me before, I am Ratko Mladić. I am the commander of the Serbian army, and you see we are not afraid of the NATO pact. They bombed us, and we took Srebrenica. And where is your country now? What will you do? Will you stand beside Alija? He has led you to ruin. . . ."

Suljić mouthed back, "I'm not interested in Alija. . . . I want to know why we've been separated from our families. Why haven't we gone with our families?"

Mladić answered him: "I've had 180 guys held prisoner in Tuzla since last year, and we haven't been able to get an exchange for them. I'm going to pick out 180 of you and make that exchange. Not a hair on your heads will be touched."

Mladić turned away from the house, and his bodyguards followed him down to the road. There were no threats and no jokes.

The Serb general hung around until dusk, when the soldiers ordered Suljić and the rest of the Muslim men out of the house and packed them aboard a pair of buses. Mladić was standing on the road. He walked up to the door of the first bus and told the driver to follow a red car parked in front of it. A soldier stepped aboard and stood next to the driver as the pneumatic door swished shut. The destination was a few miles away in Bratunac and took only a few minutes to reach. The red car and the bus stopped in front of a warehouse that was once used to store cattle feed for the farmers' co-op. Standing around were a couple of dozen soldiers in camouflage uniforms. They were in their thirties and forties and wore no insignias. The door to the bus opened.

"Let's go," one of the Serbs ordered. "One at a time. One at a time."

The men stepped into the warehouse and sat down on the floor. The silence was broken by voices from inside the building.

"Why have you brought us here?"

"We don't know anything," the Serb soldiers answered. "We were ordered here to guard you."

The men could hear more vehicles pull up outside, buses with a new group of prisoners. Then even more vehicles arrived, buses and trucks. The prisoners were squeezed tighter and tighter into the warehouse. Two or three soldiers stood guard at the door and looked for Muslims from Bratunac. They spoke to men they knew.

"Where is your brother?"

"Where is your son? Has he survived?"

"What did you do for food in Srebrenica?"

A few of the Serbs were from Bratunac. Others indicated they were from Loznica, Šabac, or Valjevo, all towns in Serbia near the Bosnian border. The chatter ended when an officer arrived. Through the doors some of the men in the warehouse heard members of the Drina Wolves receiving orders from an officer.

"The twelve of you here tonight have been given an order to carry out the task assigned you. Is that clear?"

"Clear, sir," shouted the militiamen.

The gunmen entered the warehouse with flashlights. A pool of light fell upon one Muslim.

"You! Outside."

The man wound his way to the door, turned to the left and disappeared from sight.

There were thuds, then screams, cries for help, and gurgles. Inside the building there were muffled groans.

"Do you know him? Who was that?"

"Don't know."

"He's my relative."

"Shut up."

A flashlight shone through the doorway.

"Where is Naser?" the man with the light shouted.

There was no sound.

"You! You!"

One at a time, the men were taken out. Some of them cried for help; others hardly managed a whimper. The militiamen threw a few of the beaten men, still alive, back into the warehouse, on top of the Muslims crowded together inside. The Muslims passed the beaten men to the back of the warehouse and laid them on the floor to die.

The men near the door were silent, afraid to draw attention to themselves, afraid to be the next called to go outside. Some of them shivered. Others wept. None tried to escape. No one talked of escaping. Men mumbled prayers from the Koran. Anyone who dared speak to someone nearby did so in a whisper.

"It is over for us," a voice said. "They're going to kill us all."

"Don't be afraid, man," Suljić told one of the men next to him. "Listen, if it is our fate to survive, we will survive. If it is not our fate, why should we break ourselves down, kill ourselves for nothing? We must hand ourselves over to our fate. God has handed us our fate."

The Serbs stopped the killing at dawn, and everything was quiet for about two hours.

The sound of a diesel engine approached, and the men inside the warehouse thought a vehicle was coming to take them away. Soldiers stood in the door.

"We need ten volunteers."

When no one stepped forward, the Serbs picked out ten men and led them out the door. There was silence for about twenty minutes. The engine restarted and the truck drove off. The ten "volunteers" never returned.

A Serb, about forty years old, olive skinned with black hair, walked up to the door and fired a gun into the ceiling. "Hand over all the valuables you have. Everything! If someone doesn't hand over his money, we'll shoot him and ten more as well."

Some of the Muslims pulled cash from their pockets and handed it over. The Serb fired into the ceiling again.

"Hand it all over."

There was no more. The man disappeared.

To the right of the door was a toilet, and the guards announced that the men would now be allowed to relieve themselves, one by one, in a line, each man three steps from the man in front.

"Do not look to your left on the way out. Keep your eyes to the right. To the right." Suljić made his way to the toilet. On his way back to the warehouse, he saw the Serbs bring another Muslim out of the warehouse. There were three or four Serbs on one side of him, three or four on the other side, and pools of blood on the ground in between. One of the Serbs was bringing down on the Muslim's head a squared-off metal club with pieces of iron welded into it. When the Muslim passed between them he felled him with the first blow. Another Serb hit him with an ax, and he fell to his stomach. They dragged the man around the side of the warehouse.

The second session of killing lasted until midafternoon on Friday, July 14. Then a truck approached.

"We need ten more volunteers," the militiamen shouted. "Some stronger guys. We have something for you to do."

When no one spoke up, they selected ten men and led them from the warehouse. For a few minutes, the only sound was the hiss of a garden hose. The engine restarted. The truck drove off. None of these "workers" came back either.

During the second break in the killing, one of the guards appeared at the door.

"Here is Ratko Mladić. You can complain to him about everything. He decides everything. Everything he orders comes to be."

Mladić appeared at the door. He was bareheaded, and his eyes scanned the men inside the cattle-feed warehouse.

"What are you doing to us?" the Muslim men wailed. "Why are you holding us? Why are you torturing us?"

"No one is going to kill any more of you," the general said. "We are going to take you to Kalesija for an exchange for my people. I am going to order transportation for you all. We have to count you. We must know how many of you there are so that I can organize transport."

One of the Muslims stood up and counted off the men. The last one was number 296.

"Now wait," Mladić said. "Don't panic. You will all have a ride to Kalesija."

31

SANELA was too exhausted for fear. The infant inside her had not stirred for a day, maybe two. She felt no more pain. She felt numb. And she knew nothing of what had become of Muhamed or her family. She guessed it was Thursday or Friday. Nothing except the whereabouts of her husband mattered to her when the Serb soldiers found her inside the factory building at the UN base, trying, and failing, to get some sleep on the bare metal housing of some piece of machinery. There were still lots of Muslims around the base, men and women. The Serb soldiers told everyone to get ready to leave.

"If you have a knife or a fork or razor blades, leave them behind," one of the Muslim women warned. "There might be some problems. The Serbs are confiscating family pictures."

Sanela tucked her photo album and diary into the bottom of her bag and covered them with the bibs, diapers, and baby clothes. She slid a crumpled and stained snapshot of Muhamed beneath her shirt and walked out onto the asphalt road.

"Line up, two by two," the soldiers ordered.

One of them called out the name of a Muslim man standing near Sanela. They had once been neighbors.

"How are you?" the Serb asked, as he embraced and kissed the Muslim. "Want a smoke? Don't worry, everything will be fine."

Sanela walked on. She kept her eyes straight ahead and never saw whether the Muslim took the cigarette or where he was taken. She walked to the second bus in the line. A young Serb soldier helped her climb aboard. The soldiers gave the women on the bus water, and they warned the women that the bus carried no plastic vomit bags for carsickness, as all Yugoslav buses once did.

Sanela spread out over two seats and waited in the heat and the sunshine. She shouted out to the driver:

"Excuse me, sir. Do you mind if I light up?"

"As far as I'm concerned, you can go ahead."

She pulled out a cigarette and struck a match. Everyone on the bus was rolling cigarettes and lighting up as the driver pulled away. A name flashed into Sanela's head. Nehrudin. She decided she would call the baby Nehrudin. She did not know why she picked this name. She could not remember ever having heard it.

The bus passed through Bratunac. Sanela saw three or four trucks full of young men. Some were wearing white undershirts; some were wearing no shirts at all. It was the last thing she remembered before she leaned back, rested her head, and sank into a deep sleep.

❨   ❨   ❨

"GET UP! Get out!" the male voices screamed in the darkness. "Faster! Faster! Up! Out!"

Sanela opened her eyes. Night had already fallen. She lifted herself from the bus seat, picked up her bag, and stepped from the bus into cool woodland air.

"You will go this way," one of the soldiers ordered. He pointed to an asphalt road beside a swollen river. Sanela heard the gurgle of the water. Her mind was now clear.

"Can anyone tell us where we are going?"

"Oh, my dear one, you are going to join your own," one of the Serbs said.

Sanela kept her mouth shut.

"There are some nice ones in this bunch," another Serb said. "We should let them stay behind."

The women walked into the darkness and down the road. Branches crackled underfoot in the woods to the right and left. There was a Serb soldier standing about every twenty yards. The asphalt below Sanela's feet was cracked and full of potholes, and she had to step carefully. She peered into the blackness and followed the back of a woman in front of her. The woman stopped.

"God, what is this?" Sanela asked herself. Her throat tightened. A fallen beech tree blocked the road.

"Do not go off to the right or left," a Serb shouted. "There are mines to the right and the left."

Sanela walked up to the tree. Her stomach made her too bulky to squeeze under it. When she started to climb over, a male hand grabbed her arm.

"You come this way."

The Serb led her off to the side of the road.

"Take the path there."

The path led a few yards off the road, turned sharply to the left, and came back up to the asphalt. Sanela stepped off the road carefully. The Serb had seen that she was pregnant. He led her around the tree, and she rejoined her friends.

The women stopped and smoked at a tunnel entrance. On the other side were Muslim soldiers. They had food and juice ready. Sanela passed it all by and climbed aboard one of the buses waiting there. It dropped her a few hours later at the gates of a UN base at the airport outside of Tuzla. The Swedish peacekeepers there had stopped letting Muslims inside. So she wandered into a nearby meadow, patted down some grass, and fell asleep on the ground.

Sanela went looking for her family the next morning. The sun was already up. The air was stifling. She was hungry and thirsty and walked around aimlessly, sobbing, wanting to die. She was turning back for the meadow where she had slept, when she heard someone call her name. It was Zlatija. She took Sanela to Hiba and the boys, and Sanela led them to her meadow. She was pulling branches from a tree to make some shade when the contractions started. A police officer took her in a van to a UN clinic at the airport. A doctor came in and told her to take off her clothes and get ready for an examination. Sanela stood there for an instant before she began undressing. She started to cry. She was ashamed. Her clothes were filthy. She had not bathed in days. She was wearing her husband's underpants, and she did not want to take them off. The nurse looked at her for a few seconds before she understood why Sanela was crying.

"You can keep those shorts," she said.

Sanela was in the birthing room at Tuzla hospital by midafternoon. The midwife's name was Muharema. She had once lived in Srebrenica, in a house close to Dragica's. She had known Sanela's mother-in-law, Naza. She told Sanela everything would be fine.

"When will it happen?"

"About midnight."

The midwife's guess was close enough. Nehrudin Halilović was born two days earlier than expected, at four in the morning of Saturday, July 15, 1995. Sanela took him to a tent in a refugee camp at Tuzla airport. The baby's father and both of his grandfathers might still have been alive.

THE prisoners inside the old cattle-feed warehouse in Bratunac had relaxed after General Mladić announced that he was sending them to Muslim territory, to Kalesija, a village about five miles from the refugee camp UN workers were scrambling to set up at the Tuzla airport. A little past six o'clock in the evening, half a dozen buses pulled up in front of the warehouse. The men inside stood and pressed toward the door.

"Don't bunch up," the Serb soldiers yelled. "There will be room for all of you. Single file. Single file."

The prisoners stepped aboard. Each bus had one guard up front, next to the driver. Mladić arrived again and handed down orders.

"They've drawn their share of blood," one of the prisoners in Suljić's bus said. "Now they'll let us go. There is definitely going to be an exchange. Killing us all makes no sense."

In the twilight, the buses headed out of Bratunac toward the Drina. They drove parallel to the river, downstream along its left bank. The bus stopped for about an hour when it reached a crossroads before Zvornik.

"What are we waiting here for?" the men asked the driver.

"I'm just looking at the bus in front of me. When it moves, I move."

The buses rolled on. They entered Zvornik and passed under a steel bridge across the river to Serbia from the center of town. Across the Drina they could see the minarets of mosques on the Serbian side of the border. At the village of Karakaj, the bus turned west, away from the river and toward Kalesija and Tuzla and the mass of refugee women and children gathered around the airport. The buses could have reached the front line in another fifteen minutes. But just before an overpass they turned to the right, off the main highway, and headed northwest up a narrow village road. This was no longer the road to Kalesija. The men knew it. The buses came to a stop in the village of Križevačke Njive. There was a playground in front of them, and a school building with a gymnasium next to it. The doors of the buses swished open.

"Single file! Into the gym! Move!"

The gymnasium was empty. The men sat down on the floor. Overhead were the basketball rims. Buses and trucks arrived all night with new prisoners—younger men, men like Sanela's Muhamed, his father, and brother, and Bedži Kozić, men who had been captured during the march.

The Serbs fired their guns into the gym's ceiling and shouted orders for the men to squeeze together.

"Stand up! Move back!"

"Back! Back! Back!"

The last group arrived. There were gunshots into the ceiling.

"Sit! Sit! Sit!"

The Muslims sat in one another's laps until midday on Saturday, July 15, with nothing to drink. The floor was wet with urine and shit; the air was sticky with the stench. Again sallow faces whispered prayers. Again there were whispered laments for family members taken away in unknown directions. Again Mladić appeared in the open door. His face was crimson, his uniform camouflage.

A single prisoner cried out, "They are mistreating us. They are killing us. We are suffocating here, and you have given us nothing to eat or drink. Nothing!"

"What can I do for you when your government will not take you and I have to take care of you?" Mladić howled.

"Calm down," the general said. He told the men that he was going to hand over some of them to a renegade Muslim leader named Fikret Abdić, a mafia-style businessman who had formed a private army, made a separate peace with the Serbs, and attacked the Muslim army forces in Bihać. "The rest of you will be taken to Bijeljina. We will bring you water. As you are leaving, you'll be allowed to drink as much as you want. You will go now. Immediately."

Mladić left. There was silence in the gymnasium. The men wanted to believe him. The Serbs needed men to do physical labor. A lot of the Muslim men in the gym were young and fit. They knew the Serbs had forced-labor camps set up near Bijeljina. They spoke little. They wept. Slowly the gym emptied. At the door, the men ladled water into their mouths as quickly as they could before being hustled outside.

Serb soldiers blindfolded the Muslims with sheer strips of cloth, some red, others yellow, green, or black. The soldiers were not very careful at tying on the blindfolds. The Muslims could tilt their heads back and sneak looks around. Two dozen prisoners at a time were walking on ramps into the backs of olive-green trucks with canopies but no flaps closing off the back. A red car was parked behind the trucks, and sitting in the passenger seat beside the car's driver was a soldier with an automatic who opened the front door and wedged his gun into the space between the door and body of the car.

"No talking!" he shouted. "No talking! You talk, and I'll kill you."

The red car followed as the trucks pulled out and wound their way up a village road. The trucks rounded a curve. The Muslims sitting at the back of each truck could see the corpses of Muslims who had been taken away earlier. The bodies were lying in a field, in some places two deep. Another turn in the road revealed more bodies. The men's lips twitched. No one spoke. No one tried to escape.

The trucks stopped. The tailgates swung down.

"Out, old man, out!" the soldier shouted at Suljić.

The Muslims hopped down from the truck. They were lined up in rows and told to face toward the field and away from the road.

As the trucks revved their engines, half a dozen soldiers opened fire into the Muslims' backs. Their legs gave way. They fell to the earth. The executioners searched for movement among the tangle of bodies. The twitch of a leg brought a bullet through the head.

Hurem Suljić had fallen to the ground uninjured. The slumping body of the man shot to death behind him lay atop his back. He waited there silently and stone still while the Serbs watched the two dozen men for signs of life. He lay sideways with his head resting on his arm. When the men moved off, he opened his eyes.

There were two execution areas about half a football field apart. In each one was a backhoe digging a trench. Two or three more truckloads of prisoners were driven up and shot before Mladić rode up in a car. The general stood about fifteen yards from Suljić as he watched a group of prisoners lined up and gunned down. Mladić got into the backseat of his car and drove off.

After nightfall, there was only one shooting ground. The Serbs parked the backhoes and switched on their headlights to illuminate the field. The killing went on. When the soldiers' diverted their attention to another part of the field, Suljić turned slowly onto his back and inched himself across the ground into the darkness of a thicket.

Another truckload arrived. Another few dozen prisoners were shot. A car drove up. "There aren't any more. We're done," Suljić heard the soldier in the car say.

"Should we stand guard here all night?"

"If another truck comes for you, you won't have to keep watch overnight. If the truck doesn't come, you'll stay."

The car pulled away. The soldiers left behind milled around and walked among the bodies to see whether anyone would cry out.

"If there are any of you still alive, get up and we'll bandage your wounds," one of the soldiers shouted. No one got up.

The moon rose. The soldiers stood next to the backhoes, smoking cigarettes and talking until the truck came back and drove them away. Suljić lay in the thicket silently for a few minutes.

"Is anyone alive?" he shouted.

One other Muslim, a young man named Mevludin Orić, a distant cousin of Naser, emerged from the darkness and helped Hurem hobble into the night. A few hours later it started to rain and hail. A few days later, they snuck across the front line into Muslim-controlled territory.

The killing field in Križevačke Njive or half a dozen others in the Drina basin near Srebrenica and Zvornik were the farthest that Huso Čelik, Muhamed Halilović, his father, Smail, and his brother, Hajrudin, could have made it alive. Bedži Kozić, Behadil Kešmer, Hasib Kapetanović, Uncle Ismet Čavkušić, and about eight thousand had been killed. The father, both grandfathers, and an uncle of Sanela's infant son, Nehrudin, had disappeared. It is not unlikely that they all died on the first day of Nehrudin's life.

The men who carried out the executions were reportedly under orders handed down by General Mladić and Radislav Krstić, a colonel in the Bosnian Serb army who was promoted to general and named commander of the army's Drina corps by Mladić within a few days of the killings. Among the units that took part in the killings was the Tenth Commando squad, which answered directly to the Mladić's headquarters in Han Pijesak. Men from Srebrenica, Bratunac, Kravica, Milići, Višegrad, Bajina Bašta, Loznica, Zvornik, and other towns also participated.

❨ ❨ ❨

PAJA, Senad, Deba, and the remnants of the column of Muslim men who marched out of Srebrenica were already approaching the battlefront east of Tuzla before Bosnia's president, Alija Izetbegović, called Sead Delić, the commander of the Bosnian army's Tuzla corps. Izetbegović wanted to know what the Tuzla corps was doing to help the men in the column to break through the Serb lines.

"Do you have officers standing by?" Izetbegović asked.

"No."

"Why haven't you got anyone there?" the president shouted.

Whatever the answer was, Izetbegović was not satisfied with it. He quickly called the commander of the Bosnian army, Rasim Delić.

"Rasim, what are you preparing?"

"Nothing."

"Whom have you sent to the line?"

"No one."

"Do you know what's happening there?"

The Bosnian army's general staff and the Tuzla corps did next to nothing to assist the Muslims marching from Srebrenica. Izetbegović refused to deploy the Black Swans to the front line area near Tuzla where the column of men was preparing to break through, but he did write out a personal order that gave one officer from the Black Swans permission to remove several hundred guns and crates of ammunition from an arsenal in the town of Zenica. The officer and a driver traveled to Zenica alone and delivered the weapons to Tuzla, where they were handed over to Naser Orić and about two hundred volunteers, who took them to the line east of Tuzla and waited for the column to approach.

By now, the Bosnian government was screaming that the women and children hiking across the front line were "United Nations refugees" and that it was the responsibility of the UN to find new homes for them in third countries. At a meeting of the UN Security Council in New York, the representative of France, clearly in a move to deflect attention from General Janvier and his decision not to call for air strikes against the Serbs, demanded a military operation to drive the Bosnian Serb army from Srebrenica. Great Britain's representative spoke about the need for "demilitarization" of the Srebrenica safe area, but said that the UN military force in Bosnia could not impose peace. And the Russians, whose ambassador had in 1993 promised air strikes to protect the safe areas, now said the use of force could have only negative consequences.

❝   ❝   ❝

ABOUT six miles from the Serb trenches before Tuzla, Ejub Golić and his men circled behind a group of Serbs who were setting up an ambush. The Muslims slit the throats of Serb soldiers caught off guard, and they captured a Serb captain. Golić and the other Muslim commanders told the captain they would kill him if he did not lead them along a safe route toward the Serb lines before Tuzla. The captain agreed, and the column pressed ahead. The men came to the asphalt highway between Karakaj and Kalesija and killed a Serb who happened to be driving by; then they moved northwest and skirted the execution ground at Križevačke Njive by a few miles to the west. About a mile from the Serb trenches, Golić and his men captured three Serb tanks that had been dug into the earth and were unable to move. Now the Serb captain was ordered to radio Serb commanders along the front line and instruct them to let the Muslim column pass. The Serbs stalled for an entire day and brought up reinforcements from Kravica, Bratunac, and other villages around Srebrenica. The Muslim men in the column rested in the deep grass of a meadow. Paja and Senad looked around for some kind of shelter in case the Serbs began to shell them. The men scavenged for snails and picked apples and pears.

"They're going to hit us from behind," Paja thought. "We're going to be trapped."

The hot, sunny day passed in daydreams and whisps of cigarette smoke.

WELL after midnight a cold front blew over eastern Bosnia. Rain started falling. Then a heavy hail pelted the earth. Paja and Senad took cover with a group of men under a clump of trees to wait out the bad weather. They smoked and talked. One man born and raised in Srebrenica told everyone the story of how he had managed to escape the ambush in the woods above Kravica. Then he started talking about money, about some German marks. Something about the money had upset him, but none of the men understood why. His eyes emptied, and his face turned blank. Then he reached into his jacket pocket and brought out a hand grenade. His index finger pulled the grenade's white pin. He kept his hand pressed against the clip that would set it off.

A man grabbed him from behind and held his arms to his chest so that he could not release the grenade. Paja heard someone yell, "Help me. Help me." And he and the other men scrambled for cover. The arm with the hand grenade broke free. The man upset about the money pressed the bomb to his throat and let go of the clip, and the grenade exploded. Their was silence. The man's lungs continued to suck at the air for a minute or so before he stopped moving. A jacket was pulled over the mangled flesh that had been the man's face. The other men sat nearby and smoked another round of cigarettes before they moved away from the clump of trees. Paja and Senad propped up one of the wounded, a guy who had been hit in the leg by a piece of shrapnel. He had been one of their neighbors in Srebrenica.

The rain had stopped. The sky was turning gray. The air was chilly, and the men shivered as they waited. There were more suicides. One man suffered an epileptic seizure. A soldier asleep on the ground next to Paja cuddled his automatic rifle, put his finger on the trigger, and fired a bullet through the head of the man lying next to him. The soldier did not wake up for another half an hour. When he saw what he had done, he drifted off.

THE Muslims began their assault and breakout just after dawn. They squeezed the Serbs holding out in one stretch of the trench network before Tuzla. Ejub Golić led Muslim soldiers from the column in an attack on the Serbs from the rear of the trench lines; Naser Orić advaced his volunteers on the Tuzla side of the line.

A mile from the shooting, Paja and Senad sat waiting with their wounded neighbor from Srebrenica. By about noon, Golić and his men had pried a corridor through the Serb trench lines. The waiting men were ordered to form up according to their brigades. There was anger.

"They're going to spot us," the men complained. "It's too goddamned slow."

"They're going to shell us into pulp."

"We should be spread out."

Zulfo Tursunović ordered the wounded brought forward. Paja and Senad grabbed their neighbor from Srebrenica. The men who were not carrying the wounded moved out as well. They refused to wait any longer.

"Don't go," an officer shouted. "The line is not secure."

Everyone kept going.

They hurried along a road through the woods on a hilltop just above the front line, then jumped over the first Serb trench.

They scurried down the hill, sloshed through a stream, and leaped over a second empty Serb trench.

Muslim soldiers ordered the men to stop. Only one more trench separated them from the main Muslim lines. Paja and Senad propped up their wounded neighbor.

Standing there was Naser Orić and one of Golić's men, a guy everyone called Pensioner Rambo, who was holding himself up on crutches. Two soldiers escorting the hostage Serb captain walked up. Another soldier told Rambo that a shell blast had killed Ejub Golić. Rambo took his crutches and whacked the Serb captain three or four times in the back and swore on his mother.

"Calm down," Orić told him. "It's over. It's all over. I feel sorry as well."

The soldiers turned their attention away from Paja, Senad, and the other men they had held up.

"Let's go while they are still talking. Let's use this chance," Paja said. "Senad, let's run." They urged their wounded neighbor to move quickly.

"I can't run," the neighbor said. "I can't run."

"Pička ti materina, let's go," Paja swore. They moved on. The wounded man limped quickly. Again there was gunfire, but they kept moving. After half a mile and half an hour, they crossed an asphalt road and a stream. And with that they had made it to the safety of their own lines.

Sead Delić, the commander of the Tuzla corps, was there. He was shaking the hands of the men who had made it across. Some Muslim soldiers pointed the way to a field kitchen, and Paja and Senad walked over to it. They filled their plates with food and sat down on the ground to eat. They wolfed down one spoonful after another and shook their heads. They were eating cabbage, boiled cabbage. *Kupus.*

It took another two days for them to find Hiba and Zlatija and the boys. They had been sent to a dank classroom in a village school about twenty miles from Tuzla. After one sleepless night there, Paja and Senad moved them into the fresher air of a tent in the refugee camp at Tuzla airport. Sanela arrived a few days later, after an argument with one of her aunts.

Somewhere along the way, Paja got a message to Hamed in Toronto.

32

EVEN after the fall of Srebrenica, Miroslav Deronjić, the chairman of the Serbian Democratic Party's Bratunac chapter, was still sticking to the advice of the party's president, Radovan Karadžić. In mid-April 1992, when the Bosnian war was still barely a week old, the two men reportedly sat down together in

Pale and agreed on the steps that needed to be taken "to defend" the Serbs of the Bratunac area. Before sending Deronjić home with his instructions, Karadžić gave him the same bit of advice he had given many other local Serb leaders that month. "Everything must be done on paper," Karadžić said.

A few weeks after their meeting, on April 29, 1992, Deronjić posted printed notices warning the Muslims in Bratunac that they had forty-eight hours to sign loyalty oaths to the Bosnian Serbs' rebel state. Eleven days later, before any Muslim had fired a shot in anger in the town, Deronjić spoke with a re-assuring voice to the local *hodža*, Mustafa Mujkanović, as he and 750 other prisoners were being marched away to the gymnasium of the Bratunac elementary school where half of them would be beaten, shot, and knifed to death. "Don't worry, *hodža*," Deronjić said. "You're heading for a safe place."

On July 17, 1995, as Serb gunmen from Bratunac and other towns on both sides of the Drina were executing the last of thousands of their Muslim prisoners, this same Miroslav Deronjić, now president of the Civilian Affairs Committee of Srebrenica, dropped in on the UN's main base at Potočari with an unsigned document, a kind of affidavit. He gave the paper to Major Rob Franken, the second-in-command of the Dutch troops. And in his reassuring voice Deronjić told Franken that he wanted a signature. Franken read the paper.

"I assert that the evacuation was carried out by the Serb side correctly," it said. "The Serb side has adhered to all the regulations of Geneva Conventions and the international war law [*sic*]."

Franken scratched in a meaningless disclaimer, but he signed Deronjić's affidavit just the same, and news of it went out over Serb radio stations. Franken later told Dutch army investigators that he had signed the document in order to ensure the safe departure from Srebrenica of the Dutch troops and a handful of Muslims who had been employed by the UN and private aid agencies in Srebrenica.

AFTER taking Srebrenica, General Mladić was certain General Janvier and Yasushi Akashi had given him a green light to overrun the rest of the UN safe areas in Bosnia. Mladić was further encouraged when, in secret negotiations on July 15, UN officials, including Akashi, agreed to his demand that all the Dutch troops remain in Srebrenica until July 21, days after the last Muslim civilians had been expelled and the last mass executions carried out. Thus, the UN let the Serb general keep the Dutch troops as hostages while his forces overran Žepa, the second safe area considered unviable by Janvier, Akashi, and other UN military force officials. These "hostages" gave UN officials an excuse not to use air power to deter the attack on Žepa even though by now they knew that men from Srebrenica had been summarily massacred. A few days later, Mladić's forces attacked the Bihać safe area from two directions and tried to cut it in half.

"By the autumn, we'll take Goražde, Bihać, and, in the end, Sarajevo, and we'll finish the war in Bosnia," Mladić told a Belgrade weekly magazine. "The West should understand that it cannot bomb Serbs without punishment."

THE Dutch contingent left Srebrenica, as agreed, on the afternoon of July 21. Before they departed, the Dutch reimbursed the Serb army for the fuel burned in the buses and trucks used to expel Srebrenica's women and children and to transport its menfolk to the execution grounds. Dutch officers, unlike the heads of the international aid agencies that had been working in Srebrenica, abandoned several of their translators and refused to protect their local employees' families, which resulted in the execution of women and men. Dutch troops also undertook repairs on Srebrenica's water-pumping station, the facility the Serbs had destroyed in June 1993 and over the next two years had refused to let the UN fix. Lieutenant Colonel Ton Karremans, the Dutch commander, and General Ratko Mladić were photographed raising glasses together in a toast. Karremans came away from Srebrenica praising Mladić's military acumen. He also claimed that the glass he had raised with Mladić had been filled with water.

❨   ❨   ❨

ON July 21, three years after the first London conference on Bosnia, Prime Minister John Major of Great Britain convened a second international conference in London to decide how to respond to the killings at Srebrenica and the utter humiliation of NATO and the UN. This London conference, unlike the first one, saw the United States take the diplomatic initiative. The thousands of dead and missing from Srebrenica had created the potential for real embarrassment to the American president as he was gearing up to run for reelection in 1996. The president's political interest clearly collided with the perceived absence of a vital American security or economic interest in the former Yugoslavia.

Under the authority given to NATO by UN Security Council Resolution 836 and other resolutions already on the books, the United States, Great Britain, and France drew the Serbs a line in the sand at the second London meeting.They warned General Mladić that his forces would face widespread

NATO air strikes if there were any attacks on the remaining safe areas, especially Goražde. Western leaders had no further need for the UN fig leaf they had used in Bosnia since the war began, and they eliminated Yasushi Akashi's power to veto NATO air action and extended the authority to order air strikes directly to General Rupert Smith, the British commander in Sarajevo, and Admiral Leighton Smith, the commander of NATO's forces in southern Europe. U.S. Secretary of State Warren Christopher left London saying there would be no more pinprick air strikes in Bosnia.

On August 4, with clear U.S. backing, Croatia's army attacked and overran Knin, the symbolic capital of the rebel Serbs who, at the instigation of Slobodan Milošević and the Yugoslav army, had seized a quarter of Croatia's territory and driven out their Croat neighbors in 1990 and 1991. Within hours, the tide of the wars in Yugoslavia had shifted. The rebel Serbs' leaders abandoned the civilian Serb population in Croatia. The Croatian army sent tens of thousands of these Serbs fleeing across the Croatian border into Serb-held districts in Bosnia. President Milošević, the man whose hunger for political power had led him to drive a stake into the heart of Brotherhood and Unity at Kosovo in 1989 and mount two wars to unite all the Serbs in a single state, did nothing to stop the most massive exodus of Serb civilians since the Ustaše horrors of World War II. Economically, Milošević's Serbia was on its knees. Milošević was more desperate than ever to have the economic sanctions against his country lifted. It was unthinkable to restart a war with Croatia for the sake of Knin.

The last attack by Mladić's men on a safe area in Bosnia came on August 28, when a mortar round killed thirty-eight shoppers and hawkers in the same Sarajevo marketplace where sixty-nine people had died eighteen months earlier. Again video footage of dismembered bodies and pools of blood flashed across on television screens worldwide, again the Bosnian Serb leadership denied that a Serb mortar had fired the round. Far from the cameras, however, the Bosnian Serb army mounted a large-scale attack the Goražde safe area. On August 30, General Smith quietly removed more than eighty UN troops from Goražde and called for NATO to attack Serb military targets. The Bosnian Serbs' antiaircraft missile system went up in smoke within a matter of hours. Bombs, rockets, and cruise missiles wiped out Serb arsenals, warehouses, and artillery batteries. Bridges were downed, roads blown up, and civilian and military telecommunications systems cut. On one hilltop near Tuzla, Serb soldiers manning a communications tower laughed when a single bomb landed about fifty yards feet off target and sent up a small explosion.

"Look at these Americans, they can't hit anything," the soldiers in the tower scoffed. A young Serb soldier, an electrical engineer, told me about it later on:

"They didn't believe the Americans could hit anything, and for a day after the bomb fell they were laughing it up and drinking. I told them again and again that it was a warning. I told them the Americans were signaling us to get away, and they laughed at me. . . ."

The planes returned the next day. They scored two direct hits on the tower and killed about a dozen men nearby.

EPILOGUE

1995

THEY were pure eastern Bosnia all right: broad, rustic hands, smiles punctuated by missing molars, a nasal twang to their voices. I stepped out of the car and blurted out, "*Es-salaam aleikum,*" a Muslim greeting, and they burst out laughing and loosed a couple of soul-warming cusses. We shook hands, kissed each other on the cheeks, then climbed the stairs to the upper floor of the farmhouse, slipped off our shoes, and went inside. Paja sat me down on a wooden chair. His landlord, a farmer named Šaban who was so ecstatic that I mistook him for an uncle or an in-law, broke out the brandy. Zlatija started cranking a coffee grinder, and Hiba plopped herself down on the floor next to the wood stove, cracked jokes, and giggled like a chipmunk.

It was September 1995. The Čeliks had been living at Šaban's place for about a month already. They had been driven out of the Tuzla airport by a couple of mortar rounds that crashed into a field beside the tent city where the refugees from Srebrenica had settled in. They were dud rounds, but the impacts kicked clumps of dirt onto the sides of the tents. Sanela hurried to pack up Nehrudin and her diapers and other baby things. Zlatija and Hiba got together the hand-me-down clothes and shoes and the sponge pads, blankets, and kitchen utensils they had received from an aid organization. And they all fled one last time. Even after the UN had set up the long rows of white tents, Tuzla airport had remained a Bosnian army base. Serb gunners had fired mortars into the airport for years; and their guns were so close to it that the target spotters could see people strolling on the airport tarmac. But Paja and many other Muslims who had been in the refugee camp figured the Bosnian army, the Muslims, might just as easily have fired the dud rounds, knowing they would shoo the refugees out and make it seem as if the Serbs had done it.

Sanela and Nehrudin traveled to a village about twenty miles north of Tuzla and settled in with her mother-in-law in a classroom at an elementary school jammed with other widows and fatherless children. Paja and Senad walked from farmhouse to farmhouse along the airport's periphery, looking for somewhere to live, and within a few hours they had rented Šaban's upper floor. It was the tenth place where the Čeliks had taken shelter since the war began—counting the cave in Žepa and the lean-to in the forest where they slept the night before they hiked into Srebrenica. Paja convinced Šaban he would be able to pay him thirty-five dollars a month in rent once Hamed managed to send some money from Toronto. For this amount the Čeliks got a bedroom, a storage closet, and a kitchen with a woodstove, a table, two wooden chairs, and one lightbulb that dangled by a wire from the ceiling and emitted a dirty amber glow whenever there was electricity. The drinking water came from a spigot in the yard out back, and there was an outhouse about thirty steps from the foot of the stairs. I never figured out where they bathed, and didn't ask.

The Bosnian army drafted Paja a few days after they moved into Šaban's place. He was issued a stiff new uniform and a pair of jackboots and was happy to be assigned to the kitchen of a mess hall just up the road because it meant he wouldn't have to go into the trenches for the time being. Before leaving for his first two-week tour of duty, Paja went to register the family with the local government's refugee-relief department. But the clerks there told Paja that he had come weeks too late to sign up for humanitarian food aid, so he persuaded Šaban to feed the family.

Šaban was happy to see me, and happy to share his brandy, because he knew I would be bringing the cash. He was fortunate to have tenants who could pay him thirty-five dollars a month, about ten times the average monthly income in Bosnia during the war. It was my good fortune to be back in Bosnia, too, even if only for a quick dose of freedom and the old mania. The adventure, the groin-quivering excitement of the war, and the hunt for a good story were all still there, and I was rested. Even before the dimensions of the Srebrenica massacre became clear, I knew I could not sit still in New York and let the story go by. I offered a piece about the Čeliks to the *New York Times Magazine*, but the editor there said he didn't want it; so I called *Rolling Stone*, and by the end of the next day I knew I was going to take a trip back to Bosnia, and the Čeliks weren't going to have to worry about money for a year or two. Hamed and Gordana drove down from Canada with their kids before I left home. The wives jammed everything they could into my suitcases. Diapers and lotions for the baby. T-shirts with silk-screen pictures of cartoon characters for the boys. Athletic shoes for Paja. A pair of boots for Zlatija. Several yards of fabric to make *dimije*. Some cheap plastic toys. Cartons of Marlboros. And a stack of immigration forms, courtesy of the Canadian consulate on Sixth Avenue in Manhattan.

Even under the drab glow of the lightbulb, the kitchen upstairs at Šaban's place resembled a bargain basement in Cleveland after the suitcases sprang open. The clothing and shoes and toys and candy and cartons of Marlboros flew through the air. I took Paja aside and handed him a wad of cash, most of it from Hamed. Then I translated the instructions on the Advil and Children's Tylenol bottles and tickled Edin and Mirza until they turned pink. Paja found some snapshots of Hamed and Gordana and the kids, and I told them about the doughnut shop where Hamed worked and their apartment a few minutes' walk from the mall, and the kids' thirty-gallon aquarium, and the color television, and the car, and the twenty-foot balcony. I managed to keep my notebooks and tape recorder inside my bag for the next hour or so. But after I had passed around all the snapshots and told all the stories from Canada, the tales I had come for in the first place began to trickle out.

The stories were detailed. They emerged in a chronological order that began with the day the Serb militia on Mount Zvijezda burned fluorescent-pink crosses in the night sky with their tracer bullets. Senad drew me a map showing Juz-bin's mosque, the Cross, the empty meadow called the Customs Area, the houses in Kupusovići, Odžak, and Zlijeb and the names of the families who lived in them. "Here's the schoolhouse," he said, "here, right next to Dragoljub's." Then he launched into the story about Behadil's hidden cannon and the meeting where Behadil's jealous Serb neighbor warned that he had buried his machine gun.

"Where's Behadil now?"

"Disappeared in Potočari," Hiba answered from down by the woodstove. The room went silent. Hiba shook her head and mumbled, "Oy, oy." Then she swatted one of the boys for swiping another *bonbon*, and Paja picked up the story of the meeting in the schoolhouse and hurled us back to World War II: "That's where they kept the men, right in that schoolhouse." He told me what he knew about his grandfathers, he showed me the gold wrist-watch Huso had left for him, he described making brandy with Dragoljub Radovanović and Branko Mitrašinović and drinking with Mile Janković. Paja called them all Chetniks for a while. But he wasn't convincing. I told him I would try to go to Kupusovići and talk to the Serbs. He looked at me as if I were crazy, and Hiba giggled again like a chipmunk and said it would be great if she could go too.

SANELA came to Šaban's house with Nehrudin a day or two later. She was frailer and had more resolve in her eyes than I had imagined. She smoked one cigarette After another as she told her story. I held off asking her about the last day together with Muhamed until the very end of our conversation. She started crying, and I pried for a few minutes more before she held up her hand and stopped talking.

We sat for a few minutes in the silence. Zlatija poured some colas. Sanela took a cigarette. And I pulled out an immigration application and after a few minutes was asking questions to fill in the blanks.

"Last name?"

"Halilović."

"Permanent address?"

"Primary School, Špionica, Bosnia."

"Identification card number?"

"Haven't got one."

"Passport number?"

"No passport."

"Marital status?"

"Married."

I checked off the "Married" box, slipped a question mark next to the box for "Widowed," and scratched in a sentence explaining the ambiguity.

When we finished Sanela's application, I took a second form and filled it out for Muhamed and clipped his high school picture to it. Sanela signed her name to her form, quickly and automatically in the Serbian Cyrillic alphabet, the script she had learned back in the schoolhouse in Odžak, the script Vaso Erić had taught himself to read and write as a boy so long ago when the Muslim authorities were banning the Serbs in Kravica from organizing a school. I recalled that my wife, Ljiljana had sent Gordana some children's picture books printed in Cyrillic and that Hamed sent them back; he didn't want anything printed in Cyrillic in his house.

"How can you sign your name in Cyrillic?" I asked.

"I have always signed my name in Cyrillic," she replied. "Why?"

I changed the subject. I told her it would probably take a year or more for her visa to be issued. She was happy to hear it. "I have to wait here anyway," she said.

Sanela still believed in miracles then. She had seen miracles happen for other Muslim wives and mothers. Some Muslim men had taken refuge in the forests near Srebrenica after the massacre. They straggled across the front lines at night and made their way to Tuzla with stories of other Muslim men living behind the Serb lines, sheltering in deserted Muslim villages on the flanks of Zlovrh, villages deep in the forests overlooking the gorge Jerina the Damned had cut between it and Mount Zvijezda to keep the Drina from flooding her lands. A handful of Serbs had moved into Srebrenica. The streets were piled with garbage and refuse left by the soldiers who had plundered the town. Rats and stray dogs sniffed through the trash for food scraps. The Serbs were abandoning the town at night for fear of Muslim men who were coming down to scavenge for food under the cover of darkness, and it wasn't long before I heard Serbs telling me about how people were hearing shrieks and cries for help near Srebrenica's schoolyard by night.

Sanela had gone to a *hodža* seeking information about Muhamed a few weeks after she had arrived in Tuzla. The *hodža's* name was Almir. He was pudgy, a peasant in his early twenties, with light curly hair, gray eyes, and a few missing teeth. He lived beside a lake just west of Tuzla, in a cinder block house whose interior was kept immaculately clean. On the day Sanela visited him, Almir was wearing a violet athletic suit. He showed her to a couch in a sitting room and sat in a chair across the room. On the wall above Sanela's head hung a cut-velvet, souvenir-style carpet with images of the Islamic shrines in Mecca and Jerusalem in deep golds, reds, and greens with black trim. On the side of the room facing toward Mecca hung a citation from the Koran in a frame with a towel draped over it.

Almir had gone to school to study the Koran but never finished the course. He says Allah blessed him with a mystical power, a power he discovered accidentally when he correctly prophesied that a woman from his village would give birth to a son. Some of the men on his mother's side of the family had been dervishes, and Almir refined his mystical powers by studying with a dervish for eight years. He showed Almir how to cure the sick and taught him the special prayers for exorcising demons and the art of locating missing people through numerology.

Almir asked Sanela the names of her husband and her mother-in-law and attached a number to every letter in the names Muhamed and Naza. He added the numbers together, then divided the sum, first by twelve and then by a secret number. When he obtained the final quotient, Almir opened a ring notebook in which he had arranged the tattered pages of an Arabic book protected by transparent plastic folders. He used the quotient to look up a passage from the Koran.

"Muhamed is tall . . . light haired. . . . He has a mole on his right cheek."

Sanela nodded that he was correct.

"He lived above a crossroads."

Correct. There was a small dirt road that veered off toward the north right in front of the Halilović house.

"Someone in the family was opposed to your marriage."

"His aunt," Sanela answered.

"Muhamed is alive," Almir the *hodža* pronounced. He assured Sanela that Muhamed's father, Smail, was also alive, but he could not say anything about the fate of Muhamed's brother, Hajrudin. Almir also told Sanela that he could not tell her anything more about Muhamed until he had additional information. He instructed her to find a virgin girl who would volunteer to follow a ritual and attempt to dream about Muhamed. The virgin had to have blue eyes, Almir said, and she could not be a relative. She had to recite a prayer and refrain from eating before she went to sleep, and she had to slip a picture of Muhamed under the pillow she slept on. If the girl woke up without having a dream, she had to pray again before she tried to go back to sleep.

Sanela found a virgin and returned to Almir a few days later to tell the *hodža* what the girl had dreamed.

"She saw Muhamed on a bluff, but he didn't say anything to her," Sanela told Almir. "She said he is tall. She said she walked along the bluff and came to a house where there were two old people, a couple, a man and his wife. They were separating plums, the bad from the good. One of them picked up a plum, and the other said, 'Keep that one for him. Let him eat it when he comes.' Then she said she went into the house and baked bread, dark bread. After that, she went outside the house and saw a puppy. Then she woke up."

The dream was obscure, Almir said, and problematic. But the fact that the old man and woman were selecting plums certainly had something to do with life and death. He assured Sanela again that Muhamed was alive.

Sanela visited other *hodže* and fortune-tellers every few days, seeking more information. Thousands of women who came out of Srebrenica were doing the same thing. One old mystic, a women who had visions when she kneeled to pray, passed Sanela a message that she had seen an apparition: three men, alive; one deathly ill, two of them healthy.

"He is alive," another old woman assured her. "He is imprisoned in a labor camp surrounded by water. In six months or in six years, a woman will come to you. She will come from afar. She will tell you of him. . . ."

This, Sanela told me, was the reason she was relieved that it would take a long time for her visa to Canada to be processed. This was why she wanted to wait with her mother-in-law in a classroom of a village school crowded with other widows and orphans. She wanted to wait for Muhamed.

"It was not like them to surrender," she said. "Never."

(((

PAJA, Senad, and I talked for the next five or six days, all the while swatting flies and mosquitoes and listening to the pounding of artillery that was beating the Serbs back from a front line across the lake from Almir the *hodža's* house. The weather was still hot and muggy for September in Bosnia, and, on the next to last day, Paja and I were sitting at a picnic table behind Šaban's farmhouse and talking with Muhamed's cousin about the last time he saw Muhamed and his father alive on the hillside above Kravica. American jets had bombed a Serb communications tower a few miles away the evening before, and radio reports said the Muslim army had just forced the Serbs away from a highway between Tuzla and central Bosnia.

A cool rain began to fall. From the west, we heard the rattle of machine guns and the growl and squeaky clatter of a tank approaching along an asphalt road. Tracer bullets rose into the sodden air and petered out like cheap Roman candles. Šaban and the neighbors shouted with glee. They waved their hands and smiled. Some of them ran the few hundred yards to the roadside and pulled out pistols and fired into the air. Edin began to sob. Mirza scurried after his mother, shouting and whimpering the whole while: "They're going to kill us all. They're going to kill us all." Zlatija and Hiba carried the crying boys up the stairs and into the kitchen and tried to explain to them that the happy, drunken soldiers shooting into the air were Muslims, not Serbs. The commotion was the first victory parade any of us had ever seen.

Muslim refugees who had not sunk into despair talked incessantly of fighting their way home in those days, and the victory across the lake from Almir's house cheered everyone. Paja and the rest of the surviving Čeliks, however, understood that even if the Muslims managed to advance to the east, to Srebrenica, to the Drina's left bank, there was hardly a chance they would ever be able to cross the river and return to Kupusovići and their home and fields. Mount Zvijezda would probably remain in Serb hands on any postwar map, regardless of where the mapmakers drew Bosnia's border. Or so it seemed. And the question loomed whether it would be worth returning even if the opportunity arose. There was nothing left of the house — Paja had seen that through binoculars from a hillside across the Drina before they fled to Srebrenica. He had no will to fight to liberate someone else's home, knowing he had no home of his own. He had no heart for taking vengeance upon anyone; and unlike the Serbs', his dead were not demanding it of him so that they could make their way to the afterlife. We mulled over a scheme to smuggle Paja out of Bosnia, to Croatia or up to Uncle Avdo's in Austria, but we let the idea drop. It would be best to wait for the Canadians.

THE next morning, Paja and I got into the car and drove to the refugee-relief office of the local government. Some tired, disgruntled men were hanging around outside. Tacked to the door was a notice saying that if refugees from Srebrenica had not signed up to receive food aid by some date in mid-August, they were not eligible to sign up any more.

I knocked on the door, and Paja pushed it open without waiting for word from inside. We found a couple of middle-aged women sitting in a cloud of cigarette smoke and cheap perfume behind some desks. "Good day," I said, introducing myself and Paja. "My friend here has a problem he would like to explain to you."

Paja told the women that there was no way he could have registered as a refugee, because no one was being allowed to leave the airport before the registration period ran out.

"I understand, but there is nothing I can do," one of the women said.

"Who can do something?" I asked.

"The director, perhaps."

"Where is the director?"

"She is not here."

"Who is the director's boss?"

"The district government."

"Who is the person responsible?"

She gave me a name.

"Can you call him, please?"

She got the man's secretary on the phone, and I told her I was an American journalist. I said I had to speak with him urgently to get some idea of the difficulties of managing the refugee problem in the district after the fall of Srebrenica. He agreed to meet me for an interview the next morning.

The man, whose name I have forgotten and did not bother to write down, worked in an office building in the center of Tuzla. He was wearing a burnt-orange suit when we walked in. I introduced myself and Paja, referring to him as Mr. Čelik.

"He is a distant relative of mine," I said, "and he has a serious problem that we'd like to have cleared up as quickly as possible because I have to go back to New York and don't want to leave until this matter is resolved." I explained the problem, the Catch-22, his people had created. Paja sat back, and the man in the burnt-orange suit shook his head and pretended not to know anything about the situation.

"This bothers me," I said, "because I have to go home in a day or so, and I don't want to leave Mr. Čelik and his family without being sure that they are going to have a source of food."

"And frankly," I went on, "I have to tell you that I think this is a helluva story, especially since the United States Air Force is flying overhead right now bombing the Serbs to kingdom come and the rest of the world is pouring aid into this place because of these Muslims from Srebrenica. Now, is there a way you can explain to me how it is possible that someone who has sat in a shit hole like Srebrenica for the last three years and lived through a horror that has won Tuzla a great deal of notoriety can be told by some clerk that he cannot register to obtain the food that is meant for people like him? Can you explain this to me? Because the story I'm hearing from refugees all over your area is that each family has to slip fifty or a hundred dollars under the table to register in the district. And the story I'm hearing from my friends over at the United Nations is that your people are selling food given to you by people in other countries who are trying to help people here."

The man in the suit turned burnt orange himself and shook his head again, smiled unctuously and asked me to calm down: "No problem," he lilted. "No problem."

"Yes, problem," I snapped. "Big problem."

He asked for Paja's name again and jotted down the address of Šaban's farmhouse. Then he made a phone call, and Paja got his refugee papers. I left for New York the next afternoon. A few days later, the police came around asking Šaban whether Paja had been causing any trouble.

(((

PRESIDENT SLOBODAN MILOŠEVIĆ of Serbia summoned the nationalist leaders of the Bosnian Serbs to Belgrade after the NATO bombing campaign began. He upbraided the Bosnian Serb leaders for bringing disaster upon themselves and the entire Serb nation. He chastised them for refusing time and again to follow his advice and trade land for peace. Milošević had a piece of paper for them to sign, a document authorizing him to negotiate on behalf of the Bosnian Serbs at a new round of peace talks. The humbled Bosnian Serb leaders signed the paper. The United States instructed the Croats and Muslims to halt their advance against the Serbs in Bosnia, and, ten weeks later, after stalling to see how much Izetbegović and the other Muslim leaders were willing to concede to him, Milošević put his signature to a peace treaty in Dayton, Ohio.

The Serbian president recognized the existence of the Bosnian state within its original frontiers, including the borderline running along the crest of Mount Zvijezda and down the Drina. He agreed that the Bosnian Serb army would release its hold on the suburbs around Sarajevo it had seized in 1992. He agreed to the return of all refugees to their homes and to the arrest of all persons indicted by the international war-crimes tribunal in The Hague. The deal, however, left the Bosnian Serb nationalists and their "police"—the very thugs who had started the violence in the first place—in de facto control of almost half of Bosnia's territory, including Srebrenica, Žepa, Višegrad, Zvornik, Bijeljina, and other towns whose Muslim-majority populations had been decimated and expelled. Milošević, the prime mover behind Yugoslavia's plunge into disintegration and war, was now hailed by Western leaders as a "peacemaker." American news broadcasts and talk shows bubbled over with praise for the State Department's negotiating team. By the spring of 1996, some 20,000 U.S. troops had landed in Bosnia as part of a 60,000-strong NATO force deployed to enforce the peace agreement.

1996

A CHILLING rain fell on Srebrenica the day before the anniversary. It gushed from the downspouts, flowed in sheets of gray ink down the streets, and collected in the shell holes and gutters. Policemen huddled beneath an overhang in the town square and sucked on their Marlboros. The nearby market stalls were deserted except for a haggard woman dressed in mourning who sat under a black umbrella and waited for someone to step up and buy her packs of Marlboros and throw-away lighters. It took five or six tries before I found someone who knew the way to Rudarska Street. He was the first native of Srebrenica I had hit upon, a friendly old man dressed in a woolen jacket. He took my arm, pulled me under his umbrella, and led me by the park and up the crumbling asphalt road beside the Energoinvest mining company's building. "There," he said, pointing up the hill. "Right there."

Cement stepping stones climbed into a yard overgrown with weeds before passing the apple tree. The door to the decaying, pink-stucco house hung open, and no one answered when I knocked and shouted, "Hallo." The floor of the hallway inside pitched to the left. The fusty air soured my nose and tongue. Grains of plaster crunched underfoot. The room at the end of the hall looked as if it had been the bathroom, but the tub, the hot-water heater, the toilet, and the sink had been ripped from the walls and carried off by looters. Just to the right was the room where Huso and Hiba had been living, alone at the end. Rummaging through a pile of rags, plaster dust, and the guts of a couch, I came upon a puppy-love diary belonging to one of Sanela's teenage cousins, a pair of wooden-soled clogs, shreds of Red Cross letter paper, a dented metal pot, and cylindrical pieces of wood from which Huso carved cigarette holders just like Tito's. At the top of the hill behind the house, water was pouring through a hole in the roof of the Halilović home. It had been looted and burned. Its balcony stared blankly out at the town. There was no sign of the cable that had once run down to the generator at Smail's hydroelectric dam.

Across the way from the Čeliks' place, the house Veljko Vasić had built for his wife, Dragica, was also still deserted. Sheets of orange plastic covered the hole blasted in its roof the day the crop duster growled overhead and dropped the mortar rounds. The looters seemed to have taken everything else of value. I had been hoping to find Dragica, but didn't bother to knock. Serb refugees squatting in Muslim houses nearby said they had never heard of Dragica. But a wizened old woman who had been her neighbor for years before the war invited me into the basement of a nearby house where she was living.

"Dragica's over in Serbia, at least she was," she said. "She's with her sisters in Banja Koviljača, God bless her, and just look at us here in this nightmare. Her son went off to Holland with his wife. Dragica's supposed to be going, too." The woman boiled me a cup of Turkish coffee and said she had waited out the war in Serbia. She came back to Srebrenica with her son right after the town fell. Their house was cluttered with furniture. Its walls were freshly painted, and white and red geraniums were bursting like fireworks from her flower boxes. The woman kept watch over the place while her son was at work. He had been a soldier; now he was a policeman.

"We've got nothing here now," the woman said. "Nothing to live for. It was all for nothing."

"Do you know about the people who lived here during the war? Do you know what became of them?"

"They went away," she said. "That's all I know. They just went away."

❄   ❄   ❄

By the time I moved back to Yugoslavia in June 1996, Slobodan Milošević and the nationalist Serb leadership in Bosnia had reneged on every pledge made at Dayton concerning the return of refugees and the arrest of persons indicted for war crimes. UNPROFOR had been disbanded and replaced by NATO. General Janvier had been assigned to head the French army's War College and was obeying orders not to speak to the press. Boutros-Ghali had promoted Yasushi Akashi to the position of UN under secretary-general for humanitarian affairs. I spoke once with Akashi at his office overlooking the East River in New York. We spent an hour trading questions and answers about Resolution 836 and whether the UN Security Council had ever really promised to protect the safe areas. He said he felt perfectly comfortable with the decision not to call in air attacks on Mladić's forces before it was too late. I asked him whether he and Janvier had taken into account the fact that the Serbs had warned time and again that they had a vendetta against the Muslim men of Srebrenica. "No," he answered, "this never entered into our thinking." As I got up to leave, he volunteered an insight into his feelings about Srebrenica and perhaps why the vendetta did not enter into their thinking. "Oh, those men of Srebrenica," he said, "such thieves, such a black market, such a mafia."

Despite the absence of war, Radovan Karadžić and Momčilo Krajišnik were still the predominant Bosnian Serb political leaders in the summer of 1996; Nikola Koljević, the unctuous Shakespeare professor who had bailed them out of jail, had a few more months to live before he would commit suicide; General Ratko Mladić still commanded the Bosnian Serb army from his underground headquarters near Han Pijesak and made occasional trips to Belgrade; Radislav Krstić, the man who reportedly executed Mladić's order to kill the prisoners at Srebrenica, was still the commander of the Bosnian Serb army's Drina Corps in the town of Vlasenica. A team of gunmen who were under Mladić's direct command and who executed thousands of Muslim men and boys captured after Srebrenica's fall were living quietly in Bijeljina, taking their meals at the army barracks, spending their nights drinking and whoring in a café called The Montenegro, and bilking foreign journalists out of money to tell their story. One of them, Dražen Erdemović, surrendered to the war-crimes tribunal in The Hague and testified about how he and members of his unit (who were Croats, Muslims, Slovenes, and Serbs) had been ordered by the military intelligence headquarters of the Bosnian Serb army to shoot thousands of unarmed prisoners at a poultry farm in the village of Pilići, just up the road from the farm in Križevačke Njive where Hurem Suljić had survived a similar execution. A few members of Erdemović's group would eventually enlist as mercenaries in Mobutu's army in Zaire.

The nationalist Serbs had released their stranglehold around Sarajevo that March, but only after NATO troops stood by and watched as Serb police thugs drove about eighty thousand Serb civilians from their homes in the city's suburbs and sent them scrambling to find Muslim houses abandoned in Srebrenica, Višegrad, and other captured towns in eastern Bosnia. Most of the Serb city folk who arrived in Srebrenica came in cars, and many of them were pulling trailers loaded with washing machines, beds, dressers, and other appliances and furniture. Some Serb men exhumed the bodies of their dead from the cemeteries in Ilidža and Blažuj and other Sarajevo suburbs; they packed the remains into plastic bags and carried them away to be reburied in cemeteries close to their new homes, close enough for the spirits of the departed to be attended to properly.

The Serbs who first arrived in Srebrenica occupied the best of the deserted Muslim homes and cannibalized everything that had not been looted by the soldiers a year earlier from the other houses and apartments. Garbage and trash were still piling up in the streets and gave off a choking stench. The mines were still shut down; none of the factories could operate, because all of their equipment had been destroyed or looted and taken to Serbia.

The Civilian Affairs Committee of Srebrenica, with Miroslav Deronjić presiding, became a "welcome wagon" for the arriving Serbs. The local authorities numbered the houses and supervised their allocation. They oversaw the distribution of humanitarian aid. Since everything had to be done officially, and on paper, Deronjić had printed up forms for each of the Serbs to fill out and sign. And he answered their complaints with empty promises uttered in a reassuring voice.

B Y the afternoon of the anniversary, July 11, the miserable rain in Srebrenica had been battered back by a miserable sunshine that beat down on a small group of people who assembled in the park for a commemoration of General Mladić's "liberation" of the town. They listened attentively as speakers urged them to remain true to the independence of the Republika Srpska and its future union with Serbia. "We must show the world we don't want to live with Muslims," one speaker urged. The people clapped respectfully and nodded their heads.

Toward the front of the park, near some benches whose wood had been stripped away, the civilian authorities unveiled a pair of gray slabs of polished stone inscribed with a poem, a heroic epitaph carved in graceful Cyrillic letters:

> Brave avengers of Kosovo,
> May you rest in peace
> Because you have bequeathed us better times.
> We are warmed from every direction
> By the sunbeams of freedom.
> And the wounds of Kosovo
> Are painful no more.

The stones had been hidden away by a peasant somewhere in Kara Marko's Territory for fifty-five years before they found their way into the park for the anniversary commemoration. The peasant had rescued them after the Ustaše destroyed the memorial to Major Kosta Todorović, the Serb army officer whose spy network smuggled Gavrilo Princip into Bosnia and whose rebels fought the Austrian army in the skirmish where Huso Čelik's grandfather Salih was killed. Karadžić and Mladić were supposed to attend the anniversary memorial, but neither of them showed up. Earlier that morning, the international war-crimes tribunal in The Hague had indicted them on charges connected with the Srebrenica massacre. Mladić received the news in his headquarters near Han Pijesak; Karadžić was in his capital city, Pale, still poring over maps of his domain and gnawing at his fingernails, still chirping about investment and gloating over blueprints of a "Serb Sarajevo" with shopping malls, apartment blocks for two hundred thousand people, luxury ski chalets, and a psychiatric clinic next to his official residence.

S O M E six thousand of the Muslim women of Srebrenica were seated in the bleachers on each side of the sports arena in Tuzla for their anniversary memorial on that same afternoon. They had covered the arena's entire back wall with a tapestry of pillow cases crocheted with the names of men who had disappeared after the town fell. The harsh sunlight flooded through the windows and turned the air into a chalky yellow dust. This was the first time I had been in the Tuzla arena since April 1993, when its basketball floor was covered with sponge pads and gray blankets and crowded with women and children who had jammed aboard UN food trucks and escaped Srebrenica. Many of the same women were back again, perched in the bleachers, waiting patiently to see if the authorities might use the occasion to give them some word of their menfolk. At the door, the memorial's organizers had passed out copies of a letter of support signed by distinguished women from the world over, whom none of the women in the bleachers had ever heard of; they folded the sheets of paper on which the letter had been printed and fanned themselves with them. I looked for Sanela in the crowd; she was sitting with some friends near the top row of bleachers, but I didn't see her from down on the basketball court where a small army of journalists was milling around.

The leaders of the Srebrenica women had organized and planned the memorial with the help of the American government. They designed it to remind the world of what had happened at Srebrenica rather than to comfort or diminish the grief of the women survivors. Most of the women in the bleachers hadn't had an opportunity to read anything about Srebrenica in an entire year and didn't have televisions to watch. Bosnia's Muslim leaders, afraid they might be called to account for the military fiasco that led to the deaths of about eight thousand people, had buried the issue. The only information the women had about their missing menfolk had come from the visions of fortune-tellers, from *hodža* using secret numbers and tattered books, and from men who survived and found their way across the battlefront. The women passed their information from one to the next. They told each other stories that the Serbs were holding thousands of Muslim prisoners, stories that the men of Srebrenica were slaves in Serbia and forced to live and work in underground mines, stories that Serbs were discreetly demanding thousands of dollars in ransom for each prisoner.

The women waved their paper fans and applauded politely after a speaker read a few lines of heroic verse in a defiant voice. The mistress of ceremonies then directed everyone's attention to a large movie screen just to her right. She announced that everyone would now watch a special videotaped presentation. She said the world could not deny what had happened at Srebrenica. The tape machine rolled. A narrator with a deep voice began a commentary so distorted by the public-address system's speakers that no one in the arena could understand it. But none of the women had to. Almost all of them recognized the faces on the screen immediately, for they were seeing themselves on the tape General Mladić's cameraman had shot. They were seeing themselves huddled beside a fence near the decrepit battery factory in Potočari on July 12, 1995. They were seeing themselves file down the asphalt road, carrying their bags and bedding and climbing aboard buses. They were seeing themselves huddling around Mladić, the man who had not even come out of hiding to attend the Serb memorial ceremony.

Howls and screams sounded from the bleachers as if the devil himself had materialized from the chalky air. The scene on the movie screen shifted. And now the women were watching pictures of Muslim men surrendering near Kravica, pictures of men emerging from a forest, walking through waist-high grass down the hill behind the farmers' co-op, their hands raised, their eyes silent and befuddled.

Both sides of the arena erupted in cries of anguish. Women bellowed and covered their eyes with their fingertips and screamed for the tape to stop.

"That's my husband!" a voice in the crowd shouted. "That's my husband! Ahhhhh! Ahhhh! Ahhhh!"

Women fainted, and other women around them huddled in concentric rings, signaling for attention with their hands, using the letters to fan air into the faces of the unconscious.

"Help! Help!" they called. "Stop it! Stop it!"

"My husband! My husband! That's my husband!"

No one thought to switch off the tape player, to stop the torture. More women shrieked and clutched their hands over their heads and swayed to and fro. They looked skyward, arms reaching into the dusty air, appealing to the Almighty with mouths open and teeth protruding. They sat still and shook their heads and cupped their hands over their mouths.

"Remain in your seats," a voice commanded over the loudspeaker. "Remain in your seats so we can bear witness to what has happened."

More women fainted. And each time one tumbled over and the women nearby gathered around her, the television crews on the basketball floor scurried over to catch the images of the stiff torso and flopping arms and legs being lifted up and handed down, one row to the next until she landed clumsily in the arms of policemen waiting beneath a railing on the basketball floor.

"Please sit down," the voice on the loudspeaker commanded. "Be seated! We must bear witness! Be seated!"

The crowd calmed down only when the screen went blank. There was a hushed confusion on the stage for a few minutes as more unconscious women were handed down from the bleachers and carried out into a waiting room. Then the mistress of ceremonies took the podium and introduced President Clinton's ambassador to Austria, Swanee Hunt, one of the women from the fabulously rich Hunt family of Dallas. The ambassador had been a staunch supporter of Bosnia and Herzegovina during the war and helped raise millions of dollars for the survivors of Srebrenica.

"Please, sit down," the ambassador drawled in the singsong of a Texas debutante. "Please, listen to my message." A woman translated her musical words into a barking command, and the crowd fell silent. The fainting stopped. The women sat down and seemed to listen.

"Thank you," the ambassador lilted. "Thank you." She began reading a speech. "Women of Srebrenica, . . . one year ago . . . as I watched what happened to you . . . all I could do was cry." She went on to say that as Srebrenica was falling she received a telephone call from Queen Noor, the wife of Jordan's King Hussein, and that they decided they had to do something to help.

"We could not stop your terror, but we did not forget you." The women in the bleachers waved their fans and chattered about what had appeared on the movie screen. The television crews scanned the crowd, looking for more women passing out. The ambassador spoke slowly about her conversation with the queen so that the translator would not fall behind, but the words came out sounding as if she were talking with children: "I said . . . , 'Your majesty, . . . let us . . . work together . . . for the women of Srebrenica.'

". . . So we began reaching out in your name . . . and we reached right into the hearts of women all over the world. . . . We sent out a thousand letters to women all over the world . . . the letter you now have in your hands. . . . You are fanning yourselves with it. . . . If you don't have a copy of the letter, make sure you have one today, because two hundred and fifty women leaders from all over the world have put their names on it. . . . It is with a strong sense of hope that we bring you this message. . . ."

Sitting high up in the bleachers, Sanela waited to see if anyone was going to tell her anything about Muhamed. Did they have any information? Could they tell her and any of the other women anything? She had no idea what Ambassador Hunt was talking about. She felt dizzy and worried that she might pass out or throw up.

". . . We know . . . and we care," the ambassador said. ". . . We know you must find out what happened to your husbands, sons, brothers, and fathers, and we will give help. . . . We know you need to see justice done, and we will help you. . . . We know you need help to rebuild your lives. You need jobs and schools for your children, and we will help you. . . . We've come here today to stand with you. . . . We've come with concrete support. . . ."

I was standing on the basketball floor taking all this down in my notebook, knowing full well that the State Department opposed an exhumation and identification of the remains in the three dozen mass graves around Srebrenica because it would cost tens of millions of dollars. Even a complete exhumation would have left a long list of missing people: the Serbs from Bratunac and Kravica had exhumed the bodies from a mass grave they had dug in Glogova and dumped all of their bodies in the Drina, and Serbs from other areas did the same with other graves that might have yielded forensic evidence against them. I was still taking notes and thinking about how the women of Srebrenica would probably remain on the dole for the rest of their lives, when one of my friends strolled over. His name is Ron Haviv. He is a war photographer, a New Yorker.

"You know, Srebrenica was a silver-mining town," Ron said.

"Yeah, I know."

"I wonder how badly hit Srebrenica was when the Hunt brothers fucked up the silver market twenty years ago."

THE next afternoon, Bosnia's nationalist Muslim party had its commemoration in Tuzla. An election campaign was just gathering pace, and placards with the green-and-white logo of Alija Izetbegović's Party for Democratic Action and portraits of the party's candidates were splattered everywhere in town. The candidates also wanted to stage a media event to show Muslims all over Bosnia just how much solidarity the party and the government had with the women of Srebrenica.

Even before the commemoration began, women started throwing pebbles and clumps of dirt at the local officials from the refugee-relief committee. They jeered at the local politicians. When a district official took the podium, a loud roar went up.

"Thieves! Thieves! Thieves!" the women chanted. "Where are our husbands? Where are our husbands?"

Again the official tried to mount the podium and speak, but the crowd grew even more unruly. Scuffles broke out between the women and the police.

"Thieves! Thieves! Thieves!"

Just when it seemed the commemoration would have to be postponed, a young man with a trimmed beard stepped to the rostrum. He stood behind the microphone as if at attention, and his biceps and pectorals seemed to burst through his button-down shirt when he held up his arms and signaled for attention. The women fell into a hush in an instant. The young man gazed out at them with steely, sharply moving eyes. He had no speech prepared. He was supposed to have been standing in silence behind the candidates seeking election; he was supposed to have been part of the stage setting. Now he spoke anyway. And he told the women that the truth of Srebrenica and its fall would someday be revealed. He told everyone to remain calm and remain patient. Then he stepped back, and the commemoration went on in peace.

The young man's name was Naser Orić. He was living in an apartment in Tuzla then, running a café on the lake near Almir the *hodža*'s house and cruising around town in a black Audi with no license plates. We talked a few weeks after the commemoration in an office across from Tuzla's bus station. He assumed, wrongly, that war-crimes investigators were examining his connection with the killings of Serbs around Srebrenica in 1992 and 1993. "They are attributing all that killing to me because I was the commander," he said. "But they are afraid to arrest me. They haven't gotten the men from the other side. Imagine them arresting me without having in custody the men who killed ten thousand people." Orić's face made it clear that civilian life was boring him. He inquired about life in Belgrade and asked me to get him a photograph of his house back in Potočari. "This life here is miserable," he said. "It is always miserable to be living in a place where you know you don't belong. . . . All I want to do now is to go back to my own home. To my own town. To the land of my grandfathers."

"Just give me the guns," he added, "and we'll be back there in a couple of weeks." The Bosnian army, afraid of the Kurtz-like spell Orić held over his men, later disbanded the division that had been under his command. The army's commander, Rasim Delić, gave Orić and his family the right to occupy an apartment in an army-owned building even though he had been officially discharged. President Izetbegović's inner circle in the Party for Democratic Action saw to it that Orić received seed capital to launch an imports business.

❬   ❬   ❬

IN the year after the killings, hundreds of bodies rotted away in the meadows and woodlots and forests on the hillside above the farmers' co-op in Kravica. Corpses lay strewn about the hilltop above the Konjević Polje road where Senad had watched the aid warehouse director spreading jam on his cookies. Skulls and ribs and blood-stained bandages lay along the path Paja and Deba followed down to the soccer field in Nova Kasaba. One of the piles of bones along the path had to have been Uncle Ismet's neighbor, the tobacco cutter; another, perhaps, was Deba's brother, Bedži. Across the road was the body of a man who had been tied to a cement post before he was killed.

My friend Miguel Gil Moreno and I hiked the hills above Srebrenica a few times during that July and August. Miguel is a Spaniard from Catalonia, and I remember when he rode across Sarajevo's airport on a motorcycle to write stories for *El Mundo* after becoming disillusioned with the daily grind in some

Barcelona law firm. Miguel is also a devout Catholic, and during that summer he had a cross hanging from a chain around his neck. He fashioned the cross from a piece of wire that had been used to bind the hands of one of the men whose skeleton was found inside one of the mass graves.

Miguel and I looked for the skeletons of Sanela's husband, Muhamed, and his brother and father on the hillside above Kravica. We read the names on the tattered identification cards strewn about. We used a stick to poke through layers of clothing and search for a T-shirt with "Marco Polo" silk-screened across the back. I dipped my hand into the pockets of every brown jacket I found but never turned up the snapshot of Sanela that Muhamed had tucked in his pocket the evening he kissed her good-bye.

Rodents, birds, and insects had picked all the flesh from the skeletons of men who had died in the open. Larger mammals had carried off many of their skulls. Mold, dried by the sun, had stained and stiffened the clothing, which was infested with tiny gray flies and had become twisted around bare femurs and tibiae and ranks of vertebrae. The remains of those who had been wounded, their legs and arms still wrapped in blood-stained gauze, lay on stretchers made from woolen blankets and tree branches. The bones of men who died along lumber trails had been ground into the earth under the wheels of the horse carts used by Serb refugees to haul wood for heating the Muslim homes they were squatting in. Scavengers had made off with whatever money they found, along with the gold teeth, the guns, and anything else that might fetch a price. They had left behind the volumes of the Koran, the family photos, the used syringes, and the empty red tins from the Moroccan sardines that tasted as if they had been packed in motor oil. It would take until the fall of 1996 before the Muslims and Serbs reached an agreement that allowed a Bosnian government commission to gather up most of these unburned skeletons and take them in body bags to Tuzla.

❮   ❮   ❮

PAJA had missed out on the rush by the Muslims from Srebrenica to take over Serb houses abandoned around Sarajevo in March and April of 1996. The Muslims moved into places that had been picked clean, and sometimes burned, by their owners when they left for Srebrenica, Višegrad, and other towns in the Drina valley. Muslim men beat up some of the Serbs who stayed behind, and murdered a few, but many continued to live in their homes in hopes of finding someone who would buy them out.

By midsummer, Paja and his landlord, Šaban, had had a falling out. The American army had taken over Tuzla airfield, and Šaban reckoned he could rent the place out for more money. Paja wanted a place of his own anyway, and I gave him the name of a policeman in Ilidža, a suburb of Sarajevo, who might be able to help him find a house legally. He got on a bus bound for Sarajevo a few days later and began talking with the man in the next seat, who was on his way to take over a new apartment for his sister.

"She was living in a house right on the highway but has already moved into a better place in town," he said. "I don't know anyone who wants the house."

He offered to give up the place for $200. And after Paja produced the cash, he led him to a village named Blažuj, a characterless place that lies at the foot of Mount Igman and straddles the main highway between Sarajevo and the Adriatic coast about three miles from the city.

"It's all yours," he said. With that Paja Čelik, the peasant farmer who had never had a telephone, a car, or a driver's license, the man who had not wanted to leave his house in Kupusovići or even attend high school, found himself in possession of a spread he called Paja's Ranch. It had two buildings, including a bare, three-room apartment over a mechanic's workshop, and three storefronts with room for parking and a fenced-in yard in the back.

It took a few weeks to get the place in shape. Paja took some of the money I had gotten from *Rolling Stone* and bought a woodstove, two used couches, a secondhand television set, and some beds. Within a few months, he had a chain saw and a bicycle and was earning money cutting wood and collecting UN food packages and cash sent from Canada.

The original owner had fought as a soldier in Mladić's army and had run away when the Serbs withdrew from the Sarajevo suburbs, so Paja figured he wouldn't be back. "His name was Bato something or other," Paja told everyone. "His wife's staying on in a family apartment in Sarajevo, and she's trying to sell this place." Every few days, prospective buyers came by to gawk at Paja's Ranch from the parking lot across the busy main road out front. It was a prime location, and the asking price was probably a song. But anybody who came looking would immediately notice that someone was cutting back the weeds in the yard. They would see the *dimije* and silk-screened T-shirts hanging on the front balcony. They would hear there was a refugee family from Srebrenica living there. And they would walk away. "If they buy the place, they have to find me a place to live," Paja said. "That's the law. . . . Now all I have to do is get a driver's license, buy some tools, and learn to fix cars."

1997

HALF a dozen kids were kicking around a ball in Kravica's junk-strewn schoolyard on the sunny afternoon in May of 1997 when I walked up and asked if they knew anyone in the village named Erić. Thanks to the NATO troops, Bosnia was well into its second year without war. Wobbly picket fences and shabby-looking farmhouses with cluttered yards lined the village's dirt by-ways and footpaths, and it was clear Kravica had been a poor, bedraggled place even before the war. It took a minute or so for one of the children to fetch twenty-two-year-old Mihailo Erić, the great-great-grandson of Vaso. Mihailo was a tall man with thin lips and narrow eyes, and he lumbered up dressed in blue overalls and black rubber boots that gave out somewhere just below his knees. Gruesome scars across his forehead—the bullet had entered just in front of one temple and come out on the other side of his head—led me to assume he might not be mentally competent enough to lead me to someone else in his family. I shook his hand anyway, and practically begged him to talk with me about his forefathers. Hearing a stranger mention the name Vaso Erić made Mihailo's face light up. He began speaking with fervor, as if he had been waiting a long time for someone to ask him to show what he knew about the old days. He led me up the hill behind the school, pointing out the ash pit where Nego's body had been dumped after the Orthodox Christmas attack in 1993. He showed me into Nego's house, and upstairs he pointed out the room where Krstina's burned remains were found. The roof had been repaired, the fire damage had been cleared, but the interior walls and floors were still unfinished brick and concrete.

We descended a stairway and entered a sitting room on the ground floor. Nego's daughter-in-law, Živka, broke out the brandy and made coffee. Mihailo began talking quickly about Vaso and the opening of Kravica's first school. He glowed as he told us about his great-grandfather's participation in the arch-duke's assassination, about the two great wars, and about how his great-grandmother had pleaded with Tito to spare the lives of Nego and Golub. "Vaso is my pride," Mihailo beamed. "He's the pride of the Serbs in this entire region. He was a leader here when they needed a leader, and he was no coward. My grandfather told us it was an eye for an eye and a head for a head back in Vaso's time. There was no other law."

"I'm proud of Golub and Nego, as well," Mihailo continued. "Golub was my grandfather. He was smart and decisive and self-confident. In this war, he was not afraid to go where it was dangerous. He went to fight ahead of the younger men. He told the younger men that he had lived his life.

"I saw the bullet hole in the top of Nego's skull. He killed Krstina; then he killed himself. . . . But he was still a hero. Even the Muslims thought so. We heard Naser Orić say over the radio that if there had been ten more men like Nego Erić in Kravica, the Muslims would never have taken our village."

"You were outnumbered here and had trouble getting Serbs to come and fight, didn't you?" I asked.

He nodded.

"Why was that?"

"The Muslims here were strong."

"They were angry too, weren't they, and that made them dangerous?"

"Yes."

I told Mihailo I had heard of some Serb soldiers from the far-off town of Prnjavor who had been sent to fight around Srebrenica but refused to do anything except sit in their trenches, because they knew the Muslims would not show any Serb soldier any mercy. "These Serbs heard the stories of what happened in the Bratunac school at the beginning of the war," I said. "I know what happened in the Bratunac school. I know they killed all those Muslims, and you know it too, and I'm sick of people around here telling me that they don't know what went on in that school. Half of the world knows it, including the names and addresses of Topalović and the Macedonian and the other men who killed all those Muslims and how much they were paid for each head. The guys who came from Prnjavor said they didn't want to fight for you because of the Bratunac school, isn't that right."

Mihailo again nodded. He said another group of Serb soldiers who came from Bijeljina to help defend Kravica had run away when the Muslims attacked that Christmas morning: "They were pissing in their pants. They'd been drinking all night down in front of the school, and when the attack came they got in their armored vehicle and drove off."

"After the Christmas attack, when the people from Kravica were refugees in Bratunac, the menfolk were bitter, weren't they?"

"They were angry."

"Everyone in the district was angry?"

"Everyone."

"What did they say?"

"Revenge."

"What did they tell you?"

"They said, 'Kad tad. Kad tad, sooner or later our five minutes will come.' "

"And after they took back Kravica and found all the bodies and the open graves in the cemetery?"

"*Kad tad. Kad tad.*"

"And the opportunity finally came."

"Yes."

"Vengeance?"

"Yes, blood vengeance."

"Did they come for you?"

"I was in an apartment in Bratunac," he nodded.

"They were excited?"

"Yes. Yes."

"What did they say?"

"They said, 'Grab your gun and come down to the soccer field.' "

"Their five minutes had come?"

"Yes, their five minutes had come."

"Did you go?"

"No, I went home."

"What did you tell them?"

He paused for an instant.

"It's one thing to kill someone in battle, and it's something else to kill prisoners, men who've surrendered and have no guns."

"And have their hands tied?"

"Yes."

"And they killed all of them, every one they could?"

"Yes."

"And the Muslims in the column who escaped across the road? They held them up in Baljkovica as long as they could so that they could get some men together and have one more crack at them, didn't they?"

"They came around looking for volunteers."

"Did guys from Kravica go?"

"They wanted to kill as many of them as they could."

"So they could never come back? So there would not be enough military-age men left to fight their way back?"

"Never," Mihailo said.

The door behind me swung open. A man with a construction worker's beer belly stumbled in. He had a ruddy complexion, light eyes, and light hair. It was Mihailo's father, Zoran; he had been a member of an "obligatory work brigade" called to Bratunac on the day the killings began. We stood up. I shook the father's hand and explained myself by dropping the name Vaso Erić and making a three-sentence summary of a hundred years of Balkan history that ended with the fall of Srebrenica. The father sat down in Mihailo's chair, and Mihailo stood behind him leaning against a wall.

"Was it honorable to kill them all?" I asked the father.

"Absolutely," he said. "It was a fair fight."

Mihailo stared at me from behind him with a forlorn look in his eye.

"Absolutely," the older man said again, and he turned to the woman: "Get some more brandy."

We drank one more shot together before I got up to leave. Mihailo stepped outside with me, and we walked down the hill together.

"All of Golub's books and his family tree were burned up in the fire," Mihailo said as we headed toward the schoolyard.

"I've got some of the books with the stories of Vaso and the others in them," I promised him. "I'll get them copied and send them to you."

A FEW weeks later, I made one last trip to Kravica. Mihailo had gone off to Serbia. He was doing physical labor on a farm somewhere across the border because there were no money-paying jobs to be had anywhere near Kravica. I drove up to the Orthodox church to take the opportunity to look around the cemetery.

Kravica's Orthodox church is situated on a hilltop behind the village, safe from the main road where the Ottoman soldiers would once have passed. A large gray gravestone inscribed with the names of Vaso Erić and two of his three sons, Jakov and Mikailo, stands near the front of the cemetery; none of the men are actually buried there, but Golub and his family paid for the monument so that the men could be honored by their closest kin in the place where they were born. Under a tree next to the first row of graves, a couple of women and a man were sitting on a bench, paying homage to their dead, placating spirits that will roam the earth if they are not appeased. Towels hung over the wooden crosses on the nearby graves. On the arms of one cross were an apple, a plastic cup with brandy, two *bonboni* wrapped in clear shiny plastic, a box of matches, and half a dozen unlit beeswax candles placed there with the belief that the spirit of the dead man could use them to light his pathway to heaven. The women had spread napkins over the grass and dandelions growing on the grave and set upon them slices of pork, a loaf of bread, and an assortment of other food.

"Eat, eat," one of the women urged me. "Eat or everything will go to the dogs and the wild beasts."

It is insulting not to eat at a Serb grave, so I took some bread, a bit of salad, and a slice of the pork from the grave of the woman's brother, Kostadin Popović, a bauxite miner who worked in Milići and died at age forty-five after being captured alive in Kravica on Christmas Day and tortured in Naser Orić's prison in Srebrenica. Kostadin's father, Risto, had stayed behind and died with Nego Erić and Krstina when the rest of the villagers fled.

"Drink, drink," the woman said, handing me a brandy.

"For the soul of the departed," I said, pouring some of it onto Kostadin's grave before downing the rest.

"At first I cried for the Muslims," the woman said. "They fled and left behind beautiful houses. They left everything behind. But then my father and brother were killed."

The man standing nearby was their neighbor Tomo Stojanović, and he was old enough to have finished the Kravica school before World War II. Tomo's seventy-three-year-old brother, Rajo, had also died in the Christmas attack; and when they found his body, the eyes were missing.

"There is no honor if there is no revenge," Tomo said. "And it was not easy for the Muslims when they were leaving Srebrenica. It was not pretty for them."

❨ ❨ ❨

SANELA led the way along a gravel road beside the lake to Almir the *hodža's* house. It was another sunny spring day in that May of 1997. She and Nehrudin had moved out of the schoolhouse by then. They were living with her mother-in-law, Naza, and her teenage brother-in-law in one room of a farmhouse that they shared with other families driven from Srebrenica. The UN paid the rent and provided them food aid, and Sanela worked in the farmer's fields. Her chestnut hair had become streaked with gray. She had begun chain smoking and lost a lot of weight. Sometime over the winter, she got word through a Muslim police officer that Huso's identification card had turned up in one of the mass graves excavated sometime in the fall. The police officer had no other details about Huso. He didn't know the location of the grave or whether the gravediggers had found Huso's remains. And he knew nothing of Muhamed or his father and brother.

"Sometimes I tell myself that I would like to just know the truth about Muhamed because not knowing is killing me," she said as we moved toward Almir's place. "But I do not want to know, because it's better to live with some hope, even a little. If I found out that he is dead . . . I don't know what to say . . . I don't know if it would help. But if I knew he was still alive, even if I knew I wouldn't see him for twenty years, I would somehow wait it out."

We sat with Almir for an hour and talked about numerology and dervishes and the mystical fringe of Islam. Almir was nervous at first because he knew he had a Catholic infidel in his midst. He asked me if I felt any discomfort in my chest. I'm sure it was to make me uncomfortable, but I smiled and told him I had never felt better and asked him more questions about the time he and Sanela had first met and what he had told her about Muhamed.

"I am certain he was alive when we spoke the first time," Almir said. "But now I am just as sure he is no longer living."

Sanela stared at him with a blank face and said nothing. If it had been a year earlier, she would surely have started crying; a year earlier, she was still believing what the *hodža* and the fortune-tellers were saying. We got up and thanked Almir. I offered him ten dollars for his time, but he refused to take it.

A FEW weeks later, Sanela packed her baby things and her clothes in a suitcase, and she and Nehrudin left Bosnia. The next day, they flew to Toronto and joined her brothers Hamed and Sead in a town house a few hundred yards from a huge shopping mall and a fifteen-minute walk from the doughnut shop where the brothers were working the night shift. Hamed wanted her to start helping out at the shop right away so that she could learn some English and help save enough money to make a down payment on their own house and their own shop. In a few years, Nehrudin would be ready for school, and perhaps Sanela will have gone to night school and finally learned the skills of a hairdresser or a florist or some other occupation that would support a new life.

❆ ❆ ❆

EVEN under bright sunshine, Višegrad looked like a ghost town. The streets were without traffic and seemed nearly lifeless. Most of the houses looked deserted. The riverbanks were bereft of fishermen. The mosques and the minarets were gone and replaced by vacant lots. The only people around were hacking away at the soil in the victory gardens behind their houses, or sitting on plastic beverage crates outside tiny grocery stores, or squatting beside the roadside selling plastic bottles of gasoline and individual packs of cigarettes. Few of the refugees who had moved to Višegrad had any prospect of ever finding a job there, and few had money even for gasoline. The trucks we had passed on the road from Sarajevo were transporting only logs and lumber, the same natural resources the Austrians had used the Ćiro to exploit a century earlier. Twisted pieces of scaffolding were still wrapped around the stone underpinnings of Mehmed Pasha's bridge, and the Drina was turning in turquoise swirls for no one as it slid beneath the *sofa* and on toward the shallow graves at Slap and the great gorge that Jerina the Damned had cut between Zvijezda and Zlovrh.

"Hiba, have you ever walked across that bridge?" I asked, turning around and looking at her in the middle of the backseat.

"We talked about that bridge from time to time," she said. "But it was never very interesting to me."

"That so? Never walked on it?"

"Never."

We were hurtling toward Kupusovići in a white UN car driven by Peter Deck, an American who was heading the Sarajevo office of the UNHCR. Peter was making Hiba's visit home possible. Bosnian Serb police thugs were beating up, and occasionally killing, Muslims who tried to return to their homes, and I doubted whether any Muslim had risked a return to Milan Lukić's Višegrad. In Peter's white car with "UNHCR" painted along the side, the Serb police would pose no threat; and his two-way radio and six-foot antenna would enable us to summon help in the unlikely event that the car broke down or anyone else made trouble along the way.

Lukić had left his family's homestead in Rujišta soon after he and his men had emptied Višegrad. He moved to town, expropriated for himself a sleek German car, and opened a pizza parlor, The Atina, a few blocks from Mehmed Pasha's bridge. The restaurant's decor centered on an oil portrait of Lukić in front of the old Turkish bridge, as if his exploits had made him the valley's third-most-famous son after Ivo Andrić and Mehmed Pasha himself. But much of the town was whispering about Lukić. The refugees heard from the locals about the killings on the bridge and in the fire station and the hotels. Some of them called Lukić and his men "goddamned fools" for burning houses that could have been occupied by homeless Serbs. Some of them said they hoped the international war-crimes tribunal would finally indict him and have him taken away by NATO. Only their fear of Lukić kept the towns-people and refugees quiet when journalists and other strangers came sniffing around asking questions about the killings. Many people were ashamed, but others said the Muslims got just what they deserved.

Lukić had been arrested twice during the war. In April 1993, Slobodan Milošević's police took him into custody in connection with the murder of Stanko Pecikoza, the head of Višegrad's chapter of the Serbian Democratic Party, who was gunned down in an ambush, allegedly for having failed to pay Lukić a bounty for the Muslims he and his gang had executed. Lukić was released, officially anyway, for lack of evidence. Milošević's police arrested him a second time after the abduction and killing of nineteen Muslims who were riding from Belgrade to Montenegro on a train in February 1993; Serbian police officers may have participated in the abduction, and Lukić was again freed for "lack of evidence." He sought psychiatric care in the Serbian town of Užice a few months before his second arrest and told a doctor that he was proud that he had killed so many Muslims in the early days of the war and that he had an almost uncontrollable urge to kill again.

PETER, who spent much of his free time racing around Bosnia's back roads on a motorcycle, was taking the Drina highway at a speed faster than Hiba had ever traveled in her life. We tooled across the new Drina bridge just below Višegrad, streaked downriver on the cinder road, passed a cutoff up to the hotel at Višegrad's hot springs, and a few minutes later began bouncing our way up the stone and dirt track that connects Kupusovići with the outside world. Hiba had put on an ankle-length brown skirt and a pink blouse for the occasion and had pinned up her hair without covering it with one of the flowery kerchiefs she habitually wore. She insisted that she wasn't afraid. But she whispered the whole time as if anyone walking along the roadside would be able to hear her through the closed window of the moving car.

Down beside the Drina, the fields and orchards were laden with spring; but up in Kupusovići, the wildflowers and tree buds were just beginning to pop out; and higher up on the sides of Zvijezda, the trees were still the bare brown of winter. We parked the car next to Juz-bin's mosque and locked the doors. The air was hushed except for the occasional clang of a bell on a cow grazing in the Muslim graveyard. Nothing was left of the Čelik place except the basement walls, shards of bathroom tile, white with orange half-moon designs, and broken roof tiles.

"The outhouse was over here," Hiba whispered with a cheeriness in her voice. "I buried four gold necklaces and a couple of rings here, but I dug them up before we left. . . . There's the chicken coop . . . and this was the potato cellar . . . and that was Saliha's house, right over there."

We walked down a grassy knoll to the four stone walls of the stall where Saliha had once imprisoned her cow. Hiba chortled about Šemsa straddling the tree branch and galloping around the yard to sweep the spiderwebs away. "We made that hex, a rag tied together with ash and fingernails and all, and it was sitting right here," she laughed, slapping the top of a stone wall. "Saliha's daughter put it right here the night before . . . and, you know that Šemsa never wore a skirt in her life, and she gave birth to a baby boy down in the bus stop."

Hiba examined her meadows and her untilled garden as if they were rooms of her house. She pulled the bark from a plum tree smitten by a blight and gazed over at a chestnut grove up by the Serb graveyard. "Muslim women don't go into graveyards," she said. "You won't have children if you go into graveyards. . . . I picked up a tree branch near the Serb graveyard once, a piece of stove wood. I was alone in the house then. Huso had gone to Sarajevo, and we didn't have any children yet. I went to bed that night at about one in morning, and about an hour later I started to dream that I had those moccasins, the leather moccasins the Serbs used to wear, all around me. I jumped up and heard a rooster crow, and I got that tree branch out of the house right away. I threw it back over by the graveyard, and that dream never came back."

We meandered back to the car and drove up to Odžak to visit Dragoljub. I had gotten myself assigned to the Odžak schoolhouse as an election monitor in September 1996 and had met Dragoljub then. He gave me a bed to sleep in, and his wife, Zora, and her sister, Borka, washed my clothes. They told me I was welcome in their home anytime because of my connection to Hamed Čelik. Peter parked the car in a patch of grass below Dragoljub's house, and I walked ahead into the yard.

"Yeoooo, Dragoljub," I called. "Yeoooo."

He appeared from out behind the house. "Ooooo. *Amerikanac*. Where've you been?"

"I've got someone with me. Come and take a look."

Dragoljub walked over. The glaucoma had fogged up his eyesight so badly that he had to slip on his glasses to recognize Hiba climbing the path toward his house.

The greeting was awkward. They spoke in nervous and careful tones. Dragoljub had to pause to think before he invited us, naturally enough, to sit down. Then he got up and yelled down to Zora and Borka, who were in a meadow below the house shearing sheep.

"Yeeoooo! Yeeoooo!" he called. "Come on home! Someone's come to visit."

Dragoljub went into the house and got a green bottle full of brandy and joined us at a wobbly wooden table in the yard.

"Did you go down and take a look at your place?" he asked Hiba.

"We were walking around down there."

"They came again and again taking stuff away," he said. "Where did you leave Huso?"

"Potočari," Hiba answered.

"That's over in Srebrenica?"

She nodded.

"I don't know any of the villages over there. . . ." He paused. "And you never saw him again, eh?"

"No," she replied. "That Lukić, that Milan, came and took away some of the men from up here. Novaković was there, too. So was that Pepić. They took them away, and never brought them back. That was in the evening. The soldiers separated Huso and me the next morning, and I never saw him again."

"God save us," Dragoljub gasped.

"They've come looking for money," Hiba told him. "That Lukić. He's come looking, and says he's got prisoners somewhere."

Word had spread among the Muslims from Mount Zvijezda living around Sarajevo that a Serb woman had come from Višegrad and found the family of Hasib Čavkušic´, the Muslim with the Austrian pension whom Lukić had led away in Potočari. The woman told Hasib's family that Lukić was holding 158 prisoners and was working them as slaves in four mines in Serbia. Lukić wanted $2,000 for each of the men except Hasib; the price for him was $6,000 because Lukić knew Hasib had an Austrian pension. Hasib's family demanded proof that he was still alive. The woman returned from Višegrad a few days later and said Lukić had come unhinged. She said he was nervous. He was sleeping with the lights on all night. He was driving around in a different car all the time. The war-crimes tribunal had not indicted Lukić — had not even begun investigating him — so arrest, by NATO anyway, was an unlikely grounds for his fear. Down in Goražde, however, Avdija Šabanović was not hiding the fact that he wanted Lukić and had even toyed with the idea of hiring a Serb to kill him.

Lukić warned the woman not to mention Srebrenica or the prisoners again, and the ransom demand was dropped.

"God help us," Dragoljub said again. "God help us."

I remembered Dragoljub's once telling me that the villages on Mount Zvijezda would all be empty in a generation or two. The young people were all moving away, except for the drunks and the shiftless. "When my generation dies off, no one will be left here," he said.

"All this killing was for nothing," Dragoljub told Hiba. "It did no good for anybody, and this place isn't any good any more for anybody." Folks were saying the Pepić boy had killed his own mother. A Serb who had worked all his life in Austria and come back to the mountain with pension money was murdered in his own home. A man hung himself down in the graveyard when his youngest son came home from the war front in a body bag. The rotted corpse of one of Hamed's friends had been identified only by his socks. After months of lying in bed and howling to the neighbors to put him out of his misery, Mile Janković had finally died of cirrhosis. . . . And on it went.

The conversation turned into picnic chatter when Zora and Borka climbed into the yard with their plastic bags stuffed with fleece. They kissed Hiba on each cheek, went into the kitchen, and brought out some hard-boiled eggs, a plate of soft cheese, and some bread.

"Eat, eat," Dragoljub said, pouring more brandy. "Eat all you can." Peter and I grabbed some food and went to spread the cheese.

"Haven't you got a knife?" Dragoljub laughed. "What the hell are you doing in Bosnia without a knife?" He asked Zora to bring a knife and glanced over at Hiba, who was talking with the women. "You know my father once saved her father from falling off a house!"

Across the table, Hiba was telling Zora and Borka that the Muslim women in Sarajevo were finding new husbands. "All the older ones are getting married again," Hiba said. "I was once sitting out back in Blažuj. A man came up, a tall man. He said, 'Hello, my name is Mujo.' And I said, 'I'm Hiba,' and asked myself what the hell does this one want.

" 'Is this your grandson?' he asked.

" 'Yes, it is.'

" 'Where is his grandfather?'

" 'Disappeared in Potočari.'

" 'What can you do?' he said. 'That's the way things are in these times.' "

"I was weak then," Hiba told everyone at the table. "I started crying. And then he said, 'Don't cry. What are you crying for?'

" 'I have to. I lost my man. I lost my son-in-law. I lost what was left of my youth.'

" 'Do you want to marry me?' he asked.

" 'Don't talk to me like that. . . . I could never do that, because of my children. I don't need another man again.' And the man walked away. It was the first time I had ever seen him. Even if the guy was rich, I wouldn't get married again."

"But was he good-looking?" Zora joked. And Hiba laughed and slapped her leg. Borka blurted out that she heard Hiba's cow was in a village down the mountain. And Zora coughed to shut her sister up.

"What do you think, do you think you'll be back?" Zora asked. "Do you think anyone wants to come back here?"

"No, never," Hiba answered. "Everyone's settled in near Sarajevo now, and we'll be going to Canada eventually. Nobody wants to come back."

And that was the gist of it. We posed for a snapshot outside Dragoljub's house before saying good-bye; then we climbed into the car and headed over to drop in on Petra Mitrašinović for a few minutes. Hiba and Petra hugged like the best of friends when they first saw each other. They sat on a narrow wooden bench and talked. Hiba had scared Petra by just showing up. Branko had died. She was now living alone and losing ground to fear and senility. Petra went inside her house after a few minutes and came out with three sets of bedding. Hiba smiled. And Petra smiled. And they hugged each other again before walking down to the car.

"Will you be coming back?" Petra asked.

"Oh, yes," Hiba answered. She knew it wouldn't be a day before Petra talked with Dragoljub and the others. And she knew exactly what she was doing.

"Absolutely," Hiba assured Petra, "every one of us wants to come back. You know we're all supposed to be allowed to come back. And everyone wants nothing more than to return home."

The two women quickly uttered their final farewells as Peter set the bedding in the back of the car. Hiba waved through the window as we pulled away and headed across the mountain.

She was quiet for the first few hundred yards, as if she were afraid Petra might hear her, and I finally asked her what Petra had said. "Fuck that Petra's Chetnik mother," Hiba answered, looking out the window. "I gave her my best bedding, and she told me she would keep it until her dying day. Now look what she gives me in return. She said her sons had come and sold off all of our things in Belgrade. She said they sold Paja's chain saw, too. Fucking Chetniks."

"And look at that Dragoljub," she continued. "He said he didn't take anything from any of the Muslim houses, and there he was with my wheelbarrow and a piece of my fence in his yard, and there came his women kissing me on the cheek with that garlic on their breath."

"Fuck their Chetnik mothers," she went on. "I've got asphalt. Let them bounce along on this road forever. I've got asphalt. And look at how we used to be out here in the middle of nowhere. I'd never come back here. Never. All of this land will be deserted sooner or later. It's wasteland. Mountains and rock and wasteland. Blažuj is beautiful, for God's sake. Blažuj is beautiful for now, and we're going to Canada."

We slowed down for one last glimpse at Juz-bin's mosque and the deserted Muslim cemetery and saw that gobs of algae had clogged the water trough at the spring where Hiba and generations of Kupusović's women had once gossiped the evenings away. In another minute, we had crossed above the ruins of Behadil's house in Žlijeb.

"We've got to see one more thing," I told Peter. "It'll only take a minute. But we've got to go on foot."

Peter parked the car. We locked the doors again and walked a few hundred yards along a path. The upper wall of Mount Zvijezda towered over us to the left, but there was no sign that an international border was running again along its crest. At a grassy bluff, we left the path and climbed toward the mountain wall and an outcropping of rock with a smooth face about fifty feet high and thirty feet wide and a black crust that made it look as if a huge fire had charred its surface. And there on that outcropping, etched into the living rock, were the "Roman Signs." The setting sun cast a golden tint upon the white, stick-figure eagles stretching their proud wings and unfurling their tails just above the mystical swastikas and the ancient letters. The horse soldiers wore tall, pointed helmets and held their swords and spears over the heads of their stick-figure steeds.

Peter, Hiba, and I walked up to the base of the rock. "A villainess made these signs, a foreign woman named Jerina," I told Peter. "Isn't that right, Hiba?"

"Where do you hear these things?" she giggled.

"That's what folks around here believe, anyway," I said. "Legend says a river once flowed out of the mountain wall through a hole right here, just below this rock face. The water cut away the good earth and swept it down for the Drina to carry off and left nothing but the stone behind. Jerina took sand and rags and egg whites and these stones here and plugged up that hole, and the river broke through on the other side of the mountain.

"The peasants say that someone will come along someday and reveal the secret meaning of these signs. Then the river will gush out of the rock again and devastate the land for miles around."

Experts have visited Mount Zvijezda over the last century to study the Roman Signs. A Serb ethnographer wrote in 1891 that some of the signs are actually Cyrillic letters; but he couldn't read them. An anthropologist came up the mountain after World War II and wrote that the horsemen and eagles probably date from the Bronze Age or the Early Iron Age, but he didn't explain how he had arrived at this conclusion. An Islamic scholar looked at the same signs and saw the Arabic words *Allahu ekber*, "God is great."

In the minds of the peasants for miles around, however, the observations and hypotheses of these experts have done nothing to resolve the mystery of the signs, nothing to allay the sense of doom carried within the prophecy that a torrent of water will someday wash away the side of Jerina the Damned's mountain. Sanela told me once that she had even heard the sound of the river. She told me to listen to the pile of rocks that Jerina used to plug the hole in the mountain.

"Bend over and put your ear next to the cracks, and keep really quiet," she said. "You'll hear the water. It's in there."

I did what she said, and I could hear the sound of water. Anyone can hear it there, trickling and gurgling, deep inside.

SOURCES

Prologue

INTERVIEWS
Huso Čelik, Hamed Čelik, Paja Čelik, Hiba Čelik, Sanela (Čelik) Halilović, Gordana (Todorović) Čelik.

Chapter 1

INTERVIEWS
Hamed Zahić, Medo Hurem, Hamšija (Čelik) Alić, Avdo Čelik, Latifa (Čelik) Čavkušić, Dragoljub Radovanović, Nikola Šimšić, Bismo "Penzija" Čavkušić, Sanela (Čelik) Halilović, Hiba Čelik, Muhamed Muratagić, Omer Muratagić, Fehim Ahmetagić, Hussein Ahmetagić, Momir Krsmanović, Ajdin Braco, Saliha (Čelik) Muratagić, Ratomir Lukić, Ibrahim Kljun, Vasa Čubrilović.

PUBLISHED LITERATURE
Toynbee, *Study of History*, pp. 118–20, 130, 131, 152, 160, 161, 173–78, 264, 265, 286–88, 416–17, 536, 637; Kinross, *Ottoman Centuries*, pp. 259–65, 276, 277, 279; Kann, *History*, pp. 9, 10, 277, 413, 414; Friedman, *Bosnian Muslims*, pp. 13, 17–21, 29–41, 62, 57–76, 89–100; Beatović, *Bratunac*, pp. 3–14, 41–48; Kljun, *Višegrad*, pp. 13–63; Malcolm, *Bosnia*, pp. 18, 20, 21, 47, 48, 51–69, 104–6, 123, 132–44, 150, 154–73; Donia and Fine, *Bosnia and Herce-govina*, pp. 35, 37, 40–48, 53, 55, 63, 64, 87, 93–119; Kohn, *Nationalism*, pp. 4, 9–12, 14, 15, 20, 50; Norris, *Islam in the Balkans*, pp. 116–17; Draganović, *Povijest Bosne i Hercegovine*, pp. 123, 133, 153, 570, 571; Dedijer, *Road to Sarajevo*, pp. 9–16, 42, 43, 340, 342, 343; Nile-vić, *Srpska Pravoslavna Crkva*, pp. 44, 52, 56–58, 64, 144, 163, 196; Banac, *National Ques-tion*, pp. 37, 47, 59, 60, 73, 91, 107, 272; Andrić, *Na Drini ćuprija*, pp. 18, 19, 64, 274, 278; Ćorović, *Crna Knjiga*, pp. 25–51; Wolff, *Balkans*, p. 67; Stratimirović, "Arheološki prilozi," pp. 283–93; Lampe and Jackson, *Balkan Economic History*, pp. 21–27, 33–38, 62–64, 120; Boehm, *Blood Revenge*, pp. 47, 111, 112.

Chapter 2

INTERVIEWS

Latifa (Čelik) Čavkušić, Avdo Čelik, Fehim Ahmetagić, Avdija Avdić, Bismo Čavkušić, Nikola Šimšić, Ibrahim Kljun, Momir Krsmanović, Hamed Zahić, Fehim Ahmetagić, Hamšija (Čelik) Alić, Dušan Biber, Mark Wheeler, Ratomir Lukić, Muniba (Borovac) Dervišagić, Medo Hurem.

PUBLISHED LITERATURE

Milazzo, *Chetnik Movement*, pp. 182–87; Donia and Fine, *Bosnia and Hercegovina*, pp. 137–38; Friedman, *Bosnian Muslims*, pp. 101–3; Kljun, *Višegrad*, pp. 71, 72, 99, 100; Ford, *OSS and Yugoslav Resistance*, pp. 21–22; Martin, *Web of Disinformation*, pp. 154–57; Krsmanović, *Teče krvava Drina*, vol. 1, pp. 186–90, and vol. 2, pp. 83–89; Tucaković, *Srpski zločini*, pp. 47–55, 98, 102–12, 171, 183–90; Malcolm, *Bosnia*, pp. 174–92; Dacie, *Instead of the Brier*, pp. 152–53; Wolff, *Balkans*, pp. 203–7, 211–16, 223–27; Rusinow, *Yugoslav Experiment*, pp. 1, 2, 7–9; Clissold, *Short History*, pp. 209–16, 218–19, 222–29; Singleton, *Short History*, pp. 176, 177–82, 188–89, 191–93, 198–202; Dedijer et al., *History of Yugoslavia*, pp. 591, 592, 595, 604, 615, 626, 630–58; *Encyclopedia of the Holocaust*, vol. 1, pp. 323–29, and vol. 4, pp. 1340–42.

DOCUMENTS

Assessment of the attack on Višegrad on Oct. 5, 1943, and the order by Draža Mihailović dated Oct. 7, 1943, Br. 9, *Zbornik Dokumenata i Podataka o Narodnooslobodilačkom Ratu Naroda Jugoslavije*, Tom XIV, Knjiga 3, Beograd 1983, p. 27; "A Paper Based on an Interview given by Major Archibald Jack to Mr. Conrad Wood of the Imperial War Museum, London, on March 18, 1989," Imperial War Museum, Department of Sound Records, Accession no. 10640/4, pp. 5, 18–20; Report on Mission to General Mihailović, Dec. 1942–Feb. 1944, by Colonel S. W. Bailey, Public Record Office, London, War Office 208, File 2018A.

Chapter 3

INTERVIEWS

Hamed Zahić, Avdo Čelik, Dragoljub Radovanović, Hiba Čelik, Avdija Avdić, Hajrija Čavkušić, Ratomir Lukić, Nikola Šimšić, Muhiba (Borovac) Dervišagić, Omer Harbaš, Bismo Čavkušić, Medo Hurem.

PUBLISHED LITERATURE

Malcolm, *Bosnia*, pp. 191–98; Dacie, *Instead of the Brier*, pp. 152–53; Singleton, *Short History*, pp. 202–7, 212, 215, 221–28, 238, 239, 252, 253; Clissold, *Short History*, pp. 230, 231–53, 262, 263; Clissold, *Yugoslavia and the Soviet Union*, p. 61; Dedijer et al., *History of Yugoslavia*, pp. 662–70, 699, 700, 707, 716; Wolff, *Balkans*, pp. 268, 269, 323–37, 355–64, 371–75, 391–93; Rusinow, *Yugoslav Experiment*, pp. 12, 13, 16, 17, 40, 50–55, 57, 60–64, 79–81, 95–97, 164; Friedman, *Bosnian Muslims*, pp. 150, 154, 155; Glasnik Vrhovnog Starješinstva u FNR Jugoslaviji, broj 10-12, Okt.–Dec. 1959.

Chapter 4

INTERVIEWS
Avdija Avdić, Hamed Čelik, Hiba Čelik, Dragoljub Radovanović, Nikola Šimšić, Latifa (Čelik) Čavkušić, Saliha (Čelik) Muratagić, Mehmed Mehmedović.

PUBLISHED LITERATURE
Malcolm, *Bosnia*, pp. 202–3; Petric, "On Tattooing" and "Origin of Tattooing," passim; Reuters dispatches from Belgrade, May 4, 5, and 6, 1980; Rusinow, *Yugoslav Experiment*, pp. 125–37, 209, 213, 251, 267, 268, 271, 313, 318–26, 332–39; Singleton, *Short History*, pp. 242–44, 259–60; Friedman, *Bosnian Muslims*, pp. 157, 159, 161–62.

Chapter 5

INTERVIEWS
Fehim Ahmetagić, Dragoljub Radovanović, Avdo Čelik, Hiba Čelik, Hamed Čelik, Nikola Šimšić, Paja Čelik, Sanela (Čelik) Halilović, Mikan Ilić, Hussein Ahmetagić, Gordana (Todorović) Čelik, members of the Čavkušić family from Kapetanovići, Amir Karić, Samir Karić, Muradif Karić, Mehmed Mehmedović, Ratomir Lukić, and Serb acquaintances of Milan Lukić who requested anonymity.

Chapter 6

INTERVIEWS
Radovan Karadžić, Ljilja (Zelen) Karadžić, Ivan Stambolić, Franjo Tudjman, Slavoljub Djukić, Milan Kučan, Naser Orić, Gavrilo Grahovac, Vladimir Srebrov, Marko Vešović, Boris Krstanović, Dr. Aida Hašimbegović, Nikola Koljević, Biljana Plavšić, Stjepan Kljuić, Haris Silajdžić, Velibor Ostojić, Alija Izetbegović and members of his family, members of the Belgrade diplomatic community who asked to remain anonymous, and Serbs, Muslims, and Croats who asked to remain unnamed.

PUBLISHED LITERATURE
Malcolm, *Bosnia*, pp. 196, 200, 201, 205, 208–11, 218–32; Djukić, *Izmedju slave i anateme*, pp. 122–24, 187; Djukić, *On, ona i mi*, pp. 17–18; Reuters dispatches from Belgrade, June 28, 1989; Radio Free Europe Research Reports, Yugoslavia/9, 20 July 1989, pp. 8–9; Silber and Little, *Yugoslavia*, pp. 70–73, 128–32, 205–20; Zimmermann, "Last Ambassador," pp. 2, 5–7, 9, 10, 14–16, 18; Kljun, *Višegrad*, p. 245; Coll, "Franjo Tudjman," B01; Zagorac, *Karadžić*, pp. 10, 12, 29, 63, 64, 218.

Chapter 7

INTERVIEWS
Avdija Šabanović, Murat Šabanović, Paja Čelik, Senad Sućeska, Hiba Čelik, Nikola Šimšić, Sanela (Čelik) Halilović, Omer Behman, Amir Karić, Muradif Karić, Samir Karić, Hamed Čelik, Huso Čelik, Deba and Džemal Kozić, and Serbs from Višegrad who requested anonymity.

PUBLISHED LITERATURE
Kljun, *Višegrad*, pp. 243–47.

Chapter 8

INTERVIEWS
Members of the Kupus family, Hase Tirić, Muhamed Muratagić, Serbs who spoke on condition of anonymity about the massacre of Muslims in Zvornik and the killings in Bijeljina, Boris Krstanović, Aida Čerkez, Goran Miličević, Alija Izetbegović. The biographical material on Željko Ražnatović is from Belgrade press accounts, interviews with Serbs who requested anonymity, and diplomats and police officials from the United States, Sweden, Belgium, Germany, and Interpol.

PUBLISHED LITERATURE
Mehinagić, "Smrt je stigla u zoru," pp. 28–30; Orić, *Srebrenica*, pp. 47, 79, 80; Silber and Little, *Yugoslavia*, pp. 222–30; Rieff, *Slaughterhouse*, pp. 200, 201; interview with Mendiluce, *Borba* (Belgrade), Oct. 29–30, 1994.

Chapter 9

INTERVIEWS
Avdija Šabanović, Murat Šabanović, Avdo Hebib, Paja Čelik, Hiba Čelik, Dragoljub Radovanović, Senad Sućeska, Zlatija (Sućeska) Čelik, Sanela (Čelik) Halilović, Goran Miličević, Nikola Šimšić, Mehmed Mehmedović, Serb soldiers who were deployed along mountaintops above Kupusovići.

PUBLISHED LITERATURE
Kljun, *Višegrad*, pp. 247–58; Andrić, *Na Drini ćuprija*, p. 259; Krsmanović, *Teče krvava Drina*, vol. 2, p. 83.

Chapter 10

INTERVIEWS
Paja Čelik, Senad Sućeska, Omer Harbaš, Hasan Nuhanović, Milivoje Ivanišević, Deba Kozić, Džemal Kozić, Naser Orić, Amir Karić, Samir Karić, Muradif Karić, Hamed Čelik.

PUBLISHED LITERATURE
Orić, *Srebrenica*, pp. 67–71, 150–51.

Chapter 11

INTERVIEWS
Paja Čelik, Hiba Čelik, Zlatija (Sućeska) Čelik, Senad Sućeska, Hanifa Kozić, videotaped testimony of Zehra Turjačanin, Amra (Pirić) Smailović, Biba (Čavkušić) Tabaković, Timka Kapetanović, Amir Karić, Samir Karić, Muradif Karić, Fata Pirić, and Serb witnesses from Belgrade, Višegrad, Užice, and Bajina Bašta who asked not to be identified.

PUBLISHED LITERATURE:
Kljun, *Višegrad*, pp. 248–49, 250–305; Orić, *Srebrenica*, pp. 74–78.

Chapter 12

INTERVIEWS
Paja Čelik, Hiba Čelik, Sanela (Čelik) Halilović, Zlatija (Sućeska) Čelik, and Western diplomats who requested anonymity.

PUBLISHED LITERATURE
Silber and Little, *Yugoslavia*, pp. 251–52, 258; Gow, *Triumph*, pp. 205, n. 67, 224–32, Reuters dispatches from the London conference; Gompert, "United States," pp. 133–35; Malcolm, *Bosnia*, p. 246; Maass, *Love Thy Neighbor*, pp. 50–51; Wechsler, "Inventing Peace," p. 57; Coll, "Franjo Tudjman," p. B1; Zimmermann, "Last Ambassador," p. 15; Zimmermann, *Origins of a Catastrophe*, pp. 7–8, 58–60; statements by Congressman Henry Gonzalez of Texas, the chairman of the House Banking Committee, in *Congressional Record*, April 28, 1992, pp. H2696–99, and April 25, 1991, H2547–57.

Chapter 13

INTERVIEWS
Paja Čelik, Dragica Vasić, Sanela (Čelik) Halilović, Jovan Nikolić, Mihailo Erić, Zoran Erić, Naser Orić, Ramiz Bećirović, Ibrahim Bećirović, Hiba Čelik, Zlatija (Sućeska) Čelik, Sanela (Čelik) Halilović, Paja Čelik, Senad Sućeska, Hasan Nuhanović, Avdo Muratagić, and Serbs and Muslims from Milići and Srebrenica who asked to remain unnamed.

PUBLISHED LITERATURE
Miljanović, *Krvavi Božic*, pp. 1–72; *Slobodna Bosna* (Sarajevo), July 14, 1996, p. 8; *Ljiljan* (Sarajevo), Aug. 7, 1996, p. 19; Beatović, *Bratunac*, pp. 12–14, 17–18, 24–29, 34, 41, 49; Beatović and Milanović, *Veleizdajnički procesi*, pp. 74, 77–88, 119, 123, 134, 136; Ćorović, *Historija Bosne*, pp. 334, 386, 408, 432–34, 457; Ćorović, *Crna Knjiga*, pp. 111–14, 118, 171, 190,

193; Schmitt, *Annexation of Bosnia*, p. 47; Dedijer and Miletić, *Proterivanje Srba*, pp. 318–21; Ivanišević, *Hronika našeg groblja*, pp. 11–49, 59–67, 226–55, 258–81, 283–94; Omeragić, *Satanski sinovi*, pp. 5–41, 95–98, 104–7, 136–37; Orić, *Srebrenica*, pp. 7–13, 15–21, 35–59, 162; Lampe and Jackson, *Balkan Economic History*, pp. 175–77; *Veleizdajnički proces u Banja Luci*, passim; Owings, *Sarajevo Trial*, vol. 2, pp. 395–96; Dedijer, *Road to Sarajevo*, p. 389; *Večernje Novosti* (Belgrade), Feb. 14, 1993; Bordeaux, *La Bosnie*, pp. 275–99; Cibej, "Naš marš na Drini"; "Straže na Drini," *Duga* (Belgrade), March 13, 1993; "Ono Malo Života," *Intervju* (Belgrade), Feb. 5, 1993; "Kravica Nestala u Plamenu," *Večernje Novosti* (Belgrade), Jan. 11, 1993; "Sloboda na slavu," *Večernje Novosti* (Belgrade), Jan. 21, 1993.

DOCUMENTS
Presuda okružnog suda u Tuzla, Br. K. 316/50, Dec. 20, 1950 (the official record of the trial of Golub and Nego Erić).

Chapter 14

INTERVIEWS
Jovan Nikolić, Mihailo Erić, Zoran Erić, Živka Erić, Dragica Vasić, Naser Orić, Ramiz Bećirović, Ibrahim Bećirović, Hasan Nuhanović, Džemal Kozić, Senad Sućeska, Paja Čelik, Sanela (Čelik) Halilović, and Serbs and Muslims who asked to remain unnamed.

PUBLISHED LITERATURE
Miljanović, *Krvavi Božic*, pp. 73–99; Ivanišević, *Hronika našeg groblja*, pp. 46–47, 50–58, 61, 282, 294–337; *Slobodna Bosna* (Sarajevo), July 14, 1996, p. 8; "Dosije," in *Ljiljan* (Sarajevo), Aug. 7, 1996, p. 19; *Večernje Novosti* (Belgrade), Feb. 14, 1993; Orić, *Srebrenica*, p. 162.

Chapter 15

INTERVIEWS
General Philippe Morillon, Sanela (Čelik) Halilović, Zlatija (Sućeska) Čelik, Hiba Čelik, Paja Čelik, Dragan Ćićić, Bosnian Serb army officers who asked to remain unnamed, Western diplomats who asked to remain anonymous.

PUBLISHED LITERATURE
Malcolm, *Bosnia*, pp. 247–49; Owen, *Balkan Odyssey*, pp. 88–132, 180–81; Gow, *Triumph*, pp. 142, 240–42; Silber and Little, *Yugoslavia*, pp. 265, 276, 277; Rieff, *Slaughterhouse*, pp. 28, 117–20, 145, 169, 255; *New York Times*, Jan. 12, 13, 19, and Feb. 11, 1993; interviews with Ratko Mladić, *NIN*, Jan. 1994.

Chapter 16

INTERVIEWS
General Philippe Morillon, Naser Orić, Ramiz Bećirović, Jovan Nikolić, Don Forbes, Dragica Vasić, Sanela (Čelik) Halilović, Milivoje Ivanišević, Paja Čelik, Hiba Čelik, Anders Levinsen, Michele O'Kelly, Serbs in Bajina Bašta who asked to remain unnamed, UN military force personnel, Diego Arria and other diplomats to the UN Security Council who asked to remain unnamed, ham radio operators in Srebrenica, Cerska, and Konjević Polje, U.S. military officials who asked to remain unnamed, UN civilian and military officials who asked to remain anonymous.

PUBLISHED LITERATURE
New York Times, Feb. 7, 11, 13, 14, 17, 19, 23, 28, March 1, 3, 4, 5, and 7, 1993; Reuters, March 9 and 10, 1993; Ivanišević, *Hronika našeg groblja*, pp. 329, 336–37; Silber and Little, *Yugoslavia*, p. 266; Morillon, *Croire et oser*, p. 133.

DOCUMENTS
Unpublished reports and cables of UNPROFOR and the UNHCR.

Chapter 17

INTERVIEWS
General Philippe Morillon, Naser Orić, Ramiz Bećirović, Mihailo Erić, Jovan Nikolić, Živka Erić, Paja Čelik, Anders Levinsen, Michele O'Kelly, members of the British army's 9/12th Lancers, Bosnian army officers in Tuzla, ham radio operators in Srebrenica and Konjević Polje, Serbs in the town of Bajina Bašta who asked to remain anonymous, and Brigadier General Donald Loranger, Jr., commander of the 435th Military Airlift Wing, Frankfurt, Germany, and members of his unit.

PUBLISHED LITERATURE
Miljanović, *Krvavi Božic*, pp. 86, 88–89, 91–97; Silber and Little, *Yugoslavia*, p. 267; Morillon, *Croire et oser*, pp. 175, 180; *New York Times*, March 7–11, 13–25, and 27–30, 1993; Rieff, *Slaughterhouse*, p. 169; Owen, *Balkan Odyssey*, pp. 132–36.

DOCUMENTS
Unpublished World Health Organization report on the attempted evacuation from Konjević Polje dated March 12, 1993; unpublished UNPROFOR cables and other documents dated March 13 (containing Morillon's statement and demands and describing his mission to Srebrenica and the attack on the Muslims gathered around the British vehicles in Konjević Polje), 14–16, 17 (describing the American military officer's separate communications with the U.S. government), 18, 20–21, 23–25; unpublished documents of the UNHCR, including situation reports and transcripts of conversations about the Serb attacks on Kamenica, Cerska, and Konjević Polje; unpublished UN cable dated March 25, 1993, containing excerpts from the meeting between General Wahlgren, General Morillon,

Cedric Thornberry, Judith Kumin, and President Milošević; letter from David Owen to Prime Minister Pierre Bérégovoy of France dated March 19, 1993; unpublished message from José Maria Mendiluce to François Fouinat dated March 22, 1993, and describing Morillon's deal for the exchange of the Serb population in Tuzla for the Muslims of Srebrenica; unpublished memorandum to Wahlgren from José Maria Mendiluce dated March 22, 1993, and protesting Morillon's deal for the evacuation of Serbs from Tuzla.

Chapter 18

INTERVIEWS
Naser Orić, Ramiz Bećirović, Paja Čelik, General Philippe Morillon, Serbs who witnessed the attack on Morillon's vehicle in Zvornik, Diego Arria and other diplomats belonging to nations sitting in the UN Security Council in March and April 1993.

PUBLISHED LITERATURE
Silber and Little, *Yugoslavia*, pp. 266–69; *New York Times*, March 28–April 19, 1993; Rieff, *Slaughterhouse*, p. 169.

DOCUMENTS
Unpublished background note on the situation in eastern Bosnia by the UNHCR dated April 1, 1993, and containing Mladić's notification that no further food convoys would be permitted into Srebrenica; unpublished letter from José Maria Mendiluce to General Mladić dated April 1993; unpublished letter from Sadako Ogata to Secretary-General Boutros Boutros-Ghali dated April 2, 1993; unpublished cables of UNPROFOR dated April 4 (including notes on the meeting between Mendiluce and Izetbegović as well as Silajdžić's offer for a general evacuation from Srebrenica), 6, 7, 13, 16, 17, 18, 19, and 21, 1993; UNPROFOR press releases dated April 13 and 18, 1993; unpublished UNPROFOR cable dated April 9 and containing the minutes of the meeting on the same day between General Wahlgren, General Morillon, General Mladić, President Milošević, Cedric Thornberry, and Judith Kumin; unpublished UN cable by General Wahlgren dated April 13, 1993, and containing excerpts from the meeting between Wahlgren and General Mladić in Sarajevo on April 12, 1993; unpublished message by the staff of the UN Peace Conference on the Former Yugoslavia dated April 13, 1993, and containing the account of General Wahlgren's suspicions about the Srebrenica playground shelling on April 12; unpublished review of the military situation in Bosnia and Herzegovina to David Owen from John Wilson dated April 16, 1993; letter from Radovan Karadžić to the president of the UN Security Council dated April 17, 1993; "Agreement for the Demilitarization of Srebrenica," dated April 17, 1993; unpublished message from Jeremy Braid to David Owen on the demilitarization of Srebrenica dated April 19, 1993.

Chapter 19

INTERVIEWS

Naser Orić, Ramiz Bećirović, General Philippe Morillon, UN military personnel stationed in Sarajevo during the summer of 1993, UN civilian officials who asked to remain unnamed, Diego Arria and other diplomats who participated in the Security Council debate on Resolution 836 and who asked to remain unnamed.

PUBLISHED LITERATURE

Independent (London), June 8, 1993; Silber and Little, *Yugoslavia,* pp. 269–75, 282; Owen, *Balkan Odyssey,* pp. 178–82; Gow, *Triumph,* pp. 144–45; Djukić, *On, ona i mi,* p. 157; *New York Times,* April 19–June 5, 1993; Meisler, "Inner Sanctum," pp. 23–41.

DOCUMENTS

Unpublished UNPROFOR cables, and other documents dated April 21, 22, 23, May 4, 5, 7, 8, 10, 26, 27, 28, June 3, 4, 7, 8, 10, 14, 15, 20, 23, 24 (regarding the dismissal of General Wahlgren), and 26, 1993; coded cable (MSC-945) from Kofi Annan to General Wahlgren dated June 7, 1993; unpublished account of the Srebrenica demilitarization process by an officer serving in UNPROFOR and present in Srebrenica in the spring of 1993; an unpublished assessment by NATO concerning the safe areas in Bosnia and Herzegovina, no author, n.d.; unpublished "Risk Assessment of Resolution 836," by General Wahlgren, dated June 8, 1993; memorandum by the government of France to the president of the UN Security Council dated May 19, 1993; NATO press communiqué from the meeting of the North Atlantic Council, MNAC 1 (93)38, dated June 10, 1993; UN Doc. S/PV.3228, June 4, 1993, pp. 12, 13, 46, 57, 59, 60 (the official verbatim record of the meeting of the UN Security Council at which Resolution 836 was adopted).

Chapter 20

INTERVIEWS

Hiba Čelik, Paja Čelik, Hamed Čelik, Sanela (Čelik) Halilović, Senad Sućeska, Avdo Čelik, Kasema Čelik, Mirza Čelik, Zlatija (Sućeska) Čelik, Dragica Vasić, UN refugee-relief workers and military observers, UNPROFOR senior officers who asked to remain unnamed.

PUBLISHED LITERATURE

Ljiljan (Sarajevo), Aug. 7, 1996, pp. 16–22 (on the killing of Bilal).

DOCUMENTS

Unpublished document, "Main Planning Elements for Air Support Ops for UNSCR 836," dated July 6, 1993, US NATO, 32-2-242-8837; unpublished UNPROFOR cable dated Oct. 26, 1993, and containing cease-fire violation tallies; unpublished UN cable dated July 1, 1993, and describing the water situation in Srebrenica; cables by General Cot dated Oct. 1 and 15, 1993; a UN cable dated Oct. 1, 1993, containing the Iranian government's offer to send military units to Srebrenica.

Chapter 21

INTERVIEWS
Paja Čelik, Zlatija (Sućeska) Čelik, Sanela (Čelik) Halilović, Hiba Čelik, Senad Sućeska, Lieutenant General Sir Michael Rose, Yasushi Akashi, Haris Silajdžić and other Bosnian Muslim political and military leaders, U.S. diplomats and UN military and refugee-relief officials who spoke on condition of anonymity.

PUBLISHED LITERATURE
Silber and Little, *Yugoslavia,* pp. 309–18 (for the chronology of events following the marketplace massacre in Sarajevo and, on p. 317, for the account of the meeting in Moscow between Boris Yeltsin and John Major) and pp. 324–34 (for the chronology of the Serb attack on Goražde); *New York Times,* March–April 1994; and the dispatches filed by Reuters and the Associated Press and datelined Sarajevo, Moscow, London, and other cities; Owen, *Balkan Odyssey,* pp. 262–63, 265; Gow, *Triumph,* pp. 146–47, 149–54.

DOCUMENTS
Letter from Alija Izetbegović to the president of the UN Security Council dated March 7, 1994; unpublished situation reports compiled by the UN military observers in Goražde during the Serb offensive of March and April, 1994; an unpublished cable by General De la Presle dated April 8, 1994, and containing his definition of a safe area; an official NATO press statement on the decisions for the protection of safe areas taken at a meeting of the North Atlantic Council on April 22, 1994.

Chapter 22

INTERVIEWS
Sanela (Čelik) Halilović, Avdo Muratagić, Dragica Vasić, Paja Čelik, Adem Halilović, Naza Halilović, Zlatija (Sućeska) Čelik, Hiba Čelik, Senad Sućeska.

PUBLISHED LITERATURE
Orić, *Srebrenica,* p. 167.

Chapter 23

INTERVIEWS
Paja Čelik, Sanela Čelik, Muslims who asked to remain unnamed, Hasan Nuhanović, Ken Biser, Bosnian army military officers who requested anonymity, Ibran Mustafić, French and Russian soldiers assigned to UNPROFOR, Muslims walking on Vojvoda Putnik Street in Sarajevo, a Bosnian government minister who spoke on condition of anonymity.

PUBLISHED LITERATURE
Kljun, *Višegrad*, p. 186; "Dosije," *Ljiljan* (Sarajevo), Aug. 7, 1996, pp. 18–22; Beatović, *Bratunac*, pp. 10, 59; *Slobodna Bosna*, July 14, 1996, p. 59.

DOCUMENTS
The Bosnian army's photocopy of General Kukanjac's report on the paucity of iodine in the Drina basin, "Odbrambene snage," SFRJ, pov. br. 546, dated March 3, 1992; report on the situation in Srebrenica by the Civil Affairs Office of UNPROFOR, Sector Northeast, which was based on a fact-finding trip to the safe area from Sept. 21 to 24, 1994; statements by Vehida Dedić and Šeriva Selimović given to Bosnian Serb police in Bratunac and dated April 4, 1994; unpublished UNPROFOR document, "Dealing with Srebrenica," G3 Plans, Headquarters Sector Northeast, dated Dec. 7, 1994; unpublished report by the UN military observers team in Srebrenica, dated Dec. 18, 1994.

Chapter 24

INTERVIEWS
Hase Tirić, Ramiz Bećirović, Yasushi Akashi, UN civilian and military officials who spoke on condition of anonymity, Naser Orić, ranking Bosnian army officers who asked to remain unnamed, Paja Čelik, Senad Sućeska, Hasan Nuhanović, Samir Karić.

PUBLISHED LITERATURE
New York Times, Feb. 8 and June 23, 1995; "Politics and Massacres," in *Time*, June 24, 1996, p. 24; Honig and Both, *Srebrenica*, pp. 141–59 (on the strategy of General Rupert Smith); Gow, *Triumph*, pp. 267–69 (on Smith's strategy); Atkinson, *Crusade*, pp. 383–84.

DOCUMENTS
"Réunion des Pays Contributeurs de Troupes, 24 Mai 1995, Exposé Introductif du Général Janvier, Commandant des Forces de Paix des Nations Unies"; notes taken by a representative of a Western government on the informal discussion between General Janvier and ambassadors from the troop-contributing nations after their official meeting on May 24, 1995; unpublished UNPROFOR cable dated April 9, 1995, and discussing the plan for helicopter resupply of the UN forces in the eastern enclaves in Bosnia; "Report Based on the Debriefing," pp. 13–16 (the Dutch army's report on the fall of Srebrenica, hereafter Dutch Army Debriefing); letter from Alija Izetbegović to president of the UN Security Council dated May 26, 1995; unpublished cable by General Janvier dated June 30, 1995, and referring to NATO's belief that the downing of the U.S. fighter on June 2 was a trap; unpublished UNPROFOR cable from Yasushi Akashi to Kofi Annan dated June 15, 1995, and containing General Janvier's report on the June 4 meeting: "Recontre entre le Général Janvier et le Général Mladić, Commandant en chef des Forces serbes de Bosnie de 4 juin 1995"; unofficial minutes of the meeting between Yasushi Akashi, General Janvier and General Smith in Split, Croatia, on June 9; cable sent by Janvier to Smith outlining the dialogue from the June 17 meeting between Janvier and Mladić (intercepted by Bosnia's military intelligence service and translated here from the Serbo-Croatian); unpublished UNPROFOR

cable dated June 21, 1995, and containing Akashi's response to Admiral Smith's letter; unpublished UNPROFOR cable to New York dated June 22, 1995, and containing Akashi's response to NATO's request for a clarification of whether any deal had been struck between the UN and the Serbs for the release of the hostages; unpublished UNPROFOR cable from Boutros-Ghali to Akashi (MSC-2058) dated June 22, 1995, and stating that the secretary-general held the authority to decide whether air strikes would be launched and that each request should be accompanied by a detailed explanation of the circumstances and objectives and potential implications for security of UN personnel on the ground; unpublished UNPROFOR cables dated June 28 and 30, 1995, and containing Janvier's response to the reduction of NATO's air cover over Bosnia; UN Doc. S/1995/444, May 30, 1995, pp. 3, 4, 10–13 (the report of the secretary-general on UNPROFOR's mandate and operation).

Chapter 25

INTERVIEWS
Sanela (Čelik) Halilović, Ramiz Bećirović, Serbs from Bajina Bašta who confirmed the attack through the mine tunnel and asked to remain unnamed, Hasan Nuhanović, Paja Čelik, Deba Kozić, Džemal Kozić, Dan De Luce, Senad Mustafić, Bosnian army officers who spoke on condition of anonymity on the orders to the military leaders in Srebrenica to carry out raids from inside the safe area, Muslims from Srebrenica who asked to remain unnamed, Hiba Čelik, Zlatija (Sućeska) Čelik, Mirza Čelik, Adem Halilović, Senad Sućeska, Latifa (Čelik) Čavkušić, ranking Bosnian army officers who requested anonymity, Hasan Nuhanović, Senad Alić, Yasushi Akashi, UN civilian and military officials who asked to remain unnamed.

PUBLISHED LITERATURE
New York Times, June 27, 1995, p. 3; Honig and Both, *Srebrenica*, pp. 8, 13, 15; Human Rights Watch, *Fall of Srebrenica*, pp. 8–14.

DOCUMENTS
Unpublished cable by General Janvier on the Višnjica attack dated June 28, 1995; unpublished UN military observers situation reports dated July 6, 7, 8, and 9; UN military observers assessments of the situation in Srebrenica, MIO.ASS.SREB001 dated July 7, 1995, and MIO.ASS.SRE002 dated July 26, 1995; memorandum on a meeting between Brigadier Mačar of the Bosnian army's Tuzla corps with UNPROFOR officers, Col. Brantz, Col. Raashid, Ken Biser, et al., on July 8, 1995; cable to UN Headquarters in New York by Janvier on July 9, 1995; Dutch Army Debriefing, pp. 19–46.

Chapter 26

INTERVIEWS
Sanela (Čelik) Halilović, Muslims from Srebrenica who asked to remain unnamed, Hiba Čelik, Paja Čelik, Zlatija (Sućeska) Čelik, Mirza Čelik, Adem Halilović, Senad Sućeska, Latifa (Čelik) Čavkušić, Sanela (Halilović) Čelik, ranking Bosnian army officers who re-

quested anonymity, Hasan Nuhanović, Senad Alić, Yasushi Akashi, UN civilian and military officials who asked to remain unnamed.

PUBLISHED LITERATURE
Honig and Both, *Srebrenica*, pp. 18, 20, 21–26; Rohde, *Endgame*, pp. 118–19; *Le Figaro*, March 8, 1996, pp. 4, 26; Human Rights Watch, *Fall of Srebrenica*, pp. 8–14.

DOCUMENTS
Unpublished UN military observers situation reports (sitreps) dated July 10 and 11, 1995; UN military observers assessment of the situation in Srebrenica, and MIO.ASS.SRE002 dated July 26, 1995; UN cables from Yasushi Akashi dated July 10 and July 11, 1995, and outlining the situation in Srebrenica; letter from General Janvier to General Rasim Delić dated July 10, 1995, and protesting the killing of the Dutch soldier in Srebrenica; Dutch Army Debriefing, pp. 19–46; cables from Yasushi Akashi to Kofi Annan dated July 10 and July 11; orders from acting commander of UNPROFOR, Major-General H.M. Gobilliard for the Defence of Dutchbat and the Protection of refugees in Srebrenica, outgoing fax No. 1291, July 11, 1995.

Chapter 27

INTERVIEWS
Paja Čelik, Senad Sućeska, Ramiz Bećirović, Ibrahim Bećirović, Deba Kozić, Džemal Kozić, Hiba Čelik, Zlatija (Sućeska) Čelik, Biba (Čavkušić) Tabaković, Hadžira Suleimanović, Senad Mustafić, Hasan Nuhanović, Senad Alić, Serbs from Serbia and Bosnia who asked to remain unnamed, UN civilian officials who asked to remain unnamed.

PUBLISHED LITERATURE
Silber and Little, *Yugoslavia*, p. 358; Human Rights Watch, *Fall of Srebrenica*, pp. 16–27.

DOCUMENTS
Unpublished cable from Karremans to Janvier and others dated July 12, 1995, and containing the Dutch officer's report on the meetings with General Mladić on July 11 and 12, 1995; unpublished cables from Yasushi Akashi dated July 12, 13, and 14, 1995, and outlining the situation in Srebrenica; Dutch Army Debriefing, pp. 39–40, 47–49, 56–57; UN military observers assessment of the situation in Srebrenica, MIO.ASS.SRE002, dated July 26, 1995; "Srebrenica Human Rights Report," interoffice memorandum from Michel Moussali to Yasushi Akashi dated July 31, 1995; unpublished UN military observers situation reports dated July 12 and 13, 1995.

Chapter 28

INTERVIEWS
Latifa (Čelik) Čavkušić, Hajra Čavkušić, Zlatija (Sućeska) Čelik, Hiba Čelik, Hadžira (Čavkušić) Pirić, Biba (Čavkušić) Tabaković Paja Čelik, Sanela (Čelik) Halilović, Serbs from Višegrad who requested to remain unnamed.

PUBLISHED LITERATURE
"Dosije," in *Ljiljan* (Sarajevo), Aug. 7, 1996, p. 19; Kljun, *Višegrad*, p. 20; *Dnevni Avaz* (Sarajevo), July 4, 1996, p. 7.

Chapter 29

INTERVIEWS
Paja Čelik, Senad Sućeska, Deba Kozić, Džemal Kozić, Ramiz Bećirović, Senad Mustafić, Nijaz Pilav.

PUBLISHED LITERATURE
Human Rights Watch, *Fall of Srebrenica*, pp. 27–35.

Chapter 30

INTERVIEWS
Hiba Čelik, Zlatija (Sućeska) Čelik, Mihailo Erić, Zoran Erić, Tomo Stojanović, Jovan Nikolić, Serb workers at the farmers' co-op in Kravica who asked to remain unnamed, Paja Čelik, Senad Sućeska, Hurem Suljić, Serbs in Bratunac and in towns along Serbia's bank of the Drina River who asked to remain unnamed.

PUBLISHED LITERATURE
Human Rights Watch, *Fall of Srebrenica*, pp. 16–27, 35–47.

DOCUMENTS
Dutch Army Debriefing, pp. 45; UN military observers assessment of the situation in Srebrenica, MIO.ASS.SRE002, dated July 26, 1995; "Srebrenica Human Rights Report," interoffice memorandum from Michel Moussali to Yasushi Akashi dated July 31, 1995.

Chapter 31

INTERVIEWS
Sanela (Čelik) Halilović, Hurem Suljić, Mevludin Orić, Paja Čelik, Senad Sućeska, Deba Kozić, Džemal Kozić, Ramiz Bećirović, ranking Bosnian army officers who requested anonymity, Ilijaz Pilav, Naser Orić, Hamed Čelik.

PUBLISHED LITERATURE
Le Figaro, March 8, 1996, pp. 4, 26; Human Rights Watch, *Fall of Srebrenica*, pp. 35–47; "Mass Slaughter in a Bosnian Field," *Independent* (London), July 21, 1995.

Chapter 32

INTERVIEWS
UN military and civilian officials who asked to remain unnamed, Yasushi Akashi, Ramiz Bećirović, Bosnian Serbs who witnessed the NATO bombing in the Ozren plateau west of Tuzla, Senad Alić, Hasan Nuhanović.

PUBLISHED LITERATURE
Omeragić, *Satanski sinovi*, pp. 11, 12, 26, 73; *New York Times*, July 22, 1995, p. 1; Honig and Both, *Srebrenica*, pp. 44, 45; Silber and Little, *Yugoslavia*, pp. 355–72.

DOCUMENTS
Dutch Army Debriefing, pp. 14, 69, 73; Declaration, Republika Srpska, Civilian Affairs Committee for Srebrenica, no. 07-27/95, dated July 17, 1995 (the "affidavit" signed by Major Franken and stamped with an UNPROFOR stamp), telex from Srebrenica by UN military observers dated July 18, 1995.

Epilogue 1995

INTERVIEWS
Paja Čelik, Hiba Čelik, Sanela (Čelik) Halilović, Hodža Almir, Nasir Orić.

PUBLISHED LITERATURE
Silber and Little, *Yugoslavia*, pp. 355–72.

Epilogue 1996

INTERVIEWS
Dragica Vasić, Miguel Gil Moreno, Naser Orić, Paja Čelik, Hiba Čelik, and reporting on the Bosnian Serb army's Tenth Diversionary unit in Bijeljina by Gordana Igrić.

PUBLISHED LITERATURE
Reuters, July 11, 1996; Omeragić, *Satanski sinovi*, p. 11; *New York Times*, July 12, 1996, and June 3, 1993; *Boston Globe*, May 19, 1996, p. 1; Associated Press Television video footage of Naser Orić shot by Miguel Gil Moreno in Tuzla on July 12, 1996; "Ovo je, bolan, gore od rata," *Naša Borba* (Belgrade), Aug. 31, 1996, p. 8; "Slikaj, pa nosi Slobodanu," *Vreme* (Belgrade), May 4, 1996, pp. 27–29; "Our Man in Vienna . . . Is a Woman," in *Working Woman*, Sept. 1996, p. 14.

Epilogue 1997

INTERVIEWS
Mihailo Erić, Živka Erić, Jovan Nikolić, Hiba Čelik, Dragoljub Radovanović, Ratomir Lukić, Zora Radovanović, Borka Radovanović, Naser Orić, Tim Judah, Tomo Stojanović, Hodža Almir, Sanela (Čelik) Halilović, Peter Deck, Petra Mitrašinović, Hajra Čavkušić, Biba (Čavkušić) Tabaković, Hadžira (Čavkušić) Pirić, Amir Karić, Samir Karić, Muradif Karić, Gordana Igrić, Serbs who spoke on condition of anonymity.

PUBLISHED LITERATURE
Miljanović, *Krvavi Božic*, pp. 77–82. 154–55, 157; *Arheološki leksikon Bosne i Herzegovine*, vol. 3, entry 17–305, "Stijena pod pismom," Žlijeb, Višegrad; Stratimirović, "Arheološki prilozi," pp. 283–93; *Dnevni Avaz* (Sarajevo), July 4, 1996, p. 7.

BIBLIOGRAPHY

Books and Articles

Akashi, Yasushi. "The Use of Force in a United Nations Peace-Keeping Operation: Lessons Learnt from the Safe Areas Mandate." *Fordham International Law Journal* 19 (1995): 312–23.

Andrić, Ivo. *Na Drini ćuprija*. Sarajevo: Svjetlost, 1974.

Arheološki leksikon Bosne i Herzegovine. Vol. 3. Sarajevo: Zemaljski Muzej Bosne i Hercegovine, 1988.

Atkinson, Rick. *Crusade: The Untold Story of the Persian Gulf War*. Boston: Houghton Mifflin, 1993.

Banac, Ivo. *The National Question in Yugoslavia: Origins, History, Politics*. Ithaca: Cornell Univ. Press, 1984.

Beatović, Djordje. *Bratunac i okolina u mojim sečanjima*. Belgrade: Udruženje Dobrovoljaca Oslobodilačkih Ratova Srbije 1912–20, 1981.

Beatović, Djordje, and Milanović, Dragoljub. *Veleizdajnički procesi Srbima u Austro-ugarskoj*. Belgrade: NIRO Književne novine, 1989.

Bennett, Christopher. *Yugoslavia's Bloody Collapse*. London: Hurst, 1995.

Boehm, Christopher. *Blood Revenge: The Enactment and Management of Conflict in Montenegro and Other Tribal Societies*. Philadelphia: Univ. of Pennsylvania Press, 1984.

Bordeaux, Albert. *La Bosnie populaire*. Paris: Plon-Nourrit, 1904.

Caplan, Richard. *Post-Mortem on UNPROFOR*. London: Centre for Defence Studies, 1996.

Cibej, Boris. "Naš marš na Drini." *Mladina* (Ljubljana), no. 38, Sept. 17, 1991.

Clissold, Stephen, ed. *A Short History of Yugoslavia: From Early Times to 1966*. Cambridge: Cambridge Univ. Press, 1966.

———. *Yugoslavia and the Soviet Union: A Documentary Survey*. London: Oxford Univ. Press, 1975.

Coll, Steve. "Franjo Tudjman: At War with History." *Washington Post*, March 1, 1993, p. B1.

Ćorović, Vladimir. *Historija Bosne*. Belgrade: Zadužbina Joce i Leposave Jovanovića, 1940.

———. *Crna Knjiga: Patnje Srba Bosne i Hercegovine za vreme Svetskog Rata, 1914–1918*. Belgrade: Izdanje I. Dj. Djurdjević, 1920.

Čubrilović, Vasa. *Istorija Političke Misli u Srbiji XIX Veka*. Belgrade: Narodna Knjiga, 1982.

Cviić, K. F. "The Nature of Government and Politics in Yugoslavia." In *The Soviet Union and Eastern Europe*, ed. George Schöpflin, 345–63. New York: Facts on File, 1986.

Dacie, Anne. *Instead of the Brier*. London: Harvill Press, 1949.

Dedijer, Vladimir. *The Road to Sarajevo*. London: MacGibbon & Kee, 1967.

Dedijer, Vladimir, Ivan Božić, Sima Ćirković, and Milorad Ekmečić. *History of Yugoslavia*. New York: McGraw-Hill, 1974.

Dedijer, Vladimir, and Antun Miletić. *Genocid nad Muslimanima*. Sarajevo: Svjetlost, 1990.

———. *Proterivanje Srba sa ognjišta, 1941–1944: Svedočanstva*. Belgrade: Prosveta, 1989.

Denitch, Bogdan. "Yugoslavia: The Limits of Reform." *Dissent* 36 (Winter 1989): 78–85.

———. *Ethnic Nationalism: The Tragic Death of Yugoslavia*. Minneapolis: Univ. of Minnesota Press, 1994.

Dinić, Mihail. *Za istoriju rudarstva u srednjevekovnoj Srbiji i Bosni*. Belgrade: Srpska Akademija Nauka, 1955.

Djilas, Milovan. *Land without Justice*. New York: Harcourt Brace, 1958.

Djukić, Slavoljub. *Izmedju slave i anateme: Politička biografija Slobodana Miloševića*. Belgrade: "Filip Višnjić," 1994.

———. *On, ona i mi*. Belgrade: Radio B92, 1997.

Donia, Robert J., and John Fine. *Bosnia and Hercegovina: A Tradition Betrayed*. New York: Columbia Univ. Press, 1994.

Encyclopedia of the Holocaust. 4 vols. New York: Macmillan, 1990.

Evlija Čelebi. *Putopis: Odlomci o jugoslovenskim zemljama*. Sarajevo, 1973.

Ford, Kirk, Jr. *OSS and Yugoslav Resistance, 1943–1945*. College Station: Texas A&M Univ. Press, 1992.

Friedman, Francine. *The Bosnian Muslims: Denial of a Nation*. Boulder: Westview Press, 1996.

Gompert, David C. "The United States and Yugoslavia's Wars." In *The World and Yugoslavia's Wars*, ed. Richard H. Ullman. New York: Council on Foreign Relations, 1996.

Gow, James. *Triumph of the Lack of Will: International Diplomacy and the Yugoslav War*. New York: Columbia Univ. Press, 1997.

Hadžibegović, Iljaš. *Bosanskohercegovački gradovi na rasmedju 19. i 20. stolječa*. Sarajevo: Oslobodjenje Public, 1991.

Hadžiselimović, Omer. *Na vratima istoka*. Sarajevo: "Veselin Maselsa," 1989.

Hodžic, Šaban. "Migracije muslimanskog stanovništva iz Srbije u sjeveroistočnu Bosnu izmedju 1788–1862 godine." In *Članci i gradja za kulturnu istoriju istočne Bosne*. Tuzla: Zavičajni Muzej u Tuzli, 1958. Vol. 2, pp. 65–143.

Honig, Jan Willem, and Norbert Both. *Srebrenica: Record of a War Crime*. London: Penguin Books, 1996.

Human Rights Watch. *The Fall of Srebrenica*. New York: Human Rights Watch, 1995.

International Committee of the Red Cross. *List of Missing Persons on the Territory of Bosnia and Herzegovina*. N.p., 1997.

Ivanišević, Milivoje. *Hronika našeg groblja*. Bratunac, 1994.

Kann, Robert A. *A History of the Habsburg Empire, 1526–1918*. Berkeley: Univ. of California Press, 1974.

Kinross, John Patrick Douglas Balfour. *The Ottoman Centuries: The Rise and Fall of the Turkish Empire*. New York: Morrow Quill Paperbacks, 1977.

Kljun, Ibrahim. *Višegrad: Hronika genocida nad Bošnjacima*. Zenica: Centar za Istraživanje Ratnih Zločina i Zločinaca nad Bošnjacima, 1996.

Kohn, Hans. *Nationalism: Its Meaning and History*. Princeton: D. Van Nostrand, 1965.

Kovačević-Kojić, Desanka. *Gradska naselja srednjovekovne bosanske države*. Sarajevo: "Veselin Maslesa," 1978.

Kreševljaković, Hamdija. *Kapetanije u Bosni i Hercegovini*. Sarajevo: Svjetlost, 1980.

Krsmanović, Momir. *Teče krvava Drina*. 2 vols. Belgrade, 1991.

————. *Krvave ruke Islama*, Belgrade, 1994.

————. *Tragovi mrtve brače*. Belgrade, 1996.

————. *Kletva mrtve brače*. Belgrade, 1996.

Lampe, John R., and Marvin R. Jackson. *Balkan Economic History, 1550–1950*. Bloomington: Indiana Univ. Press, 1982.

Lazarević, Djordje. "Napad Partizana na Srebrenicu juna 1943, i ustaške represalije na civilnim stanovništvom." In *Članci i Gradje za kulturnu istoriju istočne Bosne*. Knjiga VII. Tuzla: Muzej Istočne Bosne, 1967.

Maass, Peter. *Love Thy Neighbor: A Story of War*. New York: Alfred A. Knopf, 1996.

Malcolm, Noel. *Bosnia: A Short History*. New York: New York Univ. Press, 1994.

Martin, David. *The Web of Disinformation: Churchill's Yugoslav Blunder*. San Diego: Harcourt Brace Jovanovich, 1990.

Masić, Nijaz. *Istina o Bratuncu, 1992–1995*. Tuzla, 1996.

Mehinagić, Izet. "Smrt je stigla u zoru." *Svijet*, May 8, 1997, pp. 28–30.

Milazzo, Matteo. *The Chetnik Movement and Yugoslav Resistance*. Baltimore: Johns Hopkins Univ. Press, 1975.

Miljanović, Boro. *Krvavi Božic sela Kravice*. Bad Vilbel, Germany: NIDDA Verlag, 1996.

Morillon, Philippe. *Croire et oser: Chronique de Sarajevo*. Paris: Grasset, 1993.

Nilević, Boris. *Srpska Pravoslavna Crkva u Bosni i Hercegovini do obnove pečke patriaršije 1557. godine*. Sarajevo: "Veselin Maslesa," 1990.

Omeragić, Sejo. *Satanski sinovi*. Sarajevo: Ljiljan, 1994.

Orić, Naser. *Srebrenica svjedoči i optužuje*. Srebrenica: Opčina, 1995.

Owen, Lord David. *Balkan Odyssey*. New York: Harcourt Brace, 1995.

Owings, W. A. *The Sarajevo Trial*. Chapel Hill, N.C.: Documentary Publications, 1984.

Pejanović, Djordje. *Stanovništvo Bosne i Hercegovine*. Belgrade, 1955.

Petrić, Mario. "On Tattooing and Cicatrization in Prehistoric Population of a Part of the Balkans." In *Godišnjak, Centar za Balkonološka Ispitivanja*. Vol. 4, Knjiga 2. Sarajevo: Akademija Nauka i Umjetnosti Bosne i Hercegovine, 1966.

————. "On the Question of the Origin of Tattooing among the Balkan Peoples." In *Glasnik Etnografskog Muzeja u Beogradu*. Knjiga 39–40. Belgrade: Ethnografski Muzej Beograd, 1976.

Popović, Nenad. *Yugoslavia: The New Class in Crisis*. Syracuse: Syracuse Univ. Press, 1968.

Remington, Robin Alison. "Nation versus Class in Yugoslavia." *Current History* 86 (Nov. 1987): 365–68, 386–87.

Rieff, David. *Slaughterhouse: Bosnia and the Failure of the West*. New York: Simon and Schuster, 1995.

Rohde, David. *Endgame: The Betrayal and Fall of Srebrenica, Europe's Worst Massacre since World War II*. New York: Farrar, Straus and Giroux, 1997.

Rusinow, Dennison. *The Yugoslav Experiment, 1948–1974.* Berkeley: Univ. of California Press, 1977.

————, ed. *Yugoslavia: A Fractured Federalism.* Washington, D.C.: Wilson Center Press, 1988.

Šabanović, Hazim. *Bosanski pašaluk.* Sarajevo: Svjetlost, 1982.

Schmitt, Bernadotte E. *The Annexation of Bosnia, 1908–1909.* London: Cambridge Univ. Press, 1937.

Seton-Watson, R. W. *The Southern Slav Question and the Habsburg Monarchy.* New York: Howard Fertig, 1969.

Silber, Laura, and Allan Little. *Yugoslavia: Death of a Nation.* London: TV Books, 1996.

Singleton, Fred. *Twentieth-Century Yugoslavia.* New York: Columbia Univ. Press, 1976.

————. *A Short History of the Yugoslav Peoples.* Cambridge: Cambridge Univ. Press, 1985.

Stratimirović, Djordje. "Arheološki prilozi." *Glasnik Zemaljskog Muzeja u Bosni i Herzegovini,* Jan.–March 1891, pp. 283–93.

Toynbee, Arnold J. *A Study of History.* Abridgement by David C. Somervell. Oxford: Oxford Univ. Press, 1987.

Tucaković, Semso. *Srpski zločini nad Bošnjacima-Muslimanima, 1941–1945.* Sarajevo: El-Kalem i OKO, 1995.

Veleiždajnički proces u Banja Luci: Zbornik radova s medjunarodnog naucnog skupa održanog 25–27 sepbembra 1986. godine u Banjaluci. Banja Luka: Univerzitet Djuro Pucar Stari i Institut za istoriju u Banja Luci, 1987.

Wechsler, Lawrence. "Inventing Peace." *New Yorker,* Nov. 20, 1995, pp. 56–60.

Wolff, Robert Lee. *The Balkans in Our Time.* Cambridge: Harvard Univ. Press, 1956.

Zagorac, Djuro. *Dr. Radovan Karadžić: Fanatik srpske ideje.* Belgrade: Dosije, 1996.

Zimmermann, Warren. "The Last Ambassador." *Foreign Affairs,* March–April 1995, pp. 2–20.

————. *Origins of a Catastrophe: Yugoslavia and Its Destroyers.* New York: Times Books, 1996.

Newspapers and Periodicals

Dnevni Avaz (Sarajevo)
Duga (Belgrade)
Economist
Le Figaro
Independent (London)
Intervju (Belgrade)
Ljiljan (Sarajevo)
Los Angeles Times
Mladina (Ljubljana)
Naša Borba (Belgrade)
New York Times

NIN (Belgrade)
Oslobodjenje (Sarajevo)
Politika (Belgrade)
Radio Free Europe Research Reports
Slobodna Bosna (Sarajevo)
Svijet (Sarajevo)
Večernje Novosti (Belgrade)
VIP Reports (Belgrade)
Vreme (Belgrade)
Washington Post

ACKNOWLEDGMENTS

FIRST and foremost, I wish to thank those who shared their memories of Višegrad, Žepa, and Srebrenica even when the telling was painful and I goaded them to share more. I will be forever grateful to the Čeliks of North York and Blažuj; the Šimšić, Sućeska, Čavkušić, Kozić, Lukić, Karić, Kapetanović, Radovanović, Mitrašinović, Knežević, Ilić, Ahmetagić, Muratagić, and Janković families of Višegradska Župa; and the Vasić, Halilović, and Erić families of Srebrenica and Kravica.

This book would never have been written had it not been for the people at *Rolling Stone*, Jann Wenner and especially Bob Love, who believed in the project from the first message on his answering machine. I also wish to thank Gerry Howard, my editor at W. W. Norton & Company, Tom Bissell, Otto Sonntag, Lisa Bankoff of International Creative Management, and Joe Lelyveld, Bernie Gwertzman, and, my rabbi, Mike Kaufman, of the *New York Times*, who, for reasons I've never been able to fathom, took a gamble on an unknown from Cleveland, via Brighton Beach, and gave me the five best years any journalist could ever hope to enjoy. I owe a good part of my happiness, and my sanity, such as it is, to my colleagues at the *Times*: John Kifner, Fred Conrad, Jim Clarity, Dean Toda, Celestine Bohlen, Steve Weisman, Helen Verongos, Pat Steward, Tom Feyer, Ed Marks, Nancy Kenney, Kathy Rose, Linda Lake, Garry Pierre-Pierre, Cliff Krauss, Dave Kocieniewski, Marc Charney, and Tom Kuntz, as well as John Burns and Roger Cohen. I am grateful to Marie Courtney, Cynthia Latimer-Ortiz, and Francina McDuffie for solving my problems; to Dan Schneider, George Gustines, and the other clerks for making me laugh every time I called on the phone; and to Charlie Competello, Barbara Williams, and Walt Baranger, who made my life in Bosnia technically possible in two incarnations, so far.

Despite all my efforts, my life in Yugoslavia has left me with a Babel of friends and creditors who contributed to this book. I hope it provides them some assurance that their fellowship was not misdirected. My thanks to Laura Silber for her Scrabble therapy; to Aida Čerkez for her tours of North and South Korea; to Miguel Gil Moreno, who had the wire crucifix torn from his neck in Zaire but never lost his faith; to Jon Randal, the very last of the great American foreign correspondents; to Rachel Cobb for her hand tools; and to Mike Montgomery, Jon Landay, Vlatka Mihelić, Andrej Gustinčič, Tony Smith, Bob Reid, Peter Green, Carol Williams, and Tim Judah. I wish also to thank Dessa Trevisan for her lessons in press conference etiquette; Ivana Nizić and Ivan Lupis of Human Rights Watch for their soul; Enric Marti, for his night-vision driving, and Ron Pemstein, for riding shotgun; Ervin and Miriam Hladnik-Milharčič, Laura Pitter, Suzanne Keating, Eric Bourne, Bogdan Denitch, and Colin Soloway for their timely rescues; and Ron Haviv and Gary Knight and my kindred spirits in the world of photography for showing me something of the courage that is supposed to go with the insanity.

I wish also to thank Lee and Meg Sigal, Ambassador Herb Okun, Ambassador Antonio Pedauye, Ambassador Diego Arria, Joel Millman, and Aryeh Neier; Sir Terence Clark, John Fawcett, Hriar Balian, Chris Bennett, General John Arch McGinnes, Natasa Nadaždin, Anna Husarka, Samantha Power, and Mario Cvitković of the International Crisis Group; Amira Sadiković and her family of Višegrad beys; Senada Kreso and her mom for the unending stream of tea and coffee; Gordana Igrić, Anja Tomić, Miloš Vasić, Aleksandar Vasović, Dragan Ćićić, Boban Tomić, Momir Krsmanović, Milivoje Ivanišević, and Ševala Hadziefendić; Avdo Sidran, Ibrahim Kljun, Omer Vatrić, Murat Efendić, Sejo Numanović, and Sejo Omeragić; Mark Wheeler and Dušan Biber for their expertise on the Draža Mihailović's Chetniks; Alison Smale, Missy Beelman, Tedi Weyr, George Jahn, Roland Prinz, and the rest of the Associated Press staff in Vienna as well as Samir Krilić, Riki Larma, and Srečko Latal in Sarajevo; and Don Forbes, Tim Heritage, Mark Heinrich, Kurt Schork, Sabina Ćosić, Samir Korić, and the other men and women of Reuters in Belgrade, Zagreb, and Sarajevo. I am also indebted to the Cleveland Public Library, the New York Public Library, the Brooklyn Public Library, the Gradska Biblioteka of Tuzla, and the Gazi Husref Begova Biblioteka and Zemaljski Muzej Bosne i Hercegovine in Sarajevo, as well as Alija Zvizdić, president of the circuit court in Tuzla; the officers and men of the British Army's 9/12th Lancers who served in Tuzla in 1993; Ramiz Memišević of Blažuj; Rick Sudetic and Medillume III for their logistical support; Leon Twarog, Jules Lapidus, George Mitrevski, Father Mateja Matejić, Lee Becker, Jiri Hochman, Eric Fredin, John Wicklein, Bob Ehlers, Fred Schultze, and, my first mentor, the late Paul Underwood, of Ohio State University in Columbus; Jerzy Kolodziej and Henry Cooper at Indiana University's Department of Slavic Languages and Literatures in Bloomington; Chuck Crowley, Mark Lally, Joe Cook, and Ken Spiert; Kris Janowski, Peter Kessler, Peter Deck, Anders Levinsen, Louis Gentile, and John MacMillan of the UNHCR; Sylvana Foa, Fred Eckhart, Ken Biser, Gary Donaldson, Jamie Ruben, and a host of officials from the UN and the U.S. Department of State whose names cannot be mentioned.

For their unfailing encouragement along the road, I will remain always grateful to Milton Viorst, Janine and Mike Smith, Manny and Nadine Schultz, Ed Serotta, Olga Jovanović, Rob Hagan, Jimmy Pritchard and Barbara Dash, Dorothy Diffendal, Mark Nastase, Joia Turner, David Rieff, and Susan Sontag. Finally, and especially, my thanks to Peris Gumz and her mom, Zora, for luring me to Yugoslavia even as the Old Man lay dying, and to Bob Kiner, the only American flyboy I know who actually did bomb Belgrade and who told me long, long ago that I had to quit selling flowers and find a life.

INDEX

Lukić, Mikailo, xxii, 121
Lukić, Milan, xvi, xxii, xx, xxi, xxiii, xxvi, xxvii, xxxiii, xxxv, 66, 102, 107, 120–21, 124–25, 132, 139, 296
    postwar status of, 355–56, 358
    Potočari massacre and, 296–99
Lukić, Mile, 66
Lukić, Novica, 27, 66
Lukić, Rale, xxii, 298
Lukić, Sredoje, xxii, 102
Lukić, Sreten, 121

Macedonia, 84, 87
Maclean, Fitzroy, 34, 35, 274
Major, John, 127, 129, 230, 323
Mardel, Simon, xxii, 176, 177, 179, 180
Markov, Miloš, xxii, 77
Marković, Mirjana, xxii, xxiii, 77
Marković, Moma, xxii, 77
massacres:
    at Bratunac school, 149–50, 152–54, 162
    Mladić and, 307, 308–9, 311–12, 314–18, 323
    at Potočari, 296–99
    of Srebrenica refugees, 296–98, 307–12, 314–18, 322–23, 340
Médecins sans Frontières (MSF), 245
Medo, Mullah, *see* Ahmetagić, Mullah Medo
Mehmed Pasha, *see* Sokolović, Mehmed Pasha
Meholjić, Hakija, xxii, 245
Mendiluce, José Maria, xxii, 100, 183, 188
Merimée, Jean-Bernard, 211
Mihailović, Draža, xxiii, 26–28, 34, 35, 38, 90, 101, 143, 144
Miletić, Vera, xxiii, 77
Milorad (Serb peasant), 30–31
Milošević, Slobodan, xxii, xxiii, xxvi, 77, 85, 86, 87, 88, 90, 97, 99, 100, 113, 120, 121, 147, 150, 168–69, 189, 203, 205–6, 209, 210, 213, 229, 235, 253–54, 256, 263–64, 268, 324, 355
    Dayton accords and, 337, 339
    at London conference of 1992, 127–28, 130
    Morillon's confrontation with, 184–85
Milovanović, Milan, xxiii
Mitrašinović, Branko, xxiii, 59, 64, 65, 78, 105, 107, 108, 109, 111, 331, 359
    Hussein's quarrel with, 71–72
Mitrašinović, Pantelija, xxiii, 60
Mitrašinović, Petra, xxiii, 72, 109, 111–12, 359–60
Mitrašinović, Radislava, xiii, 37
Mitrašinović, Vladimir, xxiii, 27, 30, 31, 37, 46, 47–48, 61–62
Mitrašinović family, 17, 27
Mladić, Ana, 231

Mladić, Ratko, xxiii, xxvii, 114–15, 170, 171, 174, 175, 178, 182, 183, 184, 186, 188, 204, 205, 208, 209, 212, 222, 225, 229, 230, 231, 253, 266, 269, 272, 273, 288, 291, 322
    background of, 168–69
    at Belgrade meeting, 189–90
    Goražde offensive and, 232–35
    Halilović's talks with, 206–7
    Janvier's secret meeting with, 259–60, 274
    mass killings and, 307, 308–9, 311–12, 314–18, 323
    NATO air attack debate and, 233, 234, 255–60
    1995 London conference and, 323–24
    peace plan scuttled by, 210–11
    postwar position of, 339–40
    Potočari evacuation and, 292–93
    UN hostage crisis and, 261–62
    war crimes tribunal indictment of, 341
Montenegro, 12, 15, 16, 76, 77, 126, 209
Montgomery, Mike, 99–100, 102
Moreno, Miguel Gil, 346–47
Morillon, Philippe, xvi, xxiii, 169–76, 188, 203, 204, 206, 213, 223, 254, 275
    aid controversy and, 173–74, 175
    at Belgrade meeting, 189–90
    evacuation debate and, 175–76, 177
    Milošević confronted by, 184–85
    in Srebrenica enclave, 175–76, 178–84
Mount Zvijezda, Bosnia, xx, 5–6, 7, 22–23
Movement of Non-Aligned Nations, 45, 63, 206, 211, 212
Mujkanović, Mustafa, xxiii, 152–54, 322
Mundo, El, 346
Murat, Sultan, xvi, xxiii, xx, 90
Muratagić, Avdo, xxiii
Muratagić, Saliha, xxiii–xxiv, 38, 51, 52, 55, 56, 59, 60–61, 64, 68, 71, 156, 187, 221, 236, 356

Narodna Odbrana (People's Defense), xviii, 142–43
nationalism, 14–15, 72, 82
Netherlands, xxviii, 127, 225, 269
New York Times, xxxi, xxxii, xxxiv, xxxv, 79–80, 232, 249
New York Times Magazine, 330
Nicolai, Cees, xxiv, 267–68, 273
Nijaz (Sanela's boyfriend), 220–21
Nikolić, Jovan, xxiv, 162, 163
Nixon, Richard, 69
Njegoš (Petar II Petroviić-Njegoš), xxiv, 83
Noor, Queen of Jordan, 344